THE PAST AS PRELUDE:

New Orleans 1718-1968

The Past As Prelude
New Orleans 1718–1968

A Tulane University Publication
for
The 250th Anniversary of
The Founding of New Orleans

Editors:

Hodding Carter, *Editor-in-Chief*

Wm. Ransom Hogan, *Professor of History*, Tulane University

John W. Lawrence, *Dean of School of Architecture*, Tulane University

Betty Werlein Carter

Library of Congress Catalog No. 68–25161
Copyright © Tulane University
Art and copy design by Mouton Art Associates

Editorial supervision and distribution by
PELICAN PUBLISHING HOUSE, New Orleans
Manufactured in the United States of America by
Kingsport Press, Inc., Kingsport, Tennessee

TULANE UNIVERSITY

presents this volume of essays as the contribution of The Graduate School to the commemoration of the 250th anniversary of the founding of the City of New Orleans. Under the distinguished editorship of Hodding Carter, Writer in Residence at Tulane, *The Past As Prelude: New Orleans* (1718–1968) brings together a group of talented essayists to explore the variegated patterns that mark the city's growth. No one volume, indeed no encyclopedia, could recite in detail the chronicles of New Orleans. Nor could a single volume do full justice to the men and women of many faiths, diverse nationalities, contrasting cultures, and different races who have made New Orleans what it is today. But if history is a mirror to the future, the pages that follow will afford a many-faceted glimpse of the city as it reviews the first quarter of a millennium of its existence, while turning eagerly to the next.

New Orleans
February 15, 1968

HERBERT E. LONGENECKER
President

Contents

An Introduction, With Love

Hodding Carter

In this place, the rozo cane rose in a cruel thickness from the marsh and swampland. The stench of alligator musk permeated even the wheat meal, the meat and the rest of the scanty provender which Canadian Pierre Le Moyne, Sieur d'Iberville, his eighteen-year-old younger brother, Jean-Baptiste Le Moyne, Sieur de Bienville, and the French and Canadian soldiers brought with them up river in their two exploratory coastal *traversiers*, the sturdy fishing boats of Normandy, and four canoes. Already in the early springtime, the first of the hordes of mosquitoes to come plagued the air and the men who breathed it. On the higher ground beside the banks of the choppy lake and the dark, swift river and the bayous which spun off from it, moccasins slithered, and in the hot season the place would be like a sweat box and wetly cold in the winter. But the Le Moynes saw and felt more than the immediate discomfort. They were hardy men, these Canadian explorers and town builders and defenders of New France, which is why there is a New Orleans today and a river that is as American as johnnycake and fried catfish and as Creole as gumbo. The town that Bienville founded nineteen years later, in 1718, became an amoral queen among American cities, a charming Latin shrug at a runaway moon, and one of the greatest of world ports.

Save for the military man who thought of holding the Mississippi Valley and the trader who thought of golden coin, it was an unlovely place in its beginning. And some of this unloveliness

would persist in those days when the Mississippi rose in flood or
the primitively young town burned or hurricanes raged upriver
across the passes or the yellow fever death wagon creaked from
home to stricken home through the furtively quiet streets almost
without accompanying mourners or when the hated Yankee
bluecoats were taunted by the passing prostitute and the gentlewoman alike in a fallen city.

Bienville's town, New Orleans it was called, in honor of the
royal rakehell, Philippe, Duc d'Orléans, Regent of France during
the minority of the child king, Louis XV. Because Louis XIV
and Louis XV didn't know what to do with their Louisiana
colony or with their own country itself save to send its men off to
interminable wars and slaughter, it was, in its first days, virtually
the personal province of two speculative geniuses, one a Frenchman, Antoine Crozat, who was the richest merchant in all of the
France of Louis XIV, and the other, John Law, a Scotsman and
mathematical genius and gambler whom regents and kings and
nobles and poor people came to look upon for a while as a wizard
at the gaming table and among the coffers of the Crown in the
days of the Regent.

Six miles from that place in the crescent curve of the river,
which here thrust northward, spread the vast lake, a near conjunction which gave the site a rare potential. This the young
Bienville had noted.

The eastward and southern urging of lake and river alike was
to a blue gulf which ended at a semi-tropical peninsula 150 miles
away. The peninsula's sandy white and verdantly green shores
formed the outline of a pistol butt. It was called Florida by the
Spanish explorers who came and slew there more than a century
before any other Europeans and intermittently for more than
300 years the pitifully easy Indian targets. The Spanish and
the French and the British and the Americans would continue
to contend for it. Florida belonged to Spain, the Spain of a
Bourbon monarch who did not love his cousin, the Regent of
France, a fact which required counter action and scheming.
When, in 1718, the thirty-eight year old Bienville set eighty

illicit salt makers to clearing the land within the crescent, the English of the Atlantic seaboard were looking covetously toward Florida and Louisiana. Possession of the one would mean control of the Gulf of Mexico and the southeastern accesses to the continent and ownership of the other meant forests for felling and pelts and the rendered fat of bear and buffalo and, so they believed, waiting gold and jewels from the bowels of the earth. That is the way it was in 1718.

The dimensions of Louisiana had an epic but neglected vastness within which, at New Orleans and its environs on coast and lake and river, insignificant, hungry, lonely, and largely undisciplined men of the rank and file and their leaders dreamed their dreams, and some of them came true. There were those who remembered, longingly, the fleshpots of France and thought also of the waiting Indian girl and the dark Carib women who soon came as slaves and remained, many of them, as mistresses whose children were far lighter than they. Their dreams, whenever they were realized, had an earlier reality but were approved by church and state only if blessed and legalized by the married vow, which, if the women were of the right sort, the men often took. And these gaudy visions and real presences made too many forget, then and now, the good women, the faithful women, the gentle women who were the cement of city and colony. New Orleans would be a sensual town if only because the girls of the Indian tribes and the branded women of the Salpétrière made it so at the beginning and a passionate one, more tolerant than gentle, but with a history not often written in blood except when men fought over women.

The people of New Orleans were too civilized to worship the god of battle. All things pass. True, one unbelievably one-sided and important fight, the Battle of New Orleans, was fought at the city's downriver threshold on January 8, 1815, by Andrew Jackson's motley army of frontier American riflemen and Creoles, some of whom were also pirates, and free men of color and what was called the bodyguard of volunteer Anglo-American civilian newcomers. They killed more than 700 and wounded

1,400 British veterans of Napoleonic wars at a loss of only eight defenders killed and thirteen wounded.

New Orleans was less fortunate nearly fifty years later when Flag Officer David G. Farragut ran the formidable gauntlet of Forts Jackson and St. Philip and forced the all but defenseless city to surrender. Afterward, during the Northern occupation, no vengeful guerillas took to the byways to avenge what was called the Woman Order, the proclamation of General Ben Butler, the North's most hated officer, who in retaliation for what he considered the insolent snub of the New Orleans women decreed that any female whom a federal soldier or officer believed had insulted him could be considered a woman of the streets plying her trade and could be treated as such. Surely a few invaders should have paid for this monstrous edict but none did. Some folks purchased chamber pots with Butler's face appearing on the inside bottoms of the china utensils, but that was about all. Even so, New Orleans has produced its full quota of combat heroes, notably including Major Wheat's Louisiana Tigers who fought with ferocious courage in the Civil War and the Washington Artillery which has distinguished itself in every war in which it has been engaged.

This introduction cannot be thought of as a history of New Orleans. Nor can the book itself, which is a collection of studies of not necessarily related topics written by authors who know what they are writing about and who are either natives of New Orleans or who have made it their city because of affection and professional or personal interest or who wish that they could make it their city. But because some chronology may be required for guidance or as reminders, here is a brief résumé of the more important occurrences in the life of a fascinating city for 250 years with a little pertinent data concerning the years immediately preceding its founding:

1682 April 9—
     LaSalle, having descended the Mississippi River from
     Canada, places a cross near its mouth and claims all the

lands it drains for Louis XIV, naming that land in Louis' honor, Louisiana.

1698 October 24—
Iberville leaves Brest on the *Badine*, with the *Marin* and two *traversiers* loaded with French forces, to hold the Mississippi River for France.

1699 Mardi Gras Day, March 3—
Iberville, his younger brother Bienville, and other Frenchmen enter the river from the Gulf. After exploring the lower river and the passage through the lakes to Ship Island off Biloxi Bay, Iberville leaves men on the bay's shores to build a fort for protection of Louisiana.

1699 September 15—
Sixteen miles below the present Vieux Carré of New Orleans, Bienville meets an English ship anchored in the stream. He convinces the captain a large French force lies around the bend. The English turn back.

1702
The capitol of the colony is established at Fort St. Louis de la Mobile.

1717
John Law's Company of the West plans further development and settlement of Louisiana, and orders New Orleans established, naming it for the Regent of France, the Duc d'Orléans.

1718
Bienville, in charge of the colony, detaches eighty men to begin clearing the site of New Orleans, a location he had long recommended.

1720 December—
The "Mississippi Bubble," as Law's speculative development scheme came to be described, bursts, but not before several thousands of settlers had arrived in Louisiana or were on their way.

1722
Bienville moves the capitol of Louisiana to New Orleans.

1762

Louis XV gives Louisiana to his cousin, Charles III of Spain.

1769

Spain formally takes possession of Louisiana and executes five resisting patriot leaders.

1796

Louisiana's first profitable sugar crop on a large scale is harvested by Etienne de Boré.

1803 November 30–December 20—

The French flag flies in the Place d'Armes over a Louisiana retroceded to France by Spain.

1803 December 20—

The United States takes possession of the Louisiana Purchase territory in ceremonies in the Cabildo.

1815 January 8—

Andrew Jackson leads American frontiersmen and Louisiana Creoles to one-sided victory over an invading British force in the Battle of New Orleans.

1847

The University of Louisiana, the future Tulane University, is founded, taking in as its primary component the Medical College of Louisiana which seven young doctors had established in 1834.

1857

Comus presents the city's first parade-and-tableau-ball-with-a-theme, setting the pattern for future Carnival organizations.

1862

New Orleans falls to Union forces.

1872

Rex, first King of Carnival, establishes Mardi Gras as an official public holiday.

1879

Captain James Eads' jetties make a 30-foot channel at mouth of the river possible.

1905

The city's last yellow fever epidemic is promptly controlled, bringing to an end more than a hundred years of intermittent, scourging epidemics.

1927

New Orleans escapes effects of the most destructive flood in the lower Mississippi Valley's history.

1928

The United States accepts responsibility for flood control.

1935

The Huey P. Long Bridge, just above New Orleans, links east and west banks of river.

1958

The Greater New Orleans Bridge ties east and west New Orleans together.

1963

The Mississippi River-Gulf Outlet is officially opened to navigation and cuts 40 miles off the distance from city to Gulf.

This chronology is perhaps all that is needed here. But some slight elaboration must supplement even the briefest of introductions and there is room for this. New Orleans, which the visitor knows as an American city that is French, is really our nation's first melting pot. The peasant and soldier and aristocrat and noble of France, the inland Canadian, the coastal Acadian, the German tiller from the Palatinate, the Spaniard, the Englishman, the American frontiersman, the Irish, the Italian, and also the Slav adopted and were adopted by New Orleans and from their amalgam can be derived one of the valid explanations of the city's durability. Roman Catholics are numerically greater in other American cities—Boston and New York and Chicago—but New Orleans is spiritually and culturally the greatest Catholic city in the United States. More prosaically but of paramount importance to city and valley and mid-continent, the port of New Orleans, although some ninety miles above Head of the Passes, is America's second port. New Orleans was the taking-off place for the Texas-bound men, soldiers of fortune and patriots, who created the Republic of Texas and a heady base for filibusters plotting Latin American revolutions. France's colony of Louisiana, purchased by the United States in 1803, was the largest geographical area ever acquired by any nation without the firing of a shot.

And New Orleans has been America's good-time town almost from its inception: the once—but no longer—legally red light town, the river gamblers' town, the Mardi Gras town, the town for sailors and flatboatmen and country boys out for a little hell raising. New Orleans is the jazz town of "Jelly Roll" Morton, of Nick LaRocca, and the Original Dixieland Jazz Band, of the New Orleans Rhythm Kings, of Armand Piron, of Papa Celestin, of Bunk Johnson, of George Lewis, of Kid Thomas, of Pete Fountain, of Louis Armstrong, of Al Hirt, trumpeting the sensually beautiful beats into the hearts of the world. New Orleans is still the voodoo heartland of Africa in America and a despairing or vengeful lover can find an accursed pin and a proper small effigy of his wrath to stick it into. And New Orleans is the gourmet's town.

Perhaps the most enduring delight of those to whom New Orleans and the lower valley fall into special and beloved categories, and who know the city's history and that of their own families, is the heterogenous quality that unites the dissimilar and made this city of many bloods their own. Among my forebears are Frenchmen with exotic names who came early and whose plantation ruins molder; and I am sure, other Frenchmen less fortunate of whom we are not so proud and talk about seldom; and other French forebears too, one of them a Huguenot who fled to Louisiana from a German university, having killed his man in a duel. Another ancestral duellist, a Virginian, found it expedient to quit Virginia for New Orleans where he became a very solid citizen indeed, married the daughter of a Kentuckian who had come to New Orleans by flatboat with a Yale law degree in his pocket, or portmanteau, and had become in his time New Orleans' most eminent jurist. The Virginian, Louisianian by necessity, died of wounds received at Shiloh, he being a Union man who loved the state more than he liked political concepts. My father's father, who had faced up to beleaguered John Brown at Harper's Ferry and forsook his Virginia, the apple country of the valley, because he could not accept its postwar inclusion as a part of upstart West Virginia, also found a haven in New Orleans. My wife's family added to the mixture a musical young German scholar from Bavaria who didn't want to be the priest-son of the family and who married a girl from Long Island who had taught English in the same Mississippi college in which he taught and then established a still existing music business. In one way or another New Orleans unites us all. And this goes on yet.

Of all such matters some of our fellow Orleanians and Louisianians and Americans already know a little and a few much. This volume is for all of them, the knowledgeable and the uninformed alike, for there is something here for all of them: something of tropical medicine and music, of sports and sporting women, of decay and rehabilitation and education, of people and ships and the distinctive architecture and code of law. The contributions add up to a book that could be written only about one city and its people. I am happy to have had a hand in its creation as an anniversary tribute by a notable Southern university to the place of its origin and locale.

A Sazerac then and a Ramos Gin Fizz as a toast to all who move across these pages, together with a Creole feast to be selected from a *ménu* which offers: cold boiled shrimp or crabs with hot, hot seasoning; shrimp remoulade or oysters Rockefeller; crawfish bisque or turtle soup or gumbo; pompano *en papillote*, stuffed flounder, trout Marguery, soft shell crabs or Creole jambalaya; daube or grillades; soufflé potatoes; custard; and finally a demi-tasse of black, black coffee.

Or, just to prove that New Orleans hasn't been all Creole in its tastes for a long time, what about trying to recreate, at this end of our beginning, the cosmopolitan *ménu*, difficult to duplicate now, which was served up in 1882 at the dinner at which the civic and social leaders of New Orleans honored Captain James B. Eads, one-time designer of the impregnable Yankee gunboats on the lower Mississippi, for devising the jetties which insure access through the principal mouth of the river to the port of New Orleans:

Little Neck Clams
Château Yquem
POTAGES
Bisque of Clam   Consommé Chatelaine
Amontillado

HORS D'OEUVRES
Radishes   Pelitier Croustades à la Pelissier   Olives
POISSON
Pompano grillé à la Royal   Fresh Codfish, Oyster Sauce
Potatoes en Surprise   Cucumbers
Liebfraumilch

RELEVÉS
Tenderloin of Beef à la Rothschild
Saddle of Lamb à la Chancelieu
Tomatoes la Reine
G. H. Mumms Extra Dry

ENTRÉES
Sweetbreads braised à la Moderne
Suprême of Chicken à la Toulouse
Fresh Lobster Cutlets à la Victoire
Cauliflower   New Green Peas
Veuve Clicquot Ponsardin Dry

SORBET
Au vin de Champagne

GAME
Canvasback Duck   Quail Truffle   English Snipe sur Canapé
Salade Assortée
Château Lafitte

GLACÉ
Pudding à la Coburgh   Bavarois Rubane   Gelée Danzig
Biscuit Tortoni

DESSERT
Fromages de Roquefort et Brie   Fruits de Saison
Café   *Liqueurs*

But personally, most of us would stick with the Creole dishes. They're more like New Orleans.

The People of New Orleans

Charles L. Dufour

Many years before the founding of New Orleans, Jean-Baptiste LeMoyne, Sieur de Bienville, had spotted, while exploring the Mississippi, "one of the most beautiful crescents of the river."

This wide arc in the great stream brought the Mississippi and Lake Pontchartrain within six miles of each other and the land between the river and the lake had long been used by the Indians as a portage.

Here it was that Bienville decided to establish the city, which existed in name on a map in Paris almost six months before the work of clearing the canebrakes along the river's edge began.

It was probably sometime in the month of September, 1717, that John Law's Company of the West passed a resolution to "establish, thirty leagues up the river, a town which they will name New Orleans, which one may reach by the river and Lake Pontchartrain." This resolution in the company's register in Paris bears no date, but another resolution, dated October 1, 1717, named a M. Bonnaud as cashier and warehouse keeper for "the commercial office which is to be established at New Orleans."

The exact date when Bienville set to work to clear the ground for New Orleans has not been fixed, but the probability is that it was between March 15 and April 15, 1718. In June, Bienville reported to Paris that he was working "on the establishment of

New Orleans," but progress must have been very slow for Le Page du Pratz, who settled on Bayou St. John late in 1718, wrote in his *History of Louisiana* that at the time of his arrival in the colony, New Orleans "existed only in name."

One hundred and seventy-five years before Bienville founded New Orleans, the first Europeans saw the place—or could have seen it—as they went down the Mississippi to the Gulf of Mexico. These were Spaniards, survivors of Hernando de Soto's expedition, who, despairing of the long and arduous march to Mexico, built ships and floated past the site of the future French capital of Louisiana.

Three and a half decades before New Orleans was conceived by John Law, René Robert Cavelier, Sieur de La Salle, had passed the site on his way to the mouth of the Mississippi, where on April 9, 1682, he claimed all the land drained by the great river for France's Sun King, Louis XIV. Four years later La-Salle's lieutenant, Henri de Tonty, searching for his chief, twice passed Bienville's "beautiful crescent."

And in 1699, Pierre LeMoyne, Sieur d'Iberville, accompanied by his brother, Bienville, and a party of fifty, also passed the future site of New Orleans although there is no evidence that it made any impression upon Bienville at that time.

Before the Spanish, French and Canadians cruised past the site of New Orleans, the place was, of course, thoroughly familiar to the Indians of the vicinity. So it is with the Indians that the story of the people of New Orleans must begin.

The first Indians recorded in the New Orleans area were "tourists" with La Salle—eighteen Mohegans and Abnakis, with ten Indian women and three Indian children.

These Indians undoubtedly were of a higher quality than some of the tribes the French encountered on the lower Mississippi. Of the latter, one French missionary, the Jesuit Gabriel Marest, exclaimed: "Nothing is more difficult than the conversion of these savages . . . We must first make men of them, and afterwards work to make them Christians."

André Pénicaut, the articulate ship's carpenter who accompanied Iberville to Louisiana and remained for twenty-two years in the colony, described a visit to an Indian village:

"As it was near the end of August and very hot, all the savages—the men and the boys—went as naked as one's hand; but the women and the girls wore a single hank of moss which passed between their legs and covered their nakedness, the rest of their bodies being quite nude . . . Their huts . . . are made of mud and are of a round shape almost like a windmill. The roofs of the houses are made mainly from the bark of trees. There are others that are covered with the leaves of a bush locally called *latanier* . . . An observation I have made about the savages is that, however abundant their provisions may be, they do not overindulge themselves, but eat only what they need, yet very untidily, most of them eating with their fingers . . . They have some dishes made of wood and others of clay, which, even though by the hands of savages, are nevertheless very well made indeed."

The Choctaws, who abounded in the general vicinity of New Orleans, were, noted Le Page du Pratz, called Flat-heads, but for what reason he could not determine "since all the nations of Louisiana have their heads as flat, or nearly so." Du Pratz's generalizations about "all the natives of America," would surely include those Indians with whom he came in contact around New Orleans. Du Pratz wrote:

". . . Very few of them are to be seen under five feet and a half, and very many of them above that . . . they are long waisted; their head is upright and somewhat flat in the upper part, and their features are regular; they have black eyes, and thick black hair without curls. If we see none that are extremely fat . . . neither do we meet with any that are so lean as if they were in a consumption. The men in general are better made than the women; they are more nervous and the women more plump and fleshy; the men are almost all large, and the women of a middle size . . . The infants of the native are white when they are born, but they soon turn brown, as they are rubbed with bear oil and exposed to the sun . . . As the children grow up, the fathers and mothers take care each to accustom those of their own sex to the labors and exercises suited to them . . . It must be confessed that the girls and the women work more than the men and boys."

About half a century after Pénicaut and du Pratz, Bernard Romans, a Dutch surveyor in the British service, visited the area of New Orleans. The Choctaw Indians he later wrote "may more properly be called a nation of farmers than any savages I have met with." Romans described how the Choctaws became flat-headed: "The women disfigure the heads of their male children by means of bags of sand, flattening them into different shapes, thinking it adds to their beauty."

Louis LeClerc de Milford, traveling in the 1770's, found the Choctaws "cowardly, lazy and filthy." Rather than cultivate their fertile lands, "they . . . prefer a life of mendicancy. Several times a year they go down to Mobile and New Orleans to beg." Continuing his description, Milford wrote:

"These savages are so lazy and so filthy that they never clean any part of their bodies. As they go practically naked, their bodies are caked with dirt, which in the course of time becomes the color of soot."

Such, briefly, were the first inhabitants of what would become the city of New Orleans.

A certain Father Duval, who sent an enthusiastic letter about New Orleans to the *Nouveau Mercure* in Paris, must have possessed a lively imagination. The *Mercure* published in March, 1719 his comments that "the town was one league around" and was composed of "simple houses, low as in our rural regions, covered with immense barks of trees and large reeds."

Yet Le Page du Pratz, who was on Bayou St. John by the

time of Father Duval's supposed visit, stated that the city "was yet only marked out by a hut covered with palmetto leaves, and which [Bienville] had caused to be built for his own lodgings." Another Bayou St. John concessionaire, M. Pellerin, reported in April, 1719: "There are at New Orleans three houses of Canadians and a warehouse for the Company."

And Father Charlevoix, who reached New Orleans late in 1721, wrote:

"Here I am in that famous city they call New Orleans . . . The eight hundred handsome houses and five parishes which the *Mercure* attributed to it two years ago are now reduced today to a hundred huts placed without much order, to a large warehouse of wood, two or three houses which would not embellish a village in France, to half of a wretched warehouse that they have consented to assign to the Lord and of which He had hardly taken possession before they wanted Him to leave it to lodge in a tent."

Where Father Duval was a man with imagination, Father Charlevoix was a man of vision. Both saw things at New Orleans that were not there. "This savage and deserted place," wrote Father Charlevoix with the gift of prophecy, "which the cane-brake and trees cover almost entirely will one day, and perhaps that day will not be distant, be a wealthy city and the metropolis of a great and rich colony."

Although 300 concessionaires with land grants came out from France in 1718, and another hundred colonists arrived in Louisiana in the following year, it was soon obvious to John Law that volunteer colonization would be a slow process and that other means of securing colonists must be employed if New Orleans was to grow and prosper.

The simple device of deporting criminals to Louisiana assured a population in which quantity, not quality, would be the prime consideration. The riff-raff of Paris and provincial towns, thieves, cutthroats, prostitutes, were herded to French ports and among them might be found renegade sons of decent families sent to the colony to make something out of wasted lives. France was purged of its human dregs and worst derelicts, as prisons, detention houses and hospitals were emptied and denizens of the streets were rounded up and shipped to Louisiana.

One contingent of sixteen women, from seventeen to thirty-eight years of age, all branded on their shoulders with the *fleur-de-lis*, the mark of the profligate female, had such descriptions by their names on the shipping list as "thief," "perfect debauchée," "knife-wielder," "given to all vices." Another group of 299 dissolute women, sent to Louisiana in June, 1719, was deported, reported a Paris police official, because "they can cause only much trouble among the public, being of an extraordinarily depravation of habits."

Chained two-by-two, these wretched creatures were piled into carts and carried to the ports. In 1719, 600 were shipped. A similar number, but of both sexes, was deported in 1720. Among them, before they sailed, there were 108 marriages, and husband and wife, chained, mounted the gangplank together. Riots of these criminal groups frequently broke out. On one occasion, 150 of the women rebelled at a port and mobbed the handful of soldiers who guarded them. They kicked and fought, scratched and bit, and beat upon the guards with their chains. In self-defense, the soldiers fired into the milling women, killing six and wounding three times as many more. Cowed by the gunfire, the riot subsided and the women went docilely aboard ship.

With such a system of colonization, it is not surprising that between 1717 and 1721, the population of Louisiana increased twenty-fold, from about 400 to 8,000, including Negro slaves, the first large shipment of which, numbering 147, reached the colony on July 7, 1720.

This growth, however, imposing as it looked on the books of John Law's company, brought with it only a handful of respectable colonists. Father Charlevoix, writing from New Orleans in 1721, declared:

"The people who are sent here are miserable wretches driven from France for real or supposed crimes, or bad conduct, or persons who have enlisted in troops or enrolled themselves as immigrants in order to avoid the pursuits of their creditors. Both classes consider the country as a place of exile. Everything there disheartens them; nothing interests them in the progress of a colony of which they are only members in spite of themselves, and they are very little concerned with the advantages which it may procure to the state; the greater part are not even capable of appreciating them. Others have only found misery in a country for which they have incurred expenses."

Bienville's impatience grew as shipload after shipload of undesirables disembarked in Louisiana. On October 20, 1719, he protested to Paris that all he had for the defense of the colony was "a band of deserters, smugglers and scoundrels, who are all ready not only to abandon you but also to turn against you." Bienville inquired:

"What attachment also can people have for the country who are sent to it by force and who no longer have any hope of returning to their native land? . . . It appears to me that it is absolutely necessary if we wish to preserve this colony for the King to send to it as far as possible only men of good will . . ."

Even before the Regent forbade on May 9, 1720, the further deportation of criminals to Louisiana, John Law had cast his eyes on more substantial prospective colonists. Law sought families, not only for the colony as a whole, but for his own large concessions, granted him by the Company of the Indies.

Law's agents spread to Germany where landless peasants lured by the glowing propaganda of the Company and the opportunity to get a fresh start in life with land, livestock, seeds and tools, agreed to go out to Louisiana as colonizers.

Poor, and weary from the interminable wars in which they were involved, thousands of Germans from Alsace-Lorraine, the Palatinate, Baden-Wurtemburg, Mayence and Treves enlisted for Louisiana. German historians estimate that 10,000 left their homes to establish a new life on the Mississippi. J. Hanno Deiler of Tulane, a pioneer investigator of German emigration to Louisiana, believed that no more than 6,000 Germans actually sailed from France. The others, Deiler stated, either succumbed to illness, returned to their homes in Germany, or settled in France. Deiler concluded that unsanitary conditions on crowded ships took a frightful toll among the German emigrants and that "of the 6,000 Germans who left Europe for Louisiana only about one-third—2,000—actually reached the shores of the colony." Continuing, Deiler added: "By this I do not mean to say that 2,000 Germans settled in Louisiana, but only that 2,000 reached the shores and were disembarked in Biloxi and upon Dauphin Island in the harbor of Mobile . . . Many of them perished in those two places . . ."

More recent research, especially that done in 1924 by a French historian, René Le Conte, indicates that Deiler's figures may be high. Le Conte estimated no more than 2,600 Germans became John Law's *engagés*, of which about 1,600 actually sailed for Louisiana.

The first Germans to reach Louisiana, a mere handful, arrived as early as 1718 and in November, 1719, *Les Deux Frères* brought a large group to Ship Island. These were not, in all probability, the indigent peasants Law rounded up, for Pénicaut noted that they brought with them "all kinds of merchandise and personal possessions."

The survivors of the hazardous Atlantic crossing were hardy, stout-hearted, substantial stock, usually families in which no members shied from hard work. They were in marked contrast to the worthless vagabonds who had first been sent out as colonists. The Chevalier de Champigny, who was in New Orleans during the Spanish régime, noted this difference half a century later:

"You cannot find twenty of these vagabond families in Louisiana now. Most of them died in misery or returned to France, bringing back such ideas which their ill success inspired. The most frightful accounts of the country of the Mississippi soon began to spread among the public, at a time when German colonists were planting new and most successful establishments on the banks of the Mississippi, within five leagues of New Orleans. This tract still [1776] occupied by their descendants, is the best cultivated and most thickly settled part of the colony, and I regard the Germans and the Canadians as the founders of all our establishments in Louisiana."

The last significant shipment of John Law's Germans was an ill-fated one. On January 24, 1721, four vessels carrying 875 Germans and 66 Swiss colonists sailed from Lorient. The ships—*Les Deux Frères, La Garonne, La Saône* and *La Charente*—were swept with disease before the voyage was fairly underway. By the time the "pest flotilla" reached Louisiana, almost four fifths of the passengers had died from the epidemic.

Most of the Germans who settled about New Orleans spoke no French and most of the officials or priests who enrolled them knew no German, so as a consequence new "French" surnames appeared in Louisiana. A few examples are: Casbergue for Katzenberger, Cambre for Kamper, Hymel for Himmel, Delmaire for Edelmaier, Clampetre for Kleinpeter, Chaigne for Schoen, Fauquel for Vogel, Quisingre for Kissinger.

The story of what happened to Johann Zweig's name is an oft-told one. In desperation at the lack of comprehension his repeated: "Zweig! Zweig! Zweig!" drew from the notary, he broke off a small piece of branch of a tree and waved it before the official, crying out again: "Zweig! Zweig!"

The notary's face lighted up: "Ah, La Branche! La Branche!" And Johann Zweig was enrolled as Jean La Branche, which name 250 years later is still borne by a prominent Louisiana "French" family.

Amusing but purely mythical stories have existed for years concerning the Schecksnyder family, which according to Deiler's research, has had 27 variants to the name since it first appeared in Louisiana in 1721. One story relates that a Jacob Schneider, familiarly known as Jake to his shipmates, was identified as Jake Schneider when he came down the gangplank. This sounded like Schecksnyder to the non-Teutonic ear of the official and so, goes this fable, Jake Schneider became Schecksnyder. A second version of this imaginary tale has it that there were six Schneider brothers who came to Louisiana together. Identified as the "Six

Schneiders" it might be understandable, considering the language barrier, that the family name would emerge as Schecksnyder.

Unfortunately for the validity of these two legends which still persist in Louisiana, there actually was a Hans Reinhardt Schecksneider who arrived in Louisiana in March 1721 and who became the progenitor of the vast family which is still represented by many of the variants in the New Orleans telephone book.

There can be no doubt that the Germans brought the first measure of stability to the colony, as noted by the Chevalier de Champigny. This fact was remarked more than a quarter of a century later by Pierre Clément de Laussat, who came to New Orleans to prepare for a Napoleonic empire and remained to transfer Louisiana from France to the United States. Laussat wrote:

"What is called here the 'German Coast' is the most industrious, the most populous, the most at ease, the most upright, the most respected part of the inhabitants of this colony."

Although established in 1718, New Orleans did not become an ordered town until 1721 when Adrien de Pauger began, in March, to lay out what today is called the *Vieux Carré*. Pauger's New Orleans had 4,000 feet frontage on the river with a depth of 1,800 feet and this tract was divided into squares of 300 feet.

At this time, including troops, the city's population was fewer than 250, but by November 1721, enough people had settled in New Orleans to call for a census, the enumeration of which follows:

Men	145
Women	65
Children	38
White servants	29
Negro slaves	172
Indian slaves	21
Total	470

The taker of this first census of New Orleans also counted 36 cattle, nine horses, but no pigs or sheep. The metropolis on the

Mississippi envisioned by Father Charlevoix was yet in the distant future, but settlement in the environs of the infant city, both up and down the river, argued well for the eventual growth of New Orleans. The census of nearby concessions revealed that almost three times as many people lived on the outskirts of New Orleans as within its confines. These included 684 Europeans—293 men, 140 women, 96 children and 155 servants—and 533 Negro slaves and 51 Indian slaves, making a total of 1,259. Accordingly, New Orleans and its environs numbered more than 1,700 people as the year of 1721 drew to a close.

It was these people who bore the brunt of the first recorded tropical hurricane in New Orleans' history. The town was virtually wiped out by the devastating winds which struck on September 11, 1722, destroying fully two thirds of the houses and damaging the others so badly that complete reconstruction was necessary. The hurricane winds and wind-swept waters of Lake Pontchartrain and the Mississippi uprooted crops.

The people dug themselves out of the storm debris as New Orleanians have done many times since and the flimsy dwellings were replaced by more substantial structures.

To avoid the dangers of one man rule in Louisiana, the Company of the Indies created the Superior Council. Its decrees give, 250 years later, some idea of how the early inhabitants of New Orleans lived.

Seemingly, good food was an early consideration in New Orleans and the Superior Council acted to prevent profiteering in delicacies by regulating the prices of brandy, wine, venison, buffalo beef, poultry and eggs. A few years later, when the Ursuline nuns arrived, the 18-year-old novice, Sister Marie Madeleine of St. Stanislas (she was Madeleine Hachard of Rouen) wrote enthusiastically to her father of the variety of the table:

"We eat here meat, fish, peas, wild peppers, and many fruits and vegetables such as bananas which are the most excellent of all the fruits. In a word, we live on buffalo, lamb, swans, wild geese and wild turkeys, rabbits, chickens, ducks, pheasant, doves, quail and other birds and game of different species . . . They use much chocolate with milk and coffee."

Although Sister Marie Madeleine was writing in 1727–1728, she found that luxury was not unknown to New Orleans at that early date in its history:

"I can assure you that I do not seem to be on the Mississippi, there is as much of magnificence and politeness as in France. Cloth of gold and velours are commonplace here, albeit three times dearer than at Rouen . . . The women here, as elsewhere, employ powder and rouge to conceal the wrinkles in their faces; indeed, the demon here possesses a great empire."

How did the early New Orleanians spend their leisure? Two Superior Council decrees in 1723 indicate several popular pastimes. In April, legislation forbade anyone "to play billiards on Sunday and . . . feast days or at late hours under penalty of a fine of one hundred livres both against the keeper of the billiard room and against the players." Proof of the antiquity of New Orleans' addiction to gambling is embodied in a Superior Council decree issued in May:

"It is forbidden to play at home any game of chance such as lansquenet, hoca, biribi, faro, basset, dice, and all other games of chance or with stakes . . . It permits only games of recreation."

Twenty-five years after the founding of New Orleans, its first "Golden Age" was inaugurated with the arrival in Louisiana of the Marquis de Vaudreuil in May, 1743. Pierre Cavagnial de Rigaud de Vaudreuil did not come without good reason by the sobriquet Grand Marquis during his ten years as governor of Louisiana. Unlike the last ten years of Bienville in Louisiana, a decade of frustration for the founder of New Orleans, who had given almost forty years to the colony, Vaudreuil's régime was characterized generally by peace and prosperity—and by the elegance which the Grand Marquis introduced into the city. He and his wife, who was fifteen years his senior, delighted New Orleans. Balls, fêtes, banquets, card parties, promenades— everything that could divert the wealthy—soon became the rule, reaching their peak during the pre-Lenten Carnival season.

A French officer in New Orleans, writing to a friend in Paris in 1743, has provided posterity with a critical description of the people of the period. His letter, seized when the British captured the ship that was bearing it to France, was translated into English and published in a pamphlet in London in 1744. Here is an excerpt:

"The *French* live sociably enough, but the officers are too free with the Town's People; and Town's People that are rich are too proud and lofty . . . Everyone studies his own Profit. The Poor labour for a Week, and squander in one Day all they have earned in six; from thence arises the Profit of the Publick-houses, which flourish every day. The Rich spend their Time in seeing their Slaves work to improve their lands, and get money, which they spend in Plays, Balls and Feasts; but the most common Pastime of the highest as well as the lowest, and even of the Slaves, is Women; so that if there are 500 Women married, or unmarried in *New Orleans*, including all Ranks, I don't believe, without Exaggeration, that there are ten of them of a blameless Character; as for me, I know but two of those, and even they are privately talked of . . .

"Laws are observed here much in the same Manner as in *France*, or worse: The Rich Man knows how to procure himself Justice of the Poor . . .

"The Youth here are employed in hunting, fishing and pleasuring; very few learn the necessary Sciences, or at best it is what is least attended to. The Children, even of the best Sort, know how to fire a Musket or shoot an Arrow, catch Fish, draw a Bow, handle an Oar, swim, run, dance, play at cards, and understand Paper Notes, before they know their letters or their God. A Child of six Years of Age knows more here of raking and swearing than a young Man of 25 in *France*; and an insolent Boy of 12 or 13 Years of Age will boldly insult, and strike an old Man."

In 1762, by a treaty signed at Fontainebleau, the King of Spain, Charles III, reluctantly accepted Louisiana as a gift from his Bourbon cousin, Louis XV of France.

Although Spanish rule, *de jure*, over Louisiana dates from November 3, 1762, it was not until 1766 that the first Spanish governor, Antonio de Ulloa, a savant more learned in science than in the art of governing, arrived in New Orleans.

Ulloa, with only a handful of Spanish troops, never formally took possession of Louisiana for Spain and Captain Charles Philippe Aubry, the ranking French officer after the death of Jean-Jacques Blaise d'Abbadie, director and commandant of Louisiana, found himself in a most peculiar situation. "My position is a most extraordinary one," Aubry wrote. "I command for the King of France and at the same time I govern the colony as if it belonged to the King of Spain."

The Revolution of 1768, led by Nicolas Chauvin de Lafrénière, attorney general, Nicolas Denis Foucault, the French commissary, and a group of the chief merchants, lawyers, planters and military men of Louisiana, expelled Ulloa from New Orleans. This brought out from Spain General Alexander O'Reilly with a large force to establish the Spanish rule firmly in Louisiana and to punish the guilty parties.

This O'Reilly did effectively and the benign rule of Spain began, *de facto*, in 1769, to last until November 30, 1803, when the crimson and gold flag of Bourbon Spain came down in the Place d'Armes in New Orleans. The French Republic's tricolor replaced the Spanish flag, but twenty days later, it too came down and the American flag was run up the pole to signal a new era for New Orleans and the vast province of Louisiana.

It was during the Spanish régime, in the governorship of Esteban Miró, that the largest trans-Atlantic migration in American colonial history reached Louisiana in 1785, a fact completely ignored by writers of American history textbooks. These were Acadians, who had sought refuge in France after their expulsion from Nova Scotia by the British in 1755.

Although a tradition exists among the descendants of some

Acadians that their ancestors reached Louisiana and settled in the bayou country before 1760, the earliest documentary evidence is that the first group of exiles reached New Orleans in 1763 or 1764. On April 4, 1764, d'Abbadie wrote in his journal: "Four Acadian families, numbering twenty persons, arrived here [New Orleans] from New York, where they had been detained until the peace. Their passage cost them 2,200 livres and exhausted their savings." A few Acadians may have drifted in earlier, but this is the earliest record of their coming. Aubry, who assumed command for France in Louisiana on the death of d'Abbadie in February, 1765, wrote in May of that year:

"When I saw the arrival of sixty Acadian families from Santo Domingo, I did not foresee the many others who were to follow and who kept arriving and will soon make Louisiana a new Acadia. At this instant, I learned that there are 300 on the river . . . We do not speak of them in hundreds anymore but in thousands. I am told that there are at least 4,000 who have picked Louisiana as their destiny . . . This unexpected event puts me, as well as M. Foucault [Nicolas Foucault, commissary] in the greatest of difficulty. Nothing was foreseen to settle so many people; and the circumstances we find ourselves in are, to say the least, critical. Never was the colony so short of food as it is today . . . However, under such circumstances, it is our duty not to abandon them."

Aubry's estimate was high, for by 1768, when the Acadians became innocent pawns in the revolution against Ulloa, their number probably did not exceed 500. These were settled on the Mississippi above New Orleans and on the banks of Bayous Lafourche, Teche and Vermilion.

Across the Atlantic, in France, some 3,000 Acadians had eventually settled, but assistance from the King, which they had expected, never came and years of precarious existence followed one another. Meanwhile their kindred had established themselves in Louisiana where, under Spanish rule, they thrived. Doubtless word of their happy lot reached the Acadians in France. Accordingly, when the Spanish government proposed to them a fresh start in life with a promise of land, seeds, tools and livestock and free transportation to Louisiana, heads of nearly 400 families seized the opportunity.

Between May and December, 1785—thirty years after the *grand dérangement* in Acadia—more than 1600 Acadians came out on seven ships from France to Louisiana, completing the largest movement of colonists in American colonial history.

The Spanish authorities were delighted with the stability and industry of the new settlers who disembarked at New Orleans. The intendant, Martin Navarro, who located the newcomers on lands, reported to Madrid: "I can assure you that after four years these Acadians will be America's most prosperous and sturdiest colonists, because they love their new home, and are determined to give Louisiana in 1786 its best harvest." Governor Miró reported in similar tone: "The enthusiasm, industry and loyalty of these new colonists will boost the prosperity of our province and increase its local and foreign trade."

Today in Louisiana, it has been estimated that fully half a million Louisianians have Acadian blood in their veins.

During the governorship of Bernardo de Gálvez (1776–1785) a group of Canary Islanders was settled in St. Bernard and Plaquemines parishes and other Iberian colonists were settled on the Teche, one such settlement subsequently taking the name of New Iberia.

It was during Gálvez's administration that the Americans began regularly to visit New Orleans, floating down the river from the Ohio Valley on flatboats loaded with produce. Even earlier, during the American Revolution, Oliver Pollock served as American agent in New Orleans to procure from the Spanish authorities arms, powder and ammunition.

When the upriver people reached New Orleans it marked the first time that the American frontiersman had come upon a culture far superior to his own. And, as has frequently happened with Americans in a similar situation, the rough, tough, pugnacious river boatman sometimes did not know how to behave. His outrageous conduct and the impression it made on New Orleanians undoubtedly planted the seeds of antagonism which would endure between the Creoles and Americans after the Louisiana Purchase and for many decades thereafter.

But, however they misbehaved, the wild Kaintucks, as the Creoles called them, ultimately supplied the pressure on the Washington government to acquire New Orleans and with it the free use of the Mississippi River. It is not necessary to dwell here on the ramifications of the granting and withdrawal of the right of deposit of American goods at New Orleans, tax free, until transhipped up the Atlantic seaboard. The upshot of the agitation from the Ohio Valley was that Thomas Jefferson set out to buy New Orleans from France—Spain had secretly retroceded it to Napoleon—and wound up acquiring all of Louisiana, approximately one third of the present United States.

Thomas Jefferson named a young protégé, William C. C. Claiborne, as governor, first of Louisiana, and then of the Territory of Orleans, which corresponded to the present State of Louisiana. Into a free and easy Latin environment, with a French-speaking Catholic population, came this twenty-eight year old strait-laced, Anglo-Saxon Protestant. It was inevitable that they would misunderstand each other. Claiborne reported to President Jefferson that he thought the people of Louisiana "generally speaking, honest," and he continued:

"But they are uninformed, indolent, luxurious—in a word, ill-fitted to be useful citizens of a Republic. Under the Spanish Government education was discouraged, and little respectability attached to science. Wealth alone gave respect and influence, and hence it has happened that ignorance and wealth so generally pervade this part of Louisiana. I have seen, Sir, in this city, many youth to whom nature has been apparently liberal, but from the injustice and inattention of their parents, have no accomplishments to recommend them but dancing with elegance and ease. The same observation will apply to the young females, with this additional remark, that they are among the most handsome women in America."

When Louisiana became American in 1803, New Orleans was a town of about 8,000 persons, more than half of whom were Negroes. Hardly had the American flag been run up the pole in the Place d'Armes, than New Orleans experienced its first of two population explosions. The town almost doubled its population in seven years and the 1810 census takers counted 17,242 inhabitants. The heterogeneity of the population can be gathered from a comment in *The Western Gazette, or Emigrant's Directory,* published in Auburn, N.Y., in 1817:

"Here [in New Orleans] in half an hour you can see, and speak to Frenchmen, Spaniards, Danes, Swedes, Germans, Englishmen, Portuguese, Hollanders, Mexicans, Kentuckians, Tennesseeans, Ohioans, Pennsylvanians, New Yorkers, New Englanders and a motley group of Indians, Quadroons, Africans, etc."

French refugees from Saint-Domingue arrived in large numbers in the first decade of the nineteenth century, many having fled to Cuba from the insurrection, and later continuing to New Orleans. German immigrants began to arrive by shiploads, seeking a new life in Louisiana. Unable to pay their passage across the Atlantic, the Germans became indentured servants and worked for a specified time for the person who paid the ship captain for their crossing. These Germans were called Redemptioners—that is they worked under a bond to "redeem" their freedom after some years.

In the 1830's and 1840's, when the potato famine struck Ireland, and Irishmen came to the United States in great numbers, New Orleans as a port received many sons of Erin. But there had been an "Irish Colony" in the city long before then. In 1809, St. Patrick's Day was celebrated for the first time by what the Louisiana *Gazette* called "a respectable party of Irishmen in this city," and the traditional seventeen toasts were drunk.

New Orleans' second and largest population explosion occurred in the decade between 1830 and 1840, when the city more than doubled its population, due mainly to the Irish and German immigration. The 1840 census showed New Orleans with 102,193, an increase of nearly 54,000 over its 1830 population of 49,826.

On the eve of the Civil War, New Orleans' population was 168,675. Almost 41 per cent of the 155,000 whites were foreign born, the Irish with more than 24,000 and the Germans with almost 20,000, leading.

Post-war New Orleans grew unspectacularly from census to census but a decline in foreign-born inhabitants was marked as the following table will show:

	1870	1880	1890
Population	191,418	216,090	242,039
Foreign born	48,475	41,157	34,369

Of the 48,475 foreign born in 1870, the Germans (15,224) and Irish (14,693) accounted for almost two thirds. In 1880, the 17,639 Germans and 14,018 Irish represented three fourths of the foreign total. However, in 1890 the Germans (11,338) and Irish (7,923) composed together just a bit more than half the foreign born in New Orleans.

In the post-war period, a new element of immigration was added—the Italians. There were no startling gains between 1870, when 1,568 Italians were counted in New Orleans and 1890, when the Italian total reached 3,622. The biggest wave of Italians came around the turn of the century and up to the outbreak of the first World War.

New Orleans, in its 250th year, continues to be a city with a heterogeneous population, even as it was shortly after it was founded, even as it was at the Louisiana Purchase and on the eve of the Civil War.

At least half a dozen years before New Orleans was founded the first Negroes had arrived in Louisiana. When Antoine Crozat received his charter for Louisiana in 1712, there were only twenty slaves in the colony, and he did not exercise his authority to bring in more.

However, when Crozat yielded his charter and John Law's Company of the West took over Louisiana, the slave trade began to flourish. André Pénicaut recorded that in February, 1719, 250 Negroes arrived at Dauphin Island and were put to work at once unloading ships and moving merchandise into the warehouses. In 1720 about 500 more slaves arrived and a similar number reached Louisiana in 1721. These, generally, were assigned to various concessions in the neighborhood of New Orleans. The 1721 census, it will be recalled, listed 172 Negroes among the total population of 470 in New Orleans and 533 Negroes among the 1,239 suburbanites.

The *Code Noir*, or Black Code, prepared in France and promulgated in Louisiana by Bienville in 1724, was designed not only to regulate the conduct of Negroes, but to prevent cruelty and injustice to the slaves themselves. When it was issued, there were fully 2,000 slaves on the lower Mississippi. That there were, as early as 1722, free Negroes around New Orleans is evident from the record of a flogging administered the free Negro Raphael on September 13, 1722, for stealing stores from the Company's warehouse. Moreover, the Black Code of 1724 took cognizance of manumitted slaves.

The earliest advice on how to handle the Negroes seems to have come from Le Page du Pratz in his *History of Louisiana*, first published in 1758: "The Negroes must be governed differently from the Europeans, not because they are black, nor because they are slaves; but because they think differently from white men." Du Pratz declared that newly arrived slaves from Africa had a great fear of being put to death. "They imbibed a prejudice from infancy," said du Pratz, "that the white man buy them for no other purpose but to drink their blood . . . When the first Negroes saw the Europeans drink claret, they imagined it was blood . . . so that nothing but the actual experience of the contrary can eradicate the false opinion."

As early as 1729 Negroes were used as troops by Governor

Périer and in 1733 forty-five slaves, commanded by free people of color served in Bienville's campaign against the Chickasaws. And in 1746 the Marquis de Vaudreuil in reporting available forces for the defense of the colony included "200 to 300 Negroes who are to be relied upon."

The Spanish employed both slaves and free persons of color in their military forces in and around New Orleans. After the successful campaigns against the British at Manchac, Baton Rouge and Natchez, Bernardo de Gálvez reported that they "behaved on all occasions with valor and generosity as the whites."

In his book, *The Negro in Louisiana*, Charles B. Roussève summed up the nature of slavery in the state during the colonial period and contrasted it with the changes that evolved during the American domination:

"Slavery in Louisiana, as a result of the paternalistic systems of the French and Spanish was, until early in the nineteenth century, not quite the horrible institution which it came to be thereafter . . . The slave insurrections in the West Indies and the consequent tendency of slaves, urged by the free people of color, to follow the example of their brothers of the Antilles, made the Louisiana slaveholder handle his slaves with greatest vigor and subject them to increasing restrictions . . . Finally, the industrial revolution in the South, brought about through the invention of . . . the cotton gin . . . required large shipments of slaves. No more was there intimate contact between master and slave . . . Slavery had changed from a patriarchal to an economic institution."

Although the slave population of Louisiana grew steadily until the Civil War, New Orleans in 1860 had only about 13,000 Negroes and free people of color among its more than 168,000 population.

Emancipation brought many Negroes from nearby plantations into the city and in the post-war growth of the city the percentage of Negroes has risen.

Today, 250 years after the first mass arrival of slaves, Negroes represent approximately 30 per cent of the New Orleans population.

During the last years of the nineteenth century and well into the twentieth century, many other ethnic groups became represented in the population of New Orleans and its vicinity.

New Orleans, the nation's first melting pot, continues to grow as a truly international city—unlike now, as a century ago, as two centuries ago, any other Southern city.

New Orleans is a city in the South. But its French, Canadian, German, Spanish, Acadian, American, Irish, Italian, Negro and other ethnic traditions keep it from ever being a typical Southern city.

The Law with a Difference and How It Came About

Ferdinand Stone

When speaking or writing about the law in Louisiana, certain things must be kept clearly in mind. First is the curious and sadly widespread notion that a distinctive Louisiana law does not exist. People will say, "We have French law down here" or "You still follow the Napoleonic Code" or "You've pretty much succumbed to common law, haven't you?" or "Do you call yourself a civil law or a common law state?" The truth of the matter is that Louisiana has a very good legal system indeed, and the sooner she stops apologizing for its borrowings the better. What legal system has not borrowed from its neighbors when the shoe fit?

The second thing to be kept in mind is an interesting matter of prejudice: what is good in Louisiana law is attributed to France, what is medieval to Spain, and what is bad to the common law. To understand this, one must remember that Louisiana was a French colony, donated secretly to Spain against its inhabitants' wishes, and then, of all things, purchased by the United States.

The law of a people, if it is to be worth its salt, must arise from their traditions, history, lore, superstitions, religion and culture or at least from those of a dominant segment of the people. So it was that Massachusetts and the other colonies continued and preserved the common law of England as the basis of their law even after fighting a revolution to be free, since it best stated the principles and ideals which the colonies-turned-states wished to follow. So it has been that Louisiana, alone among the fifty states of the Union, reflects in her laws the fact that she was settled by French adventurers coming from Canada, was governed for a long period of her history by Spain, then became a territory and later a state of the United States. Such might have happened with other states of the United States formerly held by France or Spain, such as California, Texas and Florida, but Louisiana alone demanded and won the right to keep her laws, however alien they must have seemed to the Louisiana purchasers.

The juridical history of New Orleans begins in 1682 when René Cavelier, Sieur de la Salle went down the Mississippi from French Canada and planting a cross, claimed all the land drained by the river and its tributaries for Louis XIV. La Salle did not live to see the colonization of Louisiana to which England and Spain would also press claims. But in 1699, Pierre Le Moyne, Sieur d'Iberville erected a fort on the Mississippi, some eighteen leagues above its mouth. This was the first settlement in what is now Louisiana although the honor of being the first permanent settlement goes to Natchitoches.

Discovery, claim and first settlement over, the development of a full fledged colony was seen to require both skill and money, and Louis XIV, neither wishing to risk personal capital nor to devote much time to his Louisiana, granted to Antoine Crozat, one of the richest merchants in Europe, the exclusive commerce of the area and the task of colonization fell to him. Louisiana in 1713 had a population of 380 persons including Negroes and 100 soldiers.

According to Crozat's charter, the laws, ordinances, customs and usages of the Prevostship and Viscounty of Paris were to form the legislation of the colony. A government council, similar to those previously established in Santo Domingo and Martinique, was established, which by edicts created a Superior Council for the territory, possessing both administrative and judicial powers. This first council was superseded by an edict of September 16, 1716, which established a reorganized Superior Council composed of the governor general, the intendant of New France, the governor of Louisiana, a senior councillor, the King's lieutenant, two puisne councillors, the procureur general and a clerk.

This council served as a court of last resort for all civil and criminal cases *without cost to the litigants*. The intendant was the honorary president, while the senior councillor was president in fact. He sitting alone was a court of first instance in all provisional matters.

Of this period we know too little. Governor Antoine de la Mothe Cadillac wrote of the colony on June 22, 1716 that it "is a monster, without head or tail, and its government is a shapeless absurdity." Crozat surrendered his charter to the Crown in 1716 or, according to some authorities, in 1717. The territory had cost him several million livres.

Once again France had the problem of colonization and development. An important council of state was held at Versailles on August 13, 1717, presided over by the Duc d'Orléans, Regent of France, which decided that it "was to the interest of France that the colony of Louisiana should be fostered and preserved," and "that it had been demonstrated in the case of Crozat, that the colonization of Louisiana was an undertaking beyond the strength of any private individual" and that "whereas the undertaking would not become the King, on account of the commercial details which were its inseparable concomitant, it was resolved that Louisiana should be entrusted to the administration of a company."

The company to which the development was assigned was the Western Company or the Company of the Indies whose charter of incorporation was registered by the *Parlement de Paris* on September 6, 1717. The duration of the charter was for twenty-five years but it did not last that long. The guiding force of the company was John Law, native of Edinburgh, who was orphaned at fourteen, heir to an ample fortune, which he lost at gaming.

Law's career was never commonplace. He was at various times a bankrupt, an adulterer, a "murderer" and an outlaw, but at the time of his appointment, he was highly regarded as a financial wizard.

The charter was specific about the legal system for the colonists. All civil suits to which the company was a party were to be determined by the consular jurisdiction of the City of Paris with a right of appeal in cases involving more than a certain amount to the *Parlement de Paris*. The Superior Council of the colony had jurisdiction in other cases, but its composition was altered in September, 1719, to include *ex officio* such directors of the company as happened to be in the colony, the governor (or, as he was now called, commandant general), the two King's lieutenants (lieutenant governors), the King's *procureur général* and four other persons, one of whom was the clerk. In all civil suits before the council, the quorum was fixed at three, and, in criminal matters, at five. In the event that no quorum could be formed on account of absence or disease, the members present could complete the numbers required from the ranks of the "most respectable persons of the Colony."

The procedure in civil cases was based primarily upon the four titles of the Custom of Paris relating to real actions, actions generally, arrest and executions, and the seizure and sale of moveables. An additional source was the procedure used before the *Châtelet de Paris*, principally the *Ordonnance Civile* of Louis XIV (1667).

At the beginning, the Superior Council was the only tribunal in the country and possessed original jurisdiction, but when the population increased, it was necessary to establish inferior courts and to appoint as judges the directors of the company in the several localities where they resided. Every one of them with two of the "chief men of the vicinage" might take cognizance of any civil affair, and, with the assistance of four inhabitants having the qualifications to sit in civil matters, of any criminal matter. From their judgment, there lay an appeal to the Superior Council. Justice was kept very much within the "company town" management. But again it should be noted that by royal edict justice was to be administered without cost to the litigants.

Bienville, being governor of the colony, made New Orleans the capital of Louisiana in June, 1722. Two years later he was recalled to France. By this time it was apparent that the affairs of John Law's company were not prospering and the company surrendered its charter to the Crown in 1731, having expended some twenty million livres on Louisiana. With the surrender of the charter, the colony became a crown colony and was so governed. Bienville again became governor in 1733, a post which he continued to hold until 1743 when he returned to France.

One knows precious little about the law or legal education during this period. Charles Étienne Arthur Gayarré, Louisiana's noted historian, tells us of an early judicial trial in 1738 wherein a man, named Labarre, having committed suicide, a curator was appointed to the corpse, which was then indicted, tried, convicted and sentenced to be deprived of Christian burial, and to lie rotting and bleaching on the face of the earth "among the offals, bones and refuse of the butcher's stall." We do know that Bienville was convinced that there should be a college in the colony "at least for the study of the classics, of geometry, geography, pilotage, etc." He spoke of how ruinously expensive it was for those who sent their children to France to be educated, and he echoed a remark current today that "it is even to be feared from this circumstance that the Creoles, thus educated abroad, will imbibe a dislike of their native country, and will come back to it only to receive and to convert into cash what property may be left to them by their parents."

Despite the best efforts of men such as Bienville, the Louisiana colonial period cannot be described as a success and there is little to indicate a profound attachment of the colony to French law in this pre-Napoleon period when that law, even for Parisians, was difficult to find and apply.

Several reasons have been advanced for the failure of the French in Louisiana. One was that the form of government which a strong-willed Louis XIV had fixed upon France was too rigid to suit the needs of the colony and just as its "prying, meddling, all-directing supervision" had begun to subdue individual initiative in France, its effect upon colonial development was stultifying. As one writer also points out "in spite of opposite intentions, European custom had grafted an almost feudal system of land tenure upon Louisiana." The great tracts of land were owned by French aristocrats, most of whom never came to the colony. The colonists, even when worthy, found themselves pawns to absentee landowners. Many of the colonists who were sent out were ill-suited to colonial life and so unproductive that the main support of the colony fell upon Negro slaves. Added to all this was the fact that France's interest during this period was almost wholly taken up with European intrigues and changes.

At all events, as early as October 31, 1761, the French ambassador to Spain admitted that she could protect Louisiana no longer. Louisiana had cost France between forty and fifty million livres. For the year 1756 alone, the expenses were 829,398 livres while the revenue was almost negligible. France feared that the colony might fall to the English and she solicited Spain's aid in supplying its wants.

Finally, on November 3, 1762, by the secret Treaty of Fontainebleau, France ceded Louisiana west of the River Iberville (now Bayou Manchac) to Spain in order, as she said, to enable Spain "by the sacrifice of such part of it, as she thought proper, to ransom Cuba and to indemnify her for the loss of Florida."

The Treaty of Fontainebleau ceded to Spain "full ownership forever and without any exception or reservation whatever, from the pure impulse of his [the French King's] generous heart and from the sense of affection and friendship existing between these two royal persons, all the country known under the name of Louisiana." Ten days later, on November 13, 1762, the King of Spain accepted the donation, but it was kept secret and the King of France continued to act as sovereign, appointing Nicolas Chauvin de Lafrénière *procureur général* in Louisiana on January 1, 1763.

Spain technically became *de jure* owner of Louisiana on

November 23, 1762, but she did not replace the French flag until the summer of 1769. During the interval, France continued to manage Louisiana affairs. For example, on February 10, 1763, France decreed a reorganization of the colony and on March 16, 1763, the French King announced a reduction of the troops stationed there. Since one of France's reasons for parting with the colony was to accomplish a reduction in expenses, it was not surprising that France protested the Spanish delay.

Charles III, in 1766, finally sent Don Antonio de Ulloa to take possession of Louisiana, to govern it and organize it on a proper footing. Ulloa was a native of Seville, came from a distinguished family and was forty-six when he came to Louisiana. He was an eminent scientist: as an astronomer he had discovered a cavity on the moon which bears his name. These qualities stood him in good stead in the courts of Europe, but they did not equip him to govern an uneasy and difficult colony. Charles III instructed Ulloa not to change the administration of Louisiana's government and that "it not be subjected to the laws and usages which are observed in my American dominions, from which it is a distinct colony and with which it is to have no commerce. It is my will that it be independent of the Ministry of the Indies, of its Council, and of the other tribunals annexed to it, and that all which may be relative to Louisiana, shall pass through the Ministry of State, and that you communicate to me, through that Channel alone, whatever may be appertaining to your government."

The prime effect of the transfer from France to Spain was on the commercial relations of the colony. Ulloa's instructions called for a cessation of direct trade with France, a change not popular with French colonists whose taste was for French and not for Spanish goods. Ulloa soon realized that this could not be accomplished without firm military control which he did not possess.

Ulloa arrived on March 5, 1766 (nearly four years after the donation) to take over a colony with thirty Spanish soldiers, a comptroller, Esteban Gayarré, a commissary of war and intendant, Joseph Loyola, and a treasurer, Martin Navarro. Since Charles III wished no change in laws or government, the French authority continued and the Custom of Paris remained the applicable law. Even the charms of Ulloa's rich Peruvian wife, the Marchioness of Abrado (whom he married when he was fifty-one) were used against him. The resentment of the colonists rose to such a pitch that the Superior Council on October 29, 1768 passed a decree giving Ulloa "three times twenty-four hours to embark and render account of his conduct to His Catholic Majesty, the King of Spain." Ulloa left the colony on October 31.

Here then was a clear insult to Spain delivered at the hands of rebellious colonists of French extraction. The French flag still flew; French government still controlled; the Spanish governor had been sent home by the colonial government.

The fate of Louisiana was in the balance. The French ambassador to London suggested that Louisiana might be erected into an independent republic under Spanish protection. It seemed to him, he wrote, that a republic under Spanish suzerainty (and hence financial support) might be an example to encourage the British colonies to revolt. But nothing came of this proposal. Even the colonists, when they spoke of independence, would admit no Spanish suzerainty.

Meanwhile, Charles III summoned a Great Council which lasted from January to March, 1769, to decide what should be done with Louisiana. France had done the same thing earlier when Law's charter was surrendered. It was clear that Spain did not consider Louisiana her prime colonial jewel, no rival of her Indies, but Spain saw Louisiana as a buffer against England, and perhaps more immediately she saw this revolt as one which, if left unpunished, might easily encourage the other Spanish colonies to send home their governors. Thus Spain decided to press her claim and sent to Louisiana for this purpose Don Alexander O'Reilly, a young Irishman, whose considerable military ability had served various European sovereigns before becoming fixed under the favor of Charles III.

In contrast to Ulloa's unpretentious arrival, O'Reilly came on August 17, 1769, with a Spanish fleet of twenty-four sails. He took possession of the colony peacefully with an impressive ceremony on the following day. He went to call formally upon the French governor, Aubry, having a few days earlier received a deputation from the legislative council, headed by Lafrénière, the *procureur général*, who was regarded as Ulloa's chief opponent. The delegation had asked that the colony not be treated as conquered territory. O'Reilly replied little and made his own investigations, and shortly thereafter, he invited the chief collaborators against Ulloa to his office and arrested them in accordance with orders from the King of Spain, remarking that "the Spanish nation is respected and venerated all over the globe. Louisiana seems to be the only country which is not aware of it and which is deficient in the respect due to that nation." A court martial lasting some two months followed and there were condemned to death for insurrection the following: Lafrénière, Jean Baptiste de Noyan (nephew of Bienville), Captain Marquis, Pierre Caresse, a leading merchant, Joseph Milhet and Joseph Roy de Villeré. Thus was the insult to Spain avenged.

O'Reilly took firm control. On August 23, 1769, he issued a proclamation inviting the inhabitants of the town and its vicinity to appear before him, at his house, on August 26 at *seven o'clock in the morning* to take their solemn oath of vassalage and fealty to the new sovereign. He caused a census to be made, showing that there were then in New Orleans 3190 persons of every age, sex and color. He abolished the Superior Council and substituted therefor a Cabildo, composed of six perpetual *regidores* (offices acquired by purchase: number increased by six in 1797), two ordinary *alcaldes* (these were chosen on the first of each year by the perpetual *regidores* and each was a judge within the city of all civil cases and of criminal cases wherein the defendant did not enjoy or claim the privilege of trial by military or ecclesiastical authority), an attorney general or *syndic* and a clerk (this office also acquired by purchase).

Among the *regidores* were distributed the following offices: *alferez real* (royal standard bearer), principal provincial *alcalde* (with cognizance of offences committed in New Orleans), *alquazil* (high sheriff) and depositary-general (receiver of fines).

In addition to the judicial officers previously mentioned (*alcaldes*), there were throughout the colony *fueros ecclesiasticos* under the direction of the vicar-general, and *fueros militares* with competence among the military forces. These also served as inferior courts in the territory. Thus O'Reilly's judicial system consisted of inferior courts of first instance throughout the land with appeals allowed in minor cases to the Cabildo and in the more important ones to the Audiencia in Havana with the Council of the Indies as the final court.

Spanish law was introduced into Louisiana by O'Reilly by his ordinance of November 25, 1769 by authority of the King of Spain. This proclamation abrogated all French law except the *Code Noir* of Louis XV given in 1724. This *Code Noir* had been adopted from acts drawn up for the governance of the slaves of Santo Domingo. Spanish law being unknown to the colonists, O'Reilly proclaimed his Code of 1769 in the form of two ordinances, written in French, and in such simple form that the colonists might be won to its acceptance, no mean accomplishment since the Spanish law of that period was neither easy to find nor to interpret.

O'Reilly assigned to New Orleans its first regular revenue. It would be derived from taxes on taverns, cafés, hotels, pensions, inns, brandy, butchers and the docking of vessels. Among the many regulations given by O'Reilly were those pertaining to taverns set out on October 8, 1769. Article one directed that "public welfare demands that we permit only twelve taverns in the city." Article three ordered that they not sell liquor on "feast days nor on Sunday during High Mass nor during Vespers when there is Benediction of the Holy Sacrament." Article four provided that taverns close at 8 p.m., and article nine declared that each tavern pay the sum of 200 livres per year.

Louisiana continued under Spanish control and law until 1803. Spanish was the official language but manners and customs were French.

As early as 1779, Louisiana inhabitants made secret overtures to the French minister in Philadelphia asking that France recover the province, but the French government did not respond to these entreaties, perhaps believing that commercially Louisiana was not an important plum. Now, by the Treaty of Paris of 1783 Great Britain had restored to Spain Florida and the territory east of the Iberville which had been given to England by France in 1762. Thus Spain regained that portion of North America which pleased her most. On the other hand, Louisiana was costing Spain an annual deficit of $337,000. Spain's one concern was that Louisiana not fall to England. To part with Louisiana to France, as Charles IV saw it, was simply to have the cost of policing Spain's American frontier borne by France. On the other hand, Napoleon's desire for Louisiana was not for itself alone but as a necessary prelude to his plan to form a colonial empire in North America. In this he had the early interest of Talleyrand. Napoleon saw Louisiana as a depot for the French islands, "an empire of unlimited possibility and an effective barrier against further American settlement."

On October 1, 1800, by the Treaty of San Ildefonso, Spain receded to France the colony or province of Louisiana in such a way as to restore the status quo prior to the Seven Years' War (1755–1763). France thus recovered Louisiana "with a *pourboire* of six men of war" at no cost at all. Charles IV did not give the actual royal order for the delivery of Louisiana to France until October 15, 1802, two years after the treaty.

Pierre Clement Laussat was appointed colonial prefect for France on the retrocession, and sailed for New Orleans on January 12, 1803, reaching there March 26. He liked the Spanish little and he had little more enthusiasm for the Americans. It is interesting to note the instructions of Minister Decrés for the captain general, which had been approved by the First Consul (Napoleon) on November 26, 1802, but never issued. They directed that "English customs shall be rejected. The use of the French language shall be the only one welcomed, and the favor of the government shall be particularly attached to everything that may recall the Mother Country and its customs."

There is opinion to the effect that Laussat's occupation for France of approximately three weeks did not materially change the civil law in force, but it must be noted that Laussat destroyed the judicial tribunal for its application and enforcement when on November 30, 1803, he substituted for the Spanish Cabildo a Municipality composed of a mayor, two adjoints, ten members, a secretary and a treasurer. No provision was made for this municipality to exercise judicial power.

Napoleon by this time had other problems at hand than his dream of a North American colonial empire, and had come to the decision to sell Louisiana to the United States. The idea to sell is said to have come on April 10, 1803, but the treaty to sell was not signed until April 30. Despite doubts as to the constitutionality of the purchase, the United States Senate ratified the treaty on October 19 by a vote of 24 to 7 and on December 20 the nation received possession through its emissaries, General James Wilkinson and William C. C. Claiborne, from Laussat, representing France.

The Louisiana Purchase will continue to interest historians for generations to come. Jefferson, after much early vacillation, wrote to Livingston that "there is on the globe one spot, the possessor of which is our natural and habitual enemy. It is New Orleans, through which the produce of ⅜ of our territory must pass to market, and from its fertility it will ere long yield more than ½ of our whole produce and contain more than half our inhabitants. France placing herself in that door assumes to us the attitude of defiance. Spain might have retained it quietly for years."

Jefferson appointed Claiborne to assume control at New Orleans in preference to "Judge" Andrew Jackson, who was an applicant for the post, and after the Marquis de la Fayette had declined the President's request to serve. Claiborne, a Virginian, educated at William and Mary, read law on the side, while serving as a clerk in the House of Representatives. He began the practice of law in Tennessee at the age of 20 and in his late twenties became Governor of the Mississippi Territory and subsequently Governor General of the Province of Louisiana.

Two important questions had to be met: what form of government would be instituted in the newly acquired land? and what law would be applied there? problems which were by no means easy for the young Claiborne.

First, as to the form of government, Claiborne reported to Madison, Secretary of State, on December 27, 1803 that Laussat, the French prefect, had abolished the Cabildo, a change which Claiborne approved since the Cabildo was in his opinion "in part a hereditary Council, in action feeble and arbitrary and supposed to be devoted to the views of the Spanish Government." Laussat had substituted therefor a Municipality, of which Claiborne reported that it "for the most part" consisted of "approved Characters, and well disposed to the expected change of government; and I therefore did not long hesitate to sanction the new arrangement." But with the passing of the cabildo went also their judicial functions so that at the time of the cession the only judicial officers available were the governor himself and the former *alcaldes de barrio* (commissioners of police created by Carondelet). The need for a judicial body was both apparent and urgent and Claiborne drew upon the only experience he had had in Tennessee and Virginia and by ordinance of December 30, (written in both English and French) he established a court of justice sometimes called Court of Pleas or Court of Common Pleas, composed of seven justices three of whom would constitute a quorum. It was provided that the court meet at least once a week in New Orleans. The court's civil jurisdiction was limited to cases not exceeding $3,000 in value with the right of appeal to the governor when the amount in litigation rose above $500. It had jurisdiction over criminal matters in which the punishment did not exceed $200 and sixty days. Each of the seven justices was given authority to judge summarily all debts under $100 reserving appeal to the whole court. Detailed rules were laid down as to the court's procedure.

Apparently, the new court worked well because we find Claiborne writing to Madison on March 2, 1804, that "on my first arrival in this city, the solicitude of the inhabitants for some tribunals of justice appeared to be universal, and the general complaint was that no debts could be recovered. I immediately organized an inferior tribunal and all parties seemed pleased with the institution. Debtors have recently complained of the zeal and promptitude with which the Justices discharge their duties, and beg that some delay in the hearing and determining causes may be prescribed. I have endeavored to accommodate debtors on this point, in prescribing Rules of Proceeding for the Court which will produce in part the delay solicited."

But not all approved the action of Claiborne in setting up what was to them an alien court borrowed from England and not France or Spain. The historian-jurist François Xavier Martin wrote that in the new court of common pleas most of the judges were ignorant of the laws and language of the country and proceedings were carried on in the English language.

Claiborne's action was a temporary one, until such time as the federal Congress would make provisions for the establishment of a territory. Meanwhile, Claiborne found himself "so pressed by parties litigants, that I am compelled to exercise Judicial power." Consequently, he reported to Madison on February 13, that "the day after tomorrow I propose holding a special court, and shall set apart one day in every week for hearing and deciding of Causes until the provisions of Congress for some fixed Government shall relieve me from this painful duty." Other colonists were to complain of this court of last resort in which Claiborne "sat as sole judge, not attended, as the Spanish governors were, by a legal advisor." One pamphlet in particular was so critical that Claiborne felt called upon to explain his conduct to Madison in a letter in October, 1804: "the writer of the pamphlet has alluded to the magnitude of my late judicial powers and stated (what is quite correct) my want of information as to the Spanish laws and also of the French language. The magnitude of these powers was always a source of uneasyness to me and I refused to exercise judicial authority as long as the interest of the people would permit. But New Orleans is a great commercial city. I found myself compelled to open a Supreme Court and to preside there as the sole judge." Again and again in his letters to Madison, Claiborne alludes to the inadvisability of reviving the Cabildo as the judicial forum, a course of action which would have offended many Louisianians, and to the need for laws relating to commerce and navigation.

Congress acted on March 26, 1804, establishing the Territory of Orleans for that part of the Purchase within the present state of Louisiana and vesting the judicial power of the territory in a Superior Court and in such inferior courts as the Legislative Council, a body of thirteen appointed by the President of the United States, might establish. The Superior Court was duly established by territorial act of 1806 to be composed of three judges, any one of whom constituted a quorum and might act separately, rendering a decision of last resort.

A congressional act of March 26, 1804, also provided for the writ of habeas corpus and trial by jury in the territory. These innovations from the common law, especially the latter, produced some interesting difficulties. Martin relates how early courts were furnished with interpreters in the French, Spanish and English languages, who translated the evidence and the court's charge, but not the arguments of counsel. Where the case was opened in English, the jurors not familiar with that language were permitted to retire to the gallery. The defense, often being in French, the jurors who could not understand that language retired. This meant that the verdict of the jury was reached by each juror on what he heard which may well have been only part of the whole case.

The second and more difficult question posed by the transfer was: what law was to be applied in the new territory? According to international law, it could be argued that the law in effect at the time of the cession remained in force unless and until abrogated by legislation. This meant that Spanish law was in force unless congressional or territorial acts had repealed it. The congressional act of October 31, 1803, left the old laws unchanged and merely gave new officials the power to administer them. The congressional act which provided for the writ of habeas corpus and for trial by jury expressly declared that all laws in force in the territory at the passage of the act and not inconsistent with it, should continue in force until altered by legislation. A later act of March 2, 1805, contained the same clause, and the Legislative Council acts of May 4, 1805, and July 3, 1805, contained no repealing clause.

If then Spanish law remained in force in the territory, what did this mean in fact? For Professor J. H. Wigmore this meant: *Las Siete Partidas* (1348), which Moreau Lislet and Henry Carleton translated in 1820, the *Nueva Recopilaçion of Castile* (published in 1567 and last amended in 1777), the *Recopilaçion de los Indes* (1680) which contained the laws specially applicable to all Spanish colonies, the *cedulas* (edicts), and to a certain extent such early codes as the Theodosian Code (384), Breviary of Alaric (506), *Liber Judiciorum* (650), *Fuero Juzgo* (a corruption of the *Forum Judiciorum*), *Fuero Viejo* and the *Fuero Real.*

Copies of these older codes were rare. No complete collection was available. Of some not a single copy existed in the territory. It was easy for the Americans who were swarming into New Orleans from other parts of the United States to argue that the Spanish law being so obtuse and unavailable, it would be well for the new territory to be governed by the common law which prevailed in other parts of the United States.

But, as Gayarré points out, when the inhabitants asked what the common law was, they were told that it was that law "which draws its binding force from immemorial usage and universal reception in England" or a "body of rules, principles and customs, which derived their authority and sanctity from their filtration for centuries through the thick strata of successive British generations, and which, originating in natural justice and equity, or local customs, were only to be evidenced by the records of judicial decisions scattered through hundreds of volumes written in a language which they did not comprehend." It is not surprising that the colonists saw little advantage in such a system over that which they now knew at least in part.

Four areas of law came under early review. First, public or constitutional law, since by the cession the Constitution of the United States with its Bill of Rights became the supreme law of the territory. The treaty itself provided that the inhabitants were to be secured in their liberty, property and religion, and, as Claiborne pointed out to Madison on October 16, 1804, this clause in the treaty rendered "great innovations upon the Spanish laws and Spanish tribunals absolutely necessary." Secondly, the merchants of the city impatiently demanded of the Congress some laws relating to commerce, navigation and revenues, matters important to a great port city. Thirdly, there was widespread dissatisfaction with the Spanish criminal law, particularly in the light of guarantees contained in the American Constitution, such as the right of habeas corpus, trial by jury and prescribed methods of trial.

On May 4, 1805, the Legislative Council passed an act providing for punishment of crimes and misdemeanors, specifying a number of offenses and directing that they be construed and tried according to the common law of England. Later that year, on July 3, another Legislative Council act added a few crimes to the earlier list and prescribed a "common law trial for all other crimes" but this act was repealed in 1806. The Spanish law thus replaced included such provisions as banishment and confiscation of property of any advocate who betrayed the secrets of his client or who intentionally cited the law falsely, and directing that in many instances the sentence lay wholly within the discretion of the judge, while in capital cases, he could "at his pleasure choose as the mode of punishment, decapitation by sword, burning, hanging or wild beasts."

The fourth area in which reform or change was undertaken was in procedure and practice. At the time of the transfer, these were drawn from such varied sources as the Custom of Paris, the Code Louis of 1677 and the Regulations for Judicial Procedure promulgated by O'Reilly in 1769. Two very important changes had occurred since which made revision necessary: the adoption of the institution of jury trial, and the requirement that the testimony of all available witnesses be given in open court, a notion completely alien to French and Spanish trial procedure. Edward Livingston was appointed to draw up acts regulating practice and procedure, which acts were adopted by the Legislative Council on April 10, 1805 and are widely known as Livingston's Code of Civil Practice and Procedure.

Edward Livingston, called by Wigmore the "greatest creative jurist we have ever seen—the Bentham of American jurisprudence without the blemishes of that great critic"—, was born in 1764 in New York and educated at Princeton. A brother of Robert Livingston, who helped to negotiate the Louisiana Purchase, he read law in Judge Lansing's office in Albany, New York, and was a contemporary of Alexander Hamilton, Aaron Burr and James Kent. He came to Louisiana to repair or to recover from financial difficulties, not entirely of his own making. We shall see later the great mark which he made upon Louisiana's history.

It is certainly true that Livingston's code adopts many common law names and terms in translating the French concepts into English. One authority on Louisiana procedure, Henry George McMahon, includes that "fairly convincing evidence is available . . . to indicate that the courts and legal profession of Louisiana regarded the Practice Act of 1805 as being based primarily upon Spanish procedure."

But if change and a certain amount of innovation were accepted in public and procedural law, it was a different matter with regard to private law. The real difficulty lay in finding the Spanish law then in force in the territory. The Legislative Council made an attempt in 1806 to provide that certain portions of Roman and Spanish law should be the law of Louisiana but this act was vetoed by Governor Claiborne, provoking much furor. Still earlier on February 4, 1805 there had been a joint resolution of the Legislative Council authorizing a legislative committee to draft civil and criminal codes and to employ two counsellors-at-law to assist them in drafting such codes. Thereafter, the first Louisiana Territorial Legislature by resolution of June 7, 1806 appointed James Brown and L. Moreau Lislet "to compile and prepare jointly a Civil Code for the use of this Territory" and resolved "that the two jurisconsults shall make the civil law by which this Territory is now governed the ground work of said Code." The result of their labors was "A Digest of the Civil Laws now in Force in the Territory of Orleans, with alterations and Amendments adapted to its present system of Government." This was adopted by legislative act on March 31, 1808, and is popularly known as the Code of 1808. Section 2 of that act declared that "whatever in the ancient civil laws of this territory or in the territory state, is contrary to the dispositions contained in the said digest, or irreconcilable with them is hereby abrogated."

The source of the Code of 1808 continues to be a subject of scholarly debate. Perhaps the de la Vergne manuscript of the code with annotations and references in the hand of Moreau Lislet, which the family has recently made available for study, will throw light on the question. Judge Martin and Judge Eugene D. Saunders, a former Tulane Law School dean, were of the opinion that the drafters followed almost literally the first *projet* of the Code Napoleon. W. K. Dart considered that they followed the last *projet* of the Carabacérès Code in many particulars, but incorporated into it a part of the Spanish law which had become fixed as rules of property in Louisiana, with which opinion Hatcher agrees. H. P. Dart, Jr. is of the opinion that the code was based on the first draft of the Code Napoleon, which had been printed on March 21, 1804. John Tucker concludes that "the Code Napoleon furnished the framework and most of the substance of our Code of 1808 with Spanish elements intercalated."

Of these scholars, Judge Martin alone knew the drafters, and one is inclined to take his word that they used the *projet* and his approval of their action when he said that "although the *projet* is necessarily much more imperfect than the Code, it was far superior to anything that any two individuals could have produced early enough to answer the expectations of those who employed them."

The Digest or Code of 1808 was originally written in French and put into English by translators employed by the Legislature. With regard to inaccuracies of translation, Moreau Lislet replied that "the French text, in which it is known that work was drawn up, leaves no doubt." The digest itself in section five was less helpful when it provided that in cases of obscurity or ambiguity, "both the English and French texts shall be consulted, and shall mutually serve to the interpretation of one and the other." It is interesting to observe that a digest, presumably of Spanish law in force in the territory, appeared only in English and French.

The digest was distributed to all courts of justice and other authorities charged with the execution of the laws of the territory. Even Governor Claiborne, in reporting on the code to Madison said, "I see much to admire in the Civil Law, but there are some principles which ought to yield to the Common Law Doctrine." "Indeed," he wrote, "it has been with me a favorite policy to assimilate as much as possible the laws and usages of this Territory to those of the states generally, but the work of innovation could not be pursued hastily, nor with safety, until the existing laws were fully presented to our view."

But the old laws were not so easily laid to rest. In the case of *Cottin v. Cottin*, the court held that the old Spanish laws remained part of the written law of the territory unless repealed expressly by the Code of 1808 or otherwise, or found inconsistent therewith or with the federal Constitution. The way was thus left open again for the application of Spanish law outside or in addition to the code, and this led ultimately to the need for revision.

But before leaving the Code of 1808, it is well to look at the interesting instructions given to the drafters by the Legislature, namely, that "it shall be the duty of the two jurisconsults to attend as much as possible the superior and inferior courts of the City of New Orleans, in order that to take notice of any imperfections in the new Code, owing either to the ambiguity of expressions, or omissions or contradictions, etc., and . . . to submit faithfully their observations thereon to the Legislature, and to subjoin to those observations the additions, corrections and amendments which they may deem necessary in order to enable the Legislature to make this new Code as perfect as possible."

After considerable debate and by a vote of 77 to 36, Louisiana was admitted as a state into the Union on February 20, 1811, although many thought that Louisiana was not ready for statehood, having had little opportunity to develop self-government while a colony of France and Spain.

A state constitutional convention was held in New Orleans on November 4, 1811, which selected Julian Poydras as its president and drew up Louisiana's first constitution (the briefest in her history). The Congress had attached certain conditions to admission, these being "that the Constitution should be republican and consistent with the Constitution of the United States, that it should contain the fundamental principles of civil and religious liberty, that it should secure to the citizen the trial by jury in all criminal cases, and the privilege of the writ of habeas corpus conformable to the provisions of the Constitution of the United States, that the laws enacted by the new State should be promulgated, and all its records of every description preserved, and its judicial and legislative written proceedings conducted, in the language in which the laws and the judicial and legislative proceedings of the United States were published and conducted."

Pursuant to the Louisiana Constitution, the Supreme Court of Louisiana was created by act of February 10, 1813, and consisted of three judges (now increased to seven). Governor Claiborne became the first state governor, a post which he held until 1816 when he was succeeded by Governor Jacques Villeré. The latter, much concerned with the increase of crime in the state, allegedly due to the influx of foreigners, in his address to the legislature in 1818 recommended the adoption of measures "for the purpose of obliging foreigners, of whom there was so great an influx from all parts, to give us some reasonable assurance of their good conduct, before they shall be entitled to enjoy the protection of our laws, and participate with our citizens in the advantages afforded by our happy country." A separate criminal court was created for the City of New Orleans in that year (1818) with three judges appointed by the governor. In the governor's annual address the following year he could report that "owing to the just firmness of juries, the violators of our laws, the malefactors of every description, have suffered . . . due to their crimes."

Livingston's interest in criminal law existed before he came to Louisiana, as is attested by the fact that as a member of the House of Representatives from New York in December 1795, he moved to revise the penal code of the United States, which he said was in general too sanguinary and very badly proportioned. A committee of which Livingston was chairman was appointed to consider the matter but after a preliminary report, no further action was taken. On February 10, 1820, Livingston was authorized to prepare a penal code for Louisiana. Preliminary reports were approved by the legislature in 1822 and 1823.

Livingston describes the fate of this work in a letter to a friend, wherein he wrote, "The night before last, I wrote to you an apologetic letter, accounting for not having before that time thanked you for your letter and your book. My excuse lay before me in four codes: Of Crimes and Punishments; of Criminal Procedure; of Prison Discipline, and of Evidence. This was about one o'clock; I retired to rest, and in about three hours was awakened by the cry of fire. It had broken out in my writing room, and, before it was discovered, not a vestige of my work remained, except for fifty or sixty pages which were at the printers, and a few very imperfect notes in another place." The penal code was rewritten, but the Legislature had by then changed its mind and did not adopt it. The code of evidence was not rewritten until 1830 and it also was not adopted.

The ideas Livingston presented in his code were far in advance of his time. As he wrote in his preliminary report to the Legislature, the "object was to ameliorate punishment and not to avenge society; to reform the criminal and to prevent crime; and to clarify existing laws and write them in language comprehensible to all the people."

His work in reforming the criminal law of Louisiana, although it did not win the approval of the Legislature, yet won for him international acclaim and membership in the French Academy of Moral and Political Sciences. Belatedly, but not less sincerely, on January 16, 1832, by legislative action, the Governor of Louisiana was authorized to purchase a medal and to "tender the same to the Honorable Edward Livingston as a token of acknowledgment on the part of the State of Louisiana for the Code of Civil and Criminal Law, presented to the State by that distinguished gentleman." As with many such matters, there was not one but many reasons why Livingston's penal code was not adopted. The ideas may well have been too revolutionary, as Bentham also found in England. Judges may have been put off by the new role which they were to play in Livingston's system. The crime rate in New Orleans and the nature of the criminals involved may have persuaded the Legislature that this was no time and place to turn away from punishment as a deterrent to the concept of reformation of the criminal. It took more than a century for Louisiana to formulate and adopt a criminal code, and then it bore little resemblance to Livingston's work.

Reform of the civil code was to fare better. By resolution of March 14, 1822, the Legislature appointed Moreau Lislet (one of the drafters of the Code of 1808), Edward Livingston and Pierre Derbigny (later to be governor of Louisiana in 1828) to revise the Civil Code of 1808 by amending the same "in such manner as they will deem advisable and by adding under each book, title and chapter of the Code, such of the laws as are still in force and not included therein in order that the whole be submitted to the Legislature at its first session or as soon as the said works have been completed." The resolution further provided that the three jurisconsults should add to their work a complete system of the commercial laws in force in Louisiana, with such alterations as they might deem proper, and a treatise on the rules of civil actions and a system of the practice to be observed in the courts. The committee reported that in preparing the civil code, it would draw from *Las Siete Partidas*, the Digest of the Louisiana laws, the existing English laws, the codes of France and of Rome. The plan submitted by the draftsmen was presented to the Legislature on February 13, 1823, and approved on March 22. The *Projet* entitled "additions et amendements au code civil de l'état de la Louisiana proposés en vertu de la resolution de la legislature du 14 mars 1822 par les juristes chargés de ce travail," was ordered to be printed and distributed to members of the legislature and judiciary.

The code itself was approved on April 12, and its promulgation ordered. This took place in New Orleans on May 20 and in West Feliciana Parish on June 15. The original was written in French of which the English text is a translation. In case of conflict between the two texts, the French text was to prevail.

As to its sources, Hatcher says that approximately eighty per cent of its provisions were taken verbatim from the Code Napoleon with the rest drawn from commentators such as Domat and Pothier and from the works of Toullier on the Code Napoleon. It is said that the part of the code treating of obligations was entirely by Livingston's hand. It is true that the terminology of the English common law "crept in with the language" and some of the notions have become admixed. But as Professor Wigmore wrote, it remains thoroughly and essentially Roman, and "the Roman system of law must form a fundamental part of the equipment of a lawyer in Louisiana." One would not say that the Roman codes were less Roman because they borrowed from the Greeks, and in like manner one must appraise the Louisiana contribution. What should be said is that the Louisiana Civil Code is a code made for Louisiana after the civilian method of codification. It is Louisiana's contribution for her own governance. As such, it is more prolix than the French code (3522 articles as against 2281) but many of these extra articles consist in a proliferation of examples so that the judges who would apply the law, many of them not trained in the civil law, might understand the code more easily.

The code was to be sufficient in itself, but should there arise the so-called "unprovided-for case" then the codal directions to the judge were precise: "In all civil matters, where there is no express law, the judge is bound to proceed and decide according to equity. To decide equitably, an appeal is to be made to natural law and reason, or received usages where the positive law is silent." This provision, reminiscent of the Swiss code, is considered by many to be one of the code's most remarkable features.

This code, revised in 1870 to remove from it all references to slavery and to put in the amendments which had been made by the Legislature, remains in force today. As W. K. Dart wrote, "the tinkering of a century has only dented a few of its edges and it stands today as it stood over a century ago, a magnificent monument to human industry and learning."

Two fears possessed the draftsmen: one that the courts might again bring back the old Spanish law, holding that the repeal was not complete. The second was that the common law might be imported into Louisiana by legislative or judicial reference. In fact, in 1827, the Supreme Court of Louisiana did hold that the provisions of the Spanish law, which were not contrary to the Civil Code of 1825, and were not repealed by the new code, and articles of the Code of 1808 which were omitted from the 1825 code were not thereby repealed and continued in force. The matter was finally set at rest by an act of March 25, 1828, which abrogated all the civil laws (in the sense of French, Roman and Spanish) which were in force prior to the 1825 code. The fear that the common law might be imported into Louisiana by general reference was set at rest by the Constitution of 1812, Article IV, Section II, which provided that the "Legislature shall never adopt any system or code of laws by a general reference to the said system or code, but in all cases shall specify the several provisions of the laws it may enact."

The Code of Practice in Civil Cases for the State of Louisiana was adopted on April 12, 1824. It, like the civil code, was written in French and that text prevails over the English translation in case of conflict; also, it takes precedence over the civil code and revised statutes in case of ambiguity or conflict. According to some jurists, the Code of Practice is more Roman than the civil code and probably the "most individual of all Louisiana's legal institutions." Certainly, it shows considerable evidence of a deep knowledge of French procedural theory. This code was revised in 1870 by John Ray of Monroe and it has now been superseded by the Louisiana Code of Civil Procedure of 1960.

Some one hundred and twenty years after Louisiana rejected the penal code prepared by Livingston, she adopted the Criminal Code of 1942, drawn up by Professors Dale Bennett, Clarence Morrow and Leon Sarpy, under the direction of the Louisiana State Law Institute. While it lacks Livingston's brilliant and controversial innovation, it puts into written codal form that which before was partially written and partially unwritten. Professor Morrow wrote bitterly of "opportunities missed" and "challenges unanswered." (On January 1, 1967, the new Code of Criminal Procedure, a revision of the Code of 1928, came into effect.)

The Louisiana Code of Civil Procedure of 1960, undertaken at the direction of the Louisiana State Law Institute, is the product of ten years of study and debate. Its reporters were Leon

D. Hubert, Jr., Henry George McMahon and Leon Sarpy. In the reporters' preliminary report to the Legislature, they stated that their work would cover all of the retained procedural rules of the Code of Practice of 1870, numerous procedural rules which were to be found in the civil code, special legislation on procedure, certain procedural rules developed by the jurisprudence and some rules sanctioned by custom and long continued use by the profession. Recognizing the benefits to be derived from having state rules of procedure in harmony with those in use in the federal courts of Louisiana, the reporters adopted rules similar to those in use in those courts "wherever it could do so without violating the settled and basic theory of the procedural concepts of Louisiana." In fact, this was not so difficult since the Rules of Federal Procedure, through the presence of Louisiana's Monte Lemann on the drafting committee, had already felt the influence of Louisiana's simplified pleading.

As the chief draftsman, Henry George McMahon wrote that the code's philosophy was "essentially pragmatic," more "concerned with the utility and workability" of the rules than with any "science of civil procedure." The code represents a departure from traditional civilian method in that the redactors' comments are included in the code itself, a practice normally condemned by those who believe that the text of the law should be clear enough to speak for itself.

The common law trust concept, alien to Louisiana and the civil law, but highly desired as an import by the banking profession, has now found its way to legitimate status in Louisiana by way of the Trust Code of 1964, and trusts can now be created for limited periods. This innovation has by no means gone without criticism.

Louisiana law resembles that of her sister states in such matters as constitutional and administrative law, crimes, negotiable instruments and corporations. But there do exist important differences, some in juridical method and some deep-rooted in the political and social ideals of her origins. We can cite but a few:

First, although trial by jury in civil cases is available in Louisiana, it is seldom used since the appellate court may review the law and facts even where the latter were found by a jury.

Secondly, Louisiana like France has a firm notion that property should be freely alienable and to that purpose believes that ownership should always be in one person or body. Partly, this reflects the French Revolution's attack upon feudal tenures and partly Louisiana's desire that responsibility be centered. Thus the purchaser of mineral rights has no right to the minerals (as he might at common law) before he reduces them to possession, but only a servitude to explore and use, subject to forfeiture for non-use. Thus Louisiana has had difficulty in assimilating the trust concept, depending as it does upon the existence of two estates in land: one legal and one equitable.

Thirdly, Louisana has a profound concern for the family. Thus, a father cannot cut off his child "without a shilling." He must reserve a portion of his estate for his progeny. Further, in absence of a marriage contract to the contrary, all acquisitions of spouses during marriage become their joint property (community property) subject to certain rights of the husband during the marriage and to the survivor's usufruct in case of death. Finally, Louisiana holds the father or, after his decease, the mother responsible for the torts of their minor, unemancipated children residing with them, a provision which several other states have borrowed in cases of juvenile malicious mischief.

Fourthly, the idea is held in Louisiana that a man's last will and testament is so sacred that it can be contested only if he was mentally incapacitated at the time of making it: it can not be annulled for undue influence, or because it was made in anger, hatred, suggestion or captation.

Fifthly, the Louisiana Civil Code reflects the desire that there should be the greatest possible freedom of contract so long as no offence was given to good morals or public policy.

Sixthly, the law of tort, despite many attempts to introduce

Anglo-American common law concepts, has in essence remained simple, flexible and Roman in origin.

Finally, one should mention that the notary in Louisiana possesses some but by no means all of the traits of his French ancestor, the *notaire*.

Strong influences work to keep Louisiana faithful to her civil law heritage: her law schools with their emphasis upon civilian method and doctrine; the law reviews and their mission as partial commentators on the living law; the Louisiana State Law Institute and its emphasis upon the promotion and encouragement of the clarification, simplification and recodification of Louisiana's law; the Tulane Institute of Comparative Law which brings annually to Louisiana for teaching and research the outstanding scholars from European universities that Louisiana may keep abreast of new developments in the civil law; and finally, the judges and legislators who strive to maintain a system of law here adapted to Louisiana's history and needs.

Creole Architecture 1718–1860: The Rise and Fall of a Great Tradition

James Marston Fitch

The Europeans who, from the fifteenth century on, began the explosive invasion and conquest of the rest of the earth, faced characteristic architectural problems wherever they went: new climates, new building materials, new conditions of labor. The Portuguese in East Africa, Goa and Macao, the French and English in India and Southeast Asia, the Spanish in Central and South America, all found advanced cultures with sophisticated building technologies extant on the spot. This gave the conquerors two enormous advantages: an entire apparatus of skilled craftsmen which they could enslave; and an architecture adapted to local climates and local materials which they could co-opt. Moreover, in the case of the Spanish in the Americas, they found climates and terrains very similar to what they had left on the Iberian peninsula. This enabled them to employ their native architectural prototypes with scarcely any modification in the New World.

The very ease with which these native technologies could be chained to the imperial machine gave the colonial architecture of these regions many of its typical qualities. It resulted in relatively high levels of architectural amenity for the colonialists, often higher, in fact, than many of them would have enjoyed at home. But the very fact that colonial building was slave, or coolie, powered also gave it a conservative bias. Since manpower was cheap and abundant, there was little incentive for economy or efficiency in the use of either labor or materials.

But the Europeans who settled the North American continent were confronted by a fundamentally different situation from that which faced their contemporaries in other areas of colonial expansion. Here the Europeans exploded into aboriginal cultures, fragile and thinly spread, which were only beginning to emerge into the stage of agriculture and stable settlements. The indigenous architecture, while entirely adequate for native needs, especially along the South Atlantic seaboard and the Gulf Coast, was totally inadequate for even the lowest levels of European requirements. Moreover, the aboriginal populations did not take well to enslavement, tending instead to melt into the wilderness before the European advance. Finding the Indians intractable and unskilled, the Europeans soon resorted to a policy of methodical extermination. Thus they found themselves faced with enormous building needs and the necessity of doing all the work themselves. And this labor shortage was one of the key factors which gave North American building a fundamentally radical disposition from the very start. The incentives for invention, innovation, modification have always been very strong.

The climates of North America also forced a modification of many traditional concepts and practices. In the north, Dutch, French and English found themselves submerged in thermal régimes vastly different from and more difficult than the cool, temperate climates of Western Europe. New World winters were, on the whole, much longer and more severe, while the summers were much hotter. And when the French, English, Spanish and Danes broke into the closed lake of the Caribbean, they found themselves in a hot, humid environment for which there was no parallel anywhere in Europe. Thus everywhere in North America, from the earliest days of colonization, construction methods and plan types alike began to be modified to meet new and unfamiliar environmental stresses.

Familiar building materials such as wood and stone—together with the raw ingredients of such processed materials as plaster, cement, brick and glass—were of course everywhere abundant in the New World. Early accounts are full of rapturous descriptions of such riches of great trees, fine marbles and slates, clays and sands. But their exploitation was intimately related to the skills and quantities of available labor, as well as being dependent upon a fixed industrial plant of some sophistication: sawmills, brick kilns, lime ovens, glass smelters, etc. And one of the notable features of early North American architectural history is the speed with which this technological base was established in the wilderness.

The most important part of any immigrant's equipment is always conceptual, i.e., his fixed ideas of the proper way of accomplishing any task—burying the dead, marrying a wife, building a house. These concepts are extremely durable and the way in which they are progressively modified without being entirely relinquished is a fascinating study in itself. The building concepts which the early colonists brought with them as an integral part of their intellectual equipment turned out to be partly useful and partly sheer impedimenta. They had their origins in two related but by no means identical sources in Europe: the high style theories of the ruling classes, ablaze with Renaissance concepts of formal order; and the pragmatic conventional wisdom of the peasantry and working classes, essentially the functionalism of late medievalism.

These two currents of architectural theory co-existed in North America up until the death of Jefferson, i.e., until the full beginnings of industrialization. In fact, as we shall see, they often coalesced into extremely satisfactory architecture and town-building, at both a formal and a functional level. Indeed, at some golden point (which might be pinpointed in Philadelphia around 1790 or New Orleans at the time of the Louisiana Purchase), all American building—aristocratic and popular, urban and rural—was illuminated by shared standards of taste and styles of life. And this coalescence led to an architecture whose consistency, equilibrium and general adequacy has not often been seen, before or since.

The basic plan-type of this tradition was the single family house. It was a plan which could be expanded to a manor or a palace or, without too much violence to functional process, adapted into a barracks, a warehouse, a hospital or prison. (Shops, of course, were hardly ever free-standing buildings, being always inserted into the ground floor street front.) The Europeans had developed two variants of this basic type. With the northerners, it took the form of a compact, centralized, outward looking or centrifugal plan. For the Spanish, it took the form of the centripetal, inward-turning, blind-walled hollow square of the Mediterranean basin. Each had evolved over the centuries to meet the specific requirements of its environment, climatic and social. With the French, English and Dutch, it was fundamentally a cold weather architecture: the steeply pitched roofs, large chimneys and big south-facing glass areas were direct responses to the heavy rainfall, cold winters and scanty sunlight of the north. By the same token, this outward-turning plan could only have matured in a landscape of growing social peace and security. (Already in 1515, when Leonardo was invited to the French court, the moat and battlement could be reduced to largely decorative elements in country seats like Chambord.)

The Spanish house had developed under fundamentally different meteorological and social conditions. Its inward-turning plan was the direct inheritor of Roman and Arab experience with a climate of hot, dry summers, searing winds, intense sunlight and a semi-arid landscape. But the secluded patio was also a response to institutional necessity. It provided the necessary environment for the gynaeceum of Classic antiquity or the seraglio of the Arabs, with all its physical and psychological implications for protection from the hostile, outside world.

By the time that the French got around to establishing New Orleans in 1718, Franco-Spanish experience with adapting these prototypal house-forms to New World conditions was from a century to two centuries old. The first New Orleans house-type was, of course, French; but it reached the city from two directions (down the Mississippi from Quebec; across the Gulf from the West Indies, where it had been exposed to English, Spanish, Dutch and Danish counterparts). In coming down the river, it had remained a rural (or at least, free-standing) house, metamorphosized to meet the long, hot, humid summers of the region it was invading. The steeply-pitched, hipped roof of Quebec and Normandy was retained but it was extended beyond the walls to form galleries; and dormers were used to ventilate the attic. Ceiling heights were progressively increased and window openings were extended down to the floor and up to the ceiling. To provide better exposure to the breeze, to escape periodic flooding and invasion by vermin (snakes, insects, rodents) the house came more and more to be elevated off the ground on piers.

The same sort of metamorphosis had taken place in West Indian islands like Santo Domingo and Guadelupe but under more cosmopolitan conditions and in a fully tropical climate. Here the French prototype absorbed such Spanish warm weather inventions as the arcade, the cantilevered balcony, the metal grille and—most important device for privacy *and* ventilation —the louvered jalousie. Here also it began to be adapted to the much denser texture of the townscape.

In New Orleans, for whatever local reasons, it seems always to have been placed right up against the sidewalk (or *banquette*, as it was called) with only walled, narrow (or non-existent) side yards separating it from its neighbors. The result was a narrow corridor street not very different from what the Spanish were using in Mexico and Puerto Rico. Such a site plan automatically produced a back garden; and when the classic L-shaped Vieux Carré house plan came to be perfected toward the end of the eighteenth century, it "automatically" produced what we now call a patio. It ought to be emphasized, however, that its origins were not in the Spanish patio, the Italian cortile or the Roman atrium, even though the end result in the Creole city was much the same.

But before the prototypal French house could be employed in the building of the city, a number of very local conditions had to be solved. When the engineer Adrien de Pauger started serious construction of the city in 1722, little remained of the temporary buildings which the first Canadian immigrants had erected in 1718. Typically, they had been unable to make any use of the aboriginal building forms of the Gulf Coast: the little circular temples, tubular long houses or conical cabins, all of them consisting of bent sapling frames roofed with woven mats or thatch and walled in wattle-and-daub. Perhaps in the very earliest days, they had been compelled by circumstances to employ some of the aboriginal techniques—palisade construction, palmetto-thatched roofs, shingles or siding of peeled tree bark, *bouzillage* (mud and moss walling). But durability is never an important criterion in primitive architecture and all such constructions rotted away too rapidly to be useful. Thus, like their contemporary colonists everywhere in North America, the Louisiana men ignored the indigenous technologies and gradually adopted a policy which, in effect, called for the liquidation of the indigenous populations.

The one raw material immediately available was the fabulous primeval stands of cypress and pine. These permitted the importation of the skeletal wood frame with which all north European carpenters were familiar. Yet they soon discovered that the wooden building could not be used here as easily as it had been in Martinique or Quebec. The biggest single obstacle was too much water—in the air, on the ground and below its surface. This phenomenon raised many unfamiliar problems for the early builders, problems which they could only solve on an empirical basis. Continuously high humidities threatened all architectural fabric by encouraging attack from fungi, bacteria and insects. Heavy rains eroded roof and wall materials. Spongy, water-logged soils would support only the lightest foundations. Drainage and paving problems, before the appearance of the mechanical pump, were enormous. And standing water was the incubator of the mosquito, the cause of endless discomfort (and, of course, of high mortality rates, though it was not to be identified as the vector of malaria and yellow fever for another century and three-quarters).

All in all, the speed and sagacity with which the early builders responded to these structural exigencies is remarkable. This response can now be traced in fascinating detail, thanks to the work of local historians, including the late Nathaniel Curtis and Leonard V. Huber, Bernard Lemann, I. W. Ricciuti and Samuel Wilson Jr. The city had horse-powered sawmills, apparently as early as 1726. It had brick and tile kilns in operation at least by 1730 and seems to have been producing lime by burning oyster shells at about the same time. Such manufacturing facilities furnished the basis for waterproof surfaces—cypress shingles and clay tiles for the roofs, sawn clapboards and stucco for the walls. Brick gave the builders their first rot-free foundations. Experience taught them—as earlier it had taught the Venetians—that when wood was permanently submerged in subsurface water it could last indefinitely. Thus they could use footings of either wood piles or a solid mattress of several layers of crossed logs. A remarkable system of levees, canals, locks and drainage ditches was evolved to handle surface water. Sidewalks were paved with brick or imported cobbles or flags, while a mixture of crushed oyster shells, clay and sand provided a reasonably stable surface for the streets.

The one terrible environmental problem, which could not be solved within the limits of a pre-industrial technology, was the scourge of mosquitoes. The architect Benjamin Latrobe, in an almost clinical entry in his journal just a century after the city had been founded (and just a year before his own death from yellow fever on September 3, 1820), compared their annual assault on the city to that of a besieging army:

"The muskitoes (sic!) are so important *a body* of enemies that they furnish a considerable part of the conversation of every day and every body; they regulate many family arrangements, they prescribe the employment and distribution of time, & most essentially affect the comfort and enjoyments of every individual in the country."

Lacking any real understanding of the enemy they faced, or any real means of combatting it, the citizens closed windows, burned sulfur, drew the mosquito net around their beds; or, if they could afford it, fled the city from July through September.

A chronic shortage and consequent high cost of building labor was another phenomenon which New Orleans shared with the rest of the continent; and similar measures to circumvent it appear here as elsewhere. One of the great virtues of wood construction is that it is subject to a high degree of standardization, rationalization and prefabrication. The relatively standardized house type used in early New Orleans is itself an important measure of rationalization in construction. The use of milled lumber is a step in the direction of prefabrication, as was the panellized construction of walls where an entire house wall is fabricated flat on the ground and then tilted up into position. But there are references to prefabricated house frames among the Spanish as early as 1568. Louisiana was exporting them to the West Indies in 1727. A complete prefabricated house was stolen from a Natchez wharf in 1791. Clearly, French response here was typically North American.

By the end of the eighteenth century, the original city, the Vieux Carré, was substantially complete. From the first it had been conceived along Renaissance lines: a central square facing the river, around which were the seats of church and state; a *quai* lined with warehouses in West Indian fashion; a gridiron street system whose narrow streets (38 ft. 6 in.) formed squares of about 320 ft.; deep and narrow individual plots (60 by 120 ft.). The elaborate fortifications shown in the De La Tour map of 1723 were never realized, however: no attempt at fortifications of any sort was made until the 1760's and they were never completed. Although the city never achieved the polished symmetry claimed for it by map-makers like Thierry in 1764, it very early had an urbanity which at least impressed visitors from the north and east. The city was held in shape by its very situation—mighty river to the south, all-encompassing swamps in all other directions—and these constrictions guaranteed the intensive exploitation of expensively developed land. Such a situation was very different from most American towns where topography permitted urban sprawl; and it undoubtedly contributed to the physical urbanity and social cosmopolitanism for which the town was famous.

And, by the end of the eighteenth century, the process of architectural modification and adaptation may be said to have been completed. New prototypes had emerged which were to remain viable for a century or more (and viable still, from an environmental point of view). The little single-story house had been metamorphosized in two directions. On the one hand as a centrifugal, free-standing volume—first, the raised cottage like Madame John's Legacy (c. 1788); then the full two-story plantation house like that of the Ducayets on Bayou St. John (c. 1790); and ultimately, the classically colonnaded mansion like the Beauregard Plantation at Chalmette (1832).

The urban version of this transmutation, on the other hand, took the form exemplified by such buildings as the Merieult House of 1792, the Banque de la Louisiane (c. 1800) or the late but perfect example of the Grima House of 1831. These houses, and hundreds of others like them, were designed to abut one another along the street front. They expanded vertically to two or even three stories, topped by simple gables instead of the four-slope hipped roof. Shops uniformly occupied the ground floor along the *banquette,* while a *porte-cochère* offered both pedestrian and carriage access to the courtyard at the rear. Here, in the inner angle of the L-shaped plan, were the stairs which served the upper floors, both the main house along the street and the wing at right angles to it (commonly called the *garçonnière* because older youths, as well as guests or servants, might be bedded down there). Continuous galleries or balconies shielded both patio and street walls against sun and blowing rain, as well as providing all rooms with access to light, air and outlook.

These new prototypes represent a high point, not merely for Louisiana, but for North American architecture as a whole. Only the compact "Cape Cod" house-type of New England or the inward-turning hacienda of the Spanish-American Southwest offer a comparably high level of formal and functional response to experiential reality. And it is significant that this building is overwhelmingly the work of anonymous craftsmen. The dominance of the vernacular tradition in New Orleans architecture up until the Louisiana Purchase is obvious from a stylistic analysis of the buildings themselves. Only a handful show any clear or conscious reference to aristocratic prototypes at all. Creole craftsmen undoubtedly had some access to Parisian pattern books, which they would have used in the same way as Boston or Philadelphia carpenters followed London texts. When the military engineer Ignace Broutin came to design two important public buildings—the Barracks on the Place d'Armes (1743) and the second Ursuline Convent (1745)—he was clearly following current French fashion in *hôtel de ville* and *manoir*. The only other pre-American structures which show any obvious pretensions to upper class European taste are the Cabildo, the Cathedral and the Presbytère. But of these only the Cabildo had even approached its present appearance at the end of the century. The Presbytère was not completed until 1815 and the Cathedral did not acquire its present form until the 1850's. And even these buildings, for all their literary origins, underwent that subtle simplification of detail and clarification of form which is always the hallmark of folk practice. In the case of the Cabildo-Cathedral-Presbytère this might have been due to nothing more occult than the necessity of executing lithic motifs in a plastic medium like coarse stucco. But we find the same tendency in other buildings where no such technical problem existed.

It is a most interesting fact that the vernacular idiom only begins to be submerged after the American occupation. It is a shift in taste which might have well occurred without the Purchase, and it is partly due to the appearance on the scene of professionally-trained architects like Latrobe in 1819 and the

Galliers and Dakins after 1830. But it was fundamentally due to social and economic changes in the city and its hinterland, and relations between the two, changes of which the presence of professionals would be only an index. New Orleans from the first had served two economic functions. It was the point of transshipment for the vast generalized commerce of the river as a whole, between river barge and deep sea transport. But it was also and specifically the agent, entrepreneur and shopping center for the up-country plantations.

By one of the great ironies of history, the American democracy took control of this imperial colony at the moment when the cotton gin was converting America into the greatest slave power in the world. The gin had changed cotton from being a fiber more expensive than silk into the cheapest fiber on earth; and the impact of this change upon Delta agriculture was momentous. Its mixed economy of sugar, rice and indigo was already slave-powered. But the cotton mono-culture was destined to convert slavery from a peculiar institution (which most people had assumed to be on its way out) into the very fulcrum of Louisiana life. Creole plantation owners might well have made this conversion without the American intervention—and, of course, many of them did. But in point of fact, the great exploitation of the entire Mississippi Delta between the Louisiana Purchase and the Civil War was the work of Scots-Irish and English newcomers from the east. Rich land, mechanical ginning and Negro slavery combined to produce very rapidly a powerful new ruling class, the most arrogant and insular *nouveaux riches* in American experience.

Like all *nouveaux riches*, this new class wanted to be *au courant* in its life style: in manners, dress, furnishings, cuisine. Typically, too, they wanted their new power set forth in unmistakable fashion. This placed a whole fresh set of demands upon architecture, since architecture is always an important instrument of ideology. The stylistic transformation of the plantation house between 1800 and 1860 is a perfect mirror of the rise of this new class. Even such large and prosperous houses as Homeplace

(1790) or Whitney Plantation (c. 1800) are still fundamentally astylar. They follow the basic prototypal form of raised living floor, perimetral galleries and parasol roof—lineal descendants of the courthouse at Cahokia, Mo., or the Spanish Governor's Mansion at Baton Rouge, dating from the 1760s and 1780s. And such was the functional viability of this house-form that it was able to function as a skeleton upon which the new cotton millionaires could drape their aristocratic pretensions.

The architectural language of these pretensions was of Graeco-Roman origin, most convenient ideologically because it reflected Southern identification with Imperial Rome (as seen by Bonaparte) and Periclean Greece (as visualized by John C. Calhoun). This reactionary use of the Classic idiom was the exact reverse of Jefferson's Roman Republic or the Greek Democracy of Lord Byron because it regarded human slavery as the basis of Classic culture instead of being merely its blemish.

The plantation house was converted, step by step, from an astylar domestic form into a Classic temple, as monumental in size and scale as any court house or urban church. The progression can be traced with diagrammatic clarity in dozens of houses up and down the Mississippi—from Homeplace to Greenwood (1830) to Dunleith in Natchez (1848) to Belle Grove (1857). An astonishing change in appearance was actually accomplished with very simple means: the shift from the delicate domesticity of the early houses, with their superposed colonettes and simple railings, to the overweening monumentality of the later ones was largely a matter of replacing them with two-story columns, complete with bases, caps and cornices. The ornament gets progressively larger and more florid. As the Civil War approached, the growing crisis of slavocracy is clearly expressed in the stylistic vulgarity and confusion of its great houses. The collapse of the whole system is forecast in the Steamboat Gothic of San Francisco Plantation (c. 1856) and the preposterous Hindoo style of Longwood of 1860, Haller Nutt's unfinished mansion at Natchez.

The plantation economy was, by definition, culturally parasitical. Its style of life required a big base of craftsmanship and expertise—carpenters, cabinetmakers, dressmakers, milliners, architects and decorators. But it could not tolerate, much less produce, the free and literate craftsmen and artisans required for such a style of life. It consequently had to purchase everything abroad—in New Orleans, Baltimore, New York or Europe. The North Carolinian Winston Rowan Helper, in his remarkably prescient book of 1860, *The Impending Crisis of The South,* was lamenting just this fact when he wrote:

"We are compelled to go to the North for almost every article of utility and adornment, from matches, shoe pegs and paintings up to cotton mills, steamships and statuary; that we have no foreign trade, no princely merchants nor respectable artists; that in comparison with the free states we contribute nothing to the literature, polite arts and inventions of the age."

New Orleans, as the one great seaport of the Delta, became the great emporium of slavocracy. Economically, if not culturally, the old Creole city and the new Anglo-American plantation system were symbiotically joined. Just as the planters depended upon the factors, bankers and merchants of the metropolis to buy and sell for them, so the city depended more and more upon cotton as the century neared its mid-point. It grew astonishingly: it had a population of 8,000 in 1803 which rose to 41,000 in 1840, 160,000 in 1860.Concurrently, the old Creole entrepreneurial class was enriched and enlarged; but it, too, came to be more and more eclipsed by the Americans.

By the same historic process, New Orleans was one of the few Southern cities with a modern working class and the only one with a large community of Negro freedmen. Even slaves, under Napoleonic law, had had a legal existence and certain putative civil rights (unlike the Anglo-American South, where, being held non-human, they could not even take the oath). And that the strong Latin American influence served to insulate men of color from the ferocious practices of the plantations is clear in the pre-War novels of George Washington Cable. The quadroon and octaroon beauties who populate them belong to that same community; and many of their men would have been skilled craftsmen in the building and decorative arts, and furniture trades. In any case, black or white, New Orleans artisans would have been the only ones who could produce at least some of the cultural artifacts whose absence Helper was decrying.

These changes in the structure of Creole society are, again, accurately reflected in her architecture, both domestic and monumental. Following the disastrous fires of 1788 and 1794, much of the Vieux Carré had itself been rebuilt, with larger and more sumptuous houses. But now new residential quarters rapidly appeared—first "below" (i.e., east) of the old town; and then "above" Canal Street to the west. In these new areas, under American influence, the Creole convention of providing shops along the street fronts of the houses was abandoned: this change alone would radically alter the texture of street life. At first, along such streets as Esplanade, the free-standing house of Baltimore or Philadelphia is imported, but the Creole custom of placing it right up against the sidewalk line is still followed, with walled side-yards separating one house from the next. But uptown, in what is now called the Garden District, even this practice is relinquished. Instead, in true American style, the house is set back from the street in the center of large, tree-shaded grounds. Also, unlike the practice of the Vieux Carré, the streets themselves are planted with shade trees, often the ornamental Seville orange. The result of all this was an attractive hybrid, a kind of Philadelphia suburb in the tropics.

The new houses retained many important Creole innovations, however: perimetral galleries, tall ceilings, floor-to-ceiling windows, jalousies, grilles and louvers, etc. The houses were built of stuccoed brick, usually, and were always painted either white or very light pastels. This combination of openness and light color, of shaded forms set in a solid mat of vegetation, provided a pleasant and comfortable response to the climate, perhaps as much as the more densely textured pattern of self-shading streets and courtyards of the old town. In any case, such a tradition of upper class residences, less and less Classic as time went on, survived as a viable idiom in New Orleans right up to World War I, when it finally was submerged in the "national" proto-types espoused by national magazines for laymen and professionals.

But nineteenth century monumental architecture—religious, civic, commercial—showed no such sensitivity to local conditions, either cultural or climatic. On the contrary, Classic Revival prototypes were imported and built in the Anglo-American mode, almost as if they were flags planted on a conquered battlefield. Thus William Strickland's United States Mint (1835) is a pallid Greek Revival; A. T. Wood's United States Custom House (1849) is Egyptoid; James Gallier's City Hall (1850) is in a dry, cold Ionic style; Henry Howard's Carrollton Courthouse (1855) is a warmer, more sumptuous version of the same idiom. It is not at all that these buildings fall short of any national standard of competence or taste, but precisely because they meet them, that they stand outside the main stream of autochthonous building.

The same must be said for most of the religious and commercial buildings of the six decades between the Purchase and the War. Except for the Cathedral, finally completed after 1850, most of the new churches strictly followed "national" norms of taste—the newly arrived Protestants tending to build in the Gothic Revival style; only the Catholic parish churches clung to a kind of provincial Baroque.

The period saw the construction of two splendid hotels; the St. Louis, built by the French-trained J. N. B. de Pouilly in 1836–1840, and the first St. Charles Hotel of Dakin and Gallier, completed in 1836 and rebuilt after a fire by the Yankee architect, Isaiah Rogers in 1851. But these two long-vanished hostelries, with their Greek details and Roman rotundas, were also imported types, reflecting the truly international standards brought about by increasing travel. The most significant commercial project of the mid-century was the twin Pontalba Buildings, facing each other across Jackson Square. These buildings (whose history has been recently traced out by Leonard V.

Huber and Samuel Wilson Jr. in definitive form) are in the vernacular tradition, for all their having been built by a Parisian baronness and worked on by the elder Gallier and Henry Howard. They are almost completely astylar, revealing in only a few details (roof pitch, attic cornice, cast iron grille work) the fact that they were built at the end of the Classic Revival period.

Aside from such features as tall ceilings and taller windows, none of these buildings made any special concessions to the climate. Structurally, they were built along "American" lines, many of them employing imported materials like Baltimore brick, Westchester marble, Quincy granite. The huge size and enormous weight of these monumental structures was possible because the builders had mastered the techniques of wooden piling and wooden cribbing for foundation support. From that time forward, this expertise has permitted them to erect any type of structure, including multi-story skyscrapers, with absolute security.

The Americanization of the Crescent City has long been completed, at least architecturally; and the whole nation is the poorer for it. Our most vigorous regional tradition, flexible, perceptive and functionally precise, has been truncated. This is to be regretted, not merely for sentimental or antiquarian reasons (though, in their own way, these may be valid too) but for much more fundamental reasons as well. For the response of this architecture to experiential reality has rich theoretical implications for the modern architect, caught up as he is in his greatest philosophical crisis since the Renaissance. The national technology which has made possible the appearance of the unshaded glass curtain wall in this climate is a travesty of technology, not a victory for scientific theory. The engineering expertise which holds that mechanical refrigeration makes obsolete any need to worry about the Louisiana sun (which on any midsummer noon pumps around 250 btus per hour into each square foot of horizontal Louisiana surface) is actually not expert at all.

To take the position that the truly significant period of New Orleans architecture was brought into jeopardy by the Purchase and brought to an end by the Civil War is to be neither sentimental nor obscurantist. After that, for better or worse, the city joined the mainstream of American life. Because of the special conditions of military defeat, the city did not regain until recent times its earlier dynamism. And its architecture of the past hundred years again reflects this fact. Henry Handel Richardson, one of the very greatest of the late Victorian architects, was of course a native of Louisiana. But it was Boston and Chicago which offered the objective conditions for his development and flowering. And his one New Orleans building, the Howard Memorial Library finished by his firm two years after his death, is in fact as extraneous to the main tradition as all the other monumental structures of the period.

In such a perspective, the work of current New Orleans architects is to be criticized, not because it falls below some national average, but because, with such a splendid tradition, it does not rise above it. In this light, too, it must be understood that such tradition cannot be merely donned like a Mardi Gras costume, the way the new motels and parking garages in the Vieux Carré are attempting to do, masquerading their disastrous presence with a trickery of rusticated stucco and bowdlerized cast iron. Like all tradition, it must be studied by men and not copied by monkies (to use Greenough's immortal phrase). And in this light, finally, the preservation of the Vieux Carré from the depredations of mechanized Neanderthals becomes culturally a radical and not a reactionary task; and of national, not merely local, significance.

Pestilence in New Orleans

John Duffy

> *"Lower Louisiana is a beautiful Country, and rewards abun-*
> *dantly the Labour of man;—But the Climate is a wretched one,*
> *and destructive to human life."*

When Governor William C. C. Claiborne penned
these words on October 5, 1804, he had just suffered the loss of
his wife, daughter, private secretary and many of his friends and
co-workers to Louisiana's great killer disease of the nineteenth
century, yellow fever. Epidemic waves of this infection first
struck New Orleans in the 1790's, intensified their attack until
the 1850's, and then sullenly receded. Even in the later part of
the century, the fever occasionally lashed out in a startling fashion. Over four thousand residents of New Orleans died from the
disease in 1878, and the final onslaught in 1905 resulted in
almost 2,000 cases and over 450 deaths.

Yet Yellow Jack, or the Saffron Scourge, as it was sometimes
called, was only one of three major epidemic disorders to ravage
the Crescent City during its 250 years of existence. Smallpox and
Asiatic cholera occasionally swept through the city with devastating results. Moreover, a host of other diseases constantly
plagued the inhabitants. While these fevers, diarrheas, and respiratory complaints were not as dramatic as the major killer
diseases, in the long run they were more debilitating and deadly.
Familiar, chronic complaints, however, do not evoke the terror
aroused by the sudden appearance of a strange and deadly disor-

der. In consequence, the public, as well as the medical profession, devoted most of its attention to dealing with epidemic diseases such as yellow fever and Asiatic cholera.

The great epidemics were a major preoccupation of physicians until the end of the nineteenth century, for until the bacteriological revolution the medical profession had little understanding of the causative agents of disease. Without this knowledge, doctors were compelled to classify infectious disorders largely on the basis of symptoms. Even the many organic and degenerative ailments were understood only vaguely, since physiology was still in its infancy. Like the infectious diseases, they, too, were described and classified in terms of the obvious clinical picture.

The generic names applied to the many sicknesses which plagued old and young alike in earlier days fully reflected this emphasis upon outward signs. Contemporary writers spoke of fluxes, fevers, cancers, and consumptions, and they subdivided these general categories into equally vague classifications based upon more specific symptoms. A flux was any disorder of the intestinal tract involving flatulence and diarrhea; the bloody flux, as its name implied, was a more severe form characterized by the discharge of blood. In the case of fevers, some of the terms were descriptive enough to permit identification of specific disorders. The words fever and ague, or tertian, quartan, or quotidian fever usually referred to some form of malaria. The terms camp fever, jail fever, hospital fever, military fever, or eruptive fever ordinarily indicated typhus. Typhoid fever was generally referred to as slow or nervous fever. When a fever proved both fatal and highly contagious, it was often called a malignant or pestilential fever, a name which gave little indication of its exact nature.

While the contemporary names often provide clues to the identity of particular diseases, they supply only crude guidelines at best. Stethoscopes and thermometers did not come into general use until the twentieth century, and laboratory tests, with the exception of urinalysis, were virtually unknown. Fortunately for the historian, the three major epidemic diseases of the nineteenth century lent themselves to relatively easy identification. They involved thousands of cases, and under these circumstances the classical disease pattern usually revealed itself clearly.

Smallpox, the first of the three to attack Louisiana, is characterized by a high fever, headache, general pains, and the classic skin eruptions. These pustules vary from patient to patient, depending in part on the size of the pores, but in a certain percentage of cases they spread into one solid mass, leaving the patient's face an unrecognizable ulcerating sore. The high case fatality rate and the horrible scars on many who recovered made this disease the scourge of Europe and America in the eighteenth century. Since it was endemic in Europe and Africa, it undoubtedly must have been introduced into Louisiana on many occasions in the early eighteenth century; but in those days so many problems afflicted the early settlers that one can scarcely differentiate among them. Aside from starvation and dietetic complaints, major problems in the struggling colony, the settlers were beset with a host of fevers, fluxes, plagues, and other malignant diseases. The population, however, grew slowly; and it was 1778 before the first clear-cut epidemic of smallpox was recorded.

In this year the disease swept through the entire colony, leaving many dead in its wake. In New Orleans Governor Bernardo de Gálvez attempted to prevent it from spreading by ordering the removal of all smallpox cases to the west side of the river. He considerately ordered, however, that a parent must accompany sick children to the smallpox isolation center. When the disease returned in 1787, many of the city's residents sought to protect themselves by inoculation. This practice, one going far back into antiquity, consisted of inserting pus from an active smallpox case under the skin of a healthy individual. It had been discovered that smallpox acquired in this manner usually resulted in a mild case, and that the recipient was henceforth immune to the disease. The practice was not without danger, and, unless the disease had gained a firm foothold, the authorities usually preferred to hold it at bay by isolating all active cases. For example, when the infection was reintroduced by a cargo of

Negro slaves, the officials prevented an epidemic outbreak by quarantining all who had contracted the disease.

Ten years later, 1802, smallpox once more spread through Louisiana. As the number of cases increased, the Cabildo, or governor's council, was asked to permit the general use of inoculation. With proper controls the practice was beneficial, but it was often responsible for broadcasting the seeds of smallpox. Individuals undergoing inoculation were capable of passing a horrible and deadly sickness to all with whom they came in contact. In consequence, the use of inoculation was usually hedged by many legal restrictions. By 1802 news of Jenner's discovery of the much safer vaccination had already reached Louisiana, and the Cabildo delayed action hoping it could obtain vaccine. When the officials found it impossible either to isolate the growing number of cases or to obtain cowpox vaccine, they granted the physicians permission to inoculate. By this time a major epidemic had developed, one which remained in the city until the end of the summer. Precisely how many died during the outbreak is not clear, although the death toll mounted into the hundreds.

In 1804 smallpox returned, but on this occasion a train of events was set in motion which led to the virtual banishment of the disease for almost sixty years. Governor Claiborne had already experimented with smallpox vaccine and ample supplies of vaccine matter were at hand. Encouraged by the Governor, the city's physicians quickly began a general vaccination program which soon brought a halt to the smallpox outbreak. With the scarred faces of smallpox victims still vividly reminding New Orleanians of the horrors of previous epidemics, they accepted vaccination with little question, and smallpox virtually disappeared as an epidemic disease until the Civil War. A mild outbreak in 1825 once again brought vaccination to the fore and served as a reminder of the value of the new preventive.

Ironically, the post Civil War period, when scientific medicine and public health were making gigantic strides, saw the return of smallpox to New Orleans and the state of Louisiana on a fairly large scale. The political and economic chaos following the war scarcely lent itself to a systematic public health program. To compound the problem, freedom for the Negroes resulted in mass migrations. Thousands of Negroes formerly restricted to isolated plantations now pushed into the cities and towns or sought refuge in temporary camps established by the military authorities. Having little immunity to crowd diseases and living under the most primitive sanitary conditions, they died by the thousands from smallpox, measles, typhoid, enteric disorders, and respiratory infections.

Even when order was restored and the South slowly adjusted to the new conditions, the reduced standard of living resulted in a large depressed class, both white and colored, among whom ignorance and poverty conspired to eliminate any foresight. Among these individuals vaccination was neither economically feasible nor considered necessary. The middle and upper classes could and did protect themselves from smallpox by means of vaccination, but, except for a few public-spirited physicians and laymen, there was little concern for Negroes and poor whites. To make matters worse, towards the end of the century a strong anti-vaccination movement, led by a minority group within the medical profession, made its appearance. In New Orleans Dr. Moritz Schuppert, an able and well-known physician, was the most outspoken opponent of vaccination. Not surprisingly, the incidence of smallpox rose sharply in New Orleans in the years following the Civil War. Smallpox deaths averaged about 300 a year from 1866 to 1876. Dr. Joseph Jones, president of the Louisiana State Board of Health, estimated that the city had suffered 6,432 deaths from smallpox in the twenty years from 1863 to 1883. The disease continued to flare-up year after year, but as the century drew to a close, city and state health officials gradually gained ground in their battle for universal vaccination. Although smallpox was looked upon as a disease of the poor, it occasionally reached into the upper classes. During a widespread outbreak in the winter of 1899–1900, twelve Tulane medical students were infected. Prompt vaccination of the study body and faculty prevented further cases, but three of the twelve students died.

Steady pressure in the early twentieth century by the newly created New Orleans Board of Health gradually brought the smallpox situation under control. In 1914 a brief notice in the *Pan-American Surgical and Medical Journal* stated that Dr. Beard's private smallpox hospital was for sale. This institution had formerly treated all city smallpox cases, but, the notice read, as "a result of compulsory vaccination and the introduction of scientific preventives," the hospital was no longer needed.

As already noted, a good part of the fear engendered by epidemic diseases arose from their sudden and mysterious appearance. A city might be free of a particular disorder for fifteen to twenty years when, seemingly without any logical explanation, cases would spring into existence. Asiatic cholera, the second of the great nineteenth century epidemic diseases, was in many respects an inexplicable pestilence, yet it was the most widely heralded epidemic disease ever to invade the United States. A highly contagious and fatal intestinal disorder, it could strike its victims down within a matter of hours. The violent diarrhea and spasmodic vomiting literally dehydrated its victims, making their faces blue and pinched, and the skin of their extremities dark and puckered. In 1816 a particularly virulent outbreak in the Far East resulted in the disease slowly and steadily advancing on the Western World. By 1830 the infection was in Russia, from whence it spread over Europe, crossing into the British Isles in 1831. Early the following year Asiatic cholera invaded North America via Quebec and New York.

Occasional notices of the disease had been made in the New Orleans newspapers long before it offered a direct threat to the city. Interest in it steadily increased, and as the infection spread through Europe and Great Britain, the New Orleans newspapers avidly followed its path. The appearance of the disease in New

York led to demands upon the New Orleans city council for a rigid sanitation program. Grim accounts of the successive epidemics were published as the disorder swept through the inland waterways, taking a heavy toll wherever it struck. Its seemingly inexorable approach created an almost unbearable tension in New Orleans. The editor of the *Courier* wrote on August 1, 1832: "The cholera continues to be the all absorbing topic of public attention. Reports of its progress are looked for by our citizens with intense anxiety. Go where you will, you hear nothing talked of but the *Cholera*—which seems to be thought worse than death itself." The *Courier*, along with other New Orleans newspapers, reflected the rising fears—and contributed to them—by publishing article after article describing the symptoms, proposed methods for prevention, and possible cures. Meanwhile the disease was pursuing its course down the Mississippi Valley.

Despite a series of preliminary scares, the cholera did not make its appearance until October 25, 1832. On that day two men dying with the disease were landed from a steamboat. According to the Reverend Theodore Clapp, a crowd had gathered when a physician rode up, glanced at the two victims, and instantly declared that they had Asiatic cholera. The crowd fled in panic, leaving Dr. Clapp alone with the victims. The news spread quickly through the city, and a mass exodus got underway. An estimated 15,000 of the city's 50,000 population had already been frightened away by an earlier outbreak of yellow fever; the appearance of cholera further reduced the population.

With almost incredible speed the infection spread through the water front areas and then pushed into other sections of the city. The rapidity with which cholera claimed its victims is shown by an editorial in the New Orleans *Emporium* on November 5, only eleven days after the disease was first reported: "The people are in a state of suffering, despondency and excitement unparalleled in the history of our city. 'Death on the pale horse' for the last ten days has been rapidly engaged in the indiscriminate work of slaughter. Not less than *eighteen hundred* individuals have perished since the commencement of the disease." Four days later the *Courier* grimly noted that in fourteen days the epidemic had already caused no less than 2,000 deaths.

To the relief of New Orleans, the epidemic subsided almost as quickly as it had appeared. In the middle of November, only three weeks after the first cases were reported, the Board of Health was able to proclaim the end of the outbreak. Yet in this short time, the disease had taken an incredible toll. New Orleans physicians estimated that for a brief period the deaths were averaging 500 per day and that within the space of two weeks almost 5,000 residents fell prey to the pestilence. To complicate matters, the thousands of residents fleeing the city caused such an acute shortage of vehicles that there were not enough left to carry the dead to the cemeteries. City authorities met this crisis by requisitioning all carts and carriages. An even worse problem was that of burying the accumulating piles of corpses. In an effort to recruit additional grave diggers, the three municipal cemeteries raised wages from $2 to $6 per day.

John B. Wyeth, a New Englander temporarily stranded in New Orleans, hired out as a grave digger. His grim account of his experiences reveals the intensity of the crisis. For the first three days, he wrote, individual graves were dug for each body, but, he continued, "we soon found that we could not clear the hearses and carts. I counted eighty-seven bodies uninterred on the ground." The twenty-five grave diggers with whom he worked solved the problem by digging trenches fifty-seven feet long, eight feet wide and four feet deep. In each of these approximately 300 bodies were buried. Corpses of adults were laid in them as compactly as possible, and the grave diggers then "filled up the vacant spaces with children." Even with this mass production technique, the grave diggers fell far behind in their work. On coming to work some mornings, they found as many as 100 bodies awaiting burial.

From New Orleans the infection swept along the waterways of lower Louisiana bringing death and disruption wherever it appeared. In May of 1833 it returned to New Orleans, but, although the disease remained in the city for two months, it was not nearly so virulent. Nonetheless, when this cholera epidemic finally subsided, it left 1,000 dead in its wake. For the next few years rumors of cholera continued to arouse apprehensions, but the city remained free of the disease until the arrival in 1848 of the next great Asiatic cholera pandemic.

Like its predecessor, this world-wide outbreak, too, had origi-nated in the East and pushed westward into Europe. Its arrival there coincided with the large scale emigration of Germans and Irish, an event which virtually guaranteed that the infection would be carried to America. On December 11, 1848, a ship entered the port of New Orleans with 200 steerage passengers, a number of whom were suffering from what was soon diagnosed as Asiatic cholera. A week later the Board of Health announced that sporadic cases of cholera had led to a few deaths, but it assured the public that these deaths, 23 in all, were of little consequence. The newspapers also played down the significance of the announcement, pointing to the preventive measures taken by the health officials and stressing the excellent medical care available in the city. These assurances, however, did little to allay the fears and suspicions of the public, and events soon showed that those who fled on the first hint of Asiatic cholera had displayed admirable discretion. An editorial note in the same issue of the *Courier* which carried the Board of Health's an-nouncement decried the needless panic in the city. Within less than three weeks after its appearance, the disease had killed well over 1,000 of those who remained. The exact figure is not known, although Dr. Joseph Jones estimated the total cholera deaths at 1,646.

This time the disease did not subside as rapidly as it had appeared, but rather lurked in the city throughout the following year, occasionally flaring up in short outbursts. By the close of 1849, New Orleans had suffered 3,176 cholera deaths. For the next six years recurrent minor outbreaks occurred, but fortunately the peak of this second cholera wave had already been reached. From 1850 to 1855 the annual number of Asiatic cholera deaths ranged from 450 to 1,448, by no means an inconsiderable loss. The deaths in any particular year, however, did not compare with those for the years 1832 or 1848–49. Moreover, the city's population had increased to 150,000, three times the figure for 1832.

Following 1855, New Orleans was given another eleven year respite from Asiatic cholera, a much needed one in view of the chaos and disruption caused by the Civil War. Before the city could recover from the traumatic war years, one last explosive outburst of cholera occurred. On August 9, 1866, the Board of Health announced the presence of Asiatic cholera and warned everyone to take preventive measures. Over and above its own program of public health and sanitation, the Board recommended a policy of personal hygiene which included ample rest, moderate diet, and personal cleanliness. For those who had the misfortune to catch the disease, the Board suggested the following treatment: immediately upon developing suspicious symptoms, patients were advised to take five grains of quinine and fifteen drops of laudanum, the dose to be repeated every hour. A small dose of calomel, "say a grain every fifteen minutes, until . . . ten or fifteen grains are taken," was also recommended. The sick were urged not to give way to alarm, since this was thought to aggravate the symptoms. The Board's recommended course of treatment scarcely accords with current practice, but at least it did not include the rigorous bloodletting, purging, and blistering which had characterized earlier medical practice.

Despite all public and personal precautions, nearly 1,300 deaths were recorded from Asiatic cholera during the remaining months of 1866. In the succeeding year, sporadic outbreaks in various sections of the city resulted in another 600 to 700 deaths. This year, 1867, however, marked the final assault of Asiatic cholera upon New Orleans. Although several hundred cases occurred in 1868 and 129 cholera deaths were recorded, in the light of prevailing health conditions the disease was not considered epidemic. Nonetheless, health authorities and the public continued to worry about the threat of Asiatic cholera throughout the remainder of the century. Fortunately for New Orleans, the years following the Reconstruction period saw a steady rise in economic standards and in both public and private sanitation, all of which guaranteed that Asiatic cholera, a disease which can only flourish under conditions of primitive sanitation, filth, and crowding, would never again trouble the Crescent City.

Smallpox and Asiatic cholera, as has been shown, were frightful pestilences, but these disorders were by no means unique to New Orleans. They constantly threatened and periodically ravaged every city in Western Europe and North America. The one great epidemic disease especially identified with New Orleans was yellow fever. It was associated with the city from the first days of the American acquisition and was largely responsible for giving the port its reputation as a pesthole. This fever was not the sole cause of the city's unsavory reputation, for even such common endemic diseases as malaria and the many forms of dysentery seemed to take a particularly virulent form in the warm, humid, semi-tropical climate of New Orleans. Without question, however, the disease which terrified all newcomers and aroused the gravest apprehensions among even the oldest residents was yellow fever.

Prior to the twentieth century, the summer and fall months universally were considered the sickly season. This was the time when fluxes (diarrhea and dysentery) reaped a grim harvest among infants and children, and when many fevers exacted a heavy toll among all age groups. In New Orleans the sickly season came to be synonymous with yellow fever. During the early summer months physicians and city officials carefully watched for the appearance of multiple cases of malignant or pestilential fevers, a term applied to any fatal and contagious disease characterized by a high temperature. The two most marked symptoms of yellow fever were the so-called "black vomit," the vomiting of partially digested blood, and the jaundice or yellow hue of the skin and eyes. Since the degree of these symptoms varied from case to case, and they could occasionally be found in other disorders, it was not always easy in the days before laboratory diagnostic techniques to identify a particular fever. Generally the physicians were reluctant to make a diagnosis of yellow fever, or any other epidemic disease, until the accumulated evidence, in terms of a growing number of cases and deaths, left no alternative.

There were other reasons, too, why city and health officials were reluctant to concede the presence of even one case of a major epidemic sickness. As pointed out in connection with the other fatal communicable diseases, the rumored presence of one of them was enough to start thousands of panic stricken residents pouring out of the city. In turn, this action caused neighboring towns, parishes, and states to erect barricades, later known as shotgun quarantines, to safeguard themselves from the danger of infection. Within a few days, a city might find itself completely isolated, and its commercial and economic life abruptly halted. Under these circumstances there was justification for a cautious approach, but city officials, abetted by local newspapers, invariably delayed too long before announcing the presence of an epidemic disease, and the public pronouncement usually came only when further concealment was futile. Individual physicians or local medical societies occasionally took the initiative in warning the public, although it took great courage for a physician to announce a yellow fever case. Even after consulting with one or more of his colleagues, he frequently found himself involved in a quarrel with other members of his profession; and he was certain to be denounced by municipal officials and local newspaper editors. The chief business of a commercial port was business, and this could not be carried on when the public was alarmed and frightened. Consequently, anyone who even suggested the possibility that all was not well usually found himself the subject of bitter denunciation. Consciously or not, responsible citizens swept their fears under the rug and hoped that the threat of an epidemic would pass.

The precise date when yellow fever first appeared in New Orleans is not known. The disease was widespread in the Caribbean region during the eighteenth century and was undoubtedly introduced into Louisiana on many occasions. Probably because of the sparsity of population and the slow growth of New Orleans, it was not until the 1790's that the fever was able to gain a significant foothold. The first clearly identifiable outbreak occurred in 1796, when yellow fever broke out in August and continued until November. Compared to later epidemics, this one was not severe, but in its effect upon the community it foreshadowed all future epidemics. The intendant, Ventura Morales, wrote on October 31 that the disease "has terrified and still keeps in a state of consternation the whole population of this town." The local physicians disagreed over the nature of the outbreak, some calling it simply a malignant fever, others speaking of it as the "black vomit," and a third group insisting it was the same yellow fever which had plagued Philadelphia three years earlier.

With relatives, friends, and neighbors dying from a strange and unaccountable sickness, understandably a sense of foreboding and gloom hung over the city's residents. In a desperate attempt to drive away the miasma, or the gaseous substance which was thought to be a causative factor in epidemic diseases, the inhabitants burned tar, animal skins, hooves and horns. The resulting clouds of acrid smoke only added to the gloomy atmosphere. Residents sought to avoid each other from fear of catching the contagion, an endeavor undoubtedly encouraged by the practice of carrying garlic as a personal preventive. Futile as these practices were, they at least provided a psychological lift by giving the people a sense of doing something. Exact statistics are lacking, but an estimated 300 residents out of the town's approximate 8,500 population died during the outbreak.

Three years later, the disease was once again epidemic. The most significant result of this visit was a determined effort to improve the city's sanitation and drainage. At the close of the yellow fever season, Don Pedro Barran, the attorney general, appealed for a sanitary program on the grounds that "the public is justly frightened by the fatal ravages experienced in this City on account of the dreadful epidemic which occurred last summer." A few minor cases occurred in the following two summers, but it was not until 1804 that the fever returned in full force. This was the one which cost Governor Claiborne his wife and daughter. Early in October while the disease was still raging, he wrote: "The number of Deaths have been very great;—I verily believe, more than a third of the Americans who emigrated thither in the course of the last 12 months have perished, and nearly every Person from Europe who arrived in the City during the Summer Months."

During the outbreak Governor Claiborne had been in contact with President Thomas Jefferson. Jefferson, who had already shown wisdom through his purchase of Louisiana, expected that the lower Mississippi Valley and its key city, New Orleans, would soon become a thriving and prosperous area. He was, however, quite concerned over the threat posed by yellow fever. It was the destiny of New Orleans, he wrote, to become a great city, but there "is also no spot where yellow fever is so much to be apprehended." Both Jefferson's hopes and fears proved correct. The menace of yellow fever steadily increased in the ensuing years, but fortunately the booming prosperity of New Orleans and the lure of quick riches continued to attract merchants, brokers, and shippers in vast numbers.

Governor Claiborne's personal troubles with yellow fever were not over with the death of his wife and daughter in 1804. Five years later he sadly reported to President James Madison that he had lost his second wife to this same pestilence. These personal losses, he wrote, were attributable to the unhealthy location of the governor's mansion. It was located on the waterfront where, he asserted, "the filth and various matter for putrefaction which accumulate near the water's edge have often proved offensive to me, even when in my chamber." The deplorable condition of the water-front arose from the long-standing custom among New Orleanians of throwing their garbage, refuse, and privy contents into the river. In the late spring, when the water was high, this material was quickly carried away, but for most of the year the water's edge was well below the top of the natural levee. Following the path of least resistance, the refuse men, night soil workers, and ordinary citizens simply dumped their waste materials on the batture, the ground between the water and the top of the levee, where it festered during the hot, moist, summer months. The Governor's complaint about the disgusting condition of the batture was one which was to be reiterated for many years to come.

The recurrent outbreaks of yellow fever in these years caused serious divisions within the medical profession. Confronted by this strange disease, the physicians divided sharply over its cause and the method of treatment. The French or Creole physicians generally pursued a policy of moderation, leaving much of the cure to nature. In 1817 the Société Médicale de la Louisiane, the organization of the French-speaking physicians, requested Drs. A. A. Gros and N.V.A. Gerardin to investigate the various methods used to treat yellow fever cases. The two men reported that bleeding and vomiting, two traditional forms of therapy, had proved useless. They also condemned a practice recently introduced by the English-speaking physicians of reducing the fever by pouring cold water over the patient. Bathing the patient with tepid water, they said, was much safer and more effective. In summary the two physicians recommended "gentle evacuants, acid drinks with cream of tartar, tamarind, orange and lemon juice, [and] whey . . . ," and emphasized the need for good nursing and making the patient comfortable. Since little could be done for yellow fever patients, the advice of Drs. Gros and Gerardin was basically sound.

In sharp contrast with the French policy of supporting the patient while the disease ran its course, American physicians adopted the policy that "desperate diseases require desperate remedies;" and they fought with every weapon at their command. They had nothing but contempt for what they considered the timidity of the French doctors. Dr. M. L. Haynie of St.

Francisville wrote in 1813 that most Louisianians were of French descent and were much opposed to the use of mercury and bloodletting. This attitude, he said, was based on the assumption "that mercury never can be eradicated from the system, and that the quantity of blood is already too small, or could not be supplied if any was taken away"; an error, he added, "founded on a want of correct physiological knowledge." Dr. Haynie, whose "correct physiological knowledge" had convinced him the blood supply could be renewed within twenty-four hours, had no compunction about bleeding the patient to unconsciousness—and repeating the process whenever he felt it necessary. He also advocated generous doses of mercury, stating:

"A few hundred grains (the quantity is not dangerous) introduced into the system will excite a pulse, fuller, stronger, and more durable, than any stimulus, I have ever used." He proportioned the dosage to the violence of the disease, anywhere from two to 100 grains per hour. Epitomizing the attitude of what has since been termed the heroic school of medicine, he declared: "It is but trifling with the life of a man to give him less of a remedy than his disease calls for."

Mercury, usually administered in the form of calomel (mercurous chloride), was the chief therapeutic of the nineteenth century. Given in moderation, it passed through the system before enough of it was absorbed to do any real harm. Dr. Haynie's patients, however, were certain to develop the symptoms of acute mercurial poisoning, an exceedingly dangerous condition. Dr. Haynie's rugged therapy was completely in accordance with prevailing medical practices, for contemporary prescriptions frequently called for the administration of mercury until the patient was "salivated" or until his "gums were touched." The first symptom of acute mercurial poisoning is an excessive flow of saliva followed by ulceration of the gums and mucous surfaces. Physicians did not consider the dose of mercury effective until it was administered to the point of acute poisoning. While Dr. Haynie represented an extreme school of medicine, there can be no question that excessive bleeding, purging, vomiting, sweating, and blistering characterized a good part of the standard medical treatment.

The cold water method for dealing with yellow fever which Drs. Gros and Gerardin had criticized was graphically described by Maunsel White, a long time resident of New Orleans. Shortly after his arrival in 1801, he was seized by yellow fever and called upon Dr. William Flood. Dr. Flood, who rather appropriately was a leading exponent of the cold water treatment, first bled him and dosed him with strong medicines. On the third day White's fever rose and the situation looked hopeless. Dr. Flood did not hesitate. He and two nurses placed the semi-delirious patient in a bathtub and proceeded to deluge him with buckets of cold water. "On they poured it, unsparingly," White wrote, "bucket after bucket. It seemed as if the very Mississippi was pouring over me. The shock was great, but I had no time for reflection." White, obviously a man of strong constitution, survived both the treatment and the disease to stand a living testimonial to the efficacy of Dr. Flood's method of therapy.

During the first half of the nineteenth century the French-speaking physicians followed their moderate tactics and the American physicians continued to center their therapy around bleeding, vomiting, and the use of calomel and other purgatives. In these years only one new weapon was added to the physician's armamentarium against yellow fever. In 1820 the alkaloid quinine was derived from cinchona bark, and it soon came into general use as an "anti-fevrum." Although cinchona bark and later quinine had long been used in the treatment of yellow fever, the late 1830's and 1840's saw the introduction of what was known as the quinine method. This consisted of administering huge doses of quinine to patients in the early stages of yellow fever. It eventually proved no more effective than the traditional forms of therapy, and by the Civil War it, too, began to fall into disuse.

While physicians continued to debate the cause and treatment of yellow fever, the epidemic onslaughts steadily increased in number and in intensity. An outbreak in 1817 caused over

1,000 deaths, and the death toll two years later reached almost 2,200. In 1822 an epidemic broke out at the end of August and spread swiftly through the city. The temporary Board of Health announced on September 6 that it had established a hospital "at the lower end of Common street" for the care of strangers and the sick poor. As the city's resources dwindled in the face of the growing number of yellow fever cases, the authorities began sending the indigent out of the city. By the end of September, with the municipal appropriation all spent, the mayor asked the public for help. The opening sentences of his appeal undoubtedly reflected the prevailing mood: "CITIZENS,—Measures of Human prudence could not prevent this year the deleterious effects of an extraordinary season. Death is within our walls; mourning is general in the city; desolation in most families; and affliction within all hearts." The residents of New Orleans responded generously, but fortunately the outbreak quickly subsided. While it did not cause as many deaths as the 1820 epidemic, its effect was more devastating since the 1,400 or 1,500 victims died within the space of two months.

In the ensuing years yellow fever steadily intensified its attacks. Scarcely a summer passed without a few cases, and in most years the disease reached epidemic proportions. The violence of the disease and its widely publicized onslaughts blackened the reputation of the city far more than it deserved. On the other hand, the inhabitants literally closed their eyes to reality and insisted that, for those who were acclimated, New Orleans was a veritable health spa. The excessive summer and fall mortality was explained away on the grounds that only strangers and the intemperate poor fell prey to yellow fever. Once a newcomer had survived a two or three year "seasoning" period, the newspapers and local medical journals declared, he could henceforth enjoy the best of health, relatively safe from the respiratory disorders and other complaints affecting people in more northern climates. Even newcomers could protect themselves by leaving the city during the yellow fever season, or, if they must remain, by living a life of moderation and seeking medical aid at the first symptoms of yellow fever. The newspapers, and many members of the medical profession, cheerfully proclaimed that yellow fever was quite amenable to treatment. Those who died while under medical care (a seemingly inordinate number) invariably had sought medical help too late or else had failed to obey the injunctions of their physicians. The viability of the myth that New Orleans was a healthful city was made possible by the fact that only those who had survived an attack of the disease were around to praise the work of their physicians. The victims of yellow fever were in no position to evaluate their medical treatment.

The growing seriousness of the yellow fever onslaughts is shown clearly by the annual mortality statistics. In twelve of the thirty-five years from 1825 to 1860, no fewer than 1,000 deaths a year were attributed to the disease. The mounting population during these years seemed only to provide more and more fuel for the raging pestilence. In each of four yellow fever seasons from 1837 to 1843 no less than 1,500 to 2,000 persons were swept away, while still another outbreak in 1847 killed 2,700. Unfortunately, these recurrent outbreaks were but a prelude to the explosive outbursts which devastated New Orleans in the 1850's.

The number of deaths during the 1847 epidemic marked a new high for the city, and, in light of the intensifying outbreaks, raised serious doubts as to the city's future. The fever returned in epidemic fashion for the next two summers, but the death toll in each instance was less than 900, raising cautious hopes that the worst was over. New Orleanians were familiar with the history of yellow fever in the northeastern cities, where the disease had reached a peak between 1790 and 1810 and then had virtually disappeared. Surely, they felt, the pattern would repeat itself in New Orleans, with the great epidemic of 1847 marking the turning point. In 1850 and 1851 only a few scattered cases developed, and the earlier cautious hopes turned into buoyant optimism. In 1852 a minor outbreak led to about 450 deaths, but this merely confirmed the assumption that the disease was on the wane.

The winter of 1852–53 was an unusually prosperous one for

New Orleans. A bumper cotton crop and a wealth of produce pouring down the Mississippi from the rapidly developing Midwest lent credence to the most optimistic hopes of commerce-oriented New Orleanians. The influx of thousands of immigrants, Irish fleeing from the great potato famine and German refugees from political and social upheavals, provided an ample labor supply to meet the city's growing demands. Expressing the exuberant attitude of many civic leaders, the editor of the *Bee* declared in the spring of 1853 that business enterprise had already secured for New Orleans "a future so glorious, that imagination can scarcely conceive a more brilliant destiny." Reflecting this same spirit the editor of the city directory, after noting that five years had passed without a major yellow fever epidemic, asserted that the New Orleans medical profession now considers the disease to be an "obsolete idea." Stark tragedy, however, lay only a few short weeks in the future. Ironically, many of those who had expressed these bright hopes were numbered among the victims.

Yellow fever usually appeared in August, although in some of the more severe outbreaks cases frequently developed in late June or July. Late in May of 1853 a number of cases resembling yellow fever resulted in several deaths. Although the attending physicians could not agree upon the diagnosis, it is clear that there was some uneasiness over the situation among the profession. The newspapers, on the other hand, cheerfully disregarded the whole matter. In June, as the cases began to mount, civic leaders and newspaper editors either carefully avoided mentioning yellow fever or else dismissed the occasional published reports of yellow fever cases.

Despite their public assurances, the city councilmen indicated a few qualms over the persistent yellow fever reports by attacking the Street Commissioner, James Jolls. City streets in the mid-nineteenth century were incredibly filthy; garbage and other refuse was tossed into the streets or onto vacant lots, and the overflow from privies, slaughterhouses, bone-boiling establishments and other businesses poured into the gutters. Such street cleaning as was done was performed by private contractors. The street cleaning contracts, however, had long been considered prize political plums, and, except for rare occasions when public indignation brought a temporary reform, the work of the contractors was purely nominal. The threat of an epidemic always drastically altered this situation, for disease and dirt were associated in the public mind. Under these circumstances, the city councilmen, who were responsible for letting the street contracts, usually attempted to lay the blame upon the street commissioner. The New Orleans City Council, a particularly ineffective body, ran true to form. As the crisis worsened, it carried its criticism to the point of instituting impeachment proceedings against Jolls.

Meanwhile yellow fever was slowly spreading through the city. On July 2, Dr. Abner Hester, who had served as secretary of the previous Board of Health, irritated many civic leaders by announcing that yellow fever had caused twenty-five deaths in the preceding week. The following week the figure rose to fifty-nine and then shot up to 204 in the week ending July 16. Early in July, at a time when thousands of residents were in full flight from the city, the newspapers still denied or discounted the significance of the rising yellow fever toll. Not until the middle of July did the editors reluctantly concede that yellow fever was threatening the city. In the week from July 16 to 23, no fewer than 429 deaths were officially attributed to yellow fever.

Despite the earnest pleas of Mayor A. D. Crossman, one of the better city officials, New Orleans was still without a board of health. Under state law, the City Council was authorized to establish a temporary board each spring, but the council had done nothing. On July 25 the mayor summoned the City Council, consisting of the boards of aldermen and assistant aldermen, into session and urged that it appoint a board of health and appropriate funds for the emergency. After delaying and stalling, the two boards finally concurred and appropriated $10,000 to be used at the health board's discretion. By this time the deaths from yellow fever were averaging close to 100 a day. Filled, no doubt, with a sense of virtue, the two boards promptly adjourned for the summer, leaving their members free to join the exodus from the city. Fortunately, a minority of council members elected to remain with Mayor Crossman and the stricken city, and it was their actions which helped the residents to survive the ordeal.

During the last week in July the daily yellow fever deaths were averaging well over 100. By this time all economic activity had halted, and little was to be heard in the streets save the tolling of bells, the clumping of horses' hoofs, and the rattling of wheels on cobblestones as hearses and wagons bore coffins towards the cemeteries. In the succeeding days the number of deaths continued its remorseless climb. By August 8 it was exceeding 200 a day. Precisely at this time a crisis developed in the cemeteries which maligned the name of New Orleans by giving the false impression that its citizens were both callous and irresponsible.

As might be expected, the cemeteries were taxed to the limit, and grave diggers were in short supply. The pestilence struck hardest in the poorer sections, creating a temporary labor shortage. Although wages were tripled, bodies still accumulated in the graveyards, where, in the oppressive summer heat, they quickly mortified. The New Orleans newspapers scathingly condemned the sextons and city officials and wrote appalling descriptions of the scenes in the cemeteries. These accounts were picked up by outside newspapers and disseminated widely throughout the United States. The truth of the matter was that Mayor Crossman acted with considerable dispatch. When financial inducements could not provide enough grave diggers, he recruited gangs of Negro slaves and within two or three days had the situation under control. Unfortunately for New Orleans' reputation, the damage was already done.

When the daily death toll reached 200 a day, everyone was sure that the peak of the epidemic had been reached, but still the figure climbed. During the week ending August 14 no less than 1,526 New Orleanians perished. On August 20 a total of 269 burials was officially reported to the Board of Health. As the yellow fever intensified, Mayor Crossman seized upon any and all suggestions. Laborers were hired to clean the streets and lots, lime was generously sprinkled in all public places, barrels of tar were set afire at street corners and in public squares, and one of the artillery companies was ordered to fire its cannon in the public squares twice daily. Precisely what effect the roaring of the cannon and the leaping flames from the tar barrels must have had upon the frightened citizenry is hard to say, but the acrid smell of burnt gunpowder and the black smoke from the tar must have made the hot blanket of moist air which had settled over New Orleans in that unusually wet summer of 1853 even more oppressive than usual.

When, on August 20 the Board of Health reported the 269 burials, the announcement evoked a gloomy editorial in the *Delta* entitled "The Black Day." It was an appropriate title, for although the residents did not realize it, this dark day marked the peak of the outbreak. With so many sick and dying to care for, it was not until early September that the citizens realized the worst was over. During the week ending September 3, 749 burials were recorded, a sharp reduction over the 1,628 reported for the preceding week. As September drew on, the epidemic tide receded almost as rapidly as it had advanced, and early in October the city began to count the cost. The Board of Health figures showed that from May 28 to October 8, some 11,100 burials were officially reported, and the board estimated that almost 8,000 of the deaths resulted from yellow fever. From these figures and those of other competent observers, it is clear that in the course of the epidemic there were between 30,000 and 40,000 cases and from 8,000 to 9,000 yellow fever deaths. To appreciate the magnitude of this disaster, one has only to consider that about one-third of the city's 150,000 population had fled the city in June and early July, well before the disease reached serious epidemic proportions.

In studying this devastating outbreak, the most surprising feature is the lack of panic during the epidemic and the relatively calm way in which the city went about caring for its sick and burying its dead. A good part of the credit goes to Mayor A. D. Crossman and the few other officials who remained with him. Another large share goes to the physicians and ministers who risked—and in some cases lost—their lives in order to remain at their posts. Credit should also be given to the many volunteer organizations which did so much to relieve the sick and the poor. The most prominent of these was the Howard Association, a group taking its name from the great English humanitarian, John Howard. Its membership consisted of young businessmen who dedicated themselves to caring for the poor and sick during the recurrent epidemics. In the course of the 1853 epidemic the Association collected $225,000, established emergency hospitals, convalescent homes, and orphanages, sent nurses and physicians into countless homes, and provided housing and food for thousands of impoverished residents. Every citizen who was not sick found himself involved in some sort of welfare activity. The fact that so many individuals were drawn into the activities of emergency civic and volunteer groups may well explain why the citizenry was able to face with such equanimity the ever-increasing daily death toll.

The epidemic of 1853 proved to be the turning point for yellow fever in New Orleans history, but the events of the next five years obscured this fact to her citizens. The human loss wrought by the epidemic was more than made up for by the thousands of newcomers who flocked in to take advantage of the booming economic opportunities in the Crescent City, and by so doing, set the stage for a renewal of the yellow fever attacks. In 1854 and again in 1855 the disease struck hard at these new arrivals, killing approximately 2,500 each year. Mild outbreaks occurred the following two years, and then, in the summer and fall of 1858, the pestilence returned in full force. Once again the appearance of yellow fever cases in June and a mounting death toll in July foreshadowed a major outbreak. When the Board of Health compiled its mortality figures late in November, they showed that 4,856 residents had fallen prey to the disease, the city's second worst outbreak.

After having lost almost 20,000 of its inhabitants to yellow fever in the previous eight years, the city was understandably worried as the yellow fever season of 1859 rolled around. Unaccountably, however, the fever spared New Orleans, and another eight years elapsed before it returned in epidemic form. During most of the Civil War years New Orleans was occupied by Union forces. The military government instituted a rigid program of sanitation and quarantine, and there can be no question that this policy was a factor in keeping Yellow Jack out of the city. The success of the Union officials caused a great deal of soul-searching among local physicians. Reluctant to concede that any good could come from the administration of General "Beast" Butler and his successors, many went to great lengths to prove that the absence of yellow fever was purely coincidental.

Whatever the case, an outbreak in the summer and fall of 1867 resulted in approximately 1,600 fatalities. The return of yellow fever after an absence of eight years raised fears of a recurrence of the events of the 1850's. Happily, these apprehensions proved groundless. Although cases were reported each summer, and a minor epidemic in 1870 led to 587 deaths, no major outbreak developed until 1878. This epidemic did not reach serious proportions until August. Nonetheless, by the first of December it had resulted in 27,000 cases and brought death to some 4,050 residents. From the standpoint of New Orleans, the 1878 epidemic ranks only third in terms of cases and fatalities, but it is one of the most notorious in the United States, for the disease swept up the Mississippi Valley and caused significant outbreaks as far north as St. Louis. Of all the interior cities, Memphis bore the brunt of the casualties, losing approximately 3,500 of its inhabitants.

The following year saw a few scattered cases, but the worst was over for New Orleans. For the next 19 years a number of factors contributed to keeping yellow fever at bay. Chief among them were an improved quarantine system, a more effective drainage and sanitation program, and a rising standard of living. As the interval of freedom from yellow fever lengthened and the

century drew to a close, once again leading citizens proclaimed
that yellow fever was banished from the city—and once again
they were wrong. In September of 1897 public notice was given
of the presence of yellow fever. Remembering only too well the
tragic events of 1878, a wave of fear swept through the town.
When the mayor arranged to use the Beauregard school as a
temporary yellow fever hospital, a mob of from 500 to 1,000
nearby residents, afraid that the hospital would endanger their
lives, set fire to it. On the arrival of the firemen, the mob cut the
hoses and a battle royal ensued. This violence shocked the city.
Refusing to condone mob action, the civic officials and responsible citizens soon restored order. In comparison with previous
outbreaks, the 1897 one was almost insignificant. The official
count showed only 1,908 cases and 298 deaths. Yellow fever,
however, was no longer a familiar disease, and the new generation knew it only through grim stories heard from those who
recalled the 1878 attack. Hence the terror of the unfamiliar was
added to the real threat of this deadly pestilence.

Mild outbreaks of yellow fever developed in the summers of
1898 and 1899 following which the disease seemed to disappear.
Before it returned to New Orleans for its final assault, the mystery of this strange disease was dispelled. In 1900 Walter Reed
and his associates on the Havana Yellow Fever Commission,
capitalizing on the work of Carlos Finlay, a Cuban physician
who had pinpointed the *Aedes aegypti* almost twenty years earlier, were able to prove that the *Aedes aegypti* was the mosquito
responsible for transmitting the disease. News of Walter Reed's
findings led the New Orleans Board of Health to institute a drive
against mosquitoes. Citizens were urged to use mosquito bars
and screens and to eliminate all mosquito breeding grounds.
These appeals had little effect, for yellow fever seemed far removed, and without its imminent threat the public remained
apathetic.

On July 21, 1905 the Board of Health profoundly shook New
Orleans by announcing that yellow fever was once again loose in
the city. Dr. Louis G. LeBeuf, president of the Orleans Parish

Medical Society, recalled in later years that the news led to a general exodus and almost precipitated a financial panic. The city quickly rallied, aided by an unprecedented cooperation between city, state, and federal officials. Representatives of the medical society and the United States Public Health Service met with the state and city Boards of Health to plan a coordinated attack upon mosquitoes. Enlisting the help of hundreds of volunteers, a systematic check was made of every house and lot in the city. In the process 68,000 cisterns were oiled and screened and 753 miles of gutters were salted.

The firm decisive action of the authorities, combined with the knowledge that yellow fever could be controlled, soon calmed popular fears and put an end to the dark apprehensions that had characterized all other epidemic years. Sir Rupert Boyce, a famous English epidemiologist who visited New Orleans in September, wrote that he had never seen an epidemic city in which the citizens were so well organized or so rational in their approach to the disease. Considering the enormity of a mosquito eradication program in a day before insecticides and in a humid city such as New Orleans, the campaign proceeded with remarkable dispatch. Moreover, the success of the program in New Orleans provided a large scale demonstration that yellow fever could be stopped by the elimination of its vector, the *Aedes aegypti* mosquito. In all previous epidemics, August and September had been the peak months. Thanks to the mass attack upon mosquitoes, in 1905 the number of cases was sharply reduced by the end of August, and within a few weeks the city was completely free of yellow fever. All told, this last yellow fever epidemic to strike the continental United States had caused 3,402 cases and led to the death of 452 residents of New Orleans. Compared to the holocausts of disease which had engulfed the city in the previous century, this outbreak was indeed minor— particularly so in light of the city's population of approximately 325,000.

New Orleans did not suffer alone this year. The delay before the nature of the fever could be determined allowed it to spread far and wide through the state, with few towns of any size escaping. Fortunately, the same approach which had been so successful in New Orleans quickly enabled the rest of the state to stamp out the infection. The loss of life in the 1905 epidemic was a costly lesson, but it was one that the citizens of New Orleans did not forget. The year 1905 was not only significant for New Orleans, but it marked a major transition point in the medical history of the United States. Never again would yellow fever or any other great killer disease sweep through an American city, bringing suffering, death, and social disruption in its wake. Never again would the citizens of an American town experience the scenes of gloom and despair such as had characterized the earlier epidemic days. Communicable diseases still remain to threaten public welfare, but after 1905 the light of science was rapidly dispelling the dark fears they had formerly engendered.

Education in New Orleans

John P. Dyer

Education in early New Orleans was marked by
numerous false starts, by apathy, and, measured by anything
corresponding to modern standards, by exasperatingly slow progress. This statement, of course, could be made about education
in many if not most of the colonies and states in what came to be
the United States during the late eighteenth and early nineteenth centuries, but in Louisiana, particularly in New Orleans,
the problem was more acute than in many other areas because of
the potpourri of races, languages, religions, and customs.

Although French was the basic culture well into the American period the intrusion of other ethnic groups raised important
educational problems. What was to be taught? Who were to be
taught? By whom? In what language? These questions at the
time probably seemed relatively simple to answer. New Orleans
Frenchmen interested in education turned to the traditional
mother country's educational system administered and instructed by the Roman Catholic church through its various religious orders of nuns and priests. Thus in early New Orleans in
such schools as existed the language was French and the subjects
were religion, reading, writing, and ciphering. At first those
taught were largely poor children, orphans, and children whose
parents were not desperately poor but not affluent enough to
send them to foreign schools for their basic education. The idea
that education should be tax supported and thus under the

control of the state and open free to all classes was not considered seriously. As a matter of fact, such a system was thought of by many as being almost heretical; and it was more than a hundred years later before the idea of tax supported schools gained timid acceptance in New Orleans. Even then, public schools had competition from parochial and private school education, a rivalry which has not ceased to this day.

Bienville himself was interested in the problem of education as he saw immigrants moving into the city and surrounding countryside during the frenzied period of John Law's "Mississippi Bubble." He made repeated efforts to induce the French government to give schools to the colony under the patronage of the Crown; but it was from the church that assistance was forthcoming. The first educational institution in New Orleans was established by Father Raphael, a Capuchin and pastor of the parish church of St. Louis, who in 1725 opened a small school for boys at what is now 616–618 St. Ann Street. But the school soon dissolved in the river mists and no records have come to light to show specifically how, when or why it disappeared.

More successful and enduring were the efforts of the Ursuline nuns. In 1726 with the assistance of Father Nicholas de Beaubois, later Jesuit Superior in Louisiana, a contract was signed between the Indies Company and the order and during the next year, thirteen intrepid nuns and novices and two servants migrated to New Orleans and took up their temporary residence in Bienville's vacated home in the square bounded by the present Bienville, Chartres, Conti and Decatur streets. Thus was founded the school which became one of the proud heritages of the city. The Ursulines' stay at this site, however, was temporary for after the return of Bienville as governor, they moved to another temporary location and then in 1734 to their long awaited new building which they occupied until structural defects forced them to abandon it. A more solidly constructed building was completed on the same site in 1750 at 1114 Chartres Street; but it was not used as a school and convent after 1824 when it became the temporary capitol of the state. The Ursulines had relocated and their former building became the home of the archbishop of New Orleans in 1834. But this building still stands as the only edifice in New Orleans dating from the middle French period and as the oldest existing building in the Mississippi Valley. The present location of the Ursulines on State Street, occupied in 1912, seems new indeed when compared with the solemn and mellow beauty of the old convent and school on Chartres Street.

These nuns attended the sick, served *in loco parentis* for scores of orphans and taught many hundreds of young girls. At first pupils were orphans, daughters of the poor, and Negro and Indian girls. But as time went on more and more middle and upperclass parents found in the convent a highly desirable school for their daughters. To the basic curriculum of religion, reading, writing and arithmetic, the nuns added geography, English, French, history, the arts of homemaking, the crafts of embroidering and other skills which the homemaker and mother needed. Many prominent women in the community attended the school, including the future wife of one governor.

Thus in early New Orleans the best education available was for girls. For many years after the disappearance of Father Raphael's school there was little in the way of educational opportunities for boys, a fact which Governor Claiborne was to lament and comment on when Louisiana became American. These were occasional short lived, private, non-sectarian schools but none of them made much of an impression. The French boy, if he had wealthy parents, went to an academy in Canada or France; the son of the poor family received little or no education. It is small wonder that half the population of early New Orleans was illiterate. Why the Capuchins did not follow up Father Raphael's efforts or why some other order did not establish a boys' school is a question not readily answerable. But there are intimations as to why early education for boys was so limited. The apprentice system then in effect did not require book learning. Funds for education were scarce. But probably the best explanation in addition to the lack of funds was that the heterogeneous character of the population ranging from the cultured to John Law's adventurers and even criminals prevented any real unity of purpose or stability which would afford a climate favorable to education in the community. Too, France herself failed to visualize the growth in importance of New Orleans.

On paper at least the Spanish period from 1766 to 1803 did more for the education of boys than had the French era. Under the aegis of the King, a free school for boys, often called The Spanish School, was established in 1772 under the direction of Don Lopez de Armesto. But the venture was not a success largely because it was a Spanish language school and the community clung tenaciously to the French language. Few students presented themselves, probably never more than thirty in any one year and sometimes as few as twelve.

However, during the late Spanish period, a fresh breeze of educational endeavor blew into the city with the arrival of numerous French immigrants from Santo Domingo. During the fifteen years (roughly 1786–1800) of political and racial strife which preceded control by Touissant L'Ouverture thousands of Frenchmen left the island, some four thousand of them coming to New Orleans. (Among the émigrés was Paul Tulane's father, Louis, who settled not in New Orleans but in New Jersey. Subsequently young Paul Tulane moved to New Orleans and in his later years founded Tulane University). Many of these Santo Domingo Frenchmen were well educated and soon put their appreciation of education into use by founding several non-sectarian private schools, all, of course, French language schools. There were schools for boys, and, in direct competition with the Ursulines, day and boarding schools for girls. There were at least five of these schools and total enrollment at one time was estimated to have been almost five hundred.

The establishment of these French speaking private schools was enthusiastically welcomed by many in New Orleans, for in 1795 the people were probably more strongly French in sentiment than at any previous time. The mother country was going through a final phase of her revolution and was at war with her neighbors, including Spain. The strong feeling of patriotism caused no really serious or widespread clashes between the French and Spanish in New Orleans, but Spanish Bishop Peñalvert was not very happy over the school situation. In 1795 he reported that the Spanish school was "kept as it ought to be" but there was doubt about the French schools of which only one was "opened by authority and with the regular license." "Excellent results are obtained from the convent of the Ursulines," he wrote, "but their inclinations are so decidedly French that they have even refused to admit among them Spanish women who wished to become nuns." All in all education was rather ineffective, the good bishop thought, because regardless of what school they attended boys "retire to the houses of their parents, mostly situated in the country, where they hear neither the name of God nor of the King, but daily witness the corrupt morals of their parents."

Before Bishop Peñalvert left his diocese, however, a series of events of profound historical significance took place. In 1803 Napoleon in a secret treaty forced Spain to retrocede Louisiana to France; and then finding his dream of a French empire wrecked by L'Ouverture in Santo Domingo he surprised everyone, more especially President Jefferson, by selling the entire Louisiana territory to the United States. On December 20, 1803, in a formal ceremony at the Cabildo the official transfer was made. Outside in the Place d'Armes (now Jackson Square) the Spanish flag had been run down in November and the French flag raised. Then the French flag was lowered in December and the American flag raised. Now New Orleans was soon to be invaded by still another language and culture group—"Kaintucks," flatboatmen, pious and God-fearing, English speaking Protestants, business men, speculators—in short, Americans. New Orleans would never be the same again.

Both Jefferson and William C. C. Claiborne, the first territorial governor, were much concerned over education, or rather the lack of it, in the city, for both realized that the schools would play a major role in the Americanization process which inevitably would follow annexation. Governor Claiborne was disturbed over what he found. "New Orleans," he wrote Jefferson, "is a great and growing city. . . . I believe the citizens of Louisiana are, generally speaking, honest; and a decided majority of them are attached to the American government. But they are uninformed, indolent, luxurious, in a word illy fitted to be useful citizens of a republic." He had seen, he wrote, many youths to whom nature had been liberal but who from the "injustice" and "inattention" of their parents had no accomplishments to recommend them but "dancing with elegance and ease." In general he felt education was in a pretty sorry condition and proposed to do something about it.

In April, 1805, he urged the territorial legislative council to establish a university system with a College of Orleans at the head. The council was responsive to his wishes and in the same month passed legislation establishing the University of Orleans and the College of Orleans. The plan was to be financed by a lottery.

It must be hastily added that the "University" was nothing more than a plan for a secondary school and library in each parish plus the college in New Orleans. But whatever it was or was not, it developed so slowly that Claiborne almost despaired of it ever coming into being. The first meeting of the board of regents (largely Santo Domingo Frenchmen) was held on July 5, 1805. Claiborne was named chancellor and plans were made for the lottery. Ten thousand tickets at ten dollars each were to be offered for sale with the provision that no drawing could be held until eight thousand had been sold. Everything depended upon the success of this lottery for the act prohibited the parishes from levying a tax for education.

But the lottery went slowly and the regents were unable to secure funds even for a beginning. In 1806 Claiborne appealed to the legislature to expand the university system by providing for elementary as well as secondary schools and in May of that year there was passed "an act to provide for establishment of public free schools in the several counties (sic) of the territory."

A feature of this act was that it placed responsibility for the development of schools on commissioners to be set up by each parish. The commissioners elected by the people were authorized to take whatever steps deemed necessary to establish "free schools at the expense of the county." Again Claiborne's hopes were doomed by apathy, for two years of inactivity followed. But the governor was not daunted. When the legislature convened in January, 1808, he again urged the lawmakers to pass an effective school bill. But they were loathe to expend state funds for local schools and the bill they passed again threw the responsibility on the parish authorities. Claiborne, though obviously weary and frustrated, did not give up. In 1809 he urged the legislature to purchase a private academy in New Orleans and convert it into a free school. Again he encountered almost complete apathy; and, to make matters worse, another legislative resolution was passed to the effect that no person could be forced to pay a school tax if he chose not to do so.

Governor Claiborne did not bring up the matter of schools in 1810 but in 1811 there came a surprising turn of events. The legislature convening in January of that year found a surplus in the treasury. The governor in calling attention to this surplus urged that it be used for schools. One can imagine that he was mildly shocked when $39,000 was appropriated for schools —$15,000 for the College of Orleans and $2,000 for each of twelve parishes. At last New Orleans was to have a college, or what was euphemistically called a college, just before the territory was admitted to the Union as a state. In addition to the $15,000 appropriated for the college, $2,000 per year was to be spent for the free education of fifty indigent young men. (More and more the term "indigent" was becoming associated with free public education, a fact which did much to discredit the idea of free schools. Many parents denied their children an education rather than have pinned on them the badge of "charity").

A square of land bounded by the present Ursulines, St. Claude and Governor Nicholls streets (the site of the present St. Augustine Church) was appropriated for the campus of the new college. A large home was located on the square and this became the main building. To this were added two long barracks-like dormitories; and on November 4, 1811, the school under the presidency of a Santo Domingo refugee, Jules Davezac, opened with seventy students of all ages from seven to sixteen.

As time went on there were intimations that the college was not prospering, largely, it seems, because of inept administration. The first two presidents, Davezac and Rochefort (also a Santo Domingoan), were devoted to learning but apparently were very poor administrators. If a decision had to be made between wrestling with the financial problems of a new college and writing a poem, both men were likely to write a poem. Davezac, with the mien of a Roman senator, probably would read his poems in a stentorian voice while poor clubfooted Rochefort was likely to gather around him a few select students and quietly read them his poems in Latin. He had something of a practical side however. He was noted for giving theatre parties for the students and then sending the bill to their parents.

The state Legislature took a substantial interest in the college during its early years despite the fuzzy administrative policies of its first two presidents. In 1812, the annual appropriation for maintenance was raised from $2,000 to $3,000. In 1819, this was increased to $4,000 and in 1821 to $5,000. In 1823, the state licensed six gambling houses at $5,000 each and provided that $7,500 of this amount should go to the college. By 1824 it was clearly obvious that the college was performing poorly and the appropriation was reduced to $5,000. In 1825, during the closing months of President Joseph Lakanal's administration, this appropriation was given to the newly founded College of Louisiana at Jackson in Feliciana Parish. Poor administration during its early days, the withdrawal of appropriations, and the controversial figure of Joseph Lakanal were too much for the college and it closed its doors forever on March 31, 1826.

It is not difficult to understand why conservative Creoles would oppose Lakanal, for his life and career inspired controversy. It was not that he was an evil man, a poor administrator or a bad scholar, for he was none of these. Rather he was a healthy, strong man characterized by mildness of manner, a genuine interest in education, especially science, and a background of college and secondary school teaching and administration in his native France during the period of the French Revolution in which he was a prominent participant. Born in southwest France near the Spanish border in 1762 to middle class, respectable parents, he as a young man entered the order of the Fathers of the Christian Doctrine and was ordained a priest. (The family name was spelled with a "c" but he changed the spelling to a "k" apparently in an effort to disassociate himself and his revolutionary activities from the rest of the family.) When the French Revolution broke out, he, along with hundreds of others of the lesser clergy, joined the forces seeking to establish a new order in France. In 1792 he was elected from his home district to the national convention in Paris. Here he rose to the position of secretary and eventually to president of the committee on public education. In these capacities he could indulge his passion as a sincere republican for public education. He wrote the rules for the French Institute of which he was a member, established the *Ecole Normal*, the *Ecole Polytechnique* and the state botanical gardens at Versailles. He was a friend of all educators. Perhaps no man in the revolutionary period did more for French public education than Lakanal.

With the overthrow of Napoleon and the restoration of the monarchy in 1815, Lakanal had to leave France, obtaining asylum in the United States in Kentucky just across the Ohio River from a French colony in Ohio. From this locale he moved to New Orleans in 1822 where he had been elected president of the College of Orleans. But in this position he soon found a tempest roaring around him. At least two events in his revolutionary career rose to bedevil him: during the revolution he had married Marie-Barbe François and this made him an apostate priest. (He had declared to the convention that he had never been a practicing priest, anyway.) Too, he had voted for the execution of Louis XVI and this made him a regicide. In New Orleans, the population was divided in its opinion. There were those who defended him and many more who denounced him as a "regicide," "deist," "radical," "apostate priest" and "socialist." The uproar coupled with the cut in appropriations was enough to cause him to resign. This he did after some three years of service, and the college did not survive. Lakanal and his wife joined a French colony near Mobile where he became a planter and slaveholder and in 1836 received from Louis Phillipe amnesty and permission to return to France.

The collapse of the College of Orleans was hardly a catastrophe, however, for its birth had been premature. There was no elementary system to feed secondary schools and few secondary schools to feed the colleges which were being established willy-nilly over the state and without planning (as they still seem to be). The College of Orleans was forced into the position of being a sort of mongrel elementary and secondary school and this fact was recognized after its demise. A state financed central secondary school and two elementary schools were established immediately after the college had folded; and the new plan was considered successful. In 1828 about 250 pupils were enrolled with 100 being "beneficiaries." The small appropriation ($9,475 in 1828 with only $8,863 spent) apparently was considered adequate, but by 1831 these schools had acquired a character as schools for the indigent only and the course of study altered to fit their needs. New Orleans had taken one more step in its thinking that free public schools were "charity" schools.

The second period in the development of New Orleans schools may be said to have begun in 1841. By a legislative act of that year $7,500 was appropriated for New Orleans by the state for primary schools *on condition that the city raise half that sum.* The number of schools was fixed at one or more for each of the three municipalities of New Orleans and one on the right bank at Algiers. (Municipality No. 1 was the old city from Canal

Street to Esplanade; No. 2 from Canal Street to Felicity Street; No. 3 was the area below Esplanade to Bayou St. John.)

There appears to have been little resentment from the citizens over the fact that they were paying half the cost, for this was a period of growth and prosperity. In 1830, New Orleans had a population of 49,826 and by 1840 this figure had grown to 102,193. The wharves along the riverfront were crowded with foreign vessels and river boats. Trade was brisk and a general air of well-being pervaded the city. What did it matter if a few dollars went into public education especially when all these dollars did not come from taxes but partly from license fees on theatres and other amusements? Besides, private schools were also thriving and multiplying.

It did appear, however, that free public education had belatedly caught on. In 1844 members of the Legislature visited the new public schools in operation. Apparently they were much impressed and commented "with pride and pleasure" on the zeal manifested by the authorities of the second and third municipalities in the establishment of "numerous" public schools. (But the legislative report had no commendation for the first municipality—the French Quarter.) One must conclude that the legislative committee on education was sufficiently impressed that it was willing to re-evaluate the state's educational efforts. It came out strongly for the adoption of a comprehensive statewide public school system and at the same time brought the earlier established "colleges" of the state under sharp scrutiny. (There were, including the College of Orleans, six of these colleges established in various parts of the state between 1811 and 1839. During this period approximately $700,000 had gone to the support of these institutions which obviously were not serving any significant portion of the state's youth.) In a retrenchment mood in 1842 the legislature reduced or eliminated appropriations for most of these colleges and many of them went out of business before 1845. There appeared to be among members of the Legislature the feeling at long last that a strong elementary and secondary school system was necessary if higher education was to succeed; and New Orleans was one of the few places in the state which showed signs of progress in developing basic education, even though some of these signs were to prove illusory as time went on.

Undoubtedly the prosperity of New Orleans and the beginning of what appeared to be for its day a somewhat adequate system of public and private schools were factors in the Legislature's decision to found another institution of higher learning in the city. As a prelude, in 1834, seven young doctors had banded together to form the Medical College of Louisiana. (Another medical school, the New Orleans School of Medicine, located on the corner of Tulane Avenue and Villere Street, was formed in 1856 but soon became a Civil War casualty.) Desiring a permanent place to teach, these seven doctors made a deal with the state. In return for their professional services at Charity Hospital, the state gave to them a square of land between Baronne and Phillips (now University Place) facing Common Street. On this square the doctors began erecting at their own expense a building to be used for the teaching of medicine. (This school would be the noted Medical School of Tulane University.) When Pierre Soulé, Judah P. Benjamin, Christian Roselius and other prominent citizens convinced the Legislature that it ought to establish a university in New Orleans, there was a ready-made spot for it. In 1847 when the University of Louisiana was founded, it took in the medical school and made plans for an academic department and a school of law. Almost immediately the new university began operations after the state had made an appropriation of $25,000 to complete the building. The next year it received $35,000 for additional building. (Shortly thereafter the Legislature authorized the establishment of the Louisiana State Seminary of Learning and Military Academy at Pineville in Rapides Parish. This institution subsequently was moved to Baton Rouge and had its name changed to Louisiana State University.)

While the new university was undergoing the pains common to most new institutions of higher learning, the public schools were showing slow but continuing progress. On May 3, 1847, the first all-out state free school act was passed. For the first time in its history Louisiana now had a superintendent of public instruction, Alexander Dimitry, a native of the state and apparently a very competent school man. Under his leadership public education took another decided upward turn. In 1849, 6,720 children from a total of 14,258 were attending New Orleans public schools, and the city had raised $92,506 from millage and poll tax. There were twelve schools in the first municipality, fifteen in the second and seventeen in the third. In the second and first municipalities, the schools were graded as primary and intermediate; the third was mixed. Too, high schools had been established in the second and first. The state superintendent's report for 1860 noted that New Orleans schools were "prospering and there is a *constant demand for good teachers.* Private schools, too, are numerous and well conducted."

The phrase "constant demand for good teachers" injects still another problem into the efforts to establish respectable public schools. There existed no professional institute in the state where a prospective teacher might be trained. Nor was there a teacher training curriculum in any of the so-called colleges. An aspiring teacher took a simple examination in subject matter and on the basis of the results was certified or not. The demand for teachers was so great that few failed. Too, the salaries paid teachers were so low that there was little attraction for the superior person. There seems little doubt but what instruction in most of the private and parochial schools was superior to that of the public schools, but this isn't saying much. Neither type was really good.

The public schools thus experienced the second strike against them. The first strike was the tag of "charity." The second was the rather widespread belief that education in the public schools was always bad and that education in the private and Catholic schools was invariably good. Neither was wholly true but the belief served to retard the progress of public education.

One highly encouraging note was injected into the educational picture in New Orleans, however. In 1850 John McDonogh, a wealthy and eccentric businessman, died, leaving his estate of over a million dollars to the Baltimore and New Orleans school systems. In subsequent years thirty school buildings in New Orleans were constructed with the funds. But the gift was not an unmixed blessing, for the people of New Orleans were relieved for years from the necessity of providing adequate physical facilities for their schools, and it does not take many generations for a people to depend on gifts rather than on its own tax money.

Another potentially important step in the city's educational system was the establishment in 1858 of a normal school located in the first municipality high school. In 1859, a state appropriation of $5,000 was made for its maintenance and in 1860, this appropriation was doubled. Apparently a good teacher training foundation was being laid when the Civil War came and New Orleans was occupied.

On May 1, 1862, Farragut turned over command of the city to General Benjamin F. Butler who immediately began to make a nuisance of himself and almost as if by contrivance to bring down on his balding head the bitter hatred of New Orleans people. So far as the public schools were concerned he interfered little or none with actual internal operations of individual schools, but he did force the consolidation of the four separate municipal systems into one, (the municipality of Lafayette had been added to the three previously mentioned) obviously a wise administrative move. Each municipality had had its own textbooks, some in French, some in English. Each had had its own system of grading and promotion and when parents moved from one municipality to another there was often considerable confusion. This situation Butler corrected.

It was under Butler's successor, General Nathaniel P. Banks, that public education problems really became acute as a result of the task of providing educational facilities for hundreds of Negro youths. This problem had never arisen in Louisiana for the very simple reason that it was illegal after 1830 to educate the Negro. On January 1, 1863, however, Lincoln's Emancipation Proclamation freed all the slaves within federal lines and since New Orleans fell in this category the situation in the city rapidly became chaotic. In 1864, Banks issued General Order No. 38 which constituted a new board of education "for the rudimental education of the freed man—so as to place within his reach the elements of knowledge." To implement the task of setting up Negro schools the Freedman's Bureau was authorized in 1865 to provide for books, furniture (but not buildings) and transportation for teachers.

Although the addition of over four thousand students to the rolls of the public schools produced a crucial situation, the citizenry and school officials applied themselves grimly to the solution. William O. Rogers, native New Orleanian and former superintendent of the first municipality schools, was named superintendent in 1865 succeeding J. B. Carter, a Union sympathizer. It was Rogers who carried the almost overwhelming administrative burden of finding space and teachers for the burgeoning enrollment. Space was found but nooks and crannies had to be explored even to the extent of locating one school in a war-vacated wing of the University of Louisiana at the corner of Baronne and Common. But teachers were another matter, for even partially qualified ones were scarce, to say nothing of good ones.

Rogers' position was made untenable in 1870, however, by the action of the carpetbag Legislature and Board of Education in desegregating the schools. On April 8, 1870, Rule No. 39 under authority of the Constitution of 1868 was promulgated by the state Board of Education ordering Negro children admitted to white schools; and the anger it created was expressed by the people in a muted but none-the-less menacing swell of resentment and frustration. Demonstrations could hardly be held because of the presence of a federal army in Louisiana, but no one could mistake the community's sentiments. Not only did the white people resist, but the several hundred mulattoes, octoroons and quadroons who had traditionally been "free people of color" likewise objected to their children being forced to attend schools dominated by black children. So strong was the pressure that a special school, "Academy No 4," was established for the light colored children of free Negroes.

Conditions being what they were, Rogers resigned and devoted himself to the organization of an independent Presbyterian parochial system of schools for white children only. Citizens resorted to passive resistance; and, since there were no compulsory school attendance laws, their efforts were successful. Private and Catholic schools were flooded with white children and public education received a setback it did not deserve. It might also be added that this premature desegregation also inhibited peaceful and evolutionary attempts to solve the problem for nearly a hundred years, and even after this lapse of time there was and is stiff resistance from some white groups.

J. B. Carter who had preceded Rogers came in again as superintendent in 1870 and, in 1873, was succeeded by Captain C. W. Boothby who served until 1877 when Rogers was again named to the position.

Under the superintendency of Boothby bad conditions became worse. Although personally opposed to racial integration in the schools, it became his lot to administer most of the new programs under the new order. Space problems were acute. By 1873 the number of Negro pupils had risen to 7,000, and the local Board of Education found it necessary to construct six buildings with McDonogh money—but this did not alleviate the teacher shortage nor assure a high standard of teacher performance. It is no wonder Boothby developed ulcers.

The final solution of school integration, had it been permanent, makes interesting speculation, but the city was spared the necessity of working out the problem because, in 1877, federal troops were removed from the South and carpetbag governments toppled. One of the first acts of the Democratic Legislature under Governor Francis T. Nicholls declared:

"The education of all classes of the people being essential to the preservation of free institutions, we do declare our solemn purpose to maintain a system of public schools by an equal and uniform taxation upon property, as provided in the Constitution of the State; which shall secure the education of the white and colored citizens with equal advantages."

This resolution, with subsequent legislation, was partially the basis for education frequently referred to as "separate but equal." By 1899 the number of Negro pupils had dropped from the high of 7,000 in 1873 to approximately half that number. Education was separate but not equal and hundreds of Negroes were poorly educated or not at all. In 1899 total enrollment in the public schools was 23,886 of which 20,257 were white. The problem of desegregation had been simply swept under the rug, and the decision in *Plessy vs Ferguson* in 1896 helped keep it there.

The end of the Civil War and Reconstruction left New Orleans a city where many of the citizens knew poverty—genteel poverty among some and abject, almost degrading, poverty among others. The flower of mercantile and shipping prosperity had wilted. The mouth of the river had been partially closed by silt and larger vessels from abroad were conspicuously absent from their berths along the riverfront. Delicate ironwork which had graced French Quarter buildings rusted to a dirty brown and along the streets open drains created a nauseating stench. Disease, particularly yellow fever, small pox and even leprosy were present in menacing proportions. Red beans and rice, a cheap and filling combination, threatened to replace the Creole cuisine which had delighted the effete gourmet and the working man alike. Under these and other unsavory conditions, New Orleans had to rebuild her society, her economic well-being and her educational system.

The first and most obvious reaction to the end of the carpet-bag régime was legislative financial retrenchment, a move which seriously affected New Orleans schools. Historically, the four sources of revenue for schools had been: (1) Louisiana's pro-rata share of the proceeds of the sale of public lands other than the sixteenth sections; (2) proceeds of the sixteenth section lands;

(3) the pole tax levied upon "every male inhabitant in the state over the age of twenty-one years, which shall never be less than one dollar nor exceed one dollar and a half. . . ."; (4) a property tax of 1⅛ mills.

But these sources proved inadequate to care for the educational needs of a city such as New Orleans which was thus thrown largely upon its own resources with other parishes receiving proportionately more per student from the state. If in no other way, the financial plight of New Orleans was reflected in teacher's pay. The state (including New Orleans) average monthly pay for a white male teacher in 1888–89 was fifty dollars; for the white female teacher it was about ten dollars less; and for the colored male teacher, it was approximately thirty-five dollars; for the colored female about five dollars less.

In 1872 under the carpetbag government the salary from the State of the Orleans Parish School Superintendent was fixed at $4,000 per year while his secretary received $2,500. With the return of the Democrats to power the entire administrative budget of the Republicans was drastically reduced. The salary of the State Superintendent of Education was reduced from $5,000 to $2,000 and a ceiling of $200 per year was placed on all parish superintendents except in Orleans Parish where the salary was $2,000.

These figures reflect clearly the fiscal distress and financial conservatism in which a school system for a growing state and city was to develop. New Orleans was fortunate in having the McDonogh fund for buildings but salaries and maintenance lagged far behind the most basic needs to say nothing of respectability. Moreover, the Catholic school system and the large number of private schools caused many citizens, perhaps the majority, to oppose local taxation for school purposes. The old order of things educational changed slowly.

But public education did not completely stagnate. Perhaps it might have if it had not been for the almost heroic efforts of the school people themselves and a minority of the citizenry. Somehow, they kept alive the ideal of a good tax supported system of public education free from the stigma of charity and staffed by good teachers.

The matter of training teachers for the Orleans Parish school system had received attention, as previously stated, as early as 1858 when the legislature passed an act establishing a normal school department in the public high school. But the war and occupation of New Orleans aborted the plan. In 1870 the Peabody Normal Seminary was opened in New Orleans. It lasted fourteen years, but appropriations from the Peabody Fund were small and the institution could hardly be described as thriving. At the same time a Peabody Normal for Negro teachers was in existence, but because of financial and other handicaps neither really did a good job.

In 1885 the New Orleans Normal School, which was to be the main source of the system's white elementary teachers until 1940, was organized. It never was a degree granting institution, but offered a two year and a three year program maintaining some balance between subject matter and professional courses.

The normal school was, however, a part of the urge toward higher education (especially for Negroes) so obvious in New Orleans during the latter part of the nineteenth century and the early part of the twentieth. Most of the institutions chartered during the period 1865–1900 were important not so much for what they were, but because of what they evolved into. There was, for example, Southern University (for Negroes) founded as a state institution in 1880 and located on Calliope Street. In 1886 this site was disposed of and an entire square on Magazine and Soniat Streets was purchased, new buildings were erected and signs of permanence were evident. In 1888 an agricultural and mechanical department was added and in 1892 the institution was recognized as a full-fledged land grant college. In 1914, however, the college was closed and moved to Scotlandville in the vicinity of Baton Rouge, where it has built new buildings and increased its enrollment to the extent that a branch in New Orleans seemed a necessity. This branch was established in 1956.

Religious and philanthropic impulses were much in evidence

during the period mentioned above. Although Dillard University with its beautiful white buildings and green lawns on the edge of the city was not founded until 1930 its roots go deep into the religious and humanitarian thought prevalent during the post Civil War period. Straight College founded in 1869 was operated by the American Association of the Congregational Church and became one constituent part of Dillard. In the same year of 1869 Union Normal School, subsequently renamed the New Orleans University, came into being fostered by the Methodist church. It became the other major ingredient of the institution named for James Hardy Dillard, dean of the college of liberal arts at Tulane and ardent exponent of higher education for Negroes. (Dillard, however, has no racial nor religious bars).

Tulane University undoubtedly was the most important educational institution founded in New Orleans during the nineteenth century. It was the product of the philanthropy of the Franco-American, Paul Tulane, a long time wealthy merchant of the city. In 1882 in retirement at Princeton, N.J., he decided to give his real estate holdings in New Orleans (income of some $38,-000 per year) "for the promotion and encouragement of intellectual, moral and industrial education among the white young persons in the city of New Orleans." (The phrase "white young persons" later rose up to plague the university when it attempted to open its door to all races.)

A board of administrators of the Tulane Educational Fund was established as the controlling body of the Fund and the use to which it was to be put; and after considerable soul searching, discussion and negotiation between all parties, including Tulane, the decision was made to absorb, with its approval, the faltering and impecunious University of Louisiana with its restricted campus facing Common Street between Baronne and University Place. Act 43 of the legislature in 1884 (subsequently incorporated into the state constitution) made the decision legal and on July 5, 1884, The Tulane University of Louisiana emerged. Finding the Common Street campus much too small, the administrators in 1891 purchased a strip of land on St. Charles Avenue opposite Audubon Park. In January, 1894, the cornerstone of Gibson Hall was laid and the new campus became a reality.

Four years after Paul Tulane had made his decision, Mrs. Josephine Louise Newcomb decided to found a college for women, in memory of her deceased daughter, within the administrative structure of Tulane University. Her first donation of $100,000 was made in October, 1886, and the H. Sophie Newcomb Memorial College was opened in 1887 in a large brick residence at the corner of Camp and Howard Streets. This space proved inadequate, however, and in January, 1891, the college moved to a square in the Garden District where a lovely campus developed. In 1918 Newcomb joined the main campus in uptown New Orleans. (Both Mrs. Newcomb and Paul Tulane made large gifts subsequent to their original ones.)

Just across the fence and so close to the Tulane campus that the visitor has difficulty telling where it stops and another one begins is Loyola University of the South. But the geographic proximity does not extend to the nature of the universities. Tulane is privately endowed and non-sectarian while Loyola is a Jesuit institution.

To understand the origins of Loyola one must look into the early history of New Orleans. It has been related above how in the early days educational activities revolved largely around the Capuchins. There were, however, a few Jesuits in and around the colony engaged largely in missionary work. Their relationship with the Capuchins was marred by jurisdictional and hierarchial quarrels and finally in 1763 the Jesuits were expelled from the colony and their property sold at public auctions. This drastic action was not brought about by the Capuchins, however, but by the Superior Council of Louisiana, the governing body of the early colony. The ouster, according to Baudier, historian of the Catholic church in Louisiana, reflected a powerful enmity toward the Jesuits in France itself brought on by the "anticlerical animus that colored the whole disgraceful proceedings and very graphically foreshadowed the savagery of the French Revolution already brewing and ready to burst forth in another three decades." The Gallicans and Jensenites in France were also strongly anti-Jesuit.

Regardless of the reasons for such severe action against the Jesuits, the fact remains that the order did leave Louisiana in 1763 and did not return until 1847.

When the order was reinstated, it devoted much of its attention to education as well as to missionary work. In December, 1847, the order incorporated itself in New Orleans as the Catholic Literary and Educational Society and as such planned and broke ground for a chapel, a school and a residence at the corner of Baronne and Common streets. The school was the College of the Immaculate Conception (for boys) which opened to receive students on February 1, 1849. It was an almost instantaneous success and additional ground had to be secured and a new building erected. At last, it appeared, there was a Catholic school for boys in New Orleans as important as the Ursuline school for girls.

Immaculate Conception College carried courses beyond the high school level and in 1909 the decision was made to transfer the collegiate type courses to an uptown site opposite Audubon Park which had been purchased by the Jesuits in 1889. The institution thus founded was Loyola College which became Loyola University of the South authorized in 1912 to grant degrees. The high school portion of Immaculate Conception College was renamed Jesuit High School which subsequently was transferred to a site at the corner of Howard Avenue and Baronne Street and then to its present location on Carrollton Avenue.

Two more Catholic institutions of higher learning complete the picture in uptown New Orleans.

In 1860 six Dominican sisters from Ireland accepted an invitation to teach in the parochial school of St. John the Baptist on Dryades Street, but during the next year after their arrival, the sisters set up their own school for girls nearby. In 1865 the Dominicans purchased Macé Academy, a fashionable but bankrupt girls' school, at Greenville (now St. Charles and Broadway) and for many years operated the new uptown school for boarding girls and the older one on Dryades as a day school.

In 1908, however, the uptown St. Mary's Dominican Academy was raised to the status of a normal school whose graduates were eligible for teacher certification and in 1909, largely through the efforts of Archbishop Blenk, St. Mary's Dominican College emerged as a full four-year liberal arts college for women. (The Most Reverend James Hubert Blenk, a devoted advocate of Catholic education, was Archbishop of New Orleans, 1906–1917. It was he who organized the Catholic school system in New Orleans and appointed the first diocesan superintendent, Father Leslie J. Kavanagh, in 1907. There have been six other superintendents since that time.)

Archbishop Blenk, too, was almost solely responsible for the establishment of Xavier University (for Negroes) in 1915. Upon the archbishop's request, the Sisters of the Blessed Sacrament agreed to come to New Orleans and establish an institution of higher learning for Negroes and Indians. The order purchased the recently vacated building and grounds of Southern University and in September, 1915, opened a high school. A normal school department was added in 1917 and was subsequently designated a teacher's college. In June, 1929, property for a new campus was purchased on Washington Avenue near Carrollton and in October, 1931, the first building of the new campus was dedicated. As buildings rose the curriculum was expanded to include, in addition to liberal arts, the school of pharmacy and the graduate school. The university had been authorized to grant degrees since 1918, however.

Louisiana State University in New Orleans concludes the roll call of institutions of higher learning in New Orleans (excluding Notre Dame Seminary and Southern Baptist Theological Seminary). This branch of the state university was founded by legislative action in 1956 as a "commuters college" on a large tract of land on the lakefront leased to it by the Levee Board of New Orleans. The site was that formerly occupied by the Naval Air

Station and contained a number of usable if unbeautiful buildings which were converted to academic purposes. In September, 1958, a freshman class was admitted and in 1962 the first senior class was graduated.

Meantime an extensive building program was inaugurated and a campus has emerged, with more buildings in the planning stage. It has not, however, remained a commuters college. Legal sanction has been given for the erection of dormitories (as yet unbuilt) and the academic program has been greatly expanded to include graduate work and an evening division. It has also added an additional 150 acres of land, the former Camp Leroy Johnson tract, sixty acres of which it gave to the Gulf South Research Institute.

Meantime the public, private and Catholic school system had not been static during the early part of the twentieth century. Although space restrictions will not permit a full narrative of all the achievements, mention must be made of certain key events particularly in the public school system. These may be listed as: (1) changes in the administrative structure; (2) growing emphasis on special education; (3) passage of the compulsory school attendance law and the first free textbook act; (4) the changing base of tax support; (5) a high school for Negroes; (6) upgrading teachers; (7) salary increases for teachers; (8) new and renovated buildings; (9) curriculum revision; (10) a slowly changing image of the public school system.

Changes in the administrative structure were of paramount importance. In 1888 the Orleans Parish schools were placed under a board of twenty members, eight being appointed by the governor and twelve by the city council, an open invitation to political meddling in the schools. In 1908 the board was changed from an appointed body of twenty to a group of seventeen, one elected from each city ward, again a splendid opportunity for the ward leaders to exercise political control of the school system. In 1912, however, the present type of board was established. The ward system was abolished and provision was made for a board of five members serving terms of six years elected from the city at large. While this plan did not eliminate completely the political factor it went a long way in this direction. Closely paralleling these board changes came additions to the superintendent's staff. In 1910 came the position of first assistant superintendent; then came the purchasing department in 1912 as well as the department of educational research. Then numerous supervisors were added to the superintendent's staff—for evening schools, music, drawing, domestic science, manual training, a school nurse, kindergartens, primary grades, school dropouts, special services and even agriculture. These all foreshadowed the makeup of the superintendent's office today, a rather elaborate system of twelve major administrative departments and some thirty-eight supervisors and other lesser administrative officers (each with a staff), not including principals and assistant principals. But, it must hastily be added, the number of public schools of all categories has increased to 132 with a total enrollment in 1966 of 107,834. Between 1900 and 1960, Catholic schools showed a tremendous growth—from forty schools with an enrollment of 9,500 to eighty-seven schools with an enrollment of 48,245. In 1960, population of the Catholic schools declined slightly to 47,981 and each year thereafter has shown a continuation of the decline.

The emphasis on special education in the Orleans Parish public schools has been extremely important. Beginning in a very simple way with a program for the deaf child, the project was expanded under Superintendent Warren Easton in 1903 to include education for wayward children of both races in the Waif's Homes. Easton did not live to see the program expanded, as he had urged, to include care of the physically or mentally weak who were not able to keep pace with normal children. Undoubtedly he would take pride in the school system's modern program which takes in schooling for the slow learner, those defective in reading skills and for those with speech defects, crippled, deaf or otherwise incapable of keeping up with their peers in a formal school situation.

Special education of an entirely different character is supplied by Benjamin Franklin High School founded in 1959 for the superior student coming out of junior high school. The program is by no means as complex as one might think. The basic philosophy stems from the idea that if retarded children need special care even more so do the superior students. Therefore, the reasoning ran, let us set up a high school populated by superior students, with a stiff college preparatory curriculum and taught by the best teachers the system could provide. And the results have in most instances been very satisfactory. The superior student is challenged by high academic goals and is given the best type of counseling available. With the first graduating class, the results were obvious—national merit scholarship winners, high scores on college entrance examinations and other evidence of scholarly achievement were abundant. What little criticism existed among certain small citizen groups that the school was undemocratic and productive of intellectual snobbery one hears no more.

The New Orleans Education Association succeeded in 1909 in prodding the Legislature into passing a compulsory school attendance law requiring children between the ages of eight and fourteen to attend school for at least ninety consecutive days each year. Along with this law was another providing for free textbooks for the children of poor parents who had to comply with the attendance laws—again the poverty factor. These laws were continued and strengthened for a period of time and then changed. During the administration of Huey P. Long, free textbooks and supplies were made available to *all* children. The attendance law continued until 1960 when the Legislature under the whip of segregationist sentiment forced its repeal. "I'd rather see the children of this state grow up in ignorance than have to go to school with Niggers," one White Citizens Council member declaimed to his audience. And that about explains the rationale of repeal. Calmer minds prevailed, however, and the compulsory school law was reinstated in 1966.

Crucial to the operation of the Orleans Parish system were changes in the tax base so that something approaching adequate revenues might be realized. It has been pointed out that revenue sources were very meager before 1900. Since that date, however, the situation has improved slowly. The property tax rate (real and personal) has risen from 1⅛ mills to 13 mills and, of course, assessments have also risen enormously. In addition, revenue from a one cent sales tax adopted in 1966 has helped the financial picture. Likewise the amount of state aid has risen to approximately $24,000,000 for 1966–67. Total revenues have risen to approximately $53,000,000—45 per cent from state funds, 27 per cent from local property taxes and an anticipated 23 per cent from the sales tax. These revenues, of course, do not include money for new buildings. With the McDonogh money spent, financing of buildings has been through bond issues, the bonded indebtedness being slightly over 74 million dollars in 1966–67 with another fifty million dollar issue in the offering.

In 1917 there were 9,401 Negroes enrolled in the public schools, but they were all elementary pupils. In this year, however, McDonogh No. 13 for white boys was converted into the McDonogh 35 High School for Negroes. At the same time there was inaugurated an evening program at this school. But there was little incentive for the Negro to attend high school day or evening. During its first year, only 143 Negroes enrolled for day classes and 398 for evening courses. Since 1917 five additional Negro high schools have been built and enrollment had risen by 1966 to 8,682, slightly higher than the number of white students in senior high schools. It seems obvious that social and economic pressures among the Negro population itself as well as general community needs have had a great deal to do with the rising number of young Negroes seeking a high school education. But progress in Negro education was a long uphill pull and the problem is by no means solved. Nowhere is this more evident than in the frequent tragic failures of Negro high school graduates to succeed in the integrated colleges of the state and elsewhere, particularly the colleges and universities with high academic standards.

The upgrading of teachers is best reflected in recent statistics on degrees held and those without degrees. There has been a steady decrease in those teachers holding no degree and a significant increase in those holding bachelor's or master's degrees. Ten years ago there were 393 teachers in the public school system without degrees. Today the figure is 296. During the same period, the number with baccalaureate degrees increased from 1,-844 to 2,849. Even more impressive is the increase of those holding master's degrees—497 in 1955–56 and 919 in 1965–66. And the private and parochial schools have by necessity followed suit. Salaries, also, have shown a steady if not spectacular increase. The young inexperienced teacher with a bachelor's degree started in 1955–56 at $3,020 per year. By 1965–66 this had risen to $4,225—not a salary which had overtones of affluence, but almost as much as a truck driver earns. The new public school salary schedule has also served to increase private and Catholic lay teacher compensation.

However, in the midst of what appeared to be a definite upward turn of the progress chart a deluge of troubles swept in to confuse the picture. This, of course, was the court-ordered end of segregation which swiftly refocused the minds and thoughts of those engaged in education and enraged large segments of the general population. What had been considered an urbane and tolerant city found itself in a whirlpool of dismay, intolerance and, at times, frenzy. In Baton Rouge in 1960, a hysterical Legislature thrashed out violently in every direction in an attempt to stem the irresistible tide of affairs. Tempers flared, confusion compounded confusion and legislators vied with each other in their frenetic attempts to pass laws to keep Negro children out of white schools. The Orleans Parish School Board was shorn of its power to regulate public schools, even of the authority to approve payrolls and issue checks to teachers. For a period of months, New Orleans really had no public school system in the true meaning of the term. Moreover, the superintendent and members of the board spent days and weeks, which might have been used for other purposes, in federal courtrooms seeking solutions to the legal problems.

In one ward of the city one might have seen the moving and indeed pathetic sight of a frightened little primly dressed Negro girl with beribboned pigtails clinging to the hand of a burly federal marshal as he led her safely inside an almost deserted school building while on the street outside, emotionally stirred women carried placards, stuck out their tongues at federal marshals and, when the television cameras were pointed in their direction, waved their arms and shouted imprecations.

Such conduct was largely confined to one section of the city but that is not to say that the city as a whole approved desegregation. Sentiment undoubtedly was opposed to integration even among many moderates who would not entertain the idea of joining the White Citizens Council or participating in a demonstration. There was a relatively weak movement generated in favor of integration, but its influence was not pronounced. What really turned the tide were the decisions of the federal courts. In case after case the acts of the Legislature attempting to block desegregation were nullified. Authority was returned to the superintendent and school board and integration began to pick up speed. About the only legislative enactment to remain in force for any length of time was that permitting the establishment of private segregated schools supported by legislative grants ($360 per student) made directly to parents. About thirty of these "grant-in-aid" schools were opened in Orleans Parish and most of them managed to survive. (An interesting side light on this is the fact that many well-to-do parents in New Orleans used the grants to continue sending their children to older private schools when they were financially able to do so without state subsidy. There are also cases where Negro parents have received aid in order to keep their children in all Negro private schools.) The original plan was invalidated by a federal court decision in August, 1967; but a new plan based on "need" has been put into effect. Whether this new plan will suffer the same fate as its predecessor is undetermined. As this is written it is under attack in the courts.

The formerly all white institutions of higher learning discussed above are all desegregated—Tulane and Loyola voluntarily and Louisiana State University because it is part of the state school system.

The Catholic schools also were voluntarily desegregated and by September, 1967, public school officials said the parish system was largely integrated. There seems to be no doubt but what school desegregation has won out. Perhaps the school historian of the future will find it desirable to add a section entitled "New Orleans Schools Since Desegregation."

As for the image of Orleans Parish public, private and Catholic schools, there is no reliable and objective evidence. The city still largely follows its traditional pattern of thought. For social, educational or religious reasons the private or Catholic parochial school or the non-Catholic church-affiliated school, of which there are many, still appeals to many parents, especially those who are influential or affluent. On the other hand, if one can judge from the rather decisive vote in favor of the recent sales tax and other criteria the image of the public schools is improving. Also considerable new interest on the part of many segments of the community is being taken in the recent transformation of the Delgado Trades School into a community junior college with a strong vocational and technical orientation. Early signs indicate rapid progress for the school and this is encouraging, for New Orleans needs such an institution to round out its educational pattern, a pattern which year by year, despite the clouds and splotches, becomes brighter in its totality.

The Art Scene in New Orleans - Past and Present

Alberta Collier

In 1718, when Jean Baptiste Le Moyne, Sieur de Bienville, drove the final stakes to delineate the boundaries of New Orleans, he undoubtedly also drew a mind's-eye picture of the French-type city which would rise on the location.

This mental picture was, for many years, the only piece of fine art connected with the town.

But, today, in 1968, New Orleans, a queen metropolis, has a city-owned museum dedicated to developing an outstanding Arts of the Americas collection within the framework of its presentation of world art. It also has a state-operated historical museum, which finds more and more that the story of the past is most graphically told through the fine art that has survived from long-gone eras.

New Orleans, in addition, has a civic downtown art center, specializing in the promotion of contemporary art; a healthy group of commercial galleries, which present periodic exhibitions of both contemporary and traditional work; and a good-sized colony of top professional artists. The art department of Newcomb College of Tulane University, established in 1887, provides art instruction for both men and women; and art courses are available at the city's other universities.

But, going back to 1718, Bienville, in his struggles to wrest a city out of a mosquito-ridden swamp, could have had little time for any of the refinements that were associated with the great French culture of which he was an inheritor. Without question, he had draftsmen and artisans on his roster of assistants; he also had priests, who must have come equipped with some stock of holy pictures and statues. But the rigors and dangers associated with early life in Louisiana were hardly conducive to any immediate flowering of creative talents. The plat of a town to be and the architectural sketch were of far more immediate concern. No record exists of any serious painting or sculpture created in Louisiana in those early days.

And, though the Roman Catholic church, which came in with Bienville, could call on an iconography dating back to the Middle Ages, one can hardly believe that the missionaries were allowed to bring any treasures into a wild, undeveloped and unknown territory. (Fine ecclesiastical art was created in later years and examples may be seen in many of the city's churches but religious art remains secondary to the secular.)

The first Colonial art of any consequence appeared in the latter part of the eighteenth century after Louis XV of France had ceded the territory of Louisiana to his Bourbon cousin, Charles III of Spain. By this time, the once crude New Orleans settlement had apparently developed some kind of élite society, whose wealth was based on the rich yields of the outlying plantations and the commerce that came from the great Mississippi River Basin. With an established society, there was an accompanying demand for the graces and privileges that go with such an exalted state. And art, particularly that of the portraitist, would have been high on a list of desirables.

The evidence certainly shows that the early citizen, being human, had the desire to affirm his position through the immortality bestowed by the painted likeness.

One would assume that the first trained artists came from France but disasters such as hurricanes and the fires of 1788 and 1794 must have taken their toll on any output.

The first painters, whose names are known, are José de

Salazar and Francisco Salazar, active in New Orleans from about 1792 to 1801 or later. A signed Francisco Salazar "Portrait of Don Andres Almonester Roxas," builder of the St. Louis Cathedral, the Cabildo and the Presbytère, is now on long-term loan to the city's museum of art; other known Salazars are in public or private New Orleans collections. There are also a number of Spanish-oriented portraits, dating from the same general period, that are attributed to the Salazars but may have come from the studios of as-yet-unidentified compatriots.

The 1803 Louisiana Purchase shaped the destiny of the United States. It also changed the character and directions of both the population and the art of New Orleans.

The opening of the territory, which spurred a century of exciting American expansion, brought in a flux of immigrants: some were out and out fortune hunters; others were explorers, churchmen, homesteaders, scientists or empire builders; still others were artists.

The vanguard of the artists included a large body of portraitists. There were the hacks who advertised that they could paint anything from portraits to coaches; there were also competent painters from the Eastern seaboard; and, since New Orleans was still very much a French city, there were highly trained men who had learned their techniques in the Parisian ateliers.

All were motivated by the same impulse. They came to Louisiana to paint the wealthy Creoles and the newly-arrived Americans, and their clients were happy to assist them in this task.

A French artist like Jean Joseph Vaudechamp brought the traditions of David to the city, and his likenesses of the local pères, mères and mamères of his time speak to us today.

English-born John Wesley Jarvis won his reputation in New York but found commissions and a congenial climate in New Orleans; John Vanderlyn made his own foray into the town, as did such men as Matthew Harris Jouett, G. P. A. Healy and, possibly, Thomas Sully. Any list of names would run into the hundreds; the surviving portraits can be numbered in the thousands. And, though diverse in style, they add up to a body of work that is remarkable for its directness, honesty and simple beauty of brushwork. The advent of the Civil War brought a halt to the great age of portraiture; its death knell, however, had been tolled in 1839 with the introduction of the daguerreotype.

But the Louisiana Purchase also brought in another group of artists, the explorers and naturalists who were inspired by the grandiose ideas that went into the Great American Dream.

The earliest on the scene was J. L. Bouquet (or Boqueta) de Woiseri who, in 1803, painted a panorama of the New Orleans harbor, complete with a spread eagle banner which proclaims, "Under my wings every thing prospers." This large oil, which is owned by the Chicago Historical Society, meticulously depicts the ships, buildings and figures of that day. The sweep of the whole, however, adds a romantic feeling which was to become a part of the American style. A watercolor version is in the Mariners' Museum in Newport News, Va.

John James Audubon, who was an archtype of his generation, came to New Orleans in 1820. He did portraits for his daily bread; but his true love was science; and his ambition, as large as his Elephant Folio, was to paint every bird in America in actual size. Many of the prints in the resulting *Birds of America* were made from paintings done in Louisiana.

George Catlin, another great American artist-scientist, traveled the Mississippi River from its source to New Orleans, painting the Indian tribes who still roamed the undeveloped lands. His work, though primitive by professional standards, catches the excitement and high adventure of the times. Catlin and Audubon were only two of the many artists who flocked into the Louisiana Territory. Seth Eastman followed the Mississippi down to its mouth, sketching on his way; Joseph Rusling Meeker, who lost his heart to the Louisiana swamps, caught their exotic beauty on his canvasses.

Among the other artists of the period were the French visitor, Alfred Boisseau, who left a painting of "Indians Walking Along a Bayou" in the city; August Norieri, who captured the steamboat era on canvas; and Richard Clague, an Orleanian who painted the Louisiana oaks with the realism of the Barbizon School and the devotion of the native.

And, though he lived on until 1921, William Aiken Walker, who did genre studies of the New Orleans harbor and the Negroes and cotton fields of the surrounding plantations, was definitely related to his earlier confrères.

But there were also nineteenth century artists whose work did not fit into this Mississippi Panorama school.

There was Pierre Joseph Landry, a French-born Louisianian and a participant in the 1815 Battle of New Orleans, who left a body of naive and very delightful, allegorical sculpture.

And, much later in the 1800s, there were men like artist-educators Ellsworth and William Woodward, who painted the New Orleans scene with a freshness which reflects the advent of the twentieth century. There were Europeans like Achille Perelli and Achille Peretti, who are often confused, but who brought the technical training of Europe to the Louisiana field.

Another event of the 1800s, which has had much portent for the city, was the 1872–1873 visit of famed French Impressionist Edgar Degas to New Orleans. The sojourn, which was probably little noted outside of the family circle, was ostensibly a visit to beloved relatives. (The artist's mother, a Musson, was a native of New Orleans. Her brother and his daughter, Estelle, who had married Edgar's brother, and others of the family lived here at the time.)

Though Edgar enjoyed sightseeing, attending the races and seeing his relatives and their friends, he also found time to do a significant group of paintings and drawings. The major work of his New Orleans stay is the "Cotton Market, New Orleans," now in the collection of the Pau Museum in Pau, France. There are apparently some seventeen or twenty-odd pieces surviving from this period.

A paramount art event of the early twentieth century was the birth of the city's Isaac Delgado Museum of Art.

The natal year is given as 1910, when the benefactor, for whom the institution is named, made funds available for its construction in City Park. The doors were, however, actually opened on December 16, 1911, on what is described by the late Dr. Isaac Monroe Cline as a "well-selected" loan exhibition.

For, though Delgado had generously given the monies for the building, when the handsome neo-Greek structure was completed, it was an empty shell, waiting for future acquisitions of art.

The Art Association of New Orleans, which was founded in 1905, was called upon to contribute members to the board and probably helped with the first exhibitions. (This group was the latest in a succession of local art societies dating back to 1840, when the first was established by George Cooke, described by Cline as a "painter of some distinction.")

Public-spirited citizens soon came to the rescue of their museum and donations of art, *objets d'art* and other gifts poured in.

The most important donation of this period was that in 1914 by Mr. and Mrs. Chapman H. Hyams of their personal collection of Barbizon and Salon paintings and sculptures. These donors also established trust funds whose income is still available for the upkeep of the Hyams Room and Collection.

Among the other significant early acquisitions are a group of exquisite Chinese jades and other hard stones, given in 1914 by Morgan Whitney; and a collection of Greek pottery, assembled by Frank T. Howard and given in 1916 by his son, Alvin P. Howard.

But the Delgado, though it acquired a wide range of art from 1911 through World War II, could not be considered a modern museum until some years after that conflict was history.

Contemporary twentieth century art, as we know it, first came to the city through the Arts and Crafts Club, a non-profit organization established to develop and promote the work of living artists.

Founded in the early 1920's and located in the French Quarter, it maintained both an art school and a showroom—by the 1930's, it was an established and highly-respected art center.

A board of directors set policy and watched over its fortunes.

Among the prominent professional men who gave hours of their time to its service were art expert Albert Lieutaud and architect Richard Koch. Miss Sarah Henderson, a member of an old New Orleans family which had long been active in the art collecting field, devoted much of her time to the institution.

In 1935, when my personal knowledge begins, Charles Bein, an excellent artist-teacher, headed the school; Paul Ninas, a fine and versatile artist, was in charge of the life-painting classes; and Enrique Alferez, a highly-gifted Mexican-born sculptor, whose work may be seen all over New Orleans, was available to give sculpture lessons. A pottery section had been in operation and was re-activated shortly thereafter.

Boyd Cruise, one of the city's finest watercolorists and a dedicated art historian, had been a student and was later on the school's faculty.

The students came from all age groups and all walks of life. The tuition was kept low and scholarships were made available to talented youngsters who couldn't afford even nominal fees.

Leonard Flettrich, whose murals now adorn a number of the town's public buildings and whose easel paintings are stars of many private collections, was among the artists who received their early training at this institution.

The Arts and Crafts gallery, which was open to New Orleans professional artists, promoted both regional and national shows. It created a rapport between the local artist and the public and introduced new and frequently controversial art movements to the city. By the mid-'30s, French Impressionism and Post-Impressionism had already been digested. But pure Abstraction, Fauve art, Cubism, Surrealism and other avant garde schools were still regarded with suspicion by the ordinary art lover.

The Arts and Crafts Club made it possible for these art lovers to see the best examples that existed at the time. It was nothing to see a group of Alexander Calder mobiles playing merrily in the gallery, to glimpse the bird-like figure of Max Ernst as he checked the hanging of one of his haunting, surrealistic shows.

Of the many Louisiana artists, whose work was featured

during the late 1930's, two stand out in my memory.

These two had certain pinpoints of similarity: both were from prominent and well-to-do New Orleans families and both had taken up art later in life.

One, Josephine Crawford, had started her formal art training at the Arts and Crafts school in the 1920's and was enthusiastic enough to turn to Paris for further training. She studied under André Lhote of the noted "Section d'Or" group and she came back to apply his lessons to New Orleans subject matter. Her quietly-excellent interpretations of Creole matrons, ordinary still-life arrangements and normal street scenes were often seen in the Arts and Crafts gallery. These same pictures had retained all their validity when they appeared again in an exhibition staged in the fall of 1965 at the Delgado Museum.

The other artist, Dr. Marion Souchon, had spent a lifetime in medicine and business. But, at the age of 65, he went into semi-retirement and took up a first love, the pursuit of art. Past the age to engage in formal study, he learned his craft through extensive reading and through art discussions with professionals and others whom he respected. Weeks Hall, a fine and individual New Iberia artist who both taught at and exhibited through the Arts and Crafts, was among those whom the doctor sought out. Souchon's vital, half-Fauve, half-primitive paintings showed a touch of genius that has not dimmed over the years.

The Arts and Crafts Club survived World War II with curtailed activities; it did not, however, have the reserves to last through the post-war period and was forced to close its doors just after the mid-century.

In the mid-'30s, the Delgado Museum was a musty institution where one wandered through a plethora of nineteenth century *objets d'art* so numerous that one never saw the existing and very genuine works of art.

The Art Association of New Orleans, however, had, for some years, tried to present respectable art shows. (The city had originally taken over the onus of paying for the upkeep of the building and the salaries of the professional help; the Art Association took on the responsibility of staging and underwriting local and visiting exhibitions and other educational activities.)

Annual Art Association juried competitive displays were part of the agenda as were shows of work by such now defunct organizations as the Southern States Art League and the New Orleans Art League, a men's group which gave its name to the building located at 628–30 Toulouse.

The Art Association also sponsored exhibitions of work by Louisiana artists—the record shows that, among its coups, was a 1931 solo show of paintings by Charles W. Hutson, one of those "sport" artists whose instinctive canvasses deserve a special place in American art.

An examination of art purchased from earlier Art Association exhibitions demonstrates that an intelligent selectivity was exercised; memories of such imports as the magnificent late 1939–early 1940 Picasso retrospective show that the museum's mentors were well aware of the trends of twentieth century art.

However, the first step toward joining the ranks of modern museums was delayed until late in 1948, when the Delgado board, having persuaded the city fathers to appropriate the money, hired its first professional director, Alonzo Lansford, who had formerly headed the Savannah, Georgia, art museum and who had, more recently, been a staff writer for one of the leading New York art magazines. Lansford had no magic lantern to evoke an instant transformation of the crowded, badly-arranged old galleries. But he had the know-how and the energy. Gradually the old building began to acquire a new look.

Though there was little acquisition money available, that little was used to purchase contemporary art. With the "new look," the pace of gifts picked up and real treasures began coming into the museum collection.

Among these was a tiny bronze horse by the former visitor, Edgar Degas. This piece was among a number of sculptures that the artist had specified in his will to be cast and given to his New Orleans kin. It carries a foundry mark of "Cire/Perdue/AA

Hebrard" plus the extra stamp of "Her. D.," for "Héritage Degas," and was given to the museum by members of the family at the time that the rest of the collection was sold outside of the city.

The first real milestone in the Lansford regime was that director's successful negotiation of a Samuel H. Kress Foundation gift of thirty-one Italian Renaissance paintings, covering the fourteenth, fifteenth and sixteenth centuries. (Three of the paintings had been given to the Delgado in the 1930's; the other twenty-eight were selected by the Kress Foundation staff, Lansford, and Delgado board president, Arthur Feitel, to balance this important Italian period. Adjustments were made in the collection and one painting was added so that, when the Kress Collection gift to the nation was made final in 1961, the Delgado's share was thirty-two paintings.)

The Kress gift came in the spring of 1953. It, in a way, heralded an art floodtide which culminated in a panoramic show of French art from the Louvre and other sources (presented in the fall of 1953 in conjunction with the sesquicentennial celebration of the Louisiana Purchase) and in a retrospective Vincent van Gogh exhibition, selected from the choice collection of his nephew, Vincent W. van Gogh, and displayed at the Delgado in the spring of 1955.

But, if the tide was running high, the storm clouds were also gathering. And, in spite of continued museum progress, on March 4, 1957, the skies opened and the rains poured. They were triggered by the firing, on that day, of Alonzo Lansford, the Delgado's first professional director. The Delgado's eight-man board had, without giving any reason, precipitately dismissed a man who had apparently done a good job and had won a name for himself in the community.

One would need a book to set down all the nuances and causes that led to this sudden and seemingly strange action.

It immediately, however, became a *cause célèbre* that livened the front pages of the newspapers and split the local art world into opposing camps. The affair was, of course, also aired in the

City's Council chambers and, between the barrage of charges and countercharges, one salient fact began to emerge. It was that, regardless of any rights or wrongs in the case, the Delgado board set-up was antiquated, self-perpetuating and representative of only a limited segment of the community.

This board, which had done much good in the twilight years of public apathy, was an anachronism in the spotlight of public interest. It had the legal power to act with complete independence of either the city authorities or the general public. And it could and did make the Lansford firing stick. But it could not survive the event unchanged. And, after tempers had cooled, the men of good will (this term embraces both those on the board and those in the community at large) worked out a legal method for re-organizing the whole.

The expanded board is made up of twenty-four elected members drawn from various civic sources plus two additional members appointed annually from the City Council. Terms for the twenty-four were so staggered that now eight are elected each year to serve for a period of three years. The president is elected annually. The Art Association of New Orleans became the Isaac Delgado Museum of Art Association.

The first expanded board went into office on January 1, 1960.

The old board had, some days after Lansford's firing, issued a list of charges against him. The former director, as a member of the American Association of Museums, exercised his right to call on that organization for an investigation. A three-man team of his museum peers, after going over the case exhaustively, cleared his professional name completely.

The Delgado's next director was a woman, Sue Thurman, who took up her duties in the late summer of 1958 and served until she resigned in 1961 to accept a post as head of the Boston Museum of Contemporary Art.

Mrs. Thurman's first big presentation was "Early Masters of Modern Art," a title given to an outstanding collection, featuring French Impressionist and Post-Impressionist art, which was assembled and is still owned by a prominent New Orleans family.

Mrs. Thurman was also here for the museum's 1960 golden anniversary and celebrated the event with a large exhibition on the "World of Art in 1910."

And, although her tenure had come at a difficult time, when animosities had not completely died out, she did a good administrative job and got the boat on an even keel.

The present director, James B. Byrnes, accepted the assignment in late 1961 and came to the museum in February of 1962. He had been director of the Colorado Springs Fine Arts Center and of the North Carolina Museum of Art. But Byrnes, in mentioning any of his impressive background will glide over anything except the fact that he served as a curator and as an associate director under the aegis of the late, great art expert, W. R. Valentiner.

In spite of his Irish name, Byrnes is essentially a cautious man; and he waited until Thanksgiving of 1962 to unveil his first big exhibition, a "Fêtes de la Palette," made up of fine and decorative arts which reflected the joys of the table. Planned as a compliment to the famed New Orleans cuisine, this show, which was superbly mounted, actually reviewed Mannerist and Baroque art as developed in the sixteenth, seventeenth and eighteenth centuries in Spain, Italy, France, Germany and the Low Countries. The excellent catalog, prepared for the occasion, is still available at the museum.

If it did nothing else, this display gave some indication of the mental caliber and thinking of the new Delgado head.

So it was not so surprising when, two years later, he located and got an option on a large Edgar Degas painting that had been done during that artist's 1872–73 visit to New Orleans. A portrait of Edgar's cousin and sister-in-law, Estelle Musson, it was admittedly a natural for the Delgado, which then owned only one small memento of the French Impressionist's visit to the city. But, its price was $190,000, the acquisition coffers were empty, and it was unheard of to raise such a sum in New Orleans for a mere piece of art.

The 1964 board of directors, however, valiantly made the

effort to get donations for the project. A number of $5,000 to $10,000 contributions were pledged through their efforts; another $10,000 was made available from city funds by Mayor Victor H. Schiro; and two thirds of the remainder was raised at a dinner sponsored by the Mayor's Citizens' Committee with Seymour Weiss as chairman. But on Jan. 13, 1965, the option was running out and the Delgado was given until midnight of that date to find the last $20,000 or more needed.

The newspapers, radio and television were all called on to help in a last-ditch appeal for funds; New Orleanians, who have always loved a "photo finish," rallied to the cause and, at five minutes before the final deadline, the treasure was secured.

A loan exhibition, "Degas—His Family and Friends in New Orleans," which was a scholarly examination of the subject, was presented by the Delgado in May, 1965. Catalogs from this exhibition are also on hand at the museum.

The purchase of "Estelle" was apparently exactly the right kind of shot-in-the-arm for the institution. It was certainly responsible for the creation of the Delgado Women's Volunteer Committee, which was organized later on that year from a core of indefatigable females who had their baptism in the "Estelle" campaign. This organization is primarily a working group, dedicated to promoting any and all projects of the museum.

Immediately after the details of its set-up were cleared with the board, it asked for and got the difficult task of staging the first Delgado Art Auction, an event that had long been needed to clear out surplus and duplicate material in the Delgado collection.

Though a first effort for the ladies, who ran into many unexpected snags including the timing of Hurricane Betsy, the art auction, held on October 25, 26 and 27, 1965, netted some $39,000 for the museum's acquisitions fund. And, though the Delgado had received many gifts representative of other collectors' tastes, this was the first time that it had had any sizeable sum to exercise for its own choices.

Another significant event of 1965 was the recognition, in

principle, by the City of New Orleans that the acquisition of fine art, which increases in value each year, is a legitimate item for the Capital Improvements Budget. The sum of $15,000 was earmarked for that purpose in the 1965 budget but was preempted by the more mundane necessity of roof repairs.

The same amount was, however, included in the 1966 Capital Improvements Budget and was expended for the purchase of a Paul Gauguin drawing, "Tête d'une Jeune Tahitienne."

An auspicious year for the Delgado was 1966, and, in April, the board of trustees announced that the Ella West Freeman Foundation of New Orleans had agreed to donate $200,000 in acquisition monies during the next three years. The gift was made on a matching fund basis. The Foundation agreed to match cash funds raised by the museum as of May 1, 1967, 1968 and 1969 up to $200,000. The Foundation also asked that Mayor Schiro and the Commission Council give an assurance of intent that a Capital Improvements Budget item for the renovation of the Delgado Museum and the construction of a new wing, be updated to 1968.

The Delgado board started working immediately to get donations and pledges to meet this challenge. And later in the year, the loan of an outstanding collection of world art, which had been assembled by Mr. and Mrs. Frederick Stafford of New York and Paris, inspired a first, successful fund-raising Odyssey Ball, sponsored by the Women's Volunteer Committee.

On May 1, 1967, the Delgado had $53,135.34 in cash to put up as its first year's match for the Freeman acquisition funds.

A major event of 1967 was the offer by Mrs. Edgar B. Stern, who had already been a generous donor, to erect a series of galleries which she hoped would house an Arts of the Americas collection.

The board, in accepting her offer, dedicated $200,000 of future acquisition funds toward the building up of such a collection within the framework of its presentation of world art. Before the year was out, the board had purchased eleven examples of Spanish Colonial religious painting and issued a directive to

Byrnes to negotiate the purchase of a designated group of top-quality Pre-Columbian works and two more Spanish Colonial pieces.

And the city council, in adopting its 1968 Capital Improvements Budget, inserted a sum for the erection of an "educational and service wing to the Isaac Delgado Museum of Art."

But New Orleans also has another large institution, the Louisiana State Museum, which, though it focuses on history, has a large and important collection of art.

This museum, located on Jackson Square and occupying the old Spanish Cabildo, the Presbytère, the old Law Library building, the old State Arsenal, the Jackson House and the Calaboose, antedates the Delgado, having been created by the Louisiana Assembly of 1906, under Governor Newton Crane Blanchard.

Orleanians, who have always been proud of their history, flocked in with gifts and among these were hundreds of early portraits; examples of land, sea and cityscapes from the past; and historical paintings. The Louisiana State Museum has been built up by gifts and efforts of many interested citizens.

The museum, one of the few in the country whose actual buildings are as much a part of its treasures as are its exhibits, is now an institution with many domiciles.

Headquarters are presently maintained in the renovated Presbytère, on the other side of St. Louis Cathedral from the Cabildo. An 1850 house is a separate unit in the museum-owned Pontalba apartments on the St. Ann side of Jackson Square. The Cabildo complex, which is now undergoing a complete renovation, will eventually be available for displays, as will Madame John's Legacy, a fine and very early example of French Colonial architecture in the city, and the huge old United States Mint, which was recently turned over to the State of Louisiana.

Though the museum has had its troubles in the past and been rocked by the storms of Louisiana politics, it seems to have finally reached more tranquil waters, where both Governor

John J. McKeithen and the Louisiana Legislature evince a concern for its welfare.

Its present managing director, Mrs. Peggy Richards, has hired a staff of trained curatorial assistants, who are working at the gigantic task of cataloging and evaluating the thousands of exhibits. She has contracted with a leading art conservator, who is a specialist in the early American field, to look after and rehabilitate the old paintings.

A private organization, the Friends of the Cabildo, is dedicated to the promotion and welfare of the institution. The Friends have assembled and mounted a number of important exhibitions; sponsored a series of educational programs; prepared and published several attractive and valuable brochures; and, in 1967, campaigned and raised funds to purchase a handsome and important 1833 Vaudechamp Louisiana portrait, which was added to the museum's already extensive collection of works by that artist.

Among the museum's art treasures are a copy of Audubon's *Birds of America*; a group of sculptures by early Louisiana artist Pierre Landry; a perfect little 1861 watercolor of the "Olivier Plantation" by Adrian Persac; a delightful still-life by William Aiken Walker; a genre scene of the pirate, Jean Lafitte, and his confrères, which is attributed to Jarvis; a "Mourning Picture" of the Bernard Duchamp family, attributed to the same artist; an exquisite depiction of the old French Opera House, by Paul Poincy; a number of Mississippi River steamboat scenes by Norieri; a collection of sculptures by Achille Perelli; a large painting of the Battle of New Orleans by 1838 English court painter Eugene L. Lami, and the remarkable and extensive portrait collection.

Though New Orleans now has two well-established museums, a culture is no better than the artists it produces and, for this production, it needs good training ateliers.

The oldest now operating in the city, affectionately referred to as the Newcomb Art School, is the art department of New-comb College of Tulane University.

Founded in 1887 by Professor Ellsworth Woodward, this department first specialized in teaching the principles of draw-ing, painting, design and craftwork to the talented young ladies of the city. Under Woodward's direction, the school rapidly acquired a reputation for excellence; and, in 1896, Ellsworth and his brother, William, added a pottery department as a workshop extension of the Newcomb Art School.

The pottery, which was to win worldwide acclaim, was for the most part turned on the wheel by Joseph Fortune Meyer, who was the Newcomb potter for twenty-nine years. The decora-tion was usually done by either Newcomb Art School students or professionals who stayed on and worked (and sometimes taught) after graduation.

This Newcomb pottery, which used conventionalized botani-cal designs and was primarily concerned with Louisiana flora, was an original, indigenous and valid form of Art Nouveau. And, though it appeared simultaneously with European develop-ments, it was a purely local manifestation. The heyday of New-comb pottery, which won medals in any exposition where it was displayed, was 1897 to about 1917. And, though work in the New-comb style was produced up to the 1940's, the most vital comes from the early period.

Ellsworth Woodward, who headed the art school for so many years, was of an older generation and hardly in sympathy with the developments introduced to America in New York's 1913 Armory Show. The younger professors, however, brought the new ideas into the school. Among those who have taught or headed the department are the nationally-known painter Xavier Gonzalez; the prominent kinetic sculptor, George Rickey; and the New York Times' fine arts editor, John Canaday.

Several years after World War II, the art school began ex-panding, taking men as well as women as students and offering both graduate and undergraduate courses.

The present art department, which is headed by Professor

Norman Boothby, has a strong sculpture section and offers beginner's and advanced classes in painting, drawing, printmaking and design. Its pottery department, though far different, is still noted.

Among the Newcomb faculty are nationally-known men like Professor Pat Trivigno, James L. Steg, Donald Robertson, and Associate Professor Dirk Hubers. Assistant professors like Ryland Greene and Gabor Gergo received their master of fine arts degrees from the school and stayed on to teach other generations of aspirants.

Under Woodward's regime, the young women at Newcomb were taught professional methods of painting or designing but were not encouraged to seek out arduous careers as professional artists. But even Professor Woodward could not stand up against the enthusiasms of all of his students. And, finding that one was determined to take up the unladylike pursuit of sculpture, he finally threw up his hands and told her to seek out the best master alive—Antoine Bourdelle of France. Angela Gregory's statues now grace many of the churches and public buildings in the area—her heroic "Bienville" greets visitors as they arrive at the Union Passenger Terminal.

Ella Miriam Wood, who studied under Professor Woodward, became the most sought-after portraitist in the area; Sadie Irvine, who later taught at the school, has lived to see her early pottery become collector's items.

Among the more recent graduates are Ida Kohlmeyer, who has won a national reputation with her abstract-expressionist paintings; Kitty O'Meallie and Ann Cooper, who have both had numerous solo shows in the city; Kendall Shaw, a native Orleanian who has made good in the big city of New York; and printmakers Lois Fine and Sue Ferguson Gussow.

But New Orleans also has other institutions offering courses in fine art to talented students. Tulane University's night division, University College, has accredited courses; Xavier University has had a highly competent art department for some time.

Dillard University, which has its own art collection in an

Edgar B. Stern Family Fund gift of abstraction-expressionist paintings and sculpture, has included art courses in its curriculum for a number of years.

More recently Loyola University, Louisiana State University in New Orleans, Southern University in New Orleans and St. Mary's Dominican College, which numbers sculptor Angela Gregory on the faculty, have all added visual arts departments. All but the last is coeducational.

All of these institutions maintain exhibition programs for the benefit of their students.

The John McCrady Art School, a private, accredited institution, offers fine arts courses with McCrady, who has been active since the 1930's, heading the teaching staff.

The art wealth of a community is, however, assessed not in its public collections and facilities alone but in the strength of its private holdings.

The French Impressionist and Post-Impressionist collection, exhibited at the Delgado in 1959, is undoubtedly one that would be notable in any city. There are also other collections, representing different tastes and various periods of art. Felix H. Kuntz has an outstanding collection of Americana; there are a number of smaller holdings filled with choice gems from this field.

One Orleanian has amassed so many paintings from both American and European sources that he plans eventually to open his own museum; several other private contemporary collections are also of museum caliber.

As 1968 dawns, more and more people are bitten by the "art bug." They haunt the auctions seeking works from the New Orleans past, creations of the nineteenth and early twentieth centuries by such men as Bror Anders Wikstrom, Alexander J. Drysdale, Luis Graner or the Woodwards, and paintings, prints and drawings by artists prominent before the 1950s like Dan Whitney, Will Henry Stevens, Clarence Millet, Morris Henry Hobbs or Conrad Albrizio.

They are also flocking to the galleries to enjoy and select from the wealth of art that is presented annually.

They can go to the Carrollton section where they can find crafts or prints and paintings by the younger artists; they can stop near Lee Circle and see paintings by established names like Robert Helmer and Shearly Grode; or they can visit the old French Quarter for a walking tour of a group of select art spots.

They can find works by old masters and modern paintings and sculpture in the pioneer of today's galleries, which was opened some sixteen years ago by the late Lucille Antony; they can discover present day paintings, landscapes and abstract compositions in the civic Orleans Gallery, which is in its fourteenth year of advancing contemporary art and numbers such artists as James Lamantia, Mildred Wohl, George Dunbar, George Dureau and Lin Emery on its rolls.

These neophyte collectors can view Old Master drawings hung side by side with the wildest of avant garde art in one gallery. They can also see works by such celebrated artists as Pat Trivigno, Leonard Flettrich, Ida Kohlmeyer, James L. Steg and Robert Gorda Gordy.

They can cross the street to see the poetic interpretations of Charles Reinike or go farther downtown to look for fine works from the European or American past.

They can go around the corner to see sculptures and paintings by Juan José and Challis Calandria, a husband-and-wife team which has long worked in the city; or journey farther downtown to see prints by old and modern masters of the medium.

They can turn back uptown to find the latest in the international "hard edge" style at one gallery or cross the street to see examples of Realism and Abstraction by local or national artists.

There are other galleries where one will find all descriptions and varieties of art. But, as a final step in this walking tour, one should stop to peer in the window of a narrow, exquisitely-appointed establishment where, if the fates are propitious, one will come the full circle of New Orleans art and find examples of the early portraits on the walls.

The Creative Spirit

Albert Goldstein

The long parade of New Orleans's literary achievements is a robust spectacle of many phases and cycles. And the hundreds of men and women who produced the show have been, from the broad view, a raggle-taggle lot.

Some of them were mediocrities whose works justify little more than a casual page-thumbing. Another segment catches the eye as creators with genuine, if not always brilliant, talent. Of course, there were the giants among them, too, but only a handful.

The number of native New Orleanians in the total is negligible. The vast majority have been wayfarers from the shallower South, Yankee pilgrims, and foreign travelers who came to observe and pen their pieces. A few of them, charmed by the scene, established permanent residence.

Both the domestic and the imported saw in this city a wellspring of ideas to stimulate their imaginations. They recognized here an anomalous, often bizarre panorama. It served as their motive power for storytelling and fact-recording.

The native writers appear to have been just as wide-eyed over what always existed under their noses. What was it that so intrigued the others? Not, surely, any paradise of natural beauty; no benign climate; no illusion of a way of life unfettered by the struggle for economic security. What fascinated them, I believe, was their discovery of a city which had:

Blossomed under three separate civilizations and cultures—French, Spanish and American—and which has never, even after it matured into a sprawling United States metropolis, side-tracked that heritage.

Suffered periodically the horrors of war and civil strife, fire, floods, hurricanes and population-decimating epidemics of disease.

Became enmeshed from time to time in the skulduggery of politics, some of which had theatrical overtones.

Been burdened with the complex problem of slavery and, subsequently, that of the "race" issue.

And yet managed to come of age as an urban dwelling place of peculiarly sophisticated appeal.

New Orleans literature, down the years, reflects, for better or for worse, such matters and many more. They have been the basis for some high-caliber fiction and incisive reporting, as well as a backdrop for legend-weaving.

A considerable portion of this literature lies in its special graveyard. On the other hand, some of it suggests a near-classic quality. That the latter is mainly out-of-print and all but forgotten in the hurrahing over contemporary bestsellers, does not erase the fact that it was the work of sensitive and facile craftsmen who had something to say.

Historian Harold Sinclair takes a somewhat grimmer view. He wrote:

"The best of her (New Orleans's) native writers, artists, and musicians, with but few exceptions, have been third-rate by any international standard. Of course she produced men and women of fine talents, but invariably they were talents on a miniature scale. Even the writers who wrote best of New Orleans were not what the city thinks of as 'native.' . . . The city attracted them but did not produce them. As observers many of these writers were extremely acute, but somewhere, somehow, the essence of New Orleans escaped them. . . . No really good and honest and intelligent major novel has ever been written about the city, and when and if it ever is it should be a very fine thing indeed."

Additionally Sinclair wrote: "Books about New Orleans almost invariably fall into one of two categories. In one the writer dwells almost lovingly on the city's manifold and obvious iniquities—probably for the same reason newspapers feature gory murders in front-page headlines and bury accounts of minor good works next to the classified ads. In the other class fall the books which dwell with equal rapture upon the New Orleans of filmy, moonstruck, pseudo-romantic trappings that has no connection with reality. But oddly enough something of a case can be made for each approach."

As for Lafcadio Hearn, whom I list among the little group of titans, Sinclair believes he was "unquestionably the best proseman who ever concerned himself with the kaleidoscope of New Orleans life. The pieces he wrote for the New Orleans newspapers of the latter seventies are today as fresh and crisp as they were then, without a trace of the simpering Victorianisms which cluttered most of the contemporary writing in English. It seemed that Hearn could not write badly if he tried, and because he was an original himself, he hadn't the slightest regard for the literary fashions of the period."

George W. Cable, another in my short roster of stars, Sinclair rates "probably the best known literary man" of New Orleans in the latter nineteenth century. "Cable was uninspired and a little pedestrian, but he was industrious and made himself heard. . . ."

"Hearn," said Sinclair, "died with an international reputation which has grown after his death, while Cable, when he is remembered at all, is recalled as a mildly talented American regionalist."

Lafcadio Hearn, born in 1850 in the Ionian Islands of Irish-Greek parents, and educated in Ireland, England and France, came to the United States at the age of 19. A strange man of small stature, partially blind, and plagued with an inferiority complex, he managed to survive by odd jobs and spotty newspaper work in New York and later in Cincinnati until he pulled up stakes and headed for New Orleans, arriving in 1878.

Like many a world wanderer before and after him, he had felt the lure of the city's exotic character. He had hoped to find here—and did find to an extent that suffused him—the same kind of charm that Paris's Left Bank had offered.

Hearn became one of New Orleans's earliest bohemians. He was captivated by the town's lights and shadows, and a flavor which contrasted strongly with that of his earlier American places of residence. There must have been many an ugly aspect of the picture that Hearn shrugged off—to him the city always was a land of beautiful dreams. Nevertheless, he finally forsook this Eden, journeyed to Japan and never returned to the United States.

In the ten years he lived in New Orleans, Hearn was reporter-feature writer for, first, *The Item,* later, *The Times-Democrat.* He also operated here for a brief period a little restaurant he called The Hard Times, with each menu item priced at five cents. The venture prospered apparently, until his business associate skipped with the contents of the till (and the cook).

For all of his personality quirks and his penchant for *la vie de bohème,* Hearn was an extraordinary man of letters and a superior creative artist. His development as such was due, in part, to his career's New Orleans chapter. But in his brief stay, few New Orleanians were even aware of his presence.

George Washington Cable, a native of New Orleans in 1844, grew up to become a complete misfit in his largely Creole environment. He was a devout Presbyterian who shuddered at the life-loving behavior of his fellow townsmen. He frowned on drinking, dancing, gambling, even attending the theater. At 19 he entered the Confederate Army, was wounded, returned to New Orleans at war's end.

He found an office job and a wife, and in his spare time devoted his energies to writing. His flair for it prompted *The Picayune* to give him a news-staff job and allowed him to contribute a once-a-week column. Edward Larocque Tinker, a noted Louisiana historian and critic who made biographical investigations of both Hearn and Cable, found that he was a quiet and meek young reporter whose pieces for the paper were labored and verbose with a distinct Sunday-school flavor. When he was assigned to cover theaters and review plays, he promptly walked off the job.

He continued to try his hand at writing, turning out mainly sketches about New Orleans life and customs. During this period he seems to have been fascinated by the vast contrast between himself and the Creoles, and he was isolated from contemporary literature. Reading, like attending the theater, was, to his mind, a sinful waste of time.

Tinker observes: "Although this (isolation) deprived him of the joy and profit of many masterpieces, it also had the advantage of keeping him from the influence of poor books and allowed him to form his own style. . . . Especially did it keep him from the outworn clichés and grandiose ideology of Southern literature of his day."

When Cable was thirty-five his first book—a collection of his stories that had appeared in magazines—was published under the title *Old Creole Days*. It brought him hearty applause in the North. But New Orleanians, principally the Creole element, turned up their noses at the tales.

His first novel, *The Grandissimes*, published a year later, also was warmly accepted outside the New Orleans area. But the Creoles continued their antagonism. They disliked a writer who treated his Negro characters as flesh-and-blood rather than humble servants or comedians. Cable's works were never created to appeal to the wealthy classes of the day; from the viewpoint of many New Orleanians, he was a renegade who had let them down. But Cable managed to become a highly-respected author in the eyes of literary folk and intelligent readers in many parts of the United States and abroad.

The hatred of the community had such a depressing effect on Cable that in 1886, he went, with his family, to New York. Later he established residence in Northampton, Massachusetts. His biographers agree that he then became an outright proselytizer in several fields, and his creative work suffered accordingly.

The personal-professional story of Cable has many contradictions, but his works and his career have significance in any review of New Orleans's literary life. He was a creator who projected characters and settings with honest realism. He would have no truck with the inhibitions or conventions of his contemporaries. He was, as Tinker put it:

". . . .The legitimate father of the literary movement that is producing such splendid fruit in the South today."

"His courage freed the authors who followed him of the necessity of fulsome praise for all things sectional, taught them their right and duty to analyze and portray truthfully, even, if necessary, to criticize the social conditions under which they lived," says Tinker, who adds: "This Cable accomplished at the cost of practical ostracism among his own people. He well may be called the first martyr in the cause of literary freedom in the South."

The New Orleans Cotton Centennial Exposition of 1884 attracted to the city several editors of northern magazines and book-publishing houses. There is evidence that during their visit they were busy encouraging a few relatively obscure writers, among them Hearn, and Grace King. Cable was already earning his national reputation.

Miss King, in the thirty years following, developed a stature that was recognized far beyond the boundaries of her native New Orleans. Her novels and historical studies of her city's life and times reflect precise craftsmanship as well as interest and understanding of the diverse aspects of her environment. Although she was reared in an aristocratic atmosphere, and in a day when native literature was generally sentimental and unrealistic by tradition, her love of New Orleans is honestly projected in her fiction and in her *New Orleans, The Place and the People,* an unadorned, objective statement of fact.

Some other latter-nineteenth century New Orleans writers, remembered today, are Ruth McEnery Stuart, whose numerous books dealt mainly with recollections of her early days in the city; Cecelia Jamison, with several tales of the bygone city; and Eliza Ripley whose *Social Life in Old New Orleans* is a lively memoir of the author's childhood and young womanhood before the Civil War.

Mrs. Mary (Mollie) Evelyn Moore Davis was highly regarded in the same period as poet, short-story writer, historian and raconteuse. The home on Royal street, where she lived with her husband, Thomas E. Davis, editor of *The Picayune*, was the habitual gathering place for both resident and visiting literary lights of the day.

Cofounder in 1837 of *The Picayune*, George W. Kendall, was the author of *Narrative of the Texas Santa Fe Expedition* following his impressive performance as war correspondent in the United States–Mexico struggle. Sir Henry Morton Stanley, nineteenth century explorer who introduced himself to Dr. Livingstone in "darkest" Africa, and wrote several books about his exploits and discoveries, had a New Orleans bond: he spent his boyhood in a residence in that section of the city known today as the Irish Channel. *New Orleans As It Was*, published just prior to 1900, the work of journalist Henry C. Castellanos, is a history which researchers still find invaluable. Another newspaperman, Henry Guy Carleton, editor of *The New Orleans Times*, found time to write, in the 1890's, numerous plays, several of which were produced successfully.

In the half century before the Civil War virtually all of New Orleans' literary efforts were written in French. The city's French-language newspapers frequently printed poetry and fiction submitted to them by inhabitants who could, or thought they could, write.

Among the bright literary lights of the period were the brothers Rouquette, Adrian and Dominique. They were members of a wealthy New Orleans family and had been educated in France. As youngsters they had each published in Paris a volume of verse.

These reputedly were publicly approved by Victor Hugo. Later, Dominique became New Orleans's poet laureate—unofficially—and Adrian produced a novel about Louisiana Indians which Lafcadio Hearn applauded.

Among the nonfiction writers in French of the period were Charles Gayarré and François Xavier Martin, as two of the region's outstanding historians. Their Louisiana histories have been of utmost value to researchers.

Although he was of the early postwar period, writer-in-French Alfred Mercier was a talented New Orleanian who won wide recognition for his fiction, poetry, critical essays and scientific papers (he was a doctor of medicine).

Mercier founded in 1876 *L'Athénée Louisianais,* a serious literary group which is still active. Its official journal, *Comptes Rendus,* has printed first nearly all of Louisiana's French literature since the journal made its début.

Before the Civil War, writers in English affiliated with the New Orleans scene were rarities. Young Sam Clemens, whom the world would come to know as Mark Twain and who piloted steamboats on the Mississippi in the 1850's and 1860's, offers a penetrating picture, in *Life on the Mississippi,* of the richly-hued town he often visited. To an earlier period belongs naturalist and painter John James Audubon whose New Orleans journal tells of his arrival shortly after the first of the year 1821 and of his six-month stay. He wrote that his spirits were at low ebb but that he had seen birds of contrasting shapes, colors and habits, and recorded his impressions of them as well as of the burgeoning multi-blooded city. He noted, too, that the incessant rain depressed him and that he was "much in want of cash."

Walt Whitman was nearing his thirtieth birthday when he arrived in New Orleans with his young brother, Jeff, after a rigorous overland journey from Brooklyn in 1848. During their brief residence Walt was a reporter and feature writer for *The Daily Crescent* which printed his sketches of New Orleans customs and characters. His biographers see his New Orleans interlude as having had a formative effect on what he created in the years that followed. There is evidence, too, of a possible romantic entanglement involving Whitman and an unidentified belle.

Vincent Nolte, the international financier, lived in New Orleans in the early 1800's and wrote *Fifty Years in Both Hemispheres* which treats with the city in detail. The book furnished source material to Hervey Alley for *Anthony Adverse*, the bulky bestselling novel of the 1930's.

Two decades before the Civil War a New Orleans group of free men of color was active and, from the literary viewpoint, curiously significant.

Their leader was Armand Lanusse, born in 1812. He was an intellectual who assumed a militant, if somewhat sub rosa, position on what today would be called civil rights.

One of this group's achievements was *L'Album Littéraire*, a magazine of poetry, short stories and articles of opinion, in French, which went out of existence after three or four issues. A portion of its contents stressed, in guarded fashion, that Negroes who were not slaves would do well to strive for certain rights then denied them in the community's complex social structure. Apart from that theory, Lanusse seems to have aspired to help the Negro share rightfully in the culture of his time.

L'Album, believed to have been the first instance of the publication in Louisiana of the writing of Negroes, was followed in 1845 by another Lanusse project entitled *Les Cénelles*. This was an anthology of about 100 poems composed by Lanusse and some 15 other New Orleans-born *gens de couleur libres*. Historians have determined that this volume was the first in Louisiana in its category.

One of the most trenchant, but today unrecognized portrayers of the pre-Civil War New Orleans scene was Charles Dudley Warner, a prolific New England writer. He described eye-catching foliage, shabby streets, artistic architectural effects, a tumbledown old French Market, delicate wrought-iron and many a "fantastic" nook and corner which he said endeared the ancient city to him immediately. The Creoles gave tone to the community, Warner observed, but, in his view, their influence also affected what he called literary sympathies and literary morals.

Evaluating the canvas, Warner spoke of the "temptation" to regard the city against the romance of its past. Yet, he said, he "could fancy no ground more congenial to the artist and the story-teller."

Another forgotten nineteenth century portraitist offered a bit of advice in another vein. Henry Bradshaw Fearon, a visiting English journalist, wrote ". . . .to all men whose desire only is to live a short life but a merry one, I have no hesitation in recommending New Orleans."

The earliest recorded writing on the subject of New Orleans came from the pens of the colonists in the early eighteenth century. Naturally, it was in French.

In 1699 a *Narrative of the Expedition made by Order of Louis XIV, King of France, under Command of Pierre Lemoyne d'Iberville, to explore the (Mississippi) River and establish a Colony in Louisiana* was published. The narrative's author was the anonymous "Chronicler of the Expedition." It provides an account of passing the site from which, nineteen years later, New Orleans was carved out of the wilderness.

Two years earlier there had appeared a "mémoire" addressed to the King's Minister of Marine, Count de Pontchartrain. It dealt with the importance of establishing the colony. The writer was one de Remonville (without a given name), identified as a participant in La Salle's voyage of exploration down the Mississippi from Canada.

A roll call of New Orleans newspapermen and women, who, like Hearn, Cable and Whitman, became authors of book-length works, the majority with a strictly New Orleans-and-environs regional background, produces this motley: Dorothy Dix, Lyle

Saxon, Roark Bradford, Carl Carmer, Hermann Deutsch, Kenneth Knoblock, Charles L. ("Pie") Dufour, Catherine Cole, Harnett Kane, Hodding Carter, Gwen Bristow, Bruce Manning, John Chase, Thomas Dabney, William Sydney Porter and many more.

Miss Dix (Mrs. Elizabeth M. Gilmer) was a book writer as well as the nation's best known adviser to the lovelorn.

Saxon was the author of several books, including the highly informative *Fabulous New Orleans* and *Father Mississippi*. He directed the New Orleans Federal Writers Project in the 1930's which compiled an excellent guide book to the city.

Bradford wrote several memorable novels about Negro life, one of which, *Ol' Man Adam an' His Chillun*, was fashioned into the unforgettable stage play, *Green Pastures*.

Carmer published a small volume of verse here entitled *French Town*; his later fame stems from a nonfiction work entitled *Stars Fell on Alabama* and his authoritative books covering the history and folklore of his native New York state.

Deutsch has written novels, a biography and a Huey Long-assasination documentary.

Knoblock and Manning wrote mystery thrillers principally and Miss Bristow (Mrs. Manning, that is) has created several full-blooded novels with an Old South background.

Dufour has become a specialist in Civil War matters and Louisiana history, and Chase, historian of the New Orleans panorama, has earned a reputation as authority on the origin of New Orleans street names.

Miss Cole (Mrs. Martha Field) was best known as a travel writer.

Kane, who started out with an incisive study of the Louisiana political circus of the Huey Long regime, *Louisiana Hayride*, has published many volumes dealing factually or fictionally with events and personalities of the region.

Carter is known both for his novels and his studies of the Southern sociological and historical scenes.

Dabney's history of *The Times-Picayune* is an illuminating

study of New Orleans's face and figure during the first 100 years of the newspaper founded as *The Picayune* in 1837.

Porter, the story goes, adopted the "O. Henry" tag while hobnobbing with New Orleans fellow Fourth Estaters; later he became the all-American short story-writer.

During the whole run of the New Orleans literary extravaganza, there never were, as I see it, any great vintage years, any attention-calling period when general achievement was outright scintillating. Yet, what came about in the immediate post-World War I years does rate a special niche in the gallery of exhibits.

It was a time of resistance to the older order, a time of aspiration to do away with the traditional sugar-coated nonsense by which many a writer had, in the past, earned a reputation. It was a time when the new order demanded fresher ideas which bore a true relationship to life. It was the time of *The Double Dealer*.

Critic Henry Mencken, the arch-skeptic whose long-time pillorying of the South as "the Sahara of the Bozart" had probably wrongly identified him as an enemy of the region had begun to change his tune. His reexamination of the South's mores prompted his statement that "the South begins to mutter." Which, in Menckenisque was a radiant tribute. At any rate, he obviously was impressed by what the people behind *The Double Dealer* and one or two other Deep South journals were doing and he said as much.

Two New Orleans youngsters just out of service in France in World War I were back home, footloose, unsure of the future and suspicious of the values they had accepted before the world upheaval. They belonged, I suppose, to that fraternity which came to be called, loosely, The Lost Generation. It was this pair, Julius Friend and I, who conceived the idea of publishing a magazine.

They were not certain, at first, what kind of magazine it would be. Their original idea was a publication of shock-value material. But, somewhere along the line in their discussions, they settled for a serious literary periodical whose contents would be of highest caliber. Whether it shocked or displeased or even confused its audience, was of no importance. Two other New Orleanians, Basil Thompson and John McClure, joined hands with the founding fathers, and the project was launched. Volume 1, Number 1 of *The Double Dealer* appeared in January, 1921.

In the East and the Midwest a literary revival had taken root some ten years earlier. But nothing of the kind happened in the South until the birth of *The Double Dealer*. About the same time *The Reviewer* entered the world in Richmond and *The Fugitive* made its debut in Nashville. *The Reviewer's* aim was that of promoting Southern letters and allowing Southern writers free rein. *The Fugitive's* purpose was, largely, to present the poetry of Southerners.

The policy of *The Double Dealer*, an early-issue editorial pointed out, was no policy whatsoever, other than to print the best material obtainable, "regardless of popular appeal, moral or immoral stigmata, conventional or unconventional technique, new theme or old." The editors declared: "We mean to deal double, to show the other side. . . ."

A little later another editorial in the magazine had this to say: "It is high time, we believe, for some doughty, clear-visioned penman to emerge from the sodden marshes of Southern literature. We are sick to death of the treacly sentimentalities with which our lady fictioneers regale us. The old traditions are no more. New peoples, customs prevail. The Confederacy has long since been dissolved. A storied realm of dreams . . . . no longer exists. We have our 'Main Streets' here as elsewhere."

The lofty objective was realized, to a degree. While the editors were seeking manuscripts that lived up to it, they also were publishing the work of the so-called experimentalists—Sherwood Anderson, Lola Ridge, Babette Deutsch, Maxwell Bodenheim, Alfred Kreymborg and a few more of their stature, none of whom were Southerners.

During its first year, *The Double Dealer* published the writing of others not yet widely recognized, or those unknown. They included Malcolm Cowley, Jean Toomer, Hart Crane, Edmund

Wilson, Robert Penn Warren, Allen Tate, Donald Davidson, Ernest Hemingway and William Faulkner. The contributions of the two last named were their first published work.

By its second year *The Double Dealer* was calling itself "A National Magazine From the South." Indeed, its reception in farflung places, some of them overseas, was growing warmer than it ever had been around the hometown. Finally the magazine shifted from a regional to a national emphasis, but in its six-and-a-half-year life it remained a New Orleans creation and the nucleus of an Orleanian movement that sought, with all honesty, to kick over the traces of the established order of shopworn literary trends.

Oliver La Farge, Pulitzer Prize-winning novelist, who was a transient New Orleanian in the mid-1920's, once said of those days:

"We were still ferocious and undefeated. We had never yet toned down the truth or made use of what we knew to be inferior material for profit. We did not believe we ever would."

And Hamilton Basso, a New Orleans-born writer who circulated in the same milieu about the same time, recalled that:

"The days of *The Double Dealer* were the real, genuine, 100 per cent article. . . . We had the fact of being in our early twenties, we had a similarity of interest that made us enduring friends, we had the privilege of companionship with men like Sherwood Anderson, we had the whole page of our ambition to write upon as best we could, and we had fun. That many things don't happen to come together all at once in one place and at one time. It was our wonderful good luck that it did."

The business of publishing the magazine was, as I have indicated, a serious one with a serious goal. But the editors, and their volunteer staff, never took themselves seriously. Their working hours brought many a lighter interlude, and even on the printed page a tongue-in-cheek attitude was often unmistakable. Detractors among readers who were, or fancied themselves, litterati, labeled *The Double Dealer* second-rate. But none of them ever called it dull.

A literary critic, editorialist, and dissector of the American

scene for more than forty years, Mencken was admired or denounced by millions who followed his newspaper columns and
magazine articles. During *The Double Dealer's* first year, after
he had read "diligently" every issue, he said he was unable to find
a single reference to "the charm and virtue of Southern womanhood or to the mad way in which the slaves used to love their
masters." And he added: "It (the magazine) has the right air
. . . . it doesn't give a damn for the old gods."

It was the type of opinion which suggests the significance of
the role of *The Double Dealer* in the literary movement that
thrived in New Orleans in the vigorous 1920's.

In libraries, rummaging in the mountainous pile of literature
and less labeled "New Orleans," my eye has been caught by many
curiosa.

The stories of Mississippi River pilot Isaiah Sellers, frequent
contributor to *The Picayune*, were always signed Mark Twain.
The better-known Samuel L. Clemens appropriated the pen
name years later.

Presbyterian minister Theodore Clapp wrote *Autobiograph-
ical Sketches and Recollections during Thirty-Five Years in
New Orleans* (1857). It provides a matchless, detailed canvas of
the city's suffering during the great Asiatic cholera plague of 1832
and 1833, and the yellow fever epidemics of 1837 and 1853.

Writing about New Orleans appears to have preoccupied
authors in the late eighteenth and early nineteenth centuries. The
situation prompted one P. Forest, a traveler from France, author
of *Voyage aux Etats-Unis de l'Amérique en 1831*, to offer in his
foreword what amounts to an apology for adding his volume to
the huge collection.

The first New Orleans library, according to one researcher,
was set up in 1846 with 7500 volumes available to readers.
Another says that in 1840 a bookseller named J. A. Noble announced in the public prints that he was opening a library of

some 3000 volumes. Author-favorites of the time included Dickens, Hugo, Irving, Cooper, Poe, Longfellow and Hawthorne.

Identified as the city's first guide book, issued in 1845, is Norman's *New Orleans and Environs*. And what is called the first city directory was published in 1822 by J. A. Paxton.

Activities of the city's demimonde in the 1880's and 1890's were reported in two local periodicals, *The Mascot* and *The Sunday Sun*.

Adah Isaacs Menken, born in New Orleans in 1835, idol of theatre patrons, and friend of Whitman, Swinburne, Rosseti and the elder Dumas was the author of a volume of poetry entitled *Infelicia*. Swinburne evaluated it as "rot."

In a vastly contrasting area was the "Blue Book" of the legalized New Orleans Red Light District, world-famous playground for a quarter of a century up to World War I. Although essentially a directory of *filles de joie* in residence, the book's foreword and running commentary remain gems of preciosity in demure prose from the typewriter of an unidentified expert in the matters at hand. "Blue Books" extant are precious jewels to the collector.

My personal remembrance of the unique in New Orleans literature includes another extraordinary little volume, *Sherwood Anderson and Other Famous Creoles*. Published some 40 years ago in a limited edition, it is a slim book of 40 drawings of local arts-affiliated "personalities" who roamed the Vieux Carré and other precincts of the city in the exhilirating 1920's. Architect-artist Bill Spratling did the pictures, all in fine caricature. Mississippian Bill Faulkner, not yet a Nobel Prize-winner, not even a name in writing circles, did the preface. His 500-word commentary on the book's reason for being is a skillful parody of the writing style of titan Anderson.

While fiction writers down the years were grinding out tales of plantation life, slavery, Mardi Gras, voodoo, cuisine, Creole and

Cajun capers, etc., the biographers were preoccupied with the region's statesmen, military heroes, philanthropists and other noteworthy figures.

Among the saints and sinners covered are Huey Long, Hearn, Audubon and O. Henry. More than 35 titles dealing with these four alone can be found on public library shelves.

Other persons praised or damned by the life-story scriveners include Jean LaFitte, Zachary Taylor, Louis Armstrong, Judah Benjamin, Judah Touro, Julien Poydras, John Slidell, John McDonogh, Raphael Semmes, Alexander Porter, James Wilkinson, P. G. T. Beauregard, and Adah Isaacs Menken.

Some New Orleans biographers are Hamilton Basso, Stanley Arthur, Lyle Saxon, Louis Armstrong, Dagmar Lebreton, and James E. Edmonds.

Another phase of the city's literary history is seen in the performance of the formal historians, particularly those who flourished from the dim past through the 1920's.

Best remembered are, in addition to Martin and Gayarré, Antoine LePage du Pratz, Guy Soniat du Fossat, Alcée Fortier, Edward Rightor, Henry E. Chambers, and John S. Kendall.

From the early era to the present day, New Orleans has produced its share of poets, too. One of the earliest was philanthropist Julien Poydras, born in 1746. His *La Prise du Morne du Baton Rouge* (1779) has been identified as the first epic poem written in Louisiana. Mary Ashley Townsend's volumes of collected verse earned high critical acclaim in the 1870's and 1880's.

Among later New Orleans poets may be noted Robert Emmett Kennedy, Fanny Heaslip Lea, Richard Kirk, John Kingston Fineran, John McClure, Florence Converse, James Feibleman, Basil Thompson, Hodding Carter and Morris Williams.

The researches of Grace King discovered that Louisiana's first "dramatic effort" was *The Indian Father* which was presented for a select few in the governor's mansion. Later it was put into verse by LeBlance de Villeneuve and presented to the public in the Orleans Theater.

Books of fiction with a New Orleans regional setting have, in many instances, entered (or near-missed) the financially rewarding precincts of the bestseller. Some of their authors were:

Robert W. Chambers, Harris Dickson, Edna Ferber, Stark Young, John Erskine, Barry Benefield, Winston Churchill, Emerson Hough, Upton Sinclair, Thomas Bailey Aldrich, Evelyn Scott, Arna Bontemps, Fulton Oursler, Ben Lucien Burman, Frank Stockton, Rex Beach.

Who are the latter day writers, resident or visiting, who have told stories and provided nonfiction reports of the local scene, bygone and contemporary? A few are:

Frances Parkinson Keyes, prolific novelist and part-time New Orleanian; E. P. O'Donnell, who (in *The Great Big Doorstep*) gave evidence that he was one of the region's rarities—a genuine humorist; another humorist, James J. McLoughlin (Jack Lafaience), whose Creole-character sketches still are dear to readers' hearts; Robert Tallant, a diligent researcher of strange true stories as well as a novelist of distinction; Herbert Asbury, whose thirty-year-old *The French Quarter*, an informal history of New Orleans vice and crime, has never gone out of print; Shirley Ann Grau, Pulitzer Prize-winning author of many novels and short stories set in South Louisiana and New Orleans; and Walker Percy whose *The Movie-Goer* won high critical acclaim.

In a partial listing of others you find Elma Godchaux, Murrell Edmunds, Mary Barrow Linfield, Virginia Abaunza, Thomas Sancton, Peter Feibleman, Hilda Phelps Hammond, the Rev. Edward F. Murphy, Ella Bentley Arthur, Stuart Landry, Helen Pitkin Schertz, N. C. Curtis, Louise Guyol, George Kernion, Natalie Scott, Lura Robinson, Roger Baudier, Evans Wall, Doris Kent LeBlanc, Alice Walworth Graham, Meigs Frost.

There were (and are) also the New Orleans-based academicians who have set down in book-length form their findings from specialized examination of the city's cultural picture, past and present. Their reports have dealt separately with art, music, the theatre and like phases.

The parade is never-ending. Today's writers seem no less entranced with the New Orleans scene than those who preceded them down the centuries. They have shared in common the bright stimuli of the Creole city. The area's spectacular history, its vibrantly different customs and traditions, and a generous admixture of only locally procurable seasoning have produced a near-hypnotic effect on writers of long ago and today alike.

What about quality? How do the new compare with the old? The moderns, as I see it, are more sophisticated; they are certainly less inhibited. Are the literary artists and craftsmen of today superior, in general, to those who went before? Who can say? The titans are still in short supply.

A Sportsman's Town

Crozet J. Duplantier

Sports-minded New Orleanians, assessing their fortunes today, generally would conclude that they have never had it so good.

A new golden era of sports is underway in New Orleans as the city celebrates its 250th birthday.

The Saints, the city's entry in the National Football League, have just marched through their first season.

The Buccaneers, the New Orleans representative in the new American Basketball Association, are in business.

The Greater New Orleans Open, offering prize money in excess of $100,000, is one of the top attractions on the professional golfers' tour.

The New Orleans Mid-Winter Sports Association's Sugar Bowl, with its carnival of year-end sports activities, is still going strong.

The once mighty Tulane Green Wave, a perennial loser for too many recent years, has indicated in the past two seasons that happier days lie ahead.

Somewhere on the horizon, beyond the date when the city's superdome stadium will have been constructed, New Orleanians have already spotted a major league baseball franchise.

And, for the participant sports fans, opportunities for pleasure generally have continued to improve over the years.

All of this, coming after years of frustration when New Orleans watched its spectator sports decline while other cities moved ahead into the big league picture, certainly supports the estimate that, in sports, the New Orleanian has "never had it so good."

Surely, no sports fan who has lived only in this century would even try to dispute it.

There might, however, have been doubts among New Orleanians of other eras.

Those from one era, because they would find the modern sportsmen's fare too mild for them.

Those from another era, because they would never have been convinced that any period could approach the last half of the last century when New Orleans was the racing and boxing center of the nation and those who craved participation could choose from among such activities as racquettes, rowing, cycling, and harness racing, as well as such current sports as baseball, boxing, swimming, running and football.

But times and tastes, fortunately, sometimes change.

Little is known of the sports activities of earliest New Orleans, although there are several references indicating that the city's first residents were aware of the area's bountiful opportunities for hunting and fishing.

Most chronicles of the leisure time activities in New Orleans date back only to the early part of the nineteenth century, at which time the city's tastes for recreational sports were as varied as they have ever been.

The New Orleans City Guide noted:

"New Orleans has a history replete with strange and barbaric sports brought to Louisiana by the French and Spanish, diversified by the creoles, and added to by the Americans. . . ."

In his *Fabulous New Orleans*, Lyle Saxon points out:

"The advertisements in old newspapers prove that the people of New Orleans were always eager for novelty. In newspapers for

1820 we find notices of cockfights on Sunday afternoon. A few years before bullfights were advertised. One strange notice tells of a fight between a bulldog and an alligator, admission one dollar."

And later, he provides an account, from the *Illustrated News* of April 23, 1853, of a fight between a bull and a bear—an "athletic" contest that once was the most popular sporting event offered in the city.

Pro football, it is constantly pointed out these days, attracts the crowds because the name of the game is violence.

"Tame," would be the verdict of the early nineteenth century New Orleanian who had "participated" in the match described in the *Illustrated News:*

"In the arena was a cage about thirty feet square and twelve feet high, built of timber, grated, with bars of iron; in it stood a large powerful dark slate-colored bull, Napoleon Fourth—sole monarch of that establishment. By the side of this stood another cage, with a large and powerful grizzly bear. . . .We had just time to notice the preparatory arrangements, when the crowd from outside broke through. In rushed several thousand people; they flew like magic on to the top of the large cage, which was covered with boards, so that the cage was soon surrounded and covered in every direction by sightseers. Those from the staging and outsiders, who could not get a sight, commenced an assault on those on and about the cage, with stones, brickbats, clubs, boards, turf and everything that came handy, to clear the way and give fair play. This having the desired effect and all being ready, the slide door was hoisted and Bruin notified with a ten-foot pole that he was wanted in the other apartment . . ."

There followed a long detailed description of bear biting bull, bull throwing bear and impaling him with his horns, of blood flowing profusely, and of "bruin" finally sneaking into a corner from which he "could neither be coaxed, flattered, nor driven."

At this point, the article concluded with this paragraph:

"The bull set up a loud bellow, as he proudly walked about

the cage, pawing. The excited multitude gave one lone, loud yell for Napoleon Fourth, and departed."

What must have been the height—or depth—in the history of the sport of animal baiting in New Orleans was the event which was offered to the citizenry in an advertisement in the *Courier* of Sept. 5, 1817 which scheduled four unusual exhibitions and held out promise of a fifth. The ad listed the events in this order:

"First Fight—A strong Attakapas bull attacked and subdued by six of the strongest dogs in the country.

Second Fight—Six bulldogs against a Canadian bear.

Third Fight—A beautiful tiger against a black bear.

Fourth Fight—Twelve dogs against a strong and furious Opelousas bull."

If the tiger survived his first engagement, it was noted, another test for him was in the offing.

The cockfights had a special quality about them, too. The events were extended beyond the normal capabilities of the combatants, as their handlers blew a combination of whiskey and garlic into the nostrils of the cocks to bring them around for further action. Besides the individual battles, as a special "treat" fights were sometimes held in which as many as twenty cocks were placed in the ring at the same time, to peck and stab each other until only one remained standing.

For others, there were unscheduled but very regular boxing and wrestling contests on the streets, fights for which there were no rules.

If modern professional football would consider unfair the comparison between its sport and contests between animals, today's No. 1 contact sport might still have paled compared with another old New Orleans favorite—racquettes, described by the *New Orleans Guide* as "combining the more violent features of lacrosse, football, cross-country racing, and rioting."

Robert C. Reinders in his *End of an Era—New Orleans 1850–1860*, says racquettes, supposedly introduced by the Choctaw Indians, was played by the rowdier youths of the city. He explains the game:

"A leather ball, somewhat larger than a tennis ball, was picked up and carried or thrown with two spoonlike sticks toward an opponent's goal, a canvas target a foot-and-a-half wide placed on a tall frame . . . the teams, eighty and more men on a side, with the players shoeless, stripped to the waist, and wearing red or blue caps, made a colorful appearance. There were no sidelines and so the spectators themselves stood in the field of play. If the ball happened to fly among the refreshment stands nearby the hapless proprietors were run down by a host of athletes grubbing with their sticks for the ball . . ."

Signs that New Orleans was becoming a bit more genteel in its sports tastes began with the introduction of organized racing, which launched New Orleans as a major sports town.

The opening of the Eclipse Course in March 1837—and its immediate success—served as the spark which ignited the interest of the city's newspapers in sports and, as a consequence, the further building of community interest in sports events.

Horse racing had been, along with boxing, a New Orleans favorite for many years; but up to the time of the opening of the Eclipse Course, racing had been conducted on an unorganized basis. In fact, for many years, since about the time of the Louisiana Purchase, plantation owners had been interested in testing their horses and had been conducting match races on their own grounds.

In 1804, after the Purchase had brought New Orleans with a population of about 8,000 under the American flag, the weekly *Gazette* announced a race in what is now Audubon Park, for a purse of $100. "Barbecue and liquors" for the fans also was promised. There is record, too, of a track being operated in 1814 on General Wade Hampton's plantation.

And, in 1820, Francois de Livaudais, a wealthy sugar planter, invited the public to a race meeting at Live Oak, his estate just above the Vieux Carré.

Five years later, the first definite step in organized racing came with the opening of the Jackson Race Course built south of New Orleans, near the battlefield where Andrew Jackson had defeated the British ten years before. Regular four-day meetings were scheduled in the winter and spring of each year for "Creole," or native Louisiana, horses.

But the Eclipse Course, located near the Audubon Park site, was the first track to conduct races with only thoroughbreds participating. In March, 1837, when a six-day meeting was staged, the management announced proudly that "thirty or more blue-blooded thoroughbreds from many parts of the Union will be on hand for the races."

For the first day of racing, it was estimated that the crowd attending totaled 12,000, a figure described as "incredible" in view of the fact that the city's population totaled only 102,193 when the 1840 census was taken.

Racing was on its way.

In fact, within ten years, four tracks were in operation, and interest in the thoroughbreds was such that during the height of the Mexican War—and with New Orleans serving as mobilization and departure point for troops—the races received as much attention in the press as the war did.

Perhaps the horsemen were over-ambitious,—and besides, there were economic problems at the time—but at any rate, after the 40's only one of the race courses which had suddenly sprung to life still remained. It was the Metairie Course, built where the Metairie Cemetery is now located, which, however, was to bring the city the title of racing capital of America—and to make horse racing the only firmly established sport in New Orleans as the nineteenth century entered its second half.

And, if one event—or series of events—could be singled out for making New Orleans a racing center, it was that which started with the "Great State Post Stakes" run April 1, 1854, generally referred to today as the great match race between Lexington and Lecomte.

Actually, besides Lecomte, representing Mississippi, and Lexington, representing Kentucky, two others, Arrow, representing Louisiana, and Highlander, representing Alabama, were entered.

Owners subscribed $5,000 for each horse, providing a purse of $20,000 for the winner.

But the race was, as far as the fans were concerned, between Lexington and Lecomte.

This was a gruelling test of horse flesh, with the contest scheduled over four miles, best two out of three heats.

The race attracted some 20,000 spectators, including among them, according to the accounts of the time, governors, mayors, judges—and even former President Millard Fillmore. They had come to New Orleans from many sections and by every mode of transportation, including large delegations which had come by steamboat from Natchez, Vicksburg, Memphis, and points along the upper Mississippi.

Lexington carried the day, winning the first two heats.

But the Lexington-Lecomte feud was to carry on for another year.

For Lecomte's owner, Thomas J. Wells of Mississippi, challenged for a second duel, which Lecomte won in two straight heats a week later, his best time that day being 7:26 for the four miles, a new American record for the distance and considerably better than Lexington's best time in the earlier race—8:04. This was the only race Lexington ever lost.

Followers of Richard Ten Broeck's Lexington now demanded another rematch; and in the spring of 1855, to further interest in the event, Ten Broeck ran his horse against Lecomte's record time. On April 1, aided by a running start and spurred on by other horses entered to push him, Lexington bettered Lecomte's mark with a clocking of 7:19¾. It was estimated by the New Orleans *Bee* that some $500,000 changed hands in the betting on whether or not Lexington could top the Lecomte mark.

Thirteen days later the third match race was run—this time with the spectators traveling from all over the nation, and even from foreign countries, to see the race of the century.

Fate intervened, however, to make what promised to be the greatest of the series a dismal flop. Lecomte became violently ill a few days before the race. His owners felt he had recovered sufficiently to compete, but in the first heat, Lecomte was badly beaten and he was withdrawn from the remaining races because of the possibility of permanent injury to him in his weakened condition.

Controversy over the outcome continued, with fans demanding another rematch, the great Lexington against a healthy Lecomte—but any hope for the match faded when Ten Broeck took Lecomte to England where Lecomte died. Lexington, too, gave up the races to become a famous sire.

Although the two disappeared from the races Lexington and Lecomte had made New Orleans the most famous racing site in the nation.

Metairie flourished until the war, staging its last great race on December 10, 1861, before a small crowd, a scene (*the Picayune* noted the following day) "which hardly resembled the brilliant assemblages in the piping times of peace . . ."

The track reopened December 23, 1866, but the impoverished South could no longer support the track, nor were there sufficient horses available for competition.

Metairie struggled on until finally in 1872, it was announced that the track had been sold and would be converted into a cemetery bearing the same name.

Metairie was dead, but not racing. The Louisiana Jockey Club picked up the challenge; and this group and its successors developed the Fair Grounds which, though never the center of racing nationally that Metairie had been, has survived many crises and today, as the third oldest race course in the country, still offers top-flight racing each year, its season beginning traditionally with Thanksgiving day.

The post-war years, however, did leave one special imprint on the nation—through the performances of a jockey named Ed "Snapper" Garrison who repeatedly brought his mounts from the brink of defeat to victory in the last few strides.

It was "Snapper" who contributed the phrase "Garrison finish" to the American language.

THE PAST AS PRELUDE:

New Orleans 1718-1968

The People of New Orleans . . .

Choctaws

Jean Baptiste
le Moyne
de Bienville

Antonio
de Ulloa

Came from Many Places

LA FOURCHE PACKET-LANDING.

They Built Houses . . .

STREET-CARS, CANAL ST. TO BARRACKS.

❋ URSULINE CONVENT ❋
NEW ORLEANS.

PRINCIPAL BUILDING FACING THE MISSISSIPPI RIVER.

and Schools . . .

and Hospitals

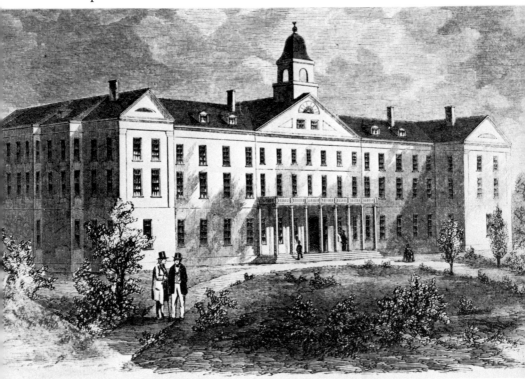

LOUISIANA.—THE BUSINESS BOOM IN THE SOUTH—A SCENE ON THE LEVÉE AT NEW ORLEANS.—From a Sketch by Joseph Horton.—See Page 319.

They Built a Great Port . . .

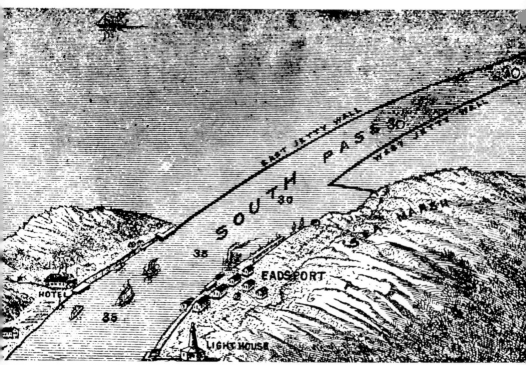

and Developed the Mouth of the Mississippi

They Produced an
Architectural Style . . .

And Brought Opera
to America

They Built More Schools

John McDonogh

Paul Tulane

and Universities and Colleges

ORLEANS COLLEGE, 1812. From design in City Library.

They Fought the Plague . . .

and Buried the Dead. . . .

Oven Tombs in our Oldest Cemetery, St. Louis No. 1.

for the Sportsman, . . .

the Athlete,

A Good Time Town

The Actor . . .

The Artist . . .

ST. CHARLES THEATRE.

MR. E. L. DAVENPORT

For a Short Season, Commencing Monday, March 8th,

IN HIS FAMOUS CHARACTER,

SIR GILES OVERREACH!

Impromptu on witnessing E. L. Davenport's masterly performance.

Wm. Woodward

The
DOUBLE·DEALER

A NATIONAL MAGAZINE FROM THE SOUTH
PUBLISHED AT NEW ORLEANS

Vol. II   OCTOBER, 1921   No. 10

25 Cents $2.50 Yearly

and the Writer . . .

G. W. Cable

Grace King

The People of New Orleans

Robert Maestri

Martin Behrman

GENERAL BEAUREGARD CALLING OUT THE NUMBERS DRAWN IN THE LOUISIANA LOTTERY AT NEW ORLEANS.

Have Their Own Brand of Politics,

and Their Own Kind of Jazz . . .

and They Have MARDI GRAS

MARDI GRAS, AT NEW ORLEANS: NIGHT PROCESSION OF THE "MYSTICK KREWE OF COMUS."—(SEE NEXT PAGE.)

CONSTRUCTING AND DECORATING THE FLOATS, FOR THE PROCESSION, IN A COTTON PRESS ON CAMP STREET.

They Have Had Fires and Battles,
Different Laws and Segregation
Struggles,

but for

New Orleans People

The Past 1718–1968

Is Prelude

List of Illustrations

At almost the same time as racing was being developed, boxing began in New Orleans, but its maturation period was much longer to a great extent because of legal restrictions that existed from time to time.

Nat Fleischer's *Ring Record Box* lists as the city's first official prize fight an encounter on May 6, 1836, between James Burke, alias "Deaf" Burke and Sam O'Rourke.

Fleischer's account of the event suggests—as in the case of the bear and bull fight—that it was typical of New Orleanians of the era to become participants in events to which they came as spectators.

Burke, according to Fleischer, was leading in the third round when a gang of O'Rourke's thugs broke into the ring and Burke had to run for his life.

Burke was described in *the Picayune* of March 4, 1837, as "the celebrated pugilist and champion of England," who operated one of a number of clubs teaching the manly art of self defense.

Burke's club, "Boxiana," proclaimed in an ad in *the Picayune* five days later:

"Gentlemen, after taking a few lessons, will be able to chastise those who may offer insult, and protect themselves against the attack of the ruffian."

Boxing contests continued irregularly during these early years, New Orleans city ordinances against the sport notwithstanding.

John L. Sullivan, almost singlehandedly, was responsible for New Orleans' emergence as the boxing center of the nation in the post-war years. In fact, when Sullivan began using New Orleans as one of his major bases of operation, boxing became an instant success—despite the fact that the bare-knuckled contests were against the law.

The city had been conditioned for the Sullivan invasion, for his major illegal bare-knuckled fights, promoted in New Orleans and fought in Mississippi, and for the greatest event—his battle with James J. Corbett, with gloves, in New Orleans.

On May 13, 1866, for instance, *the Picayune*, taking note of the fact that fighting was illegal, announced there would be "another prize fight" in the city the next day. "We will not state where," it added "for the simple reason that we do not know."

The article continued:

"These exercises in the 'manly art of self defense' possess great attractions to many, but we beg to be excluded from the number . . ."

Apparently, however, it was no problem for the residents of the city to learn the location of the fight—and apparently, also, *the Picayune*'s petition for exclusion was denied. The day after the bout the newspaper reported:

"The prize fight which took place yesterday, between the two noted pugilists, King of this city, and Farrell of Philadelphia, resulted in the total discomfiture of the latter. The greatest interest was manifested by thousands in this great trial of strength, and from an early hour in the morning, before the 'peep o' day,' until 8 o'clock, the road to the Half Way House was filled with vehicles of every description and pedestrians, all hastening to the scene of action . . ."

A city which could attract thousands to a fight for which no location was announced obviously was the place to plan Sullivan's illegal battles.

It was February 7, 1882, when Sullivan, the Boston Strong Boy, wrested the bare-knuckle heavyweight championship from Paddy Ryan of Troy, New York, in front of the Barnes Hotel in Mississippi City, Mississippi, before a crowd of 1,500, most of whom had left New Orleans by train at 3:30 a.m. for the noon meeting.

All kinds of deceptions had been employed to get the crowd there without the law in pursuit.

Reports were that sheriffs in the area were sent on a wild goose chase at fight time and sports writer Pete Finney, in his *Evolution of the New Orleans Sports Page*, noted:

"For the fight, the story goes, lookouts were posted to warn of approaching police, a peculiar turn of events since some say the audience included such distinguished gentlemen as Frank and Jesse James."

Seven years later, even bigger things were in store for Mississippi, with a big assist from New Orleans, as Sullivan defended his title against Jack Kilrain on July 8, 1889 in Richburg, Mississippi.

This bout was another exercise in deception. New Orleans was excited about the forthcoming event days in advance.

Promoters obviously would have been delighted to stage the event in the city, but Governor Francis T. Nicholls had called out the militia to prevent that occurrence.

Mississippi was chosen, in spite of the fact that the state had recently strengthened its laws against prize fights by making fighting and its promotion a crime punishable by imprisonment up to twelve months or a fine of $1,000, or both.

Still one has to question the determination of the lawmen to enforce an unpopular law when 3,000 fans, most of them from New Orleans, but some from far parts of the nation, could find their way to a little sawmill town of 200 persons in time for the contest.

The place of the bout was never mentioned in the advance notices. Fans bought railroad tickets to an unannounced destination.

On the morning of the fight, the crowd on Canal Street was said to resemble a Mardi Gras turnout.

Two trainloads of fans departed New Orleans, every seat filled, to see the contest in which Sullivan beat Kilrain in 75 rounds during most of which time the temperature hovered at 108 degrees.

An indication of New Orleans' interest in the bout was *the Picayune's* coverage of the event the next day. It reported the fight in twelve columns of six-point hand-set type, nearly 20,000 words, or about twice the size of the average section of this book.

The decision by the governor of Mississippi to prosecute the "criminals who have outraged the decency and defied the laws" accomplished exactly the opposite of what must have been intended.

Though the principals were convicted, they became overnight heroes.

Sullivan was found guilty of prize fighting and sentenced to a year in jail. Kilrain, despite the fact that he had been beaten, was convicted of simple assault and battery, and sentenced to two months in jail and fined $200. Both appealed to the state Supreme Court and finally settled for fines of $500 each. The referee of the fight, John Fitzpatrick, was fined $100.

While they were awaiting the final decision on their appeal, Sullivan and Kilrain went on tour, boxing with gloves and building new interest in the sport.

When the principals came to Purvis, site of the circuit court, the city was decked out with flags in their honor; and so great was the crowd gathered to welcome Sullivan that police were needed to clear a way between his train and his hotel. After the appeal was heard, bonfires were lighted in Purvis in honor of the battlers.

And the referee? John Fitzpatrick went on to become mayor of New Orleans.

A sequel to the bout also was the decision by the Louisiana Legislature the next year legalizing contests between fighters wearing gloves. This decision, making Louisiana the first state to legalize fighting, set the stage for the greatest fight extravaganza in the history of boxing. And "extravaganza" is not too strong a word.

On three successive days, September 5, 6, 7, 1892, the city's Olympic Club, located on Royal Street, hosted three championship bouts.

First, there was Jack McAuliff against Bob Meyer for the lightweight title; then George Dixon against Jack Skelly for the featherweight title, and, finally, what is still perhaps the most memorable of all prize fights, John L. Sullivan opposing James J. Corbett.

All the drama of sports was tied up in this one.

The Boston Strong Boy against Gentleman Jim.

The rough customer against the fancy dan.

The puncher against the boxer.

The old-timer, the people's choice, the fading hero, against the young upstart.

For newspapers around the country, it was the biggest sports night in their history—as people waited on downtown street corners to hear and see "flashes" of the fight's progress. It was the night, also, more than any other, that sportswriting came alive, as reporters, caught up in the drama, discussed Corbett's surprising victory and Sullivan's equally surprising magnanimous reaction to his loss.

"Gentlemen," he was quoted by *the Picayune* as saying to the press after the fight, "all I have to say is that I've stayed once too long. I met a young man. I'm glad the championship remains in America, with one of her own people."

New Orleans' claim to being the ring capital of the nation was undisputed for many years . . . and was re-established for a few years again between 1910 and 1915. During those two periods, every boxer of note appeared in New Orleans and the city hosted championship bouts in every weight division. From then on, New Orleans would be an occasional fight town, a good one generally, but not big time. The area would produce several champions, like Pete Herman, Tony Canzoneri, Willie Pastrano, and Ralph Dupas, and a number of near champions including Joe Mandot, Martin Burke, Happy Littleton, Johnny Coulon, Pal Moran and Tony Marullo, to name but a few of the professionals. And the top amateur was Loyola's Eddie Flynn, an Olympic winner.

What else was there to do in the New Orleans of the last century, as it grew, during the ante-bellum years, into a cosmopolitan city, and put aside some of its meaner pastimes?

There was, indeed, plenty—for spectators or participants.

Fencing which had been a way of life—and death—became a sport, with organized groups, including the Orleans Fencing

Club and the Bayou St. John Fencing Club, providing public exhibitions at such places as the Grunewald Hall, at a site now occupied by the Roosevelt Hotel.

One not-so-gentlemanly recreational experience, which developed in the '50's, after all the animal fights except those between cocks had been banned, was the "rat hunt."

This highly unpalatable sport, which continued even after the war, provided sport for dog owners and some relief, presumably, for the city's residents.

In these events which were held irregularly, dog owners paid an entry fee of $2.50 for their animals to enter a contest to determine which could kill the greatest number of some 1500 rats which would be released for their pleasure. Prizes for the dog collecting the most rats ran as high as $500 in cash or prizes.

And, aside from the citizenry which benefitted from the elimination of many rats, there were others who profited also— the rat collectors who, taking advantage of an offer made through a newspaper ad, provided rats for the hunt masters at the rate of 15 cents a dozen.

There were at the middle of the century, carriage racing opportunities, under the sponsorship of the New Orleans Trotting and Pacing Club. Their course was the Old Shell Road leading to the lake.

In 1849 the Southern Yacht Club, antedated today in the United States only by the New York Yacht Club (founded five years earlier), already was holding regattas. And within a few years there was another, the Crescent City Yacht Club, which restricted its races to craft smaller than those of the SYC.

Rowing clubs proliferated, beginning as early as the '30's, with racing on the river, on Lake Pontchartrain and on the New Basin Canal.

The Empire Baseball Club and the Louisiana Baseball Club were operating in 1859 and met each other in September of that year in a monumental battle which the Empires won 77–64.

The Crescent City Cricket Club and the Pelican Cricket

Club were playing each other and teams from Mobile on a regular basis.

And, surprisingly, about the time of the war, the most popular spectator sport had become balloon ascensions, the spectators lured not only by the mysteries of flight but by the fact that there were extensive wagering opportunities—bettors guessing how far the balloon would travel before being forced down.

There was swimming in the river, in canals, and in the lake, at the old resort known as Milneberg.

In vogue for a while, also, was "pedestrianism", a sport which generally included professional runners traveling the nation, competing against each other, or against time.

A favorite of the '40's and '50's was William Jackson who, on one occasion, attempted to walk eleven miles in one hour for a purse of $2,000. *The Picayune* noted that he failed by ten seconds.

Women, too, performed in this specialty, traveling from town to town. Occasionally, local champions were developed to compete against the visiting stars.

In fact, what is believed to be the last important walking race in New Orleans, on March 11, 1878, was a 400-mile contest between Henry Schmehl and Ellen Wicker on an indoor track in Grunewald Hall. Schmehl won in 119 hours, 41 minutes and 5 seconds and received a $1,000 purse. Mrs. Wickers, a young widow with an infant child, so impressed the audience, however, that they took up a collection for her.

There was bowling and target shooting and gymnastics, and billiards, a sport which also had its touring experts coming to town to give exhibitions.

And although bull-baiting had been banned, there were occasional bull fights, featuring matadors from Mexico.

Another unusual post-war sport was the ring tournament, modeled after the contests of the knights of another era. Riders, armed with lances, rode horseback along a prescribed course and attempted to pierce rings which had been suspended above the track on frames resembling gallows. The riders called themselves knights and their contests jousts. They rode for "the honor of fair southern maidens," and after each tournament the winner was allowed to chose a "Queen of Love and Beauty."

In the last part of the nineteenth century, another sport which was in vogue for about twenty years was cycling, first with the tall-wheeled bicycles and later with models which approximated the bikes of today.

Regular races were run and on occasions there were special events, such as endurance rides from the city to Baton Rouge. Perhaps the highlight of the whole period was the feat of three New Orleanians who, in 1886, rode high-wheelers from New Orleans to Boston in thirty days, covering more than 1600 miles. They crossed rivers and bays en route by riding over railroad bridges and even used the railroad right of way when country roads were impassable.

As the century was drawing to a close track and field events were begun, sailing still had its enthusiasts, hunting and fishing were still good, tennis was being played, golf had been introduced, and croquet, trapshooting and roller skating were popular. Steamboat races captured columns of type in the newspapers. And for about twenty-five years after the start of the twentieth century polo, played at Jackson Barracks, had a dedicated following.

Hunting good? Well, one description of hunting at the turn of the century would develop a massive case of envy in the modern hunter, restricted as he is by game regulations:

"The hunting trains during the hunting season over the Louisville & Nashville railroad, are always crowded with regular hunters and their friends, whom they are taking over, and when they return Sunday night the amount of game that is brought in is something extraordinary. Over every seat is hung a bunch of ducks, and the baggage car besides is loaded full."

New Orleans also, through the talents of Miss Clara G. Baer, director of physical education at Newcomb college, presented the nation with two new games—"basquettes" and "Newcomb."

Basquettes was somewhat like basketball, with seven players

on each team, each player being assigned to a particular sector of the court, the baskets at diagonal corners of the court rather than at each end. It was designed primarily for girls. Newcomb was a version of volleyball, with a rope replacing the net, the players allowed to throw or bat the ball across the rope, and the court adjustable to accommodate any number of players. Apparently both achieved widespread—and short-lived—popularity.

But the three most significant things as the nineteenth century drew to a close were the increase in the popularity of baseball, the introduction of football, which was to become, in time, the No. 1 spectator sport for New Orleanians, and the sudden growth of opposition to racially mixed competition. Up until then mixed teams competed in baseball and racquettes, Negro jockeys rode alongside white ones and Negro and white boxers fought each other regularly. By the turn of the century such mixed competition had all but disappeared, not to reappear again until the second half of the twentieth century.

Baseball and football along with horseracing, were easily the principal items in the New Orleans sports diet until well into the twentieth century.

The rise and fall of professional baseball in New Orleans began with amateur and semipro teams, some of them of enough consequence that they toured other cities to perform, and some of them good enough so that Finney noted that New Orleans was the place where the Cincinnati Red Stockings "discovered five different amateur teams capable of beating them."

For many years New Orleans was baseball crazy—and, in fact, the participation phase of the sport still draws thousands of residents of the area.

As the professional sport was being developed, there were teams representing social clubs. There was a Catholic League; a league for every kind of worker, banker, jeweler, telegrapher, government employee; a Commercial League, a Rowing Club League, an Association of Gymnastic Clubs; there were women's teams; there were all Negro teams and there were teams of whites and Negroes.

That the city was a baseball town should have been obvious to any promotion-minded individual who read *the Daily Picayune* of March 10, 1899:

"The B.A. (baseball) season having opened, there is still ground for hope that there is life in the old land yet, and that whatever be the condition of the state debt . . . the sweet consciousness remains that the baseball business is being properly attended to."

A professional team representing the city participated in the Gulf League early in the '80's and in 1886 New Orleans became a member of the Southern League, later to become the Southern Association. The following year the club won its first pennant, under manager-pitcher Abner Powell.

Powell was an organizer, financier, promoter and idea man. It was he who kept pro baseball alive in the south at the outset, helping finance other clubs as well as his own . . . and at one time he was part owner of four of the teams in the league.

It was Powell who introduced Ladies' Day and the "rain check" to professional baseball.

The New Orleans team, the Pelicans, was in its heyday under the managership of Larry Gilbert, who directed the club from 1922 to 1938, and won pennants in 1923, 1926, 1927, 1933 and 1934.

With Gilbert's departure to become manager and general manager of the Nashville team in the same association, the Pelicans' fortunes dwindled—and so did their fans.

From then on the demise of the Pelicans and of minor league baseball in a cosmopolitan city seemed only a matter of time.

Eventually their playing field, Heineman Park, later Pelican Stadium, at Tulane and Carrollton avenues, was sold and turned into a motel. The Pelicans gave up the ghost in 1959 in a makeshift ball park in City Park stadium, a site which provided 25,000 seats for a few hundred fans nightly, and a left field so short that the kids behind its screen caught more baseballs than did the left fielder.

New Orleans has been noted nationally, however, for the players it produced.

Natives of the metropolitan area who made it to the big leagues included Mel Ott, a member of baseball's hall of fame, and other such stars as Zeke Bonura, Mel Parnell, Howie Pollet, Hal Bevan, Bo Strickland, Al Flair, Al Jurisich, Johnny Oulliber, John (Fats) D'Antonio, Connie Ryan, Chuck Klein, Oyster Joe Martina, Dutch Leggett, Carl Lind, Eddie Morgan, Ray Yochim, Jack Kramer and Rusty Staub. And, of course, there was the city's No. 1 baseball family, the Gilberts. Larry, who had played with the Boston Braves' "miracle team" of 1914, sent two sons, Charlie and Harold (Tookie) to the big leagues.

Baseball is still big here with massive summer kid programs offering leagues for players of all ages, primarily through the city's recreation department and another New Orleans novelty, its Commercial Athletic Association, made up of business houses in the city.

Both the recreation department and the commercial league also offer a wide variety of sports throughout the year to New Orleanians who want to play.

Racing was in trouble as the century grew to a close. The character of the horsemen had changed over the years. No longer were wealthy plantation owners racing their stock against each other. It had become a big business and, without the careful kind of supervision the sport receives today, the manipulators got a foothold.

Fixers began operating, arranging the races to profit on the gambling. Soon the idea grew that all racing was dishonest and the citizenry began complaining. Finally, in 1908 the state Legislature was prevailed upon to outlaw racing and tracks were closed until Jan. 1, 1915, when the Fair Grounds reopened under new controls designed to prevent the fix.

After that the Fair Grounds regained its place among the outstanding tracks in the country and has remained among the better ones, although with the development of tracks in the East, in Florida and on the West Coast, New Orleans long ago lost its place as the racing capital of the nation.

Football, which is generally agreed to be the city's top spectator sport, was slow in arriving in New Orleans.

"Intercollegiate" football, in fact, was introduced to New Orleanians several years before the city had its first team, the Tulane club of 1893.

The game was introduced in 1889 by a number of college students on vacation from Princeton, Yale, Massachusetts Institute of Technology, Virginia and Notre Dame and some students from Tulane.

They divided themselves into two teams which they labeled Princeton and Yale and staged a contest.

Yale won 6–0 in a game which ended before it was due to. The contest had to be terminated because one of the players kicked the only ball they had into a canal adjoining the playing field and it could not be found.

Tulane's first team played three games losing two of them but winning the one which has become traditionally its most important—the match with Louisiana State University.

The following year the season was extended to four games and the full trappings of the game were added. There were prepared cheers, organized cheering sections and cowbells, horns and musical instruments to add to the enjoyment.

And the fans—and the newspapers—also—already were demanding winners.

In fact after the 1894 Tulane team lost all four of its contests *the Picayune* published a cartoon which recommended that the university abandon football for more suitable games like marbles or croquet.

Tulane's Green Wave enjoyed many successful seasons and produced a number of outstanding players, including such All America team selections as Charles (Peggy) Flournoy, Willis (Bill) Banker, Jerry Dalrymple, Don Zimmermann, Claude (Monk) Simons Jr., Ralph Wenzel, Harley McCollum, Tommy O'Boyle, Ernie Blandin, Lester Gatewood, W. A. Jones, Paul Lea, Eddie Price, Jerome Heluin, Tony Sardisco and Tommy Mason.

Most memorable team was that of 1931 which went undefeated in eleven contests, while allowing the opposition a total of

35 points. This team was selected for the Rose Bowl where it finally had its string snapped on Jan. 1, 1932, with a 21–12 loss to Southern California.

The Greenies defeated Temple 20–14 in the first Sugar Bowl game on Jan. 1, 1935 after a 9–1 season. In its only other bowl appearance, in the 1940 Sugar Bowl, Tulane lost to Texas A&M 14–13 after posting eight wins and one tie during the regular season.

Since 1956, the Tulane team had not had a winning season, until the 1966 season when a new coach, Jim Pittman, provided the spark which enabled them to win five games, while losing four and tying one.

The only other major college football in New Orleans was played for a few seasons by Tulane's next-door neighbor, Loyola, which abandoned the sport during the depression years. Their greatest star was Bucky Moore whose running exploits rivaled those of the great Red Grange. Loyola made one lasting contribution to the game, introducing night football to the area.

The rise and fall of the Pelicans, the departure of Loyola from the grid scene and the decline of the fortunes of Tulane, would have made the sports scene in New Orleans in the recent past very grim indeed had it not been for the development of the Sugar Bowl, the Greater New Orleans Open Golf Tournament and, just recently, the entry of New Orleans into professional football and basketball circles.

There were occasional happenings which relieved the city's hunger for sports heroes and heroics.

Occasions when New Orleans athletes like Emmett Toppino, Roland Romero, Sidney Bowman and Lloyd Bourgeois were named to the U.S. Olympic track teams; when Gilbert Gray captured the star class Olympic sailing title in 1932 and when Gene Walet Jr. sailed in the 1956 and 1960 Olympics.

Occasions, such as in 1954 when the Loyola basketball team won the National Association of Intercollegiate Athletics championship—the high water mark in basketball in a city which has not generally taken to the game.

Or when Marian Turpie won the Southern Women's Golf Championship in 1926, 1928, and 1931. She still is the only New Orleanian ever to hold that title.

Or when Tulane's tennis teams, traditionally among the nation's finest, brought National Collegiate Athletic Association titles to New Orleans with the rackets of Ernie Sutter, Jack Tuero, Ham Richardson, Jose Aguero, Ron Holmberg and Crawford Henry. Sutter and Richardson won the singles titles twice, Tuero and Aguero, once each, and Holmberg and Henry won the doubles crown twice.

Or when Fred Lamprecht and Vince D'Antoni won the NCAA golf titles, and golfers Nelson Whitney and Freddie Haas brought fame to New Orleans.

When the Papoose, and then the Jesuit team, won the American Legion's Little World Series.

When the power boat races were being staged on Lake Pontchartrain or when the pro bowlers finally picked New Orleans as one of the top on their tour.

But it was the Sugar Bowl and the New Orleans Open which continued to give New Orleans a regular place in the nation's sports sun.

In view of the time at which it began, the Sugar Bowl was a daring venture.

Business leaders who formed the New Orleans Mid-Winter Sports Association in 1934, with an appeal to residents of the area to subscribe funds to guarantee the proposed events, were running against the depression tide.

As with pro football, action did not come quickly.

For seven years sports editor Fred Digby of the New Orleans *Item* battled for the establishment of a program to rival the Rose Bowl, before the community acted—almost exactly the same number of years, incidentally, which transpired between the time when a sports columnist in the *New Orleans States-Item* started a campaign for pro football for New Orleans and the date, in 1967, when the Saints became a reality.

But in October, 1934, the sports association was able to

announce that $30,000 had been subscribed to guarantee participating teams $15,000 each, and that a game would be played the following January 1.

As a matter of fact the promotion was an instant success, the Tulane-Temple game attracting 22,026 fans to Tulane stadium and providing each team with $27,800, a much larger return than the guarantee.

The growth of the Sugar Bowl's popularity is reflected in the growth of Tulane stadium, for which the Mid-Winter Sports Association agreed to provide funds in return for use of the structure for its annual games.

In 1937 some 14,000 seats were added; two years later 20,000 more and in 1947 approximately 12,000 more, giving the stadium a current capacity of 80,985.

The Sugar Bowl program is much more than a football game. In addition to its principal attraction, the sports association offers a regatta, a tennis tournament, a track meet and a basketball tournament. Amateur fights once were part of the program but were eliminated as colleges dropped boxing from their roster of intercollegiate athletics.

Today the Sugar Bowl is a tradition, bringing New Orleans and tens of thousands of visitors an exciting week of sports each year.

It was noted in the *Standard History of New Orleans* in 1900 that "The game of golf is recent in New Orleans, but is firmly established here, as in all large American cities who have followed the fashion of England and New York in reviving the ancient game of Scotland. In Audubon park there are several golf links, and the players operate upon them frequently."

However firmly established it may have been then, golf still was a slow starter in New Orleans.

A Scotsman named George Turpie, father of Marian, is generally conceded to be the father of golf in New Orleans.

Turpie who had caddied for Henry Vardon when Vardon won the British Open, came here as a teaching pro.

His fame was considerable, for he divided his teaching time

between New Orleans and Pasadena where he wintered. Among his pupils was John D. Rockefeller.

Joe Bartholomew was also a famous teacher and a designer of golf courses and many golfers say that had he not been a Negro he also would have been a champion player.

In spite of their efforts, golf in New Orleans long remained a rich man's game and as late as 1957 there were only seven courses in the area. Since then nine additional courses have been added, and all of them generally have players waiting in line to tee off.

Significantly all of this building has occurred since a number of golf enthusiasts got together in 1957 to plan to have New Orleans added to the professional golfers' tour.

Early efforts to secure sponsors for the first New Orleans Open were directed at a modest tournament offering a total purse of $20,000.

The first two tournaments were successful and for the third one, in 1960, the purse was raised to $27,000. It was raised again the following year to $30,000; in 1963 to $40,000; in 1964 to $50,000, and in 1965 to $100,000, making the New Orleans stop one of the top tournaments on the pros' tour.

It is a favorite of the professional golfers, as each year almost all of the ranking players participate in the New Orleans Open.

It was the success of the New Orleans Open, as much as anything, that prompted the beginning of a campaign to bring a professional football team to New Orleans.

One straw man after another had to be knocked down.

And then, finally, in 1966, came the announcement of the awarding of a National Football League franchise to New Orleans; the approval by the voters of the state of a bond issue to finance the construction of a new "superdome" stadium; the selection of New Orleans for a franchise in the new American Basketball Association, and the glut of rumors, pending the construction of the stadium, that New Orleans would acquire a major league baseball franchise.

New Orleans, which had once been the sports center of the nation, was arriving again.

New Orleans, which had been the leader, had watched the parade pass it by. Its citizens developed a complex that their city was a "two-bit town."

And now suddenly everything was coming its way again.

New Orleans, on the eve of its 250th birthday, was big league again—in every way.

The Music of New Orleans

Henry Arnold Kmen

Ask someone nowadays what comes to mind when New Orleans is mentioned in connection with music, and the answer will usually be jazz. The birth of jazz is reason enough to tell the story of music in New Orleans. But there is another compelling reason: had you asked someone the same question during much of the nineteenth century, the answer given would have been opera. For New Orleans also gave birth to America's first, and for a long time its only resident opera company. Many held the New Orleans French opera to be as good as or better than any in France outside of Paris, and it was high on the traveler's list of things to be seen.

Many Americans who never got to New Orleans saw and heard the New Orleans opera during the eight tours it made to New York and other cities of the Northeast between 1827 and 1845.

Along with the opera in New Orleans was a multitude of other musical activities. Someone once said that he always found this city to be half way between a ball and a parade—an apt description that was even more true throughout the nineteenth century. As for balls, a well-known actor who played in New Orleans in the late 1830's described the city as "one vast waltzing and gallopading Hall." And as for parades, by 1838 the New Orleans *Picayune* reported that the passion for horns and trumpets had reached the stage of "a real mania."

Concerts too were abundant, ranging from intimate rooms with four to eight instrumentalists and singers, to large halls in which a full orchestra played overtures, symphonies, and accompaniments for vocal and instrumental solos. It was not unusual for an orchestra or other combination of instruments to perform in church, often as part of the service. On one such occasion in 1837, an orchestra of sixty musicians played a Grand Mass and a Te Deum in the St. Louis Cathedral.

Amateurs were as numerous as professionals, frequently combining with the latter in concerts and occasionally augmenting the opera orchestra. One society of amateurs, Les Amis des Arts, joined with the boat clubs of New Orleans to offer a spectacular floating concert. The orchestra played on an illuminated barge with the tug and escort boats also bedecked with lights. Followed by a flotilla of other craft, they sailed slowly down the river to constant applause from the crowds lining the shores. So successful was this nautical concert that the next year the musicians filled two barges.

Music stores were so plentiful that the music trade was a major industry in New Orleans. By 1840 close to one thousand pianos had entered the city and over eighty businesses had dealt in music. In the decade 1831–1841, out of twenty-six stores which handled music, twenty-one were in music exclusively, ten carried large stocks of pianos, and two published music largely composed locally.

Music simply permeated New Orleans, and until the 1850's this city was undeniably the musical capital of America. Indeed it was the site of a cultural flowering in the Old South that in its own way rivaled the literary flowering of New England. And since the latter-day end product was jazz, the importance of New Orleans' music is doubly evident.

The first milestone in the growth of music in New Orleans was the year 1792. On October 4 the first public ballroom opened. Dancing of course was already a favorite pastime, occurring wherever there was a suitable place such as a warehouse or hotel. But the Condé Street Ballroom was the first building devoted exclusively to dancing. To hear the delighted residents tell about it, it was superior to any in the world, but in truth it was simply a one-story wooden building measuring about eighty by thirty feet. During the next fifty years, however, over eighty identifiable locations for dancing plus a host of unnamed taverns and cabarets would appear. At one end of the scale were ballrooms rife with disorder, thievery, and prostitution, while at the other end were ballrooms such as the Orleans, the St. Charles, and the St. Louis—unsurpassed anywhere in splendor and decorum.

Thus every class and condition of people in New Orleans could find a compatible place to dance. And this was well because already by 1803 when the Americans took possession of the city, dancing was a necessity of life. In a very short time Commissioner William C. C. Claiborne discovered that one of his immediate and pressing problems concerned dancing. The only serious disorders confronting the new régime occurred in the ballrooms when arguments arose over the choice between French or English dances. These fights erupted into near riots. Moreover, when a delegation of anxious Frenchmen called on Claiborne, he found that their most pressing concern was dancing: rumors had spread that the Americans intended to clamp down on the ballrooms. Claiborne hastened to reassure them on this vital point, and began attending the dances himself in order to give further assurance. Six weeks after his arrival, Claiborne reported on all this to Secretary of State James Madison. He apologized for bringing up a matter that must seem trivial to Madison, but he assured the secretary that in New Orleans dancing was foremost in the mind of the public.

Dancing was a popular recreation throughout the Western World at that time, but it was much more than this in New Orleans. Travelers from all over Europe and America were struck by the absolute passion for dancing that they observed in this city. As one put it, "in the winter they dance to keep warm, and in the summer they dance to keep cool." Others declared that

New Orleanians danced in the city, in the country, and everywhere; that they would pass all their days and nights at dancing if they could; that neither severe heat nor cold ever stopped them from dancing; or that they could dance for days in a row without tiring. There was one tired resident, though, who complained that if the love of dancing in the city became any worse people would never see bed again. Since some of the dances began in the afternoon, and some even in the morning, to be followed by others that ran until dawn, his fear is understandable.

The majority of the balls were simply public affairs where one paid at the door. Here whatever selectivity existed was determined by the price. The really select balls were open to subscription only wherein one signed for a series of six to ten balls.

But whether public or select, the masked balls were the most popular. One could be so much bolder when disguised. Protected by the anonymity of a mask, a stranger could ask a lady to dance and not be refused. Neither birth, wealth, nor color made any difference, observed one entranced witness. Another was struck by the sight of a teen-age apprentice being familiar with a lady of high social standing. Moreover, covering the face encouraged uncovering elsewhere. Thus, wrote a man who claimed to disapprove, the ladies often had "every other part of their bodies exposed, if not to sight, at least to touch." The restraint on sight served more than a moral purpose: properly disguised, "there is no discovering whether they are black or white." No wonder the dance was so attractive in New Orleans.

In the beginning, the isolated location of the city and the polyglot nature of its population made dancing simply the most feasible recreational and social function. Then as the city grew, other factors kept dancing preeminent. Fine food and drink, gambling, summer gardens, trips on the lake and river, free carriages, entertainment, and the chance to "turn on" by inhaling laughing gas, were only a few of the attractions that went with dancing. Add to this the opportunity for masked adventures and few could resist.

In case anyone could, however, New Orleans had something special in reserve. This was the so-called quadroon ball. This attraction first appeared in November, 1805, when one Auguste Tessier advertised dances on Wednesdays and Saturdays for white men and free colored women only.

For some years prior to 1805 balls had been held ostensibly for the free colored people of New Orleans; but in actuality these affairs were attended by numerous slaves as well as by soldiers, sailors, and other whites. In addition were the taverns—it was charged that they could be found on every street corner—where "white and black, free and slave, mingled indiscriminately." To these came fathers and sons together without shame "to revel and dance . . . for whole nights with a lot of men and women of saffron color, or quite black, either free or slave."

But the exclusion of all except white men and free colored women was something new. Thus restricted, these dances proved an instant success with the result that soon there were several ballrooms in the city where such restrictions were applied two or more nights a week.

The quadroon balls became so popular, in fact, that they cut seriously into the supply of white male dancers—to the detriment of the white balls. Men who began their evening at a white ball had a habit of slipping away to a quadroon ball at the first opportunity, leaving the white ladies short of partners and tempers. When the ladies thus neglected complained, one man defended his fellows by accusing the ladies of being too cold. So the men, as he put it, desert "the white privets to gather black grapes." "Every clerk and scrivener," wrote the actor Louis Tasistro, "who can muster up a few dollars, hurries to these unhallowed sanctuaries, and launches unreservedly into every species of sensual indulgence; every flat-boatman or cattle dealer . . . finds his way to these abodes of enchantment. . . . Nor is it unusual to see members of the legislature mingle freely with these motley groups."

But why dwell on dancing? Did it contribute to the growth of serious music? In New Orleans it did. In fact, it was vital. Had dancing been only a peripheral activity, it would have little importance; but the fact that it was central, that there were so many ballrooms, and so many dances, makes the sheer quantity important. For here was the extra employment necessary to attract and keep the caliber of musicians needed to staff the opera. Furthermore, the income from dancing helped directly and indirectly to make up opera deficits. Ballroom proprietors underwrote the city's first theatre, opened the second one, and finally built the Orleans Theatre.

As if to emphasize the connection between dancing and opera, the city's first theatre, a small building on St. Peter Street, opened on the same day (October 4, 1792) as did the first public ballroom. There is, however, no specific record of any opera until May 22, 1796, when a little group performed *Sylvain* by André Gretry. It is clear that there had been previous performances of *Sylvain* and other operas, but they are recorded only indirectly.

The company was made up of actors and musicians who sought refuge in New Orleans from the upheavals of the age. They came not in a body but individually from France, from the West Indies, and from the United States. Almost at once they were in financial trouble, and in 1799 the owner of a ballroom on St. Philip Street undertook to make good the theatre's losses in return for the exclusive right to run dances for the free colored. Later this same man, Bernardo Coquet, converted his ballroom into the city's second theatre.

In 1800, after eight years of precarious existence, the little house on St. Peter Street was forced to close, ostensibly because of a seating dispute between the civil and military authorities. For two years it remained closed, then opened briefly. By the end of 1803 the house was so decrepit that the authorities declared it unsafe. After a minimum of repairs the theatre opened again late in 1804.

Beginning with the season of 1805–1806, the record of opera performances in the theatre on St. Peter Street is fairly complete and certainly impressive. In a period of a little over five and one-half years, New Orleans was treated to at least three hundred and seventy-four performances of ninety-two operas. The leading opera composers of that day—Pierre Monsigny, Nicolas Dalayrac, André Gretry, François Boieldieu, Etienne Mehul, Domenique Della Maria, and more—were all familiar to New Orleans. And on December 10, 1805, the opera was Giovanni Paisiello's *Il Barbiere di Siviglia,* playing very probably for the first time in the United States.

When the theatre on St. Peter Street finally closed on December 9, 1810, the company simply moved four blocks to another theatre ready and waiting on St. Philip Street. This had been the ballroom owned by Bernardo Coquet wherein he had run dances for the free colored, and where took place the first dances restricted to white men and colored women.

Coquet had been intensely interested in the theatre ever since he financed it in 1799. As the inadequacies of the St. Peter Street structure became more and more apparent, Coquet decided to venture fully into the theatrical world. He gathered some disgruntled performers from the original theatre and put benches on his ballroom floor. Promising a larger stage than the one on St. Peter Street, Coquet opened the St. Philip Street Theatre on January 30, 1808, with the opera, *Une Folie* by Mehul.

So now there were two theatres. Both, according to an impressed observer, were generally crowded. But the city then contained only about 15,000 people all told, scarcely enough to crowd two opera houses once the novelty wore off. Furthermore there simply were not enough singers and instrumentalists to supply two opera companies. So long as the two houses offered performances on alternate nights they were in trouble only at the box office; but as soon as they both tried to run on Sundays, the most lucrative day, they faced an impossible situation in the orchestra.

Everyone concerned knew that a solution had to be found. So Coquet proposed that they all use the older house exclusively while he remodeled his ballroom on St. Philip Street. When all was finished, they would sell the theatre on St. Peter Street and move to the new one. For eighteen months they stalled and argued before they finally realized that this was the only feasible plan. Throughout most of 1810, opera played only on St. Peter Street, while the alterations on St. Philip Street progressed. Chiefly these consisted of pitching the flat ballroom floor, and building "upper boxes for women of color."

The remodeled St. Philip Street Theatre opened on December 20, 1810, with a double bill of operas: Gretry's *Sylvain* and Dalayrac's *Adolphe et Clara.* For the next nine years the converted ballroom would be the principal opera house in the city, until the first really suitable structure, the famous Orleans Theatre, opened its doors.

During those nine years New Orleans saw no fewer than five hundred performances of well over one hundred different operas. Among these was the American premier of Mehul's *Joseph* on April 21, 1812. *Joseph* required an all-male cast and musically it marked an important advance in the development of opera. It was a remarkable achievement for what was still a frontier town, and for a decade marked by war and invasion. When the St. Philip handed the baton to the new theatre on Orleans Street, New Orleans stood on the threshhold of its great days of opera.

We must now go back some years to the time when the first of two men came to this city. Their names were Louis Tabary and John Davis. Early in 1803 Tabary emigrated from Provence, where he was born, to Saint Domingue. Some time between the summers of 1804 and 1805 he moved to New Orleans. For the next quarter-century he was a part of the theatre—acting, directing, planning, and building. In July, 1805, his name first appears on a letter he sent to the City Council proposing a new theatre. The following March he became director of the theatre on St. Peter Street, but he had already purchased land and hired an architect. The 70-by-153 foot lot was located on Orleans Street between Bourbon and Royal. Here on October 6, 1806, with the governor, the city officials, and the shareholders looking on, Tabary laid the first brick of the Orleans Theatre.

It would take nine long years to complete—years full of strife and struggle for Tabary. When he was not in the middle of the frequent quarrels among the actors and musicians, he was involved in lawsuits, sheriff's sales, and other financial troubles connected with the new building. Somehow he kept on directing and improving the opera, and he kept on building and raising the money until on October 19, 1815, the new theatre opened with Pierre Gaveaux's opera *Un Quart Heure de Silence.*

The event should have marked the end of the St. Philip Street Theatre, since the new house, seating 1,448, was not only larger but had been from the beginning designed for opera. But in its very first summer Tabary's new theatre burned to the ground, forcing him and his troupe sadly back to St. Philip Street.

There is no telling what the future of opera in New Orleans might have been if John Davis had not now taken a hand. Davis had come from Saint Domingue seven years before. In New Orleans he rapidly prospered in several business ventures, including the operation of ballrooms. At the time of the fire he had been planning to lease the ballroom belonging to the Orleans Theatre and destroyed with it.

Before 1816 ended Davis bought the grounds and ruins. He promised to rebuild everything in the shortest possible time and more elegantly than before. He pledged also to recruit new artists and musicians in Europe.

Davis hoped to have his theatre completed early in 1819, but as it turned out the structure was not ready until late in that year. It was November 27 when New Orleans' newest home for opera opened with a double bill—Boieldieu's *Jean de Paris* and Henri Berton's *Les Maris Garçons.*

The theatre was part of a complex of buildings that included Davis's Hotel and the Orleans Ballroom. Never seating many over thirteen hundred, it was not a pretentious building. The loges were not as well placed as they might have been; there were seats where one could neither hear nor see well; and the sound from the corridors intruded at times. But for the time and place it was a splendid achievement. One interesting feature was a section of latticed boxes for people in mourning who did not wish to be seen enjoying an opera.

On the stage and in the orchestra was a considerable number of fresh faces from Europe as Davis had promised. The newcomers took most of the opera leads, the first chairs in the orchestra, and the conductor's podium. On the other hand, Tabary was named manager of the new company. More struggles and more despair were yet to come, but from the opening of the second Orleans Theatre the general course of opera in New Orleans would be upward.

Each year Davis recruited more personnel from Europe, and in 1822 he brought the first regular ballet troupe to the city. (Hitherto local dancing teachers had supplied the choreography.) Thus by the season of 1822–23, opera at the Orleans Theatre was performed by a company almost wholly imported, of substantial size and artistry, and possessed of a proper ballet. One notable event that season was the introduction of Gioacchino Rossini's *The Barber of Seville* on March 4, 1823.

The New Orleans opera was by now without equal in America, but Davis continued to find himself beset with financial problems. Were it not for his profits from the ballroom, hotel, and the gambling room in the theatre, he might well have been forced to let the opera go under. For one thing, he faced competition. Not only had an American theatre been built on Camp Street, but a second French theatre operated from time to time in the old St. Philip Theatre. It was composed of artists and musicians who, for one reason or another, were no longer in the Orleans company. The biggest problem though was simply the long hot summer. Davis kept going through four summers until June, 1824, when he was forced to close the Orleans Theatre for the first time since its opening.

In the following January, Davis got his theatre running again. With remarkable faith he continued to improve the company each year, bringing it to a new artistic high with the premiere of Boieldieu's masterpiece *La Dame Blanche* on February 6, 1827.

But summer had no regard for excellence and the problem persisted. Why not simply close each summer? The trouble here lay in the fact that the troupe was imported. If Davis hired his artists for one season only, he would have to pay two-way passage each year as well as annual recruiting costs. If he engaged the company for longer periods, he had to find a way to get through the summers. It was for this reason that Davis took his entire company to the cities of the North in the summer of 1827.

For the next seven years—from 1827 to 1833—the French Opera Company of New Orleans toured the major cities of the Atlantic seaboard during the summers, except in 1832 when cholera crippled most theatrical life. The reception accorded these tours affords a good index to the caliber of Davis's company. In the North they were performing before audiences who had no considerations of Creole patriotism or civic pride to color judgment.

Moreover, the company's introduction to New York occurred shortly after that city had its first prolonged taste of grand opera. Less than a year had elapsed since Manuel Garcia and "the first Italian opera troupe to visit the New World" had departed after a "very successful" season which ended in September, 1826. (That an authority on the period could write in 1949 that "American opera really began with the Manuel Garcia Company" only illustrates how unaccountably little is known about New Orleans opera.)

In the North the New Orleans company won an overwhelming critical success. Their balance of quality was especially praised. "It is not often the same troupe has five good singers," said the New York *American*. "This company is as good as those heard in the provinces of France and superior to those heard in the Capitals of Europe outside France."

The orchestra was hailed as the largest and best ever heard in the North, and this was before Davis enlarged it with more musicians just in from Germany. In Philadelphia it was the first time the audience heard the horn properly played. As one listener there put it, "not a single fault was committed by the instrumental performers, and this itself furnishes a great treat to those who, like us, have generally been obliged to make great allowances, even for the best orchestra we could assemble." In Boston one newspaper gladly conceded that "we have never before heard so good theatrical music."

And what a feast of opera was laid before those Northeastern cities. In their six summers, the New Orleans players presented 61 different operas by 24 composers for a total of 251 performances. New York heard 100, Philadelphia 109, Boston 12, and Baltimore 30.

Yet on their home grounds the company too often drew high praise but poor attendance. While the combination of a Sunday night with an opera like Carl Maria von Weber's *Der Freischutz* (*Robin des Bois*) could occasionally bring in enough money to repair the losses of Tuesdays and Thursdays; or the introduction of a new opera might fill the house for a while, these were insufficient props. Sundays came only once a week and new operas soon turned into old fare. Invoking patriotism and pride might help a little. The public was urged to remember that its French opera was unique in America; that if the Greeks had their Parthenon and the Romans their Pantheon, New Orleans had its French opera. "It is the pride and hope of the generation raised on the ruin of the old French régime."

Nor did the tours really help. However much acclaim the company received in the North, the cost and the road hazards of transporting a troupe now numbering over fifty persons made these tours dubious ventures and engendered internal dissension. When the company returned to New Orleans after the summer of 1833, it arrived "sadly bruised and wounded—it had had enough of the nomadic life." John Davis himself would never try the road again, although his successors did take the company to New York in 1843 and 1845 where again it won much praise but gained little profit.

At home, in the fourteen years since 1819, the Orleans Theatre had staged almost a thousand performances of over two hundred operas. Boieldieu's *La Dame Blanche,* Daniel Auber's

La Muette de Portici, Rossini's *Le Comte Ory*, and numerous others were introduced to America in New Orleans. The accomplishment is all the more striking when one considers that in New York the thirty years from 1825 to 1855 recorded nothing but a succession of companies and impresarios that failed.

By now Davis's job was nearly done. The growing population, the constantly improving quality of performance, the increasing pride New Orleanians took in their unique institution, and a genuine appreciation of the opera were combining to assure support. In fact the French opera was becoming so prestigious that its very success generated its most serious challenge—the introduction of Italian opera by John Caldwell in his new St. Charles Theatre.

Caldwell came to New Orleans in January, 1820, in charge of a theatrical group called the Virginia Company. Since this was the first season of the Orleans Theatre, Caldwell was able to rent the St. Philip. He was successful from the start, and in February he moved into the Orleans Theatre for four nights a week. He was soon building his own theatre on Camp Street in the American section of the city.

On January 1, 1824, the American theatre opened. While not primarily an opera house, by the end of its first decade it was presenting such musical fare as *The Beggar's Opera, Guy Mannering, Rob Roy, John of Paris, Masaniello, Fra Diovolo, The Barber of Seville,* and *The Marriage of Figaro.*

Early in 1835 both the Camp Street Theatre and the Orleans Theatre began rehearsing Giacomo Meyerbeer's *Robert le Diable.* To the consternation of the French, the Americans got their production staged first, on March 30, 1835. But the French were consoled by producing a much better version on May 12. *Robert* played eight times in the American theatre and seven in the French. So it was that within a three-month period that spring a theatre-goer in New Orleans could have heard two productions of *Robert le Diable* fifteen times. Though probably no one did.

Caldwell had leased out his theatre a year before and was now busy building on St. Charles Street the largest theatre in the United States. It opened on November 30, 1835, and the city now had three theatres for a population of only about 60,000, 25,000 of whom were whites, 20,000 slaves, and 15,000 free colored.

Within a week pleased patrons of the St. Charles Theatre concluded that its thirty-piece orchestra was "probably the best in the United States" with but one exception—the Orleans Theatre orchestra. Encouraged, Caldwell now prepared to contest the Orleans Theatre more directly. He enlarged his orchestra and engaged the G. B. Montressor Italian opera company, fresh from successes in London, New York, and Havana. For their opening on March 6, 1836, the Italians chose Vincenzo Bellini's *Il Pirata*. "Caldwell and his Italian opera company have taken the town by storm," said the New Orleans *Bee* with little exaggeration. *Il Pirata* played eight times; Rossini's *Otello* and his *Zelmira* four times each. The biggest success was Bellini's *Norma,* given ten times. For those Americans resentful of French superiority in opera, it was a happy time.

English opera continued at the St. Charles Theatre as well as on Camp Street. Thus the spring of 1836 saw a wealth of opera in New Orleans. On a Tuesday night in April, for example, one might attend the St. Charles Theatre to hear Rossini's *Cinderella* in English, or go to the Camp Street Theatre for Bellini's *La Sonnambula* in English, or to the Orleans Theatre where Auber's *Le Cheval de Bronze* was playing.

Next night the choice lay between Bellini's *Norma* at the St. Charles or his *La Sonnambula* at the Camp Street. During the single week of April 18–24, 1836, there were fourteen performances of nine operas. Four companies, two of them unsurpassed in the United States, played in three theatres, one the largest in the country. No other city in America offered so much certainly, and the next season promised to be even better as both major theatres strove to outdo each other.

Caldwell strengthened his already fine orchestra and prepared for the arrival of the best Italian opera company in this hemisphere, the Havana troupe directed by Francis Brichta. For his part, Davis recruited no fewer than thirty-six fresh artists from France plus twenty-one additional instrumentalists.

Caldwell's challenge, however, precipitated a crisis in the Orleans Theatre; and the shareholders, having grown increasingly restless under the one-man control of Davis, now persuaded him to step down. On April 15, 1837, a newly formed Orleans Theatre Company took over the administration from John Davis. Apparently he had sold his properties and contracts to the company.

The change from control by a single man to that of several was generally approved. *Le Moqueur*, a local journal devoted to music and opera, pointed out that in Paris, opera cost the government immense sums, and the paper further argued that a company should "be able to undertake expenses that a single director couldn't without risking his future." The journal expressed the hope that this would not be Davis's "last battle," but it proved to be precisely that. He died a little over two years later on June 13, 1839.

John Davis' contribution to opera in America has never been adequately recognized. His six tours of the Northern cities with his entire company were tremendous feats, the influence of which can never be measured. At the very least, Davis's tours kept Northern interest in opera alive during what were otherwise woefully bleak years.

But it was in New Orleans that all could see visible evidence of Davis' work. Before he died, he himself had the satisfaction of seeing his company successfully withstand the challenge of Caldwell's Italian opera and begin its years of greatness with the arrival of Julie Calvé in the fall of 1837. In truth the presence of a fine Italian company, imported expressly to rival the company

Davis built, was more a credit to him than to Caldwell. Fittingly, the Brichta company, introduced by Caldwell in the spring of 1837, ended its stay in New Orleans in Davis's theatre following a quarrel with Caldwell.

Most of all Davis had helped create an atmosphere conducive to the growth of music. As one grateful citizen declared: "We have now, in this place, what no city in America, and few cities in the world can boast of . . . strong companies in the English, French, and Italian languages, and what is more, they are all extremely well patronized." Or, as some others put it, "the opera . . . in New Orleans is unexceptionally the best which has ever been . . . in America."

With a city aware that it alone "formed a bright exception to the tasteless apathy and soullessness which have characterized the reception of opera in every other city in the United States," the future for opera in New Orleans looked secure, and indeed the French company played with few interruptions to 1919.

Before leaving the musical theatre of New Orleans it should be mentioned that both the French and English theatres brought much drama to the city. The permanent French company was a dramatic as well as a musical company. Those performers who were primarily actors usually sang in the chorus or took minor roles in the operas, while the operatic leads doubled in similar fashion for the dramas and comedies. Thus, over the years, the entire repertoire of the French dramatic theatre was presented in this city.

The English theatre relied more on touring companies or visiting stars. In this way the best plays and performers of the English stage came regularly to entertain New Orleans. Tyrone Power, James Hackett, Edwin Forest, and Joseph Jefferson were just a few of the great actors who appeared here.

In the end, however, the dramatic theatre in New Orleans was never more than a prime stop on the circuit, an echo of the New York theatre. As such it left no lasting impression to compare with that of the musical stage.

When *The Picayune* described New Orleans' love of brass as "a real mania" in 1838, it was not far off the mark. New Orleans surely did love a parade. Any occasion from the laying of a cornerstone to the blessing of a flag was reason enough for a parade. Because of the many nationalities in the city, there were an unusually large number of national holidays on which to parade. Militia companies, fire companies, secret lodges, and other organizations abounded—all with their marching bands.

On Sundays parades began bright and early, multiplying in number and increasing in fervor as the day wore on. It was not uncommon for a minister to have his sermon overpowered by the din of drum and trumpet. The organ and choir in the St. Louis Cathedral were often subdued by the sounds of fife and drums from the Place d'Armes directly across the street. On Sunday the whole city became a vast field of war, wrote one visitor, while another concluded that "the Sabbath in New Orleans exists only in its Almanacs." Bishop Henry Whipple sadly observed in his diary that "Sunday in New Orleans is a day when the music is dedicated to the God of war & not to the God of peace."

By the 1850's, New Orleans' reputation for Sunday parades had so spread that a slave in northern Alabama told Frederick Law Olmstead that slaves dreaded being sold down the river in New Orleans simply because there was no Sunday, no day of rest in that city where "dey drums and fifes de whole bressed day." But few in the city would have understood such a view. There might be an occasional complaint about bands "going about the city early on Sunday mornings, squeaking and rattle-te-banging away . . . and waking everybody." Most however were ready to join with the "boys, negroes, fruit women and whatnot" who fell in behind the bands "shouting and bawling and apparently delighted."

Less predictable but equally popular was the funeral parade. Marching to bury the dead was already a custom when Benjamin Henry Latrobe came to New Orleans in 1819. These burial parades were, he said, "peculiar to New Orleans alone among American cities." Latrobe thought the practice might have grown out of the Catholic procession of the Host. Whatever its origin, by 1808 at the time of the funeral of Colonel Macarty, a wealthy Creole planter, the procession had evolved into a full military parade. No doubt the Napoleonic wars and victories enhanced the appeal of military funerals.

By the 1830's frequent notices of funeral parades appeared in the newspapers. Members of militia companies, veterans of the Revolution and of the War of 1812, Masons, fire companies, benevolent societies, mechanics' societies, and numerous others all marched to bury their dead. It seemed only proper that the Masons parade in the funeral of a Catholic priest, Père Antoine: had not the good father always paraded in theirs?

Nor did the deceased necessarily have to be present. The death of a hero anywhere was sufficient reason to hold a parade—or even two, as when Lafayette died.

Only during epidemics did the city experience a surfeit of the "mournful notes of the death march customarily played by full brass bands en route to the grave." People, especially those in hospitals, were reminded all too often of their mortality. On the more cheerful side, the bands did strike up a "gay and lightsome air as they returned from the grave."

No hour was too extreme, no occasion too trivial, for a parade. The bands marched at 7 a.m. and they marched after midnight. At ten o'clock one summer night a Spanish militia company paraded with its band—wheeling a large cake before them. On holidays bands were out in every part of the city long before noon. And indeed why not? As *The Picayune* boasted in 1838, "our numerous martial bands . . . are perhaps unrivaled on this side of the Atlantic."

The mania for marching in New Orleans fitted perfectly with the love of dancing and the opera. Musicians who came to the city to join one of the theatre orchestras were usually able to augment their incomes by playing in bands and dance orchestras. Most of the band directors and orchestra leaders were theatre musicians.

It was a two-way street: the quality of dancing and marching music in New Orleans was vastly improved by the presence of so many imported musicians; while the money made available by means of these other activities enabled the theatres to attract the best musicians. Since most taught and gave frequent concerts in which they played with their students and with other professional and amateur musicians, the general level of music in New Orleans was significantly raised. Those who could played, and those who couldn't tried. You could hardly turn a corner, said *The Picayune* in 1838, without running into someone trying to blow.

Such then was the state of music in New Orleans as the nation drifted toward the Civil War. During the 1840's and 1850's the opera, now an established institution unique in America, enjoyed its best years. All visitors were urged to hear it, and all business men who hoped to do any business were practically forced to attend.

Few were disappointed. To a New Yorker this was not one "of your mushroom establishments which exist one day and are defunct the next . . . ; none of your half-and-halfs, whose orchestra is . . . temporary; . . . but an opera . . . worth your while; always good management; always good singing; always good instrumentation in the orchestra; always an agreeable fashionable and critical audience." To English visitors this opera had "perfection . . . found nowhere else"; its orchestra was the "best in America"; and the "Italian opera in London was never better." Best of all was the judgment of a French visitor who heard Meyerbeer's *Le Prophete*. Not only did he find the New Orleans opera better than anything in New York; it reminded him of Paris!

Once established, the pattern of music in New Orleans persisted. The opera remained a vital institution until 1919, although after the Civil War it gradually lost pre-eminence among the opera companies of the United States. Dancing and parading lost nothing in popularity, and in the end it was these vernacular activities that produced jazz.

Since the Negro played an indispensable part in the creation of jazz, we must now consider his relation to music in New Orleans. The free Negroes had been holding balls for some time prior to 1799 at which time the practice came under attack. The objection was that such dances "impudently imitated" those of the whites and that they drew "the majority of the slaves of this city."

Despite these objections the Free Colored dances never abated and the style of dancing and the music continued "impudently" to imitate the white. Nonetheless, tradition has long assigned to the Negroes a more primitive kind of dancing performed on the levees and in the public squares, especially Congo Square. Here the slaves of the city gathered on Sundays to relax until sundown. It is true that during the early years these dances resembled those of the West Indies, being accompanied with homemade drums and instruments. In 1819 Benjamin Latrobe came upon such a gathering:

"They were formed into circular groups in the midst of four of which . . . were two women dancing. They held each a coarse handkerchief extended by the corners in their hands, & set to each other in a miserably dull and slow figure, hardly moving their feet or bodies. The music consisted of two drums and a stringed instrument. An old man sat astride of a cylindrical drum about a foot in diameter, & beat it with incredible quickness with the edge of his hand & fingers. The other drum was an open staved thing held between the knees & beaten in the same manner."

But as early as 1799 fifes and fiddles were being used, and before long banjoes, triangles, jews-harps, and tambourines. In short order the violin became the favorite instrument. Similarly, quadrilles, jigs, fandangos, and Virginia reels were the favored dances.

The fact is that, as fast as he possibly could, the Negro discarded West Indian influences in favor of the dances and music surrounding him in New Orleans. From one side flooded over him the music of Europe; from the other the songs and dances of the American backwoods. He could attend the white balls to look and listen. In the theatres, where his patronage was needed and sought, he heard the operas and other music of the day. On the docks and in the taverns he worked and danced to the music funneling down the Mississippi from the heart of America. In the ballrooms he supplied much of the music and on the streets he paraded with the rest of New Orleans, often to the music of his own marching bands.

Many free Negroes in New Orleans were taught music by the French, German, and Italian musicians abundantly present, and some Negroes were even educated abroad. The result was that by the late 1830's there was in New Orleans a Negro Philharmonic Society of over one hundred members. In addition two theatres by and for Negroes were opened although neither lasted long. As the Civil War approached, Negro musicians in New Orleans were playing for dances, teaching, parading in bands, and composing music from songs to a symphony.

After the war the Negroes were able to perform in places hitherto not available. For example in August, 1865, they gave concerts in the Orleans Theatre, featuring a symphony "enthusiastically received on the French stage." It was composed by Edmond Dede, a Negro. And in 1877, to take an example at the end of Reconstruction, Negroes held a concert in the Masonic Hall wherein an orchestra of twenty musicians played overtures by Auber, Donizetti, Rossini, and that old favorite, the overture from *La Dame Blanche*. Along with these were compositions by Negro composers like Samuel Snaer. There was no lack of trained Negro musicians in New Orleans after the Civil War.

Nor was there any shortage of marching bands. In the 1870's two of the best Negro bands were the St. Bernard Brass Band and Kelly's Band. "With these two bands and some others," wrote a contemporary, "the people of New Orleans are always well supplied with the best of martial music." Over a dozen of the city's Negro bands turned out for President Garfield's funeral parade in 1881. Four years later the Excelsior Brass Band led a march to the New Orleans Exposition of 1885 and then gave a concert to mark the opening of the colored exhibits.

The Excelsior was one of those bands we hear of in the early history of jazz. Before long such famous bands as the Onward, the Alliance, the Tuxedo, the Eureka were making their contribution to the new music.

Four things need to be said about these brass bands. The first is that they were in the New Orleans tradition of loving a parade—so much so that after the Civil War the parade became an end in itself for the Negro. More and more he marched not for some occasion or celebration, but simply to have fun. Since this was his goal, the atmosphere changed; and the music became less martial, less formal, and acquired more lilt, more swing.

Second, after the war the white funeral parades gradually diminished in number as fraternal societies like those of the firemen became fewer. But the Negroes took over this custom. Burial societies multiplied, one of their chief purposes being to provide a fine band for the funeral. The procession to the grave was slow and stately, with the band playing hymns. The return however was given over to the bright, almost dance-like music of the good time parades. It was in these burial parades that Negro religious music influenced the brass bands.

Third, there were so many societies, so many parades, so many demands for bands in New Orleans that these bands were seldom large. Most of the time ten or twelve musicians did all the blowing. This meant that the bands were of a size suitable for the larger dance halls. All through the nineteenth century military bands in New Orleans had played for dancing, so it was only natural to hire these bands for dances. But the style of dancing was changing with the cakewalk, turkey trot, and foxtrot replacing the more formal dances of the earlier period. When a band now played for dancing, it had to play a looser kind of music. Often the brass bands had a string orchestra associated with them to play in smaller places, and frequently bandsmen joined with string players to make a dance orchestra.

Fourth, the brass bands of New Orleans were increasingly used for ballyhoo. Many of the dance halls possessed porches or balconies where the band could play to promote the dance. Or the bands mounted upon wagons in order to advertize a business opening, a picnic, an election speech, or some similar event. Here such instruments as a string bass, a banjo, or a guitar could join the brass and reeds.

Somewhere towards the end of the nineteenth century, as the bands played for parades, funerals, picnics, ballyhoo, and dancing, the music they made became discernibly different from any heard before. Something new, something distinctively American, was being added to the music of the world.

White musicians too played this new music, and as it happened, it was a white band, the Original Dixieland Jazz Band from New Orleans, that first recorded the new music. These five men scored the initial popular success for jazz, and in 1919 they took their music to Europe for the first time. Ironically, in that same year the French Opera House in New Orleans burned down and resident opera ceased.

Why New Orleans? Why was jazz born here? Of course the musical setting described above was necessary. It supplied the skills, the repertoire, the tools for jazz. But something more was needed, something that gave the music its soul.

America had been changing enormously since the Civil War. The emerging nation was urban rather than rural. Its Anglo-Saxon culture was being profoundly altered by a huge influx of immigrants. Power was shifting to merchants and men of business, and religion was making a place for Roman Catholicism. The southern Negro was moving into the cities.

These things were new in America—but not in New Orleans. This city, with its polyglot population and strong Catholicism, its trade and commerce, its large proportion of Negroes, and above all its joy in expressing itself through music, offered a preview of the nation to come. In a very real sense New Orleans pioneered on the road America would follow. It is only natural that a music to speak for and to the new America would first appear in New Orleans.

Good Time Town

Phil Johnson

Thank God the French got here first.

Can you imagine what New Orleans might have been had the Pilgrims gotten off at Pilottown instead of Plymouth?

It's frightening . . . we might have been burning witches instead of *café brûlot*; or preaching to the quadroon beauties, instead of dancing with them; or spending eons eating boiled beef and potatoes, instead of *écrevisse Cardinal*, or *pompano en papillote*, or gumbo.

Poor Pilgrims! They spent so much time merely existing that they never really learned how to live. Between fighting the Indians and fighting sin, there was little time to do anything else, and so little else for them to do.

But the French. Ah, the French! They came here full blown with life and love; not refugees, God centered and narrow; but adventurers, gamblers, fat with a culture that made living a love affair of the senses, and secure in the knowledge that while sin was the work of the devil, its nearest occasions were the particular art of the French.

And this is why New Orleans is unique even today among the cities of America: The French gave us not only life, but a glorious way of living it, as well. Of course, the Spanish came, and made their contributions. And the West Indies tossed filé into the jambalaya. But by the time the Anglo-Saxons had filtered down, the pattern was set, the mold had been cast. They could live in New Orleans, these Americans, they could grow rich upon it, and they would govern it. But they would never change it. Rather, they would be changed by it. New Orleans was, and is, and is destined always to be a city in love with life, a city of graciousness and style and character; a city imperfect, as all beauty is imperfect; a city sometimes so taken by its past that it neglects its future; but overall, a city in which each day can be lived as an adventure, and each night is made for dreams.

Some cities take years, even decades, before their directions can be established and their personalities set. But not New Orleans. It was only a few months after he founded the new city on the Mississippi that Bienville established a character and a tone that was to prevail for the next 250 years and, hopefully, beyond. In a message to the King of France he said, "Send us some women."

We don't mention this frivolously, or for vicarious effect, but to show once again the uniqueness of the spirit and the ethic which was present at the beginning of this city and upon which this city has thrived for lo! these two and a half centuries. Had Bienville been of Anglo-Saxon heritage, for example, he might never have sent such a message. Instead, he would have preached to his men about the fear of God and about damnation and sin. And he would have lifted his eyes to heaven, the better not to see his soldiers sally off into the woods after the Choctaw chippies.

But, being a true Frenchman, Bienville did the sensible thing. And the King did send women. In fact, at least one historian ranks him as New Orleans' very first procurer.

Now, you must realize that New Orleans being what it was at the time, a crude settlement of log houses on a bend in the Mississippi, it was not easy to recruit women to come here. So the King, with that great Gallic pragmatism, did what came naturally. He merely emptied one of Paris' prisons onto a boat. And in February of 1721, eighty-eight former inmates of La Salpétrière arrived in New Orleans, whores, harlots, cutpurses and pickpockets, bawds all, the founding mothers of New Orleans.

Of course, it must be mentioned that the whores, while first, were not the only women to come to New Orleans. Several years later the Mississippi Company began sending boatloads of proper young Frenchwomen to the city as brides for the men. They had middle-class backgrounds and became famous as the "casket girls," because of the small chests, containing a dowry of clothing, given them by the company. It was all very proper. They were well guarded in New Orleans, locked up at night and brought out by day so that the men could see them and make a choice. All apparently married, because, as the report of a French official of the time put it, "this merchandise was soon disposed of."

(Herbert Asbury, in his book *The French Quarter*, wryly points out the amazing fertility of the Casket Girls, and the almost unbelievable barrenness of the strumpets who preceded them. As proof, he explains that almost all of Louisiana's first families trace themselves in unbroken lines to the Casket Girls, while none claim descent from their predecessors.)

And so the pattern was set, a pattern of permissiveness, of earthiness, of life and the Latin joy of living, that was to fix the course of New Orleans for all time to come.

By shortly after the turn of the nineteenth century, great changes had come over New Orleans. It was no longer French or Spanish but American. Its society had become stratified. At the top were the Creoles, descendants of the original French and Spanish settlers, who lived in the Vieux Carré, and whose gayer young men knew well the cock pits, gambling houses, cabarets, coffee houses and fashionable bordellos of the old city. At the bottom, was the dissolute underworld whose gathering place was the "Swamp," a six-block-long section of town about a mile up-river from the French Quarter, on Girod Street, where the flat-boatmen from Kentucky and Tennessee came for their pleasure, to be loved, and mugged, and oftentimes murdered. And in between socially were the American newcomers, unaccepted by the Creoles. They were to build their often stately homes several miles upriver, in what is now known as the Garden District.

Separate from each of these groups were the Free People of Color made up in part of descendants of the earliest white settlers and the Negro slave women and greatly from West Indian immigrants and refugees of mixed blood whose food and clothing had such a lasting effect upon the taste and fashions of the city. And of course there were the African slaves.

Then, along about 1850, New Orleans became aware of two great changes that had taken place: for one, it was no longer a small settlement on the Mississippi, but something of a metropolis, with almost 125,000 people; for another, it was probably the prostitution capital of all America, with the income of its whores ranking second only to the port, itself, in dollar volume. Wantons of all sizes and nationalities proliferated throughout the city. The Swamp still held its low dives and barrelhouses. But elsewhere more enterprising strumpets were erecting huge pleasure palaces, where as many as a dozen or fifteen ladies were available for a gentleman's pleasure.

New Orleans responded to this threat with direct action, action which proved that, despite its Americanization, there was a little French logic in the old girl yet. The City Council, in 1857, voted not to outlaw the strumpets, but to tax them. And to this end the Council established certain licensing requirements. It was a good try. But one destined for failure. In May of that same year a madame named Emma Pickett applied for a license to operate a bordello at 25 St. John Street, between Gravier and Perdido. She paid for her license, but stipulated in writing that she was doing so under protest. Then she sued to recover her fee and, within two years, she was upheld in the courts, and the law was declared unconstitutional.

Clearly, this was a great victory for New Orleans prostitution. And the madames and their ladies celebrated with what one historian calls ". . . one of the lewdest spectacles in American history." And he continues: "It was made up of hundreds of bawds, carriage borne, driving through the city streets, variously costumed, a great many nude. The whores shouted obscenities,

. . . and snatched male bystanders with whom they improvised erotic displays along Canal Street and in the French Quarter. They left little doubt in the public mind that a victory had been won by the sin industry."

And with this victory, prostitution in New Orleans boomed, it exploded, it figuratively engulfed the town. Within the next thirty years houses of ill repute would be scattered throughout the city, causing great anguish among the purer minds of the community, and a great increase in neighborhood business.

But only in one neighborhood did it settle down and really become famous—on Basin Street.

It was on Basin Street in the last half of the nineteenth century, that the world's oldest profession was to achieve a peak of elegance and style heretofore unknown on this continent. It was here that the great houses were to be built, and great fortunes made, and great scandals unfolded, and even greater legends formed.

One of the first of the pleasure palaces to rise on Basin Street was that of Hattie Hamilton, at 21 South Basin. (It should be noted that South Basin Street was across Canal Street from North Basin Street, which later became famous as the main street of Storyville.)

Hattie was a veteran strumpet when she arrived in New Orleans from Cuba. In her day she worked in some of the meanest brothels in New Orleans. But her luck changed when she met and took up with Senator James Beares, a member of the post Civil War black and tan Legislature and as corrupt as they come. With the senator's influence—and money—Hattie rebuilt an old whorehouse into a minor palace. Nothing was too good for the "21." Light was provided by statues holding glittering flambeaux; plate glass mirrors reflected gilded furniture; oriental rugs, bright in reds and blues, covered the floors; and paintings of full-blown but delicate nudes looked down in repose from the walls.

It was a sybarite's dream. And it attracted the best people.

And it made much money. But it didn't last too long. One night Hattie and her senator had a fight. And Hattie shot him. He died almost immediately. The Negro butler, attracted by the shooting, saw the senator lying bleeding on the floor, and Hattie standing over him with the pistol in her hand. Such was justice in those days that Hattie never went to trial. In fact, she wasn't even arrested. The Negro butler was held for a time, however, as an accessory.

Things were never the same at "21" after this. The senator's death threw a damper on things and after a year or so Hattie was forced to sell. She died twelve years later, a strumpet to the end, leaving an estate of $719.20.

She was succeeded, however, by one of the great characters of all of whoredom—Kate Townsend. Kate came early—at age eighteen—and stayed to become the most celebrated madame of her time. She built one of the most magnificent brothels in the Western Hemisphere, at No. 40 South Basin Street; three stories high, of marble and brownstone, and decorated like a miniature Versailles. Her own apartments in the house were said to have cost $40,000, with white marble mantels, black walnut paneling and plush carpets of the reddest velvet. Even the chamber pot was embossed in gold. And all this before she was thirty.

Many say Kate owed her meteoric rise to her friendship with the politicians of the day. One story tells of the wife of an alderman who, in disguise, entered the house to see if her husband was there. And there, it is claimed, she found not only her husband, but the mayor and the members of the Common Council, as well. Kate Townsend's place was operated strictly on snob appeal. You had to be someone to get in. And you had to spend money to stay in. Champagne sold for $50 a quart. And at $100 for the night, her ladies were the highest priced in America. But it was an elegant house. She insisted the men come in evening clothes, and she dressed her girls in the latest Paris fashions.

Always the innovator, she became the first madame of any reputation to have charge accounts. A man's standing in the community could sometimes depend on whether he had an account at Kate's. And there are reports that some banks consulted her when considering applications for loans.

Kate reigned for seventeen years. And her end, when it came, was quick, and bloody, and quite sensational. She was stabbed by her "fancy man," a pimp named Troisville Sykes. She died immediately. He was arrested, tried and acquitted! She was buried in Metairie Cemetery in a metallic casket. Her house was taken over by the public administrator, who leased it to another, less selective madame.

There were other madames of the period who, while not operating on the scale of Kate Townsend, were just as colorful. There was a beautiful Negro madame who called herself "Minnie Ha-Ha." She claimed to be an Indian, and a direct descendant of Indian royalty. To prove it, she had an elaborately framed oil painting mounted in the parlor of her house. It was a picture of two Indians. And beneath it, the caption read: "Mr. and Mrs. Hiawatha." Her parents, who else?

And then there was Fannie Sweet, who used voodoo to lure and hold customers; and Gertie Livingston, whose chief attraction was a coy wench named Josephine Clare. They called her "Josephine Ice-Box," because she was utterly frigid. And Gertie offered large cash rewards to any man who could move her. Many tried but all failed. And it's said that when she died, one of those gentlemen had this line engraved upon her tombstone: "Here lies Josephine Clare, no colder now than when she was alive."

There was Mary Thompson, who ostensibly ran a cigar store, but whose real business was furnishing virgins for assignations, for which she received between $200 and $500 each. She once had a runaway virgin arrested "for stealing her own person." Mary said she paid the girl's mother for her, and had already completed her sale to a man for $350.

And there were others who made a living furnishing "new" girls to the houses of Basin Street. One Agnes Herrick, better known as "Spanish Agnes," actually ran an employment agency at 94 Burgundy Street but used it primarily to guide young maidens into the sporting life. Others of the city's major pro-curesses were Nellie Haley, Mother Mansfield of Bienville Street, and Emma Johnson, who was to gain later fame in Storyville for her sex circuses.

For the way-out, there was Miss Carol's on Baronne Street, which found young boys for affluent homosexuals and actually established a house of assignation on Lafayette Street, bossed by a gross, hairy-chested fag who called himself "Big Nellie."

But in addition to all this, there were houses being estab-lished all over town. Sin had become a rampaging epidemic. New Orleans, in the last half of the century, had turned into one enor-mous den of iniquity.

Something had to be done, and not just for the usual moral reasons. The economy of the city was suffering. Property values fell with every new brothel erected, and whole neighborhoods were made worthless by the sudden appearance of a madame and her girls, moving into a house just down the block.

There were two ways of dealing with the problem: total suppression, or control.

Sensible voices called for control, the setting up of laws to regulate the brothels and to limit their spread. As one wise editorialist of the day wrote: "Young men can no more be made continent by legislation than gamblers can be forced to cease gambling . . ."

But other voices called for suppression, many because they knew that suppression was impossible.

Among these were landlords who, making a fine living rent-ing houses to whores, didn't want to lose the business if the girls were forced into a downtown district. And business people who catered to such women and their "fancy men" and so did not want to see them go. Even the motives of some churches, pro-testing against more containment, came into doubt when it was discovered that these churches owned some of the land upon which many of the targeted whorehouses stood.

Out of all this clamor, this confusion, came one thin voice of reason, that of Alderman Sidney Story. In the first week of

January, 1897, he rose before the City Council and, in a flat, calm voice, proposed a law. It was simple enough: the City of New Orleans should establish a "certain district, outside of which it will be unlawful for prostitution to be carried on . . . and further, that the City of New Orleans should see to it that this ordinance be strictly enforced." As soon as he finished, he was greeted with applause, unprecedented in the City Council chamber. There were a few questions but no debate and a few weeks later, on January 26th, 1897, the City Council passed Mr. Story's ordinance.

For the first time in the history of the Western Hemisphere, there was established by law a district wherein prostitution could be practiced as a profession, and carried on as a business, with the full support of the law. Nothing like it has ever been done before or since in the Western world.

The vixens had almost a year to get ready. The law setting up the District, as it was known in New Orleans, did not go into effect until January 1, 1898. But when it did, brothels all over New Orleans closed their doors . . . except in Storyville. These would be open wide for years to come.

The boundaries of Storyville match almost exactly those of the huge public housing project which now rises in its place. It was bounded on the river side by Basin Street; on the lake side by N. Robertson; by Iberville (then Customhouse Street) and St. Louis. It consisted of only thirty-eight blocks but within a very short time those blocks became the most celebrated red light district in all America as well as one of the chief tourist attractions of the New World.

It was gaudy, loud, crude, cheap, sinful. But it was legal. And that made the difference. At its peak Storyville packed 2200 registered whores into those thirty-eight blocks. And business was brisk. There were about thirty-five really big houses doing business, chiefly on Basin Street, which became the district's main drag. These were the elaborate mansions, presided over by imperious madames and boasting stables of from twelve to twenty girls. Next in the social order were the so-called "parlor houses."

There were several hundred of these, usually staffed by only two, maybe three girls; a small house containing a front room, or parlor, with the bedroom just behind. And last in line were the "cribs." These were simply tiny cells, about seven feet wide and ten feet deep, containing a bed and a chair, with one door that opened onto the street. There were over 1000 "cribs" in Storyville which, in its heyday, were operating day and night. Usually, they were rented by the day. The procedure was simple, much like the way hotel rooms are rented today. The rental agent, usually the corner bartender, had a board in back of the bar, with the keys to all the cribs hanging from individual nails. When a doxie wanted to open for business, she would give the bartender a dollar, or maybe three, and he would hand her a key which made the crib hers for the day. It sounds piddling, but not a few New Orleans fortunes were made from the rental of cribs in Storyville.

But, of course, that which gave Storyville its character, which set it apart from other sin centers, which made it interesting aside from the mere fact of legalized sex, were its madames. The madames were the *Grandes Dames* of Storyville society, its social arbiters, its miniscule "400." It was the madames who gave Storyville what personality it had, who infused it with a character and a bent all its own. As the madames went, so went the reputation of Storyville. And for these madames, the sky was the limit.

Undoubtedly the Queen of all Storyville madames was Lulu White, a short, chubby Negro woman who ran the classiest, best known, best remembered brothel of all—Mahogany Hall.

Lulu White was the epitome of all madames from all times. She was cheap and brassy, with a strident voice and terrible taste. She wasn't pretty but she dressed so that you didn't notice. She wore a red wig, bright red. And, always, a long, formal gown, usually silk or satin. She preferred white. And diamonds . . . she wore diamonds everywhere: in her hair, around her neck, on her fingers—thumbs included—and on bracelets running up her arms from wrist to shoulder. There is even talk of a special dental bridge she had made to give her the only diamond-encrusted smile in town.

To frame such a picture, Lulu built Mahogany Hall, in its day the gaudiest, most expensive sporting palace ever. It was built primarily of marble and mahogany, with crystal chandeliers, oriental carpets, gilded mirrors—the works. It was also highly functional. Four stories high, it contained five parlors, all on the ground floor, with fifteen bedrooms on the upper floors, all with private baths. It even had an elevator.

The "Blue Book", a small brochure published in the District to advertise the charms of the various houses, had this to say about Lulu White and Mahogany Hall:

"Nowhere in this country will you find a more popular personage than Madame White, who is noted as being the handsomest octoroon in America, and aside from her beauty, she has the distinction of possessing the largest collection of diamonds, pearls, and other rare gems in this part of the country. To see her at night is like witnessing the late electrical display on the Cascade, at the late St. Louis Exposition. Aside from her handsome women, her mansion possesses some of the most costly oil paintings in the Southern country. Her mirror parlor is also a dream. There's something always new at Lulu White's that will interest you. 'Good Time' is her motto. There are always ten entertainers who get paid to do nothing but sing and dance." This last reference is obviously a status remark, emphasizing that Lulu's girls were able to concentrate on their work.

Mahogany Hall operated in grand style throughout the life of Storyville, closing with the rest of the brothels, in 1917. Shortly afterwards, Lulu retired, and ran a small saloon on the corner of Basin and Bienville, right next door to Mahogany Hall. In fact, the bottom story of this building still stands today in New Orleans. Mahogany Hall was razed in 1949, but the engraved marble curbstone and the front door knob and lock were saved and are on display at the Jazz Museum on Dumaine Street.

If Lulu White was the undisputed Queen of Storyville, its

unchallenged King was a big, handsome, mustachioed man named Tom Anderson, state representative from the Fourth Ward, financier, restaurateur, stool pigeon, whoremonger and pimp.

Tom Anderson was forty years old when Storyville came into existence. For much of those years he had done many favors for the politicians and powers of the day so that when he was ready to make his move, all doors opened for him. For example, he had known before Mr. Story introduced the ordinance setting up Storyville that it was coming. He quietly bought out the Fair Play Saloon on the corner of Basin and Iberville. Thus, when Storyville was born, he had a base of operations that was to make him the most powerful man in the District, the richest, and one of the prime movers in New Orleans politics.

Tom Anderson's Saloon was always the first stop for anybody who was anybody on a tour of the District. And it was a sight to see. It was the first saloon in America to use electric lights for illumination. There were over 100 bulbs stuck in the ceiling, as well as a huge sign outside, spelling out Anderson's name with a brightness to rival the stars. The bar was half-a-block long, a small highway of polished black mahogany. The back bar was of carved cherrywood, with gilded cherubs, and five enormous arched mirrors. The floor was tile, studded with bright brass spitoons. Upstairs was a whorehouse.

It was here that Anderson ran "Anderson County," as Storyville came to be known by the insiders. It was here that he set 'em up for the likes of John L. Sullivan, Babe Ruth, Ty Cobb, George M. Cohan, Lew Dockstadter, and many other luminaries of the day. Even Carrie Nation visited the Saloon, and, without her hatchet, preached for hours against the demon rum, until an indulgent policeman finally ran her out.

Anderson's power grew with the size of his purse. Before long he owned or controlled over a dozen brothels and bars in Storyville. His word was law. And it is said that even the policemen assigned to the District took their orders directly from him. He bossed Storyville with an iron hand. And, apparently, the politi-

cians preferred it that way. As long as they took care of Tom,
they reasoned, Tom would keep the District in line, and take
care of them.

Whenever there was trouble in Storyville, whenever a pimp
stole somebody else's girl, whenever there was a question of
equity between madames, Tom Anderson was the mediator. It
was he who settled the argument, who made the decisions, who
banished, who punished, who rewarded. After all, Storyville was
Anderson County.

As King of Storyville, Anderson had his pick of the madames
and the girls. And his many affairs were usually well known and
well chronicled throughout the District.

One of these was with a neighbor, Josie Arlington, whose
"Arlington" mansion at 225 Basin Street was one of the few in
Storyville that could match Lulu White's in splendor and gaudi-
ness. At least, Josie had imagination. The "Arlington" was a
narrow house, four stories high, with a byzantine cupola at its
peak. Inside was a succession of parlors, outrageously outfitted,
but at the time the talk of the District. There was a Japanese
parlor, and a Turkish parlor and a Viennese parlor, all, of course,
suitably decorated. There was a Hall of Mirrors, and seemingly
dozens of elaborately furnished boudoirs, where a gentleman
could, supposedly, lose himself in the splendors of far-off places.
The parlors, of course, served only the finest wines and cham-
pagnes. Music was provided, as in most of the fancy houses, by a
Negro "professor" at the piano.

This is what the "Blue Book" had to say about the "Arlington:"

"Nowhere in the country will you find a more complete and
thorough sporting house than the Arlington. Absolutely and
unquestionably the most decorative and costly fitted out sporting
palace ever placed before the American public. The wonderful
originality of everything that goes to fit out a mansion makes it
the most attractive ever seen in this or the old country. The
Arlington, after suffering a loss of many thousand dollars
through a fire, was refurnished and remodeled at an enormous

expense, and the mansion is now a palace fit for a king. Within the great walls of this mansion will be found the work of great artists from Europe and America. Many articles from various expositions will also be seen, and curios galore."

The fire mentioned above occurred in 1905. During the re-building Josie and her girls moved next door, over Tom Ander-son's place. This became known as the "Arlington Annex" which, even after the original Arlington was rebuilt, remained in business.

Josie retired in 1909, wealthy beyond the dreams of many men, to a fashionable home she had built on Esplanade. She died five years later. Even in death she still contributed to the folklore of New Orleans. She was laid to rest in a marble tomb in Metairie Cemetery. Years later it was said that a traffic signal installed nearby caused a red light to glow on the tomb all night.

Josie Arlington could not be called a typical madame, be-cause there were no "typical" madames. They were all different . . . different sizes, different tempers, even different colors. All they shared was a common lust for money.

One of the most genuinely evil madames in Storyville was a tall, almost masculine, harridan named Emma Johnson. As a working prostitute, she was an exhibitionist. She soon learned there was more money to be made by performing before an audience, than locked away in a bedroom with just a single customer. Also, she was a trafficker in young virgins and in acquiring young boys for aging homosexuals. A lesbian, herself, she took a masochistic pride in controlling the young women of what became her "harem." No perversion was too odious or too difficult for Emma Johnson, no crime too low.

So when Storyville came into being, she went into business in grand style. She didn't run a regular house but specialized in producing "shows," or "sex circuses," at which deviations of all kinds would be performed on a raised stage, surrounded by an audience. The "Blue Book" referred to her as "The Parisian Queen of America." It was the custom in those days to refer to anything out of the ordinary, sexually, as "Parisian."

Countess Willie Piazza wasn't a "Parisian," but she was most everything else. An octoroon who had traveled widely, the Countess could speak seven languages, sported a monocle, affected a cigaret holder as long as her arm, and ran one of the most cosmopolitan houses in Storyville. The 1910 revolution in Honduras was actually planned and plotted in the Countess' house. And on at least one occasion Willie personally shot dead a customer, with highly placed relatives in New Orleans, who had misused one of her girls.

But if Willie Piazza is to last in the history books, it will not be because of anything she did, but because of whom she hired. It was at Willie's that the great piano men played—Jelly Roll Morton, and the equally great, but lesser known Tony Jackson.

Willie was a master of public relations. On all big public occasions, such as the opening of the Fair Grounds, or at Sunday Mass at the Cathedral, Willie would be on hand with her girls, shepherding them like a mother superior, all the while dressed in the height of fashion.

"It takes a heap of loving to make a home a house."

Embroidered in finest needlepoint, against a pure linen background, this was the motto that hung framed and centered in the parlor of Antonia Gonzales, an octaroon madame at 1535 Iberville. It could have been the motto of Storyville, itself.

Other famous madames who worked hard at making houses of their homes were Hilma Burt, Gertrude Dix, Gypsy Schoefer, Martha Clark, who ran a small, but select house (two girls) at 227 Basin Street; Willie O. Berrera, who smoked cigars and was known as the toughest madame on Basin Street; and May Tuckerman, who ran the best known parlor house in the District.

While the madames were the stars of the drama being played out in Storyville, the whores, themselves, were prominent supporting players. The "Blue Book" previously mentioned was a directory of all the whores in the District, published by Billy Struve, a former reporter on the *Item*, who managed most of Tom Anderson's properties. Struve's writing abounded with the archaic constructions of the day and gave evidence that he was well advised to abandon the writing profession to become a manager of real estate. In addition, many of the madames, like Lulu White, published their own brochures, extolling the virtues of their most particularly gifted ladies. So meet now some of the ladies of Storyville, as they would have been introduced to you those many years ago in Lulu White's sales brochure, or the "Blue Book:"

"The beautiful Estelle Russell, now a member of high standing in Miss White's famous Octaroon Club, and a few years ago one of the leading stars in Sam T. Jack's Creole Show, which assertion alone should test the capacity of Miss Lulu's commodious quarters every night. Gentlemen, don't fail, when visiting Miss White's, to ask for Miss Estelle, for you miss a treat if you do not."

"Victoria Hall, a member of Miss White's Club, as accomplished as she is beautiful, a form equal to Venus, a voice not unlike Patti. How could a more accurate description be printed, what more could be said."

"Clara Miller . . . demure, everybody's friend, can sit up all night if necessary, and handicap to put a friend on to a good thing. Why? Because it is her disposition. And who don't want to meet such a young lady? Not one with real blood in his veins. She has been in the principal cities of Europe and the Continent and can certainly interest you as she has a host of others. When we add that the famous octaroon was born near Baton Rouge, we trust you will call on her."

"Corine Meyers. The poet has said that there are others, lots of others, but there is only one Corine Meyers. And we do not stretch the point when we re-echo and say that this is true. She can sing a song and rob the canary of its sweet voice. She can perform on any musical instrument, and is a bosom friend in a short while."

"Miss Eunice Deering who is known as the 'idol' of the society and club boys, needs but little introduction as she is known by the elite's from New York to California."

"Miss Margaret Bradford, if ever there was an affable person, it is certainly portrayed in full when the name Bradford is mentioned. If it was within my power to name Kings and Queens, I would certainly go out of my way to bestow the title 'Queen of Smile' on Miss Margaret. She is one of the few women who can say she has friends, who are friends in deed, and who are with her in all her adventures."

"Miss Grace Simpson, there are few women in this country who are better known than Grace. Grace has always made it a mark in life to treat everyone alike and to see that they enjoy themselves while in her midst. There are few women who stand better with the swell people than Grace. A visit once will mean a long remembrance and friendship."

The ladies and the madames and the pimps of Storyville lived high for a long time. But while the good times rolled, they did not roll forever. Somehow the novelty of legal sin wore off as the years wore on. Maybe New Orleans was growing up. Whatever the reason, Storyville faced its end as only a shadow of its former self. Contrasted with the 2200 bawds who registered for business when it opened in 1898, less than 400 answered the rolls when it closed in 1917.

Its closing, in fact, was almost anti-climactic to the many dramas which had been played out in Storyville during its twenty tempestuous years of life. The order to close came from the federal government. Four sailors had been killed in Storyville (World War I was in full swing then) and Secretary of the Navy Josephus Daniels issued an order prohibiting open prostitution within five miles of a naval base. He told Mayor Martin Behrman that unless the city closed Storyville, the Navy would. The mayor went to Washington to try to reverse the order, but to no avail. Reluctantly, on October 2, 1917, he introduced the ordinance which closed Storyville. It was adopted on October 9, to be effective after midnight November 12. On November 13, Storyville was no longer Storyville, but just a collection of tired houses and unemployed whores.

But they weren't unemployed long. They simply scattered to new quarters. The payoffs were bigger, the graft line longer, but business remained the same, as it has to this day, proving, no doubt, the validity of that very old saying: "You can make it illegal, but you can't make it unpopular."

Of all the stories that have arisen from the mists of fact and fancy that surround Storyville and its place in New Orleans' history, none is more persistent, more popular, nor more erroneous than that concerning jazz. Jazz was born in Storyville, they say, the bastard child of the honky-tonk piano and the spasm bands. And when the prostitutes wrapped up their belongings at Storyville's closing, they sachayed out to the strains of the first jazz band playing "Nearer My God To Thee."

It's romantic. But it just ain't so!

True jazz historians point out that jass music, as it was known then, was already being played even before Story was elected to the Common Council. Joe Clark, Sr., one of the early greats, had played his piece and died even before there was a Storyville. And Charles "Buddy" Bolden, one of the great jazz trumpet men of all time, was already on his way to immortality, with songs like "The Bucket Got A Hole In It," this by 1897, a full year before Storyville was begun.

No, jazz was not born in Storyville. It was born in the streets of New Orleans, in the camps at Milneburg, in parades, at lawn parties. It was played in Storyville where the District did give employment to some of the early musicians. But as one definitive historian puts it, "Jazz did not generate in a whorehouse environment."

This same historian points out one important contribution that Storyville did make to jazz: It broke down the color line . . . not between black and white, but between the Negro sub-ethnic groups: between the downtown, light-skinned Creole Negroes, and the uptown, dark-skinned Africans. Both had great contributions to make to jazz. But until Storyville, they lived on different levels, with the lighter musicians not deigning to play with their darker uptown neighbors. The easy life in Storyville broke down this wall between these two groups, and jazz is the richer for it.

Jazz, after all, is largely a product of Africa, picked up musically from the chants of the African slaves working the plantations. In these African chants, there was always a leader, who provided a dominant line; and answering chants, or counterpoint, one masculine, and one feminine. Then the rest of the tribe would join in.

The jazz band was an instrumental extension of this, with the trumpet or cornet taking the lead, the clarinet providing the feminine counterpoint, the trombone the masculine counterpoint, and the piano, or banjo, and other rhythm instruments joining in.

Martin Williams, in his book *Jazz Masters of New Orleans,* repeats a theory that New Orleans jazz resulted "from the juxtaposition of the Creoles' musicianship and the freed slaves' passion and feeling. Downtown sophistication plus uptown rhythm. To the downtown sophistication belongs a transplanted European musical tradition, ranging from the opera house to the folk ditty. And to the uptown tradition belongs the work song, the spiritual and the field holler, an already developed African-American idiom. Put them together and an old French quadrille becomes 'Tiger Rag.' "

Whatever it was, it came out just fine. By the beginning of 1900, jazz was making itself felt. Buddy Bolden, as we said, was one of the first great New Orleans trumpeters. King Oliver was another, who gained an even greater fame by being recognized as a mentor of Louis Armstrong. And one of the very best was Freddie Keppard. He succeeded Bolden as King of the Horn in the first decade of the new century. And as such became one of the first to export jazz to the rest of America. Around 1912, he, along with Eddie Vinson on trombone, George Baquet on clarinet, Dink Johnson on drums, Jimmy Palao on violin, Leon Williams on guitar and Bill Johnson on bass, formed the Original Creole Ragtime Band. Later, with a new drummer, they were booked on the Orpheum circuit out of San Francisco as the Original Creole Orchestra.

But the white musicians in New Orleans were also developing jazz in their own style. "Papa" Jack Laine was the leader of the white musicians, forming as early as 1888 a "Reliance Brass Band" for parades, concerts or what have you. By 1915 the first white jazz band was ready for export. Tom Brown's bunch, consisting of Brown, himself, Gus Mueller on clarinet, Ray Lopez, cornet; Arnold Loyocano, guitar; Stêve Brown, bass and William Lambert on drums, moved north to play in Chicago. They were billed as "Brown's Band from Dixieland."

It was not until the following year that another white band made the trip north—with Johnny Stein on drums, Nick La-Rocca on cornet, Alcide "Yellow" Nunez on clarinet, Eddie Edwards on trombone and pianist Henry Ragas. They played in Chicago and New York with some success. But the big break was to come in another year. It came in New York, with LaRocca leading a band composed of himself on cornet, Larry Shields on clarinet, and Edwards, Ragas and Stein. They opened on January 15 at the Paradise Club on Eighth Avenue and 58th Street. They were a great success and were billed as "The Original Dixieland Band—Creators of Jazz."

And jazz was on its way to becoming a national, then a worldwide institution—America's only original art form.

But there is something more which New Orleans has traditionally offered its own people and the visitor for their enjoyment, something which is as memorable an identification as jazz itself. That something is food.

Why is New Orleans cooking so good? The answer to that question begins with the very first line of this chapter: Thank God, the French got here first. Indeed, it was the great and good influence of the French chefs that set New Orleans on the proper path to gastronomic greatness. But notice, we said influence, and perhaps that's the real secret of New Orleans cooking. Because while it was influenced by the French, the New

Orleans cuisine was not dictated by the French. Along the way we picked up a little from the Spanish, a little more from the Free People of Color, many of whom came in as refugees from the West Indies. And also a little from the African slaves. What evolved from all this was the distinct New Orleans culinary idiom called "Creole."

We'll give you an example of what we mean:

Bouillabaisse is that fabulous fish soup of Southern France. Most of the great fish of the warm Mediterranean find their way into it, as well as the prawns and lobsters. It is delicious.

Of course, the French wanted *bouillabaisse* when they came to New Orleans. But the fish here were different from those found off Marseilles. So they compromised. Instead of prawns and lobsters, they used the hard shell crabs and the delicious native shrimp. And they added the salty oysters found on the floor of the bays around New Orleans, the redfish and the pompano, the aristocrats of the Gulf of Mexico. And, *voilà! bouillabaisse*, New Orleans style.

But it didn't stop there. Along the way the Spanish added peppers, to give it a little fire. The African slaves, many of whom did the cooking in Creole houses, added okra, to give it a body, and a tang. And the émigrés from the West Indies contributed filé, an exotic powder, concocted by pounding sassafras leaves into dust.

It was an orderly, slow, patient evolution. When it was complete *bouillabaisse* was no more. In its place something infinitely better—New Orleans Creole gumbo. Of course, the evolution continued even beyond that, and, in fact, branched out into several directions at once. So that now it is possible to eat, in many New Orleans homes, a more specialized dish, such as chicken gumbo, or shrimp gumbo, or even simply okra gumbo. Under any name, however, if prepared with love and an old New Orleans recipe, it is fabulous.

Good cooking in New Orleans remained pretty much a private, at-home affair during the early years of the city's existence. It was not until the Spaniards came that anything resembling a restaurant began catering to the tastes of New Orleans' residents.

But the emphasis in these early inns was on drinking and music, with food served as more of an afterthought.

The American purchase of Louisiana began a period of great wealth for New Orleans, however, and soon restaurants began blossoming in the city to accommodate the newly acquired habit of dining out. The St. Louis Hotel, the Creoles' hotel, was built in 1835 and was said to have an excellent kitchen. Later, its manager, Pierre Maspero, left to open a restaurant of his own.

Along about this time, in 1840 to be exact, an émigré from Marseilles named Alciatore opened a boarding house on St. Louis Street. It was a favorite place of the artists and opera singers who came to New Orleans, not simply because it was a quiet place to stay, but because the proprietor was such a superior cook.

Shortly afterwards, word of his culinary skill circulated so throughout the city that he enlarged his establishment, keeping the rooming house on the top floor, and opening a restaurant beneath. He gave it his name—Antoine . . . and Antoine's it is to this very day.

And although it bloomed under Antoine's expert cookery, the establishment really made its mark under his son, Jules. Jules took to cooking like butter to a roux. He gave it a flair. And in 1874 he invented a dish that has become famous throughout the world—Oysters Rockefeller. It's a sauce, really, a heady sauce fat with butter and greens and a hint of absinthe. And it makes an oyster an aristocrat. Why the name? It was a rich sauce. And Rockefeller was the richest man in America at the time. N'est-ce pas?

He also created a dish that even today, better than half a century later, is a favorite of New Orleans, Pompano en papillote. He did it for a banquet honoring the famous French balloonist, Montgolfier, who was passing through New Orleans. He wanted something that would taste good, and yet would pay proper honor to the intrepid aerialist.

The solution—fresh Gulf pompano, covered with a rich sauce of white wine, baby shrimp, tiny oysters, mushrooms and pearl onions, and cooked wrapped loosely in a paper bag. The steam from the sauce caused the bag to inflate. And when it was served—*voilà!*—a balloon.

Now the restaurant is into its third generation of Alciatores, with Roy, son of Jules, *grand chef de maison.*

Soon followed other restaurants that would become famous: Leon Lamothe's Restaurant and Oyster Saloon, at 137 St. Charles, on the "American" side of Canal Street; Bégué's, near the French Market, featuring breakfasts lasting for hours; Tujaque's, with no ménu, you just walked in—as you still do—and were served, you ate, and it was delicious; and Maylie's, started in 1878 as an informal market restaurant, which also still serves its heterogeneous patrons.

The French Quarter saw a boom in new restaurants: Galatoire's on Bourbon Street; Broussard's, with its lovely patio; La Louisianne, started by Louis Besaudin and Antoine Alciatore's son, Ferd, on Iberville; and Arnaud's, on Bienville.

Also in the nineteenth century the St. Charles Hotel was built, the "American" answer to the Creoles' magnificent St. Louis. It was the grandest hostelry of its time, boasting a fabulous solid gold dining service that was brought out only for special affairs. It, too, had a good kitchen, although it lost luster with age.

One of the truly unique directions in New Orleans cookery came sometime before the turn of the century, with the establishment of restaurants on the shores of Lake Pontchartrain, at West End and Milneburg and at the Spanish Fort. These specialized in seafood, of course. And the shrimp and crabs and lake trout served there were gastronomic delights. Even today there are several of these restaurants remaining at West End and they are always crowded, especially on Fridays.

The period between the World Wars saw a dramatic increase in the growth of New Orleans. And restaurants expanded to meet that growth. Commander's Palace in the Garden District catered to the tastes of the descendants of the Americans who settled there so long ago. The neighborhood restaurants came into their own: Gentilich's on N. Rampart; Manale's on Napoleon Avenue; Zibilich's, on S. Claiborne Avenue; Pittari's on N. Claiborne; Tranchina's on Carondelet (which has operated since under a variety of owners and names); Delmonico's on St. Charles Avenue. There are four fine Italian restaurants: Sclafani's, originally in the Third Ward but now moved into Jefferson Parish; Moran's, which put a Roman zest into the old La Louisianne; Tortorici's (née Tortorich's) at Royal and St. Louis; and best of them all, Turci's, originally at 223 Bourbon Street, but now located on Poydras, just off Baronne. It was founded by two opera singers, Signor and Signora Ettore Turci. And Mama Turci, well into her eighties, still supervises the preparation of the pasta and of the incomparable Veal Parmigiana. Nor must we forget Kolb's, the city's famous German restaurant, in the 100 block of St. Charles.

The popularity and influence of New Orleans cookery is attested to by the unending establishment of new restaurants which serve it. In the 1940's Owen Brennan, who operated the Absinthe House on Bourbon, one day walked across the street and took over the Vieux Carré Restaurant. Soon, it was one of the most famous French restaurants in America, thanks in part to Owen's brilliant personality and public relations, but also because of its delicious foods. Shortly before he died, he moved the restaurant to the old Paul Morphy house on Royal Street, where his sister, Ella Brennan Martin, continues the novel tradition of a fine French restaurant operated by Irishmen.

About the same time Brennan, a saloon keeper, was establishing his restaurant, a Third Ward druggist named Ernest Masson had similar dreams. He was blessed with two sons. One, Ernest, Jr., he sent to Paris, to bolster his already formidable cooking prowess with several years at Cordon Bleu. And the other, Albert, he sent to the vineyards, to learn about wine. Shortly, both were ready. And Masson's Beach House, located in what was formerly a notorious roadhouse, on Pontchartrain Boulevard, near the lake, opened for business, with Ernie, Jr., as chef, Albert as sommelier and maître d'hôtel, and Ernest, Sr., as best customer. It continues today one of the city's very best.

Two other smaller gourmet restaurants are the Bon Ton, situated near the Board of Trade on Magazine Street; and the Andrew Jackson, in the 200 block of Royal.

As a personal aside, if I were asked to pick New Orleans' best restaurants, however, I would have to name in alphebetical order Antoine's, the Caribbean Room of the Pontchartrain Hotel, and LeRuth's, the newest, located, almost incongruously, in Gretna, across the river from New Orleans. Owner-Chef Warren LeRuth is not yet forty. But he is, without doubt, a worthy successor to the great masters of the past.

All of New Orleans is, in fact, a deserving successor to what has gone before. We have had many flags flying over this city. We have had jazz, and good food, and high living, all of which have helped to make this city a rare and vital entity.

But will it change? Will the future, with its technology and its mechanization, make something different of New Orleans?

We think not.

We believe the New Orleans of the next 250 years will be little different from the fantastically marvelous city of the last 250.

Why?

Well, just this year District Attorney Jim Garrison of Orleans Parish interrupted his investigation of the assassination of President John F. Kennedy to go into criminal court and intercede for a certain Miss Linda Brigette, a quite beautiful, quite fabulously built, strip tease dancer, who had been arrested and charged with giving a lewd performance.

Miss Brigette, said the district attorney, should not be prosecuted, because the dance was not lewd, and besides, she is married and the mother of two fine sons.

We believe that as long as New Orleans has district attorneys like Jim Garrison, and strip tease dancers like Linda Brigette, and the enormous capacity not only to tolerate, but to enjoy both, it will not change, never in a thousand years.

Besides, who would want her to?

Gateway to the Americas

James P. Baughman

As currently defined for the purpose of collecting federal commercial statistics, the "Port of New Orleans" includes "both banks of the Mississippi River, from mile 127 above Head of Passes to the mouth of the Passes; Innerharbor Navigation Canal, 5.5 miles; Mississippi River-Gulf Outlet, from its junction with the Innerharbor Navigation Canal to Bayou Bienvenue, 7 miles; and Harvey Canal, 5.5 miles." These components of the modern port can serve as reference points while tracing the history of navigational and waterfront facilities in the city.

Three aspects of New Orleans' location have had great relevance to her physical evolution as a port. First, has been the character of the Mississippi River between the city and the Gulf. Second, have been the possibilities of connecting the city's riverfront with Lake Pontchartrain to the north and with the bayou network of southwestern Louisiana. Third, has been the nature of the river at the "front" of the city and its effect upon port operations. All three of these circumstances have persistently tested the ingenuity of individuals and agencies responsible for or inclined toward improving the port's natural state.

Few would question the assertion that location has been a major determinant of New Orleans' comparative advantages in domestic and foreign commerce. The city lies at Lat. 29° 56′59″ N., Long. 90°04′09″ W., athwart the ocean end of North America's most extensive river system. She commands the Gulf coast-line from the Florida Keys to Yucatan. She has easy access to the sealanes and ports of the Caribbean and the Atlantic. And in many ways, the commercial growth of the city can be explained in terms of geographic determinism.

In this brief history of the port, however, geography serves as a point of departure. It seems more appropriate here to characterize the process by which the city's location has interacted with her residents' propensities to improve their natural situation, and to analyze the results of that interaction in terms of the historical patterns of trade.

Of all the facets of the port's history, two can best be used to illustrate the process of interaction between man and nature. First, has been the gradual but continual striving to improve the city's natural navigational and waterfront facilities. Second, has been the evolution of conscious port administration and its transition from mere police regulation to active trade promotion. In identifying the timing, the individuals, and the organizations most important to these interrelated developments, and in evaluating causes and effects of their incidence, the process of New Orleans' maritime history can be captured in microcosm. And against this background, the undulations in the statistical record of the port's commerce, past and present, can be more fully understood.

Questions of the navigability of the lower river have been major threads in the port's history. For 110 miles below Canal Street, the Mississippi loops its way toward the Gulf: around the big bend at English Turn; past Jesuit Bend; past Fort Jackson and Fort St. Philip; past Venice and the Jump; past Quarantine; past Pilottown (where the "bar pilots" and the "river pilots" exchange responsibilities). At Head of Passes, 95 miles below the city and 2,320 miles below its headwaters in Lake Itasca, the river divides itself into three natural outlets to the Gulf: South Pass, Southwest Pass, and Pass à l'Outre. These passes and the lower river plagued the city in the seventeenth, eighteenth, and nineteenth centuries in a manner best described by Walter Lowrey:

" . . . the Mississippi, like most rivers of its type carried . . . minute particles of sediment in tremendous quantity. These it deposited when its current slowed . . . as the river neared the sea [and] created what might be called a mud blockade at the river entrance . . . Above the mud bars a channel of fifty feet or more was commonly available. At the entrances, however, the average depth of water was approximately twelve feet . . . in the summer and fall . . . the volume of water carried by the stream decreased and the amount of sediment declined. Then the depth of the river mouth might increase to as much as eighteen feet. In the late winter and spring, however, as flood waters poured soil-choked water into the channel, the bars would enlarge . . . and almost overnight reduce the depth of water to twelve feet or less. Then, in effect, the river and its port would be shut off from all major foreign commerce. Ships caught inside the river might be delayed there for months, while those outside had to wait patiently for the waters to subside and the entrance to deepen . . . "

The threats posed by these natural phenomena to the livelihood of the port were recognized as matters of great public concern from the earliest days of French rule. Royal engineers continually studied the problem and experimented with solutions. In 1722, the Duke of Orleans (then Regent of France) went so far as to offer 10,000 *livres* to anyone who could achieve and maintain fifteen to sixteen feet of water on the bars. The prize went begging, however, and, in 1725, royal pilots were stationed at the passes. As difficulties persisted, they and their Spanish and American successors did their best to outguess the river the engineers could not tame.

Among those concerned for the well-being of New Orleans' water-borne commerce, debates over the lower Mississippi centered upon two questions. First, which of the natural passes should be improved and how? Second, could and should an artificial outlet between the river and the Gulf be constructed to replace and/or supplement the passes and, if so, where and how?

The first question was hotly contested prior to, but was

solved by, 1879. Between 1836, when Congress designated them responsible for river-mouth improvements, and 1873, the Army's Corps of Engineers expended millions of dollars and countless man-hours in studies of and attempts at improving the natural passes. With only a few exceptions, the officers of the Corps persistently advocated massive and continual dredging as a solution to siltation of the passes. They just as consistently underestimated the power of the river to undo their best efforts. Their dredges ultimately became local laughing-stocks because of their furious but futile assaults upon the Mississippi mud.

The construction of jetties, so as to narrow the passes and induce them to scour themselves to greater depths, was the alternative to dredging most often suggested. The idea was as old as the city itself, but was not seriously tried until the mid-nineteenth century. Crude jetties were built by the Louisville firm of Craig and Rightor between 1856 and 1859 under a federal appropriation of $330,000, but with no success. Since only a minority within the Corps of Engineers favored jetties instead of dredging, the idea languished until after the Civil War.

Debates over the situation below the city peaked during 1873–1875, after a particularly severe closure of the port and in response to a set of public proposals made by James B. Eads of St. Louis. Eads, supported by General John G. Barnard (against his peers in the Corps of Engineers), revived the jetty idea. In January 1874, Eads offered to construct a 600 × 28-foot channel in Southwest Pass within two years. His price if he succeeded: $1,000,000 upon achievement of a 20-foot depth; $1,000,000 for each additional two feet of depth up to 28 feet; and $500,000 per year for maintaining the channel for ten years after completion. His price if he failed: zero!

After extended public and private debate, Congress approved Eads' plan for South Pass (rather than Southwest Pass), and, on July 8, 1879, Eads' jetties and channel had achieved and were maintaining 30 feet on the bar. Successful completion of the original Eads jetties ended 160 years of frustration for the port and began an extended series of further improvements of the lower river, usually at federal expense, but often at local initiative.

Between 1879 and 1928, the prime movers in this process were the Mississippi River Commission and the New Orleans Board of Trade. Created by Congress on June 28, 1879, the commission reported to the Secretary of War and was charged "with the preparation and consideration of plans to improve the river channel, protect its banks, improve navigation, prevent destructive floods, and promote and facilitate commerce." The board, a cooperative venture of New Orleans' Produce Exchange, Chamber of Commerce, and Merchants and Manufacturers Association, maintained a dialog with the federal agency.

The board was successful, between 1896 and 1911, in persuading the federal government to assume the Eads contract at South Pass upon its expiration (in 1901) and to install and maintain similar jetties at Southwest Pass. After passage of the Flood Control Act of May 15, 1928, by which the Mississippi River Commission was reconstituted as an advisory and consulting agency to the Chief of Engineers, U.S. Army, the Corps of Engineers became the federal party to national-local interest in the river.

Although responsible for the whole Mississippi, the numerous surveys and recommendations of the Corps after 1928 paid particular attention to the navigability of the lower river. Their suggestions were consolidated and translated into national strategic and economic policy in an act of March 2, 1945, when Congress charged the Corps with maintaining the following channels:

Baton Rouge to New Orleans	40′ x 500′
Port of New Orleans	35′ x 1,500′
New Orleans to Head of Passes	40′ x 1,000′
Southwest Pass	40′ x 800′
Southwest Pass Bar Channel	40′ x 600′
South Pass	30′ x 450′
South Pass Bar Channel	30′ x 600′

The second set of man-made waterways which has evolved to improve the natural navigational conditions of the port comprises the canals between the river and the lake and between the river and the coastal bayous and bays. Among the former, the Carondelet (or "Old Basin") Canal and the New Basin Canal were precursors and the Innerharbor Navigation (or "Industrial") Canal historically the most important. The prime river-bayou-bay connection has been the Harvey Canal. Each developed in its own unique mixture of national, state, and municipal initiative.

The Carondelet Canal was begun as a public work in 1794–1795 from the lake end of Bayou St. John. In 1805, the Orleans Navigation Company was chartered by the Territorial Legislature to resume and improve the Spanish governor's start and spent $375,000 dredging out the waterway seven miles to a basin just off Congo (now Beauregard) Square. The New Basin Canal was the project of the New Orleans Canal and Banking Company, dug during 1832–1838 from the "West End" of the lakeshore 7.5 miles to a basin behind Rampart Street between Julia and Delord.

Both of these canals were lockless and both were heavily travelled by shallow-draught vessels. Neither was ever connected to the river despite periodic proposals to do so (because of a fear of flooding), but both gave small ocean and lake vessels waterside access to the city center. Their existence and commerce were part of the port's history until they were filled in in the 1940's.

Part of the reason for the obsolescence of the Carondelet and New Basin canals, and much more significant in the modern maritime history of the city, was the development of the Innerharbor Navigation Canal. In contrast to the federally financed projects at the mouth of the river, the history of the Industrial Canal is particularly instructive on how state and municipal initiative could also effect a vital waterway improvement.

The canal was created, according to a port handbook: "primarily to provide deep water frontage for unlimited industrial development, and to provide the port with an inner harbor in which the commercial wharf system could be extended with the advantages of a constant water level." The project took eleven years to complete. On July 19, 1914, the State Legislature authorized the Commission Council of New Orleans to locate, and the Board of Commissioners of the Port of New Orleans (locally known as the "Dock Board") to build and operate the proposed waterway between the river and the lake. Implementation was delayed by World War I and a change in state administrations; but between February 10, 1918, and December 10, 1919, a site was selected, construction plans approved for locks and a canal, financial arrangements were made, lands were expropriated, and excavations begun.

The site was bounded by France and Lizardi streets and joined the river on the east bank, 2.9 miles below Canal Street. From there it ran north to Florida Walk and thence to the lake. The Dock Board paid $1,493,532.24 (or $1,665 per acre) for the site and ground was broken on June 6, 1918, under the supervision of George W. Goethals Co., Inc., consulting engineers.

Costs of expropriations and construction were financed by $19,500,000 in 5 per cent, 40-year bonds sold by the Dock Board to a syndicate composed of the Hibernia, Interstate, and Whitney-Central banks of New Orleans, the William R. Compton Investment Company of St. Louis, and Halsey, Stuart Company of Chicago. The principal of these bonds was secured by the canal itself, while interest payments were guaranteed by four sources of funds: net receipts from canal tolls; annual subsidies from the New Orleans Public Belt Railroad Commission ($50,000) and the Board of Levee Commissioners of the Orleans Levee District ($925,000); and rentals derived from leasing industrial sites along the canal (terms: 99 years, 10-year tax exemption, $1,200 per acre land rental per year).

On May 2, 1921, the Industrial Canal locks were formally dedicated, as was the canal itself on May 5, 1923. By explicit Dock Board policy, the canal has never been developed at the expense of the river, but it has added eleven miles of prime industrial waterfrontage to the port and serves as part of both the Mississippi River-Gulf Outlet and the Intracoastal Waterway. As presently maintained, the lock has usable dimensions of 640 × 75 × 31.5 feet, and the 5.5 mile canal a controlling depth of 28 to 29 feet from the lock to Seabrook Bridge. Some idea of current usage is gained from traffic statistics for 1965:

VESSELS	NORTHBOUND	SOUTHBOUND
Passenger and dry cargo	277	275
Tanker	5	5
Towboat	6,261	6,266
Dry barges	9,290	9,302
Tank barges	823	825
Other	2	1
Total	16,658	16,674

Like the Industrial Canal, the Harvey Canal was created by man as a supplement to New Orleans' natural waterways. In the latter's case, however, its evolution was less coordinated and much longer and was the result of the interaction of private enterprise and the federal government.

As early as the 1830's Captain Nicholas Noel Destréhan began improving the bayou connections between Barataria Bay and his plantation on the west bank of the Mississippi, opposite New Orleans. By the 1850's a 5.3-mile canal associated by name with Destréhan's son-in-law, Captain Joseph H. Harvey, was in operation but did not connect with the river. Between 1880 and 1909, the Harvey family added a lock gate which could be opened when river and canal levels were the same, but extensive development of the waterway lagged until the 1920's. On March 10, 1924, the Harvey family sold their canal to the federal government for $425,000, and the latter spent $1,775,132 building a 425 × 75-foot lock which joined the river's west bank, 3.3 miles above Canal Street.

Opening of the Harvey Lock on March 13, 1934, began a new phase in the port's history, as it and part of the Industrial Canal became sections of the Gulf Intracoastal Waterway. Congressional acts of March 3, 1925, and January 1, 1927, authorized completion of the New Orleans–Corpus Christi segment of that system via the Harvey and Industrial canals. An act of July 23, 1942, extended the waterway from Apalachee Bay, Florida, to the Rio Grande, placing the port of New Orleans squarely in its center. By 1945 traffic was already so great that, on March 2, Congress authorized construction of a second connection between the waterway and the port. In April 1956, the Algiers Lock and Canal were opened to ease congestion at the Harvey Lock. The Algiers Lock is 10.3 miles below the Harvey Lock and 7 miles below Canal Street, a 760 × 75-foot facility, costing $5,215,700. Its canal is 9 miles long and intersects the Intracoastal Waterway 6 miles behind the Harvey Lock.

The various projects to improve the natural river, however, have culminated in the most ambitious new waterway of all, the Mississippi River–Gulf Outlet. Proposals for an artificial ship canal to avoid the passes had never died, with the most thorough exposition of the idea being made by State Engineer Benjamin Buisson in 1832. A canal scheme was revived by the Chief of Engineers, General Andrew A. Humphreys, during the debate of the 1870's, but was put aside in the euphoria of Eads' success. By the twentieth century, however, the idea was again heard, but talk had shifted from a canal to proposals for a tidewater ship channel of the variety built at Houston between 1910 and 1914.

Prime advocate of the plan in New Orleans, from the 1920's on, was Colonel Lester F. Alexander (1879–1954), a local consulting engineer and organizer of the New Orleans Tidewater Development Association. Later leaders of the group were A. B. Freeman and George S. Dinwiddie. Their proposals argued for the obvious advantages of a shorter, more dependable passage to the Gulf, the strategic value of a third entrance to the port, as well as recognition of the extensive opportunities to develop industrial frontage along such a waterway.

Local proposals for a "Tidewater Channel" finally bore fruit in the Rivers and Harbors Act of March 29, 1956, which budgeted some $100,000,000 in federal funds for excavation of a "Mississippi River–Gulf Outlet." The project called for "a seaway canal" (36 feet deep × 500 feet wide from Michoud, Louisiana, southeasterly to Lake Borgne, and across Chandeleur Sound to the 38-foot contour of the Gulf of Mexico) and for "an inner tidewater harbor" (a 1,000 × 2,000-foot turning basin) connected by a 36 × 500-foot channel to the Innerharbor Navigation Canal via the Gulf Intracoastal Waterway. Access to and from the Mississippi River was to be "by means of the Innerharbor Navigation (Industrial) Canal Lock until such time as this lock becomes obsolete or economic justification necessitates construction of an additional lock with suitable connections in the vicinity of Meraux, Louisiana."

Excavation for the waterway was begun by the Corps of Engineers on December 10, 1957, and the final breakthrough to the open Gulf was made on March 18, 1961. The outlet was officially opened to navigation by *Del Sud* on July 25, 1963, and by January, 1967, the Corps of Engineers reported "that the controlling depth for the entire 76-mile length . . . has reached the planned 36-foot level." The outlet cuts some 40 miles off the old 110-mile river trip, and freight traffic has steadily increased from 178, 746 short tons in 1960 to 2,091,888 in 1965.

Opening of the Tidewater Channel certainly marks a new chapter yet to be written in the history of the port. In context, however, it is but the current stage in the continual physical evolution of maritime New Orleans. The 200 years from the city's founding until the close of World War I were required to solve the navigational problems of the natural outlet to the Gulf. Then, between the two world wars, local, state, and national funds were mobilized to create man-made waterways which bisected the riverfront and linked the port more directly with the eastern and western Gulf coasts. Since 1945, a third major effort has produced an alternative route to the sea. Few American ports can claim such a persistent and productive effort to improve their natural state.

The planning and execution of these public works were, of course, the task of those official agencies and private individuals and organizations which concerned themselves with the port's welfare. How such agencies, individuals, and organizations evolved, who they were, and what they did to improve the operation and commerce of the port must now be considered.

During both French and Spanish times, all waterfront facili-

ties in New Orleans were public property and were regulated in the military and commercial interests of the Crown. Royal governors, in implementing port policy, might confer with town officials, but were not required to do so. Thus, as the era of American government began, there was little tradition of municipal port administration. And, during the territorial period, responsibilities for the waterfront divided pragmatically between governor and City Council. On December 29, 1803, only nine days after the transfer of sovereignty from France to the United States, William C. C. Claiborne, Governor General and Intendant of the Province of Louisiana, issued the first set of American port regulations. These created the office of harbor master, established a scale of fees to be charged vessels using the port, and prescribed anchorage and berth regulations. Claiborne's ordinance was carried over as the Territory of Orleans was established on March 26, 1804 (effective October 1), with him as governor.

On December 4, 1804, however, when the charter to incorporate the City of New Orleans was approved (effective March 1, 1805), the town was allowed to reinstitute the Spanish port charges instituted in 1769 by Governor Alexander O'Reilly and current until 1802. Municipal officials were permitted to levy a flat fee per ship for the benefit of the wharves. Actually, the major public controversy concerning the port area during the territorial period did not relate to port fees or administration, but to the ownership of the batture deposited by the river in front of Faubourg Ste. Marie. These deposits of silt persisted between Felicity Street and Jackson Square and were gradually augmented with solid fill to extend the riverbank. In 1880, for example, it was estimated that 1,500 feet of batture had been created at the foot of Delord Street since 1718. In general, the batture was privately developed.

As Louisiana organized herself as a state, port affairs in New Orleans became more and more a local matter. It was not that the state relinquished sovereignty over the waterways, levees, and wharves within the city. It was rather that the duly elected government of the city gradually evolved as the state's agent in such matters. General authority for the city to act for the state in port administration passed in the city's charter of 1805 and in the state constitution of 1812. And over the next two dozen years a variety of municipal ordinances appointed harbormasters, port wardens, and wharfingers to police the port and to collect various fees. Waterfront improvements were left to the initiative and, usually, to the financial resources of the mayor and City Council.

The new city charter of 1836, which divided New Orleans into three municipalities, reserved to the general council (composed of the three municipal councils) the right to fix uniform wharfage rates for the city as a whole. Local authority in these matters was again implied in the state constitution of 1845. Each municipality erected its own administrative, collection, and policing establishment. Since the wharfage charges imposed were far above the token port fees of earlier periods, two important lawsuits were brought to test the new powers being exercised by the general and municipal councils. In both cases the finding was for the city, and the principle of municipal wharfage, if for the purpose of port maintenance, was first fixed in Louisiana jurisprudence.

Between 1852, when the city was reunited and enlarged under a new charter, and 1865, a new pattern of port administration emerged. Because of the shaky financial condition of the city, there was much more state intervention in local affairs. The pattern, as far as the port was concerned, became one of pragmatic municipal ordinances predicated upon the city charter and the new state constitution of 1852; one of periodic subsumation of local laws by state legislation; and one of constant judicial review. State acts of 1855, 1857, and 1859, for example, codified and clarified the duties and remunerations of the harbor masters and port wardens of New Orleans, and were then rigorously challenged in the courts.

In general, these acts stood the test of judicial review. Port officials were authorized to collect fees when they actually performed services, but the older, broader principle of their collecting fees "whether called on to perform any services or not" was declared unconstitutional. The leasing of the public wharves to private operators willing to maintain them was also upheld. But if the volume of litigation on wharf leasing is any guide, the system apparently brought no great improvement in the physical condition of the waterfront. Little changed during the federal occupation, when the port was operated at the pleasure of the military commandant.

A state act of 1865 reasserted state sovereignty over the New Orleans waterfront and reenacted the port legislation of 1857 and 1859. Implementation, however, was still left to the city. The city was authorized to lease the public wharves and landings to the highest bidder and to set the rates of wharfage he might collect. From 1865 to 1881, the firm of Eager, Ellerman & Co. leased and operated all public waterfront facilities under these conditions.

In addition to the public-wharf leasing arrangement, however, there was renewed effort to coordinate state and local port laws: Sections 1681–1684 and 2218–2230 of the Revised Statutes of 1870 as amended by Act No. 3 E.S. of 1877, dealt specifically with the powers and duties of the now-called "Board of Harbor Masters of New Orleans"; city ordinances published uniform charges for use of the port; and an important federal case upheld the right of the Legislature through the City Council to charge "reasonable" fees to regulate and improve waterfront facilities, regardless of the services performed by port officials.

Between 1881 and 1891, the practice of farming out the waterfront was continued, and the public wharves were leased to Joseph A. Aiken & Company. Aiken guaranteed to spend at least $25,000 per year for waterfront improvements and $40,000 annually to police the port and pay the salaries of the wharfingers. In 1891, the public wharves were again let on competitive bids, again for ten years, to Charles K. Burdeau. Burdeau's Louisiana Construction and Improvement Company agreed to spend $465,000 for wharf improvements during its first two years of operation and at least $35,000 per year thereafter. In addition, the company paid $40,000 per year for policing and salaries.

These wharf lessees fulfilled their contracts in good faith, and New Orleans' waterfront facilities were upgraded as a result. But during their tenure, the port's comparative advantage declined so noticeably as to induce a complete reorganization of its administration. The process began in the 1880's at the initiative of several interested groups of businessmen.

Besides the Chamber of Commerce, which had led the fight for improvement of the passes, the prime organizations lobbying for port improvement were the New Orleans Cotton Exchange (organized in 1871), the New Orleans Produce Exchange (organized in 1880), and the New Orleans Maritime Association (organized in 1880). The role played by the Cotton Exchange was primarily informational, through the efforts of its secretary, Henry G. Hester, who was the most assiduous statistician the port has ever known. The Maritime Association was a group of shipowners, agents, brokers, and import-export merchants. It had standing committees on "customs and abuses," "underwriting," "arbitration," and "legislation" and published "rules and regulations" for the conduct of maritime trade in the city. The Produce Exchange proved to be the catalyst in formation, in 1889, of the most influential group of all, the New Orleans Board of Trade. The standing and special committees of the Board of Trade were those who became most often heard in public councils. Their target was the wharf-leasing system.

The Louisiana Construction and Improvement Company had agreed to spend twice as much on waterfront improvements as had their predecessors, and to accept a 20 per lower schedule of wharfage rates. Even so, New Orleans' port charges remained higher than those of any American port of comparable size and her facilities less than modern. As a result, a committee of the Board of Trade, headed by Hugh McCloskey, began investigating the situation in 1895 and drafted a city ordinance calling for municipal repurchase of the wharf lease and a review of the rate structure.

McCloskey's proposals were enacted on February 12, 1896, but were repealed by an incoming city administration four months later. The Board of Trade now changed its tactics and sought a reassertion of state authority over the port. The group was successful on July 9, when the Legislature passed "An Act to establish a Commission for the Port of New Orleans; to define their powers and duties; to provide a revenue therefore, and to repeal conflicting laws." The new state agency was to be known as the "Board of Commissioners of the Port of New Orleans" or, more popularly, the "Dock Board."

The purposes for establishing the Dock Board were clearly stated. First, it was recognized that "the Port of New Orleans has been gradually extended until it has reached beyond the limits and jurisdiction of the City of New Orleans." Although Lafayette (1852), Algiers (1870), Jefferson (1870), and Carrollton (1874) had been annexed by the city, the legal limits of the port had remained unchanged since 1804. In 1875, these were codified so as to correspond to the boundaries of Orleans Parish on the east bank (roughly from Monticello Avenue down to Jackson Barracks).

Between 1888 and 1896, however, law, if not administration, caught up with reality. On July 23, 1888, the port limits were extended to include all of Orleans Parish on the west bank (including Algiers), plus that portion of Jefferson Parish on the east bank between the upper line of Orleans Parish and the upper line of Carrollton (including Southport). On March 20, 1896, the limits were further extended to include: (1) a 4,000-foot depth of Jefferson Parish on the west bank (including West-wego, Amesville, Marrero, Harvey, Gretna, and McDonoghville) between the west-bank upper line of Orleans Parish and a point opposite the east-bank upper line of Orleans Parish; and (2) a 3-mile length × 4,000-foot depth of St. Bernard Parish below the east-bank lower line of Orleans Parish (including Chalmette).

With this physical expansion of the port area, and without some administrative reform, it was argued, the "divided authority of three parishes and the multiplicity of officials with their various fees and the development of contiguous rival ports will act injuriously and prejudicially to the traffic of the port." Furthermore, "the tax on shipping exacted for various fees, charges, etc., is of such proportions as to threaten to divert the trade to less expensive ports." But, it was proposed, "the supervision and control of an intelligent Board of State Commissioners can consolidate the services of Harbor Masters and Wardens, Wharf Superintendents, Wharfingers of the three parishes into one set of competent exployees at a reduced expense; can operate and improve the wharves and other terminal facilities of the port and greatly develop and expand its commerce."

As originally established by Act No. 70 of 1896, the "Board of Commissioners of the Port of New Orleans" consisted of five members appointed by the governor for five-year staggered terms. All members had to be United States citizens and residents of either Orleans, Jefferson, or St. Bernard parishes. All had to be "prominently identified with the commerce or business interests of the Port." The duties of the board were clear:

". . . to take charge of and administer the public wharves of the Port of New Orleans; to construct new wharves where necessary and to erect sheds thereon; to protect merchandise in transit; to place and keep the wharves, sheds, levees and approaches in good condition; to maintain sufficient depth of water and to provide for lighting and policing such wharves and sheds; to defray said expenses . . . charge upon the shipping visiting the port, for the use of wharves, etc. . . .

To avoid misunderstanding, "all laws and ordinances regarding the appointment and fees governing Harbormaster, Masters and Wardens, Wharfingers, Wharf Superintendents and any and all laws in conflict with this act are hereby repealed and the authority and control heretofore vested in them is hereby vested in the Board." Most important, however, the Dock Board was "authorized and impowered to acquire by purchase or by expropriation the lease of the wharves now held by the Louisiana Construction and Improvement Company," and it was "made the duty of the Common Council of the City of New Orleans to provide for the payment of the price of such purchase of expropriation."

Since the lease of the Louisiana Construction and Improvement Company did not expire until May 29, 1901, the Dock Board had plenty of time to organize itself and establish liaison with other agencies and interested groups. The Board assumed its duties on September 5, 1896, with Hugh McCloskey as its first president, and in 1901 took over the public wharves on schedule.

The first task of the Dock Board was to take stock of what it had acquired. It inherited nearly six miles of public wharves, primarily on the east bank between Jefferson and Napoleon avenues and between Louisiana and Jourdan avenues. Nearby were several large private facilities which had been granted revocable wharf privileges by the state between 1870 and 1900: (1) the Illinois Central's Stuyvesant Docks (between Louisiana and Napoleon avenues) and Southport Terminal, a total of 5,200 feet of wharves and warehouses, including four grain elevators with a combined capacity of 3,500,000 bushels; (2) the Texas and Pacific's Westwego Terminal, 3,700 feet of frontage, two elevators with a total capacity of 1,800,000 bushels, and a car ferry to the east bank; (3) the Southern Pacific's terminals at Gretna and Algiers, 1,000 feet of wharves and a car ferry; and (4) Port Chalmette, operated by the New Orleans Belt and Terminal Company, 3,800 feet of wharves and a 500,000 bushel elevator.

In determining priorities for implementation of its powers and responsibilities, the Dock Board acted first regarding its rate structure. It then turned its attention to waterfront facility improvement. By August 31, 1901, the New Orleans Maritime Association reported real progress: "as soon as the Port Commissioners took possession a minimum reduction of 25 per cent and a maximum reduction of 83⅓ per cent in wharfage fees on all vessels went into effect." By July 3, 1908, it was reported to the State Legislature that the Board had, "out of its revenues" since May 29, 1901, "practically rebuilt the entire wharf system received from . . . [the] Louisiana Construction and Improvement Company, built new wharves, erected steel sheds on the wharves and landings . . . constructed paved roadways and approaches thereto, provided suitable dredge and tugboats for dredging and fire protection purposes; has maintained sufficient depth of water and provided for the lighting and policing of the wharves, landings, sheds and appurtenances thereto."

Even as these improvements progressed, however, the Dock Board realized a paradox in its purposes. It had no taxing power and its sole income was from its harbor, wharfage, sheddage, and wharf tollage fees. Yet, if the public interest demanded that these fees remain low, how could sufficient funds be accumulated to finance large-scale port improvements? Lack of funds was serious enough in the early days to cause some Board members to draw against personal lines of credit to cover public expenses.

One additional source of credit was developed prior to 1908 —"advances against contracts." In return for "preferential assignments" to particular wharves, shipping lines advanced funds to the Board for improvement of those facilities. This practice is still common and the non-interest-bearing loans are liquidated by rebating wharfage. The first of these contracts were probably those with the Leyland Line (July 9, 1903) and the Harrison Line (November 28, 1903). As part of a contractual advance, or separately, water carriers could also purchase a "first-call-on berth privilege," payable quarterly in advance.

Since 1908, however, the Board has been authorized to issue negotiable bonds for the purpose of waterfront improvement. As of June 30, 1965, seventeen issues totaling $97,712,000 had been made, of which $54,870,000 was then outstanding. Funds from these bond sales are invested in short-term securities until needed. The principal and interest on these bonds are funded from net earnings, depreciation accumulations, and, since 1921, by a portion of the revenue from the state gasoline tax. Also, between 1918 and 1960, the Board of Levee Commissioners of the Orleans Levee District and the Public Belt Railroad Commission contributed $925,000 and $50,000 per year, respectively, to fund interest and maturities of the four issues of

Industrial Canal bonds discussed above. Between 1921 and 1959, the Board's statutory debt limitation was $35,000,000. Since December 5, 1958, its limitation has been $95,000,000.

For what improvements have these monies gone? First, of course, has been betterment and expansion of the public wharves. The wharves under Dock Board ownership and control in 1920, for example, totaled 28,872 linear feet of frontage and 4,230,894 square feet of area (2,784,144 sq. ft. covered; 1,446,750 sq. ft. open). By June 30, 1965, these facilities had increased to 49,067 linear feet of frontage (a gain of 41 per cent over 1920) and 9,944,576 square feet of area (a 57 per cent gain). Covered wharf area had increased by 59 per cent (to 6,747,788 sq. ft.). The major new wharves constructed since World War II have been those at Jourdan Avenue (1953), Thalia Street (1955), Perry Street (1960), Nashville Avenue (1962), Napoleon Avenue (1965), and Henry Clay Avenue (1965).

Prior to World War II, in addition to its wharf projects and besides its construction of the Industrial Canal, the Dock Board built a number of cargo-handling facilities. Between January 27 and August 1, 1915, it completed a seven-unit Public Cotton Warehouse between Napoleon Avenue and Soniat Street (now known as the Public Commodity Warehouse and enlarged in 1953–1954). The port's first Public Grain Elevator was completed at Dufossat Street between October 9, 1915 and February 1, 1917. Its original capacity of 2,622,000 bushes was increased to 5,122,000 in 1953 and to 7,122,000 in 1960. This facility passed the billion bushel mark in receipts and deliveries during fiscal 1954–1955, and in 1964 was leased under competitive bidding to private operators. A Public Coal and Bulk Commodity Handling Plant was built at Nashville Avenue between September 3, 1919 and September 1, 1921, and operated through World War II. This facility has since been replaced by construction of the Nashville Avenue Wharf. Besides these projects of its own, the Dock Board leased and operated two sections of the Army Supply

Base which was built between Poland Avenue and the Industrial Canal during 1918–1919.

In 1947, the Dock Board embarked on two of its most ambitious projects—one successful; one not. In the demobilization rush following the war, the Board, exercising its authority to form and develop industrial districts, acquired the Michoud Industrial Facility located on the Intracoastal Canal. Over the next four years, several firms were induced to locate manufacturing operations at the facility, but as the Korean War loomed, the federal government retook the site for defense purposes. The Dock Board facility was closed down on January 18, 1951, federal possession taken on May 1, and condemnation of fee simple title proceedings begun on December 23, 1952. This litigation was finally ended in December, 1964, with the payment of $2,750,000 to the Dock Board in final settlement of its claims. In the meantime, the National Aeronautics and Space Administration had converted the facility into its Saturn rocket plant.

More successful, from the Dock Board's standpoint, was the development of Foreign Trade Zone No. 2. The Foreign Trade Zone Act of 1934 had authorized public port authorities to operate preferential customs areas under grants obtainable from the department of commerce. The Port of New York Authority was the first to open such a facility, but the foreign commerce committee of the New Orleans Association of Commerce began formal study of the idea in 1942. Their favorable report prompted the Dock Board to seek a trade zone grant. Permission to operate the 18.6-acre Foreign Trade Zone No. 2 was forthcoming on July 17, 1946, and formal dedication of the facility followed four months later. It opened for business (in the Public Commodity Warehouse) on May 1, 1947.

Within the trade zone "the Customs laws governing imports are not applicable until the goods are withdrawn for domestic U.S. consumption. No duties are levied against foreign commodities transshipped through the Zone to other foreign destinations. . . . Goods normally dutiable can remain duty-free

indefinitely in the Zone, and products may be processed, manip-
ulated, manufactured or otherwise treated in any manner to
enhance their value or change their tariff classification." Processing facilities presently located in the zone include: a manufac-
turer and exporter of fishing nets who uses imported raw materials; a kiln for drying imported lumber before it is shipped to
U.S. destinations; a vacuum fumigation plant; an international
department store's warehouse. Success of Foreign Trade Zone
No. 2 prompted a Dock Board application for a sub-zone to
handle oil, oil derivatives, and petrochemicals in April, 1964. On
March 23, 1967, the department of commerce granted the Board
authority to operate Foreign Trade Sub-Zone 2A on a 79-acre
site at Taft, Louisiana.

Of equal importance since World War II, of course, has
been the Dock Board's involvement in completion of the Mississippi River-Gulf Outlet. The Board has acted as assuring agency
for the state in this project for purposes of obtaining rights of
way and relocating existing facilities. In addition, it has constructed a Public Bulk Terminal (since 1960) on the Tidewater
Channel to handle ores, rock, shell, sand, gravel, coal, concen-
trates, and raw sugar.

In the planning and execution of these projects, the organization of the Dock Board has undergone a metamorphosis. Between Act No. 70 of 1896 and the state constitution of 1913,
Board members were appointed by the governor for five-year
terms. Act No. 69 of 1920 amended that constitution to extend
the term to six years and detailed a thorough reorganization of
the administration of Board projects. These changes were incorporated into the state constitution of 1921. Act No. 388 of 1940
ended the tenure of the existing Board, changed the term of
membership to five years, and named five organizations to serve
as nominators for Dock Board vacancies: the New Orleans Association of Commerce; the New Orleans Board of Trade; the
New Orleans Clearing House Association; the New Orleans Cotton Exchange; and the New Orleans Steamship Association. Act
No. 760 of 1954 further provided that one member of the Board

must reside on the west bank, substituted the Chamber of Commerce of the New Orleans Area for the Association of Commerce on the nominating committee, and added the West Bank Council of the Chamber of Commerce and International House as nominators.

Much of the Dock Board's work since World War I has also concentrated on liaison with other public agencies such as the U.S. Corps of Engineers, the Levee Board, the Public Belt Railroad Commission, and the authorities which constructed the Huey P. Long Bridge (1935) and the Greater New Orleans Bridge (1958). An important recent development has been the formation of the Mid-Gulf Seaports Marine Terminal Conference. In 1966, the dock boards of New Orleans, Baton Rouge, and Lake Charles requested permission from the Federal Maritime Commission to work cooperatively on revisions of their rates, charges, rules, and regulations. When federal approval came on January 19, 1967, an organizational meeting elected W. J. Amoss, director of the Port of New Orleans, as chairman of the conference.

Effective July 15, 1967, revised wharfage rates went into effect "designed to provide additional revenues essential to the continuance of capital construction programs in the three ports, and to the orderly development of public port facilities capable of meeting the increasing demands of commerce." At New Orleans, where the Dock Board's "Facilities Program" budget for the years 1964–1974 is $193,076,062, "the new wharfage charges on cargo making use of public facilities will generally range from 35 to 50 cents per ton, depending upon the commodity." These rates supplant a rate of 15 cents per ton dating back to 1921 which "no longer provides revenues sufficient to the task of meeting the port's development needs."

Besides liaison with public agencies, however, the Dock Board has increasingly cooperated with carriers, shippers, and other interested groups in organized efforts at trade promotion. The Board established trade solicitation offices in Chicago (1928), New York (1935), St. Louis (1950), and Cincinnati

(1957), as well as overseas. It has worked closely with the Board of Trade, the Chamber of Commerce, the New Orleans Steamship Association (founded 1912), and International House (incorporated 1943) in such projects as the annual Mississippi Valley World Trade Council Conference (twenty-three meetings through April, 1967) and in International House's Trade Missions overseas (fifty-nine through September, 1967). The Board itself has also financed the construction of the $13,500,000 Port of New Orleans Exhibition Center at the foot of Canal Street.

Thus, in the development of organized administration and betterment of its waterfront, just as in the improvement of navigational facilities, the history of the Port of New Orleans reflects the persistent and productive interaction of man and nature. The process has blended private and public interests and has gradually consolidated municipal and parish agencies into a unified, powerful, and aggressive state board. This board sets policies and supervises the overall activities of the port and provides most of the terminals and waterfront facilities. Private enterprises own and operate some facilities, lease others from the Dock Board, and provide all stevedoring, pilots, and other shipping workers. It now remains to summarize the patterns of waterborne trade which have stimulated or reenforced these physical and administrative changes in the Port of New Orleans.

From the large body of available commercial statistics, three sets are most useful in characterizing the historical patterns of New Orleans' waterborne trade: those relating to river commerce; those pertaining to the coasting trades; and those reflecting the contours of foreign trade. Since the data come from such diverse sources and have been gathered for such diverse purposes, they do not always fit together in continuous and comparable series. Nevertheless, by using selected series for different periods, the general patterns can still be discerned.

The best available measure of New Orleans' river commerce prior to the twentieth century is the dollar value of downriver freight received at the port. For the years 1801–1807, the first period for which reliable data exist, the total value of such receipts was $31,799,000. From 1816, the first successful year of steam nagivation on the river through 1861, receipts totaled $2,956,643,000. And, according to antebellum experts, "the shipments up stream from New Orleans averaged about . . . 57 per cent in value of those coming down the river." Banner individual years were those ending in 1859 ($172,953,000), 1860 ($185,-211,000) and 1851 ($196,924,000). As to the nature of this trade, it has been estimated that in 1816 cotton accounted for only 12 per cent of downriver receipts. By the years 1823–1825 cotton comprised 49 per cent of receipts; sugar and molasses, 12 per cent; and tobacco, 6 per cent (the remainder being grain, produce, spirits, and package freight). During 1841–1845, cotton comprised 53 per cent of receipts; sugar and molasses, 12 per cent; and tobacco, 10 per cent. During 1856–1860, the comparable percentages were 54, 13, and 6.

Between 1862 and 1890, downriver receipts at New Orleans totaled $4,476,903,000, with banner years in 1883 ($200,-019,000), 1870 ($200,820,000), and 1866 ($201,501,000). Even the worst postwar years never fell below $127,000,000 per year: 1868 ($127,298,000) and 1879 ($127,207,000). More significant during this period was competition between water and rail carriers. For example, downriver carriage by rail was 31 per cent of that by water in 1873; in 1880 rail ran 50 per cent of water; by 1887, rail ran 118 per cent of water carriage. Regardless of the changing methods of transport, however, the fact remains that between 1821 and 1890, $7,433,546,000 of downriver freights were received at New Orleans.

Better data are available for the twentieth century, but are compiled in tonnage rather than in dollars. This is because the most significant river traffic in this century has been barge transportation of bulk products such as grain, petroleum, ores, and chemicals. For the years 1915–1919, internal receipts and shipments by water at New Orleans totaled 44,514,000 short tons. During 1921–1940, receipts totaled 39,012,000 short tons and shipments 24,039,000. Receipts during 1941–1965 were at least 278,374,000 short tons and shipments, 152,628,000. To summarize these data another way, for the period 1921–1940, internal receipts and shipments accounted for an annual average of 21 per cent of the port's waterborne freight tonnage; for the period 1941–1965, at least 47 per cent.

Coastwise trade is much harder to document, especially for the nineteenth century. Data exists for only 19 of the 32 years, 1830–1861, and none earlier. For these 19 years, however, the value of New Orleans' coastwise shipments totals $362,020,000. High years were 1856 ($28,031,000), 1849, ($28,384,000), and 1854 ($30,695,000). Low years were 1834 ($9,930,000), 1833 ($9,058,000), and 1830 ($8,358,000). The only figures available for the postbellum years of the nineteenth century are those for 1885 and 1886, when coastwise shipments totaled $75,404,000 in value. A better understanding of the coasting trades' share in New Orleans' nineteenth-century waterborne commerce comes when the value of coastwise shipments is calculated as a percentage of the port's value of exports of domestic products. This comparison averages 53 per cent annually for the 19 years for which data are available, 1830–1861. Thus, in those years, New Orleans shipped just under twice as much abroad as she did coastwise (by value). For the years 1885–1886, coastwise shipments averaged 47 per cent annually of domestic exports, indicating that New Orleans was then exporting just over twice as much as she shipped coastwise (by value).

For the twentieth century, of course, the picture is more complete and the effects of such navigational improvements as the Harvey, the Industrial, and the Intracoastal canals are clear. During 1910–1930, coastwise receipts and shipments accounted for an annual average of 26 per cent of the port's waterborne commerce. During 1931–1937, under the combined effects of a depression in foreign trade and the opening of the Intracoastal Waterway, coastwise receipts and shipments accounted for an annual average of 47 per cent of the port's waterborne trade. From 1941 through 1965, coastwise receipts have totaled at least 17,056,000 short tons; shipments have risen in volume and have totaled at least 185,408,000 short tons. Yet, because of the growth of both foreign and internal trade, coastwise receipts and shipments accounted for an annual average of only 20 per cent of the port's commerce, 1941–1965. Since 1959, however, this annual average has been 25 per cent.

The table presents selected foreign trade data for the period 1821–1965, arranged to identify contours in that important segment of the maritime history of New Orleans. Note that for 1821–1960, the average annual value of both exports and imports increased, New Orleans' share in total American foreign trade increased, but the ratio of imports to exports in the city's own trading mix declined. Antebellum record years for the port were 1843, when she handled 33 per cent of American exports and 19 per cent of imports; 1853, when she handled 34 per cent of American exports; and 1859, when she handled 35 per cent of American exports—her all-time high. The effects of the Civil War are quite apparent.

During the first period of wharf leasing, 1866–1880, exports rose above prewar levels and imports almost so. Yet there was decline in the share imports played in the city's foreign trade and a decline in the proportion of American foreign trade which moved through the port. Record year for the period was 1867, when 28 per cent of American exports and 3 per cent of American imports moved through the port. Prime export commodities were cotton and cotton products, tobacco, wheat, corn, wood and wood products, wheat flour, and pork products. Imports were primarily coffee, iron, and steel products, sugar and molasses, wines and spirits, and cotton textiles. As of June 30, 1871, Europe took 96 per cent of New Orleans' exports and shipped 65 per cent of her imports; Latin America accounted for 3 per cent of exports and 30 per cent of imports; Asia took no exports of New Orleans and provided only 1 per cent of her imports.

In the second period of wharf leasing, 1881–1890, New Orleans' export level held its own, but her imports declined absolutely as well as relatively. The city's share of total American foreign trade also continued to decline. During the final period of wharf leasing, 1891–1900, both exports and imports increased,

SELECTED PATTERNS OF NEW ORLEANS FOREIGN TRADE,
1821–1965

Period (Inclusive)	Average Value Exports / Yr. ($million)	Average Value Imports / Yr. ($million)	Average Tonnage Exports / Yr. (millions)	Average Tonnage Imports / Yr. (millions)
1821–1835	15	7	*	*
1836–1851	35	10	*	*
1852–1860	78	16	*	*
1861–1865	4	3	*	*
1866–1880	85	13	*	*
1881–1890	87	11	*	*
1893–1896	77	17	*	*
1891–1900	97	17	*	*
1901–1910	150	37	*	*
1911–1916	184	81	4	2
1917–1921	443	146	5	4
1922–1930	330	186	5	5
1931–1940	162	100	3	3
1941–1945	304	240	3	3
1946–1956	845	513	6	4
1957–1965	*	*	12	5

Notes: For 1821–1842, dollar-value years end September 30; for 1843–1956,
dollar-value years end June 30. For 1911–1965, tonnage years are
calendar years. For sources see text.
  * No comparable data available.

the latter regained some of their share in the port's commerce, but no improvement in New Orleans' share of national
trade is apparent. Also, note the depression in exports during
1893–1896, which precipitated formation of the Dock Board.

The effects of the Dock Board's wharfage reductions and
trade promotion are clear. During 1901–1910, the first decade of
Board control, New Orleans' exports rose 55 per cent and imports 101 per cent over the previous decade. There was also
improvement in the import share and in New Orleans' share of
American foreign trade. Since these increases ran 90 per cent and
168 per cent of national increases during the same period,
changes in port administration must be credited with some por-

SELECTED PATTERNS OF NEW ORLEANS FOREIGN TRADE,
1821–1965

N.O. Imports as % N.O. Exports by value (annual average)	N.O. Imports as % N.O. Exports by Tonnage (annual av)	N.O. Exports as % U.S. Exports by value (annual av)	N.O. Imports as % U.S. Imports by value (annual av)
49	*	18	8
29	*	29	9
21	*	30	6
48	*	3	1
15	*	19	3
13	*	11	2
22	*	9	3
17	*	9	2
25	*	10	3
44	44	7	5
32	72	7	4
56	103	7	5
62	105	7	5
80	103	4	6
60	63	6	6
*	48	*	*

tion of the betterment of New Orleans' trade. During 1911–1916, there was continued growth in exports, imports, and the share of the latter in the city's commerce.

Between the world wars, there was a significant increase, 1922–1930, in New Orleans' foreign commerce and a noticeable advance in the proportion represented by imports, followed, during the depression years of 1931–1940, by a decline which affected exports more than imports. And, despite local fluctuations, New Orleans' share of national foreign trade held firm. Unlike World War I, World War II increased the import share of New Orleans' foreign trade, and, from 1946 through 1956, there was exceptional growth in the value of both exports and imports—particularly in the latter. New Orleans' postwar proportion of American foreign trade has remained stable.

The prime export commodities of New Orleans since World War II have been wheat, corn, soybeans, sulphur, wheat flour, lube oil and grease, raw cotton, machinery and vehicles, steel-mill products, and industrial chemicals. Her largest imports have been sugar and molasses, bananas, bauxite, coffee, industrial chemicals, sisal, jute, burlap and bagging, fertilizer materials, rubber, newsprint, and coal and petroleum derivatives. Petroleum and its products and grain are the leading products handled by water in the port. Since 1961, New Orleans has been the world's leading exporter of grain, accounting for 25.7 per cent of all United States grain exports in 1962; 26.4 per cent in 1963; 27.9 per cent in 1964; and 23.9 per cent in 1965.

In contrast to the situation 90 years earlier, Europe now takes about 44 per cent of New Orleans' exports and provides only 18 per cent of her imports (as of June 30, 1961). Latin America now receives 26 per cent of the city's exports and sends 54 per cent of her imports; Asia's shares are 22 per cent and 18 per cent respectively. In 1965, the rank of nations by value of exports taken from New Orleans, was Japan, West Germany, Italy, the United Kingdom, Venezuela, and the Netherlands. By export tonnage, the rank was Japan, Italy, the Netherlands, and West Germany. By value of imports brought to New Orleans, the rank was Brazil, Japan, Mexico, and West Germany. By import tonnage, the rank was Japan, the Netherlands Antilles, and Mexico.

In a sense, these statistics of foreign trade encapsulate the history of the Port of New Orleans. Only the Civil War and the depressions of 1893–1896 and 1931–1940 have seriously interrupted a steady growth in the annual value and tonnage of the city's exports. In value, imports have always lagged exports and, occasionally, the proportion has become so lopsided as to require vigorous trade promotion to restore the desired balance. It has always been easier for the port to attract high-bulk imports than high-value imports, and, in the twentieth century, import tonnage has sometimes exceeded export tonnage. Since 1946, however, this phenomenon has not occurred. Finally, New Orleans has seen her proportion of American foreign trade decline precipitously in the late nineteenth century and stabilize in the twentieth. Since World War II, she has reigned second only to New York among American ports in total value of trade.

Thus, a location well-endowed by nature and aggressive management and port development by man brought New Orleans to the billion dollar annual level of waterborne trade in 1946 and pushed her over the two billion mark in 1965. She has fully exploited her natural exporting position and vigorously attended to the quantity and quality of her imports. She has continually bettered her navigational and cargo-handling facilities as corollaries to her promotion of trade. She has diversified the commodities she handles and their points of origin and destination. And, she has sustained herself as a leader in American commerce. With this record of achievement, the port faces the challenges of the future.

The Post-Civil War Segregation Struggle

Roger Fischer

The nine men who sentenced Jim Crow to death in 1954 set in motion a racial revolution without parallel in the South since the one begun by Abraham Lincoln's historic stroke of the pen more than ninety years earlier. This second struggle to determine the "place" of the Negro came to New Orleans in the autumn of 1960, when a handful of colored children gained entry into the white public schools of the city despite a festival of fanaticism staged by diehard segregationists. Color barriers fell in quick succession after that. New Orleans Negroes soon rode in the front seats on buses and street cars, sat side by side with whites in theatres and restaurants, and sent their sons and daughters in ever-increasing numbers into the white schools and colleges.

It was clear to those who witnessed the changes that a way of life was dying, a code of conduct that had governed relationships between the races for as long as memory could recall. Faced with a present they could neither control nor understand, many white New Orleanians looked longingly to a hazy, heroic past, to a time when giants such as Frederick Ogden and Francis Nicholls walked the earth and Negroes knew their proper place. Preachers and politicians, editors and educators invoked the gray ghosts of an earlier lost cause to witness the shame of their progeny. Had they chosen to explore the past rather than exploit it, they might have discovered the irony of their current crisis. It had all happened once before.

The first campaign against the color line in New Orleans was waged during the decade of Radical Reconstruction that followed the Civil War. Slavery died at Appomattox, and the Northern conquerors were determined that a new and more subtle system of servitude would not rise out of the ashes of the old order. So they decreed that the ballot be given to the Negroes and taken away from many of the whites who had served the cause of the Confederacy. This missionary mathematics delivered control of the Louisiana state government into the hands of the Negroes and their white Radical Republican allies. As a vital part of its struggle to remold Louisiana life, this coalition declared total war on racial segregation.

The system of segregation was already very old in New Orleans by the time the guns fell silent. In the rural regions surrounding the city, plantation slavery had been its own stern segregator, maintaining direct discipline over the Negroes and rendering any secondary reminders of their inferiority altogether unnecessary. But in ante-bellum New Orleans the situation had been very different. Race discipline had been virtually nonexistent. Many of the Negroes, the Free Persons of Color, were quite literally masters of their own souls. Most of the slaves were household servants whose domestic duties made possible a certain independence. Others were "hired-out" to employers and given the freedom to secure their own lodgings with part of their wages. Nearly all New Orleans Negroes enjoyed a latitude of liberties unknown on the plantations. Unrestrained by any direct discipline, the city Negroes made a mockery of their lowly station. Colored crowds often harangued passing whites outside the numerous taverns that catered illegally to their trade. The more brazen Negroes assaulted whites with pistols, knives, razors, clubs, bottles, brickbats, horsewhips, cold chisels, and pool cues. Rare colored Don Juans even defied the greatest taboo of Southern society by engaging in *affaires d'amour* with white women.

The nature of city life made direct, personal control over the Negroes impossible. In its place segregation evolved as a public approach to the problem, a secondary line of defense for white supremacy.

Public facilities were strictly segregated in New Orleans throughout the ante-bellum period. An ordinance passed in 1816 required theatres and public exhibitions to seat whites and Negroes in separate sections. The most famous of all such arrangements was that of the French Opera House, where a section of boxes in the upper gallery was set apart for the free colored élite. Separate street cars were operated for the two races, with Negro cars identified by large stars painted on the sides. City jails provided separate accommodations, as did Charity Hospital. Even the cemeteries were segregated, first by local custom and after 1835 by city ordinance. Negroes were simply excluded from such white facilities as restaurants, hotels, and the public schools. On the eve of the Civil War, when mounting tensions led to increased suspicion of interracial contacts, a series of city council ordinances spread segregation to drinking, gambling, and prostitution. Many Negroes resented these restrictions bitterly, but manifestations of their discontent were largely limited to sporadic eruptions, like their attack on a street car that had refused to carry a group of them to Lake Pontchartrain in 1833. Lacking the power to change the system, there was little else they could do.

Negro hopes were raised when New Orleans fell to the Federals in 1862. Free Negro spokesmen petitioned General Benjamin F. Butler—the "Beast" of local legendry—to end segregation in the public schools and on the street cars. They tried to mix the schools in 1862, but Butler personally put down the attempt. The street cars were desegregated briefly in 1863, but the car companies soon won a judgment giving them the right to reinstitute separate cars for white and colored passengers. General Nathaniel P. Banks, Butler's successor as occupational commander, allowed the ruling to stand. Desegregation received no better reception from the native Unionist faction that assumed provisional power in the state in 1864. Delegates to the constitutional convention of that year were of one voice in condemning the mixing of the races in the public schools. Military defeat and occupation brought no changes in the segregation patterns of New Orleans places of public accommodation. Negroes were still assigned to "nigger heavens" in theatres and halls and excluded altogether from coffee houses, restaurants, ballrooms, and hotels. It began to appear to colored critics that the Northern victory meant little more than a change of masters.

But the First Reconstruction Act, passed by Congress on March 2, 1867, altered the picture suddenly and dramatically by giving the Negroes the power of the ballot. The Carpetbaggers who came to claim Louisiana in the name of the Radical Republican party soon realized that their hopes hinged to a great extent upon their ability to cooperate closely with the "colored Creole" spokesmen who had assumed leadership of the New Orleans Negro community. These colored aristocrats had long viewed segregation with great bitterness and they now made its abolition one of the prices for their allegiance. The point was not lost on the Radicals. One of their orators drew a thunderous ovation from a Negro audience in April, 1867, by asking them, "If my colored brother and I touch elbows at the polls, why should not his child and mine sit side by side in the school room?" Republican organizers lost no opportunity to remind their colored audiences of the new casteless society that would be theirs as soon as the Republican reign began.

But the Negroes did not wait for the dawn. In April, 1867, the New Orleans *Tribune*, a militant Negro daily edited by "colored Creoles" J. B. and Louis Roudanez, revived its running attack on the "star" system of segregated street cars. On April 28, Negro William Nichols tried to board a white car and was bodily ejected by starter Edward Cox, an action that sparked a series of suits and counter-suits. The Nichols incident set in motion a number of Negro attempts to ride the white cars. To keep the peace but retain segregation, the car companies instructed their personnel not to assault colored intruders, but to halt the cars until the Negroes departed.

The week-end of May 4–5 brought the city to the brink of violence. On Saturday Negro crowds gathered on Love Street in the Third District and began attacking white cars. One belligerent demonstrator overpowered a white driver and stole his street car. When police were called to the scene, the mob grew uglier. A police dispatch described the assemblage as "a crowd of colored men in open riot." Squads of police from neighboring stations reinforced the embattled Third District patrolmen and prevented the violence from reaching epidemic proportions. But tensions remained dangerously volatile. On Sunday afternoon colored crowds again gathered and again waged war on passing white cars. Scattered fights erupted between white and colored gangs throughout the city. The focal point of the unrest was Congo Square, traditional slave dancing ground before the war, where a mob estimated at five hundred gathered and began attacking white street cars. Their fury abated only after Mayor Edward Heath, a moderate Republican with a well-earned reputation for fairness among the Negroes, promised the rioters that the proper authorities would consider their grievances.

General Philip Sheridan, commander of the Fifth Military District, met the following day with Mayor Heath and car company executives to settle the matter. When Sheridan refused to support the "star" system with Union troops, the businessmen decided to abandon street car segregation altogether. Company personnel were ordered to admit all passengers to all cars. Actual change came more slowly. Most Negroes continued to ride in the "star cars" at first, but they gradually followed their bolder brethren into the white carriers. One white mob roughly ejected the colored passengers from a mixed car, but other than that the white reaction was surprisingly calm. The *Times* dismissed the controversy as "a clamor for shadows" and the *Crescent* welcomed its settlement for averting "a collision of races." But the

Daily Picayune saw more clearly that the car crisis was "simply the introductory step to more radical innovations, which must materially alter our whole social fabric."

The Negroes apparently learned the same lesson, for they followed up their street car victory with attacks on segregation in other areas of city life. Several colored crusaders demanded service in white theatres, restaurants, retail stores, and taverns. The *Tribune* renewed its demand for public school desegregation and unleashed a vehement attack against a proposed "star" school system for colored children. But white resistance stiffened and both ventures failed. Mayor Heath issued an executive proclamation in May affirming the right of a private business to serve whomever it desired. The separate school system for Negroes was put into operation in the autumn of 1867, despite the loud and angry protests of militant colored leaders.

While the desegregation debate raged, the issue was being resolved elsewhere. Under the guidelines set by the First Reconstruction Act, 82,907 Negroes and 44,732 whites had been registered during the summer of 1867 as voters to select delegates to a convention to rewrite the Louisiana constitution. The hopelessly outnumbered white Democrats boycotted the elections, thus making inevitable a Radical runaway. Ninety-six of the ninety-eight delegates were Republicans. Half were Negroes. Most of the whites were Carpetbaggers. During its deliberations which lasted from November, 1867, into March, 1868, this "black and tan" assemblage wrote a theoretical racial revolution into the laws of Louisiana. Segregation was expressly forbidden in the public schools and places of public accommodation. A new oath of office required all state officials to "accept the civil and political equality of all men, and agree not to attempt to deprive any person or persons, on account of race, color, or previous condition, of any political or civil right, privilege, or immunity enjoyed by any other class of men."

The "black and tan" constitution of 1868 was a declaration of war on the social system of the South and the white New

Orleanians knew it. The *Crescent* called the crisis "a question of liberty, of civilization, of social existence." The *Times* saw it as "a time of great danger to every interest of our civilization, our social system and the supremacy of the white people." The *Bee* branded the document a "condensed charter of all the turpitudes and monstrosities which negro depravity and fanatical partizanship are attempting to impose upon us" and advised its readers, "If you don't want your mothers and sisters, and wives and daughters insulted by insolent and depraved negro vagabonds, go to the polls and vote against the new Constitution. If you are opposed to amalgamation and miscegenation, vote against the new Constitution."

The election to ratify or reject the "black and tan" document was held on April 17 and 18, 1868. This time there was no white boycott, for the verdict was too vital to be determined by default. But Democratic dedication was not enough to overcome the great Radical registration majorities. By a vote of 51,737 to 39,076, the constitution became the law of Louisiana and sent Radical egalitarianism careening toward a collision with white customs, prejudices, and convictions of racial superiority.

In the same elections the Radicals captured control of both houses of the State Legislature. During the summer of 1868 colored lawmakers began to press for the adoption of stringent civil rights legislation to implement the general constitutional provisions. R. H. Isabelle, a New Orleans Negro, introduced a measure that defined racial discrimination in places of public accommodation as a criminal act and set severe fines and jail sentences for convicted violators. State Superintendent of Education Thomas W. Conway, a white Radical from New York, gave his blessing to a bill that demanded the compulsory attendance of all children in the mixed public schools. But these brotherhood-by-bayonet proposals were killed by the new governor, Henry Clay Warmoth, a moderate Republican from southern Illinois who favored a "moderate and discreet" approach to the segregation question. Warmoth vetoed the Isabelle bill and saw to it that the Conway measure died in committee. In 1869 the Radicals won acceptance of milder measures. The school bill was passed after its obnoxious compulsory provision was abandoned. Governor Warmoth signed into law a public accommodations act that deleted criminal prosecution for violators.

The Radicals had made their law, but they had yet to put it into practice. In the country parishes they never did. Rural Negroes were too deferential; federal forces were too far away; and white shotgun sovereignty remained the law of the land. But in New Orleans conditions were altogether different. The city Negroes demanded desegregation, their Radical representatives enacted it, and occupational garrisons of bluecoats stood near to support it. The war against the color line in Louisiana would be waged in the streets and saloons and schools of New Orleans.

The drive to desegregate places of public accommodation in the city began in earnest in January of 1871, when Civil Sheriff C. S. Sauvinet, a Negro, demanded a drink in the Bank Saloon at 6 Royal Street. Proprietor J. A. Walker told the sheriff that the tavern did not cater to colored trade and ordered him to leave. Sauvinet promptly brought suit against the barkeep, demanding $10,000 in damages and revocation of the Bank Saloon's liquor license. The case was decided in April by Judge Henry C. Dibble, a Northern-born Radical, who allowed Walker to retain his license but awarded Sauvinet $1,000 to "sanctify the principle involved and deter others from inflicting the same injury."

Despite the severity of the Dibble decree, segregation survived in places of public accommodation. Few Negroes followed Sheriff Sauvinet's example by testing personally the strength of the color line. Those who did ran the risk of stirring white wrath. A colored state senator from Plaquemines Parish boarded the steamboat *Bannock City* in March, 1871, and took a seat in the cabin facilities reserved for white travelers. A steward asked the legislator to leave peacefully, and when he refused he was seized by a group of white passengers, beaten over the head with an iron bar, and thrown out onto the deck. Everywhere segregation proved stronger than the law. A new, tougher civil rights law enacted in 1873 failed to bring changes or even many challenges.

Five years after the passage of the "black and tan" constitution, New Orleans Negroes still ate in separate restaurants, drank in separate saloons, and sat in separate theatre sections.

But the mighty power of the federal government came to the assistance of the local Negroes on March 1, 1875, when President Ulysses S. Grant signed into law the controversial Civil Rights Act of 1875. The pet project of Radical Senator Charles Sumner of Massachusetts, the law prohibited racial segregation in theatres, inns, common carriers, and all other places of public accommodation and amusement. Upon conviction, a violator could be fined as much as $1,000, imprisoned for at least thirty days, and directed to pay the injured party $500 in damages. The Sumner law revitalized the drive for desegregation in New Orleans. The *Daily Picayune* complained that to "the general herd of blacks the signing of the bill is looked upon as a second emancipation proclamation, by which they are to gain some sort of indefinite privileges which they suppose the whites to enjoy." On March 9 two local Negro politicians gained entry into the white seating section of the St. Charles Theatre to see the play *Sir Giles Overreach*. The white patrons deserted their seats, but the Negroes were not disturbed. Throughout the city Negroes demanded service in white restaurants and taverns.

Unwilling to cater to Negroes but unable to challenge the awesome power of the federal government, local proprietors devised ingenious ways to circumvent the law. The manager of the Varieties Theatre discouraged two would-be colored patrons by telling them that although admission was free, it required the purchase of a $2.50 "beer ticket." Restaurants forced to serve persistent Negroes often saturated the food with salt, pepper, or vinegar. Bartenders were unexcelled in their wizardry at rendering drinks unpalatable. George McCloskey served a Negro a soft drink doctored with a liberal dose of cayenne red pepper in his saloon at 76 St. Charles. The gasping Negro tried to have McCloskey arrested, but according to the *Times* the policeman considered the dispute "entirely a matter of taste." A donnybrook developed in a saloon on Canal Street after a bartender served salted soft drinks to three colored customers.

Gradually the testing subsided and the movement died. In rare cases Negroes continued to challenge the color line until Reconstruction itself died in 1877, but they never again mounted a sustained drive to destroy segregation in places of public accommodation. The crusade failed in part because white proprietors dared to defy the law rather than cater to colored trade, but it failed primarily because few New Orleans Negroes found the incentives worth the obstacles. Most of them could not afford the white luxuries, and few wanted to endure certain white hostility for the uncertain rewards of salted food or doctored drinks.

The Negroes enjoyed greater success in their drive to desegregate the New Orleans public schools. The local colored leadership had long regarded mixed public education as an essential step toward real racial equality. Free Negro spokesmen had waged an unsuccessful struggle to get colored children into the white schools in 1862 and the colored community had mounted a bitter protest against creation of a separate Negro school system in 1867. Their viewpoint finally prevailed in the constitution of 1868, which outlawed "separate schools . . . established exclusively for any race by the State of Louisiana."

For more than two years the Negro triumph proved no more than a paper victory. Every attempt to mix the public schools was repelled by the staunchly segregationist New Orleans Board of School Directors. When the principal of the Bayou Road School admitted twenty-eight Negro girls, the school directors took their stand. The unfortunate principal was censured and almost dismissed, the colored girls were transferred into a Negro school, and other school administrators were "hereby instructed not to receive any children of color."

The Negroes had followed their dreams too far to surrender them without a struggle. The *Tribune* attacked the Board and its race policies with bitter words, but the Negro masses chose to wage war with different weapons. When the white Fillmore School turned away some colored applicants on September 25, 1868, an armed and angry Negro mob marched on the school to dispute the decision. When the young Negroes were again denied admission, the mob opened fire on the building. Police put down the protest, but the Board of School Directors did nothing to alleviate the discontent that had caused it. For two years it blocked every Negro move to mix its schools. Finally in 1870 the Radicals established a rival school authority by instituting individual ward school boards, packed with "safe" personnel to guarantee integrationist policies. When Judge Henry C. Dibble upheld the validity of the new boards in November, 1870, the door to desegregation swung open at last.

Change came suddenly. During the first week of classes after the Christmas holidays, the three adopted daughters of Lieutenant Governor Oscar J. Dunn were enrolled as students in the Madison Girls' School, six colored boys won admission into the Bienville Boys' School, and five more joined the student body of the St. Philip Boys' School. By the end of January color barriers had been breached in as many as a dozen more white schools. Most of the colored children remained in Negro schools, but the migration into white classrooms continued steadily.

The changes stunned and sickened the powerless white population. One outraged Orleanian summoned the spectre of "Lee, Jackson, Hill and a host of their compeers standing upon the eternal shore with faces veiled in shame and sad tears rising at the scene of their people so fallen." Others reacted less eloquently but more effectively by removing their children from the mixed schools. Wherever colored children were introduced a massive white exodus followed. Nearly two hundred white boys were withdrawn from the Bienville Boys' School the morning after the six Negroes were enrolled. Similar boycotts decimated the ranks in schools throughout the city.

Unwilling to send their sons and daughters to school with Negroes, many white parents were forced to look to private institutions free from state control. Private education had all but died out in New Orleans during the ordeal of civil war and occupation, but it revived amazingly when Radical politics threatened the color line in the public school system. There had been only ten private schools operating in the city in 1868, but by 1871 there were more than one hundred. Catholic authorities, anxious to build a parochial system to combat the secular influences of the public schools, took advantage of the white unrest to increase the number of their institutions from eight to forty-nine. The Presbyterians and Episcopalians fashioned parochial systems of their own, and the Lutherans and Methodists also supported schools. Most numerous of all were the independent private schools, conducted by individuals to eke out livelihoods, usually in their own homes. A few achieved permanence and quality, but most of them lasted only a year or two, offering their pupils white classmates and little else. However jerrybuilt, these varieties of private schools taught a majority of the white school children in New Orleans from 1871 until the restoration of Democratic rule in 1877.

The white exodus from the public schools was by no means universal, for the public school system was never desegregated completely. More than half of the white schools escaped integration altogether. Others admitted colored children, but segregated them internally by requiring separate seating arrangements, separate playground areas, and even totally separate classrooms. In such schools where the color line was upheld, white students continued to come in large numbers. A few public schools actually succeeded in totally integrating their student bodies without triggering chaos. The principal of the Bienville Boys' School, badly decimated by a white boycott in January, 1871, reported a year later, "Two-thirds of the pupils are white and one-third colored. It is but seldom that the usual peace and good order of the school are disturbed by any exhibitions of prejudice on account of race or color." While his success remained an ideal rarely achieved, it did renew the hopes of the Negroes and Radicals that school desegregation was a practicable step toward a caste-free society.

Tensions over the school situation eased considerably during 1872 and 1873. Colored children continued to trickle into already mixed schools, but few new targets were selected. The Democratic newspapers, involved in a campaign to recapture the state government by seducing Negro voters away from the Radical ranks, contributed to the calm by silencing their bitter attacks on the mixed schools. In September, 1872, the *Daily Picayune* wrote of "the strongest indications of the continued and deep affection of the people for our public school system." Nine months later the *Times* found the totally integrated Bienville School to be "in fine condition morally, mentally, and physically." White animosities abated so markedly that many private school pupils began to transfer back into the public system.

This period of peace between the races was shattered suddenly and violently in September, 1874, when a white supremacist organization known as the White League led a three-day insurrection that temporarily toppled the Radical government and restored white Democratic rule in New Orleans. The revolt was finally crushed by federal troops, but the bitter resentment that caused it continued to smolder.

Three months later, in an atmosphere still crackling with tension and race hate, the Negroes decided to test the color line in the white high schools, the last real citadels of segregation in the public system. For nearly four years the three high schools had defied the desegregation movement. In that time they became symbols of the larger struggle, representing resistance to whites and oppression to Negroes. On December 14, 1874, delegations of colored girls marched on the two girls' high schools and demanded that they be enrolled. The white students met and decided to boycott classes until the matter was resolved. When officials at Upper Girls' High School turned away the colored girls and hastily closed the school, an angry Negro mob assembled outside the building and reportedly shouted that "they were Tenth Ward niggers and meant blood." Their wish was soon granted. On the morning of December 17 a group of young Negroes tried to desegregate the Central Boys' High

School. When enraged white students barred their way, the colored boys returned with adult reinforcements and a free-for-all ensued. The great school riots of 1874 were under way.

After the school was closed by its nervous principal, the young men of the student body organized themselves into a vigilance committee to purge the white public schools of their colored pupils. They marched first to the Lower Girls' High School, where they assembled the young ladies for a skin inspection and expelled some twenty girls they judged too dark to suit their tastes. Throughout the afternoon the high school vigilantes made the rounds of nearby grammar schools, ejecting the colored children and warning them never to return. They eventually came to Keller School and ousted two small Negroes as a finale to their festivities.

As they left the building they were attacked by an angry gang of boys from a nearby Negro school, cheered on by a few colored adults. During the fierce fighting that followed an elderly Negro fell dead with a broken neck. As wild reports of violence and death swept through the city, both mobs were swelled by newcomers, older men crazy with hate. For several hours the whole Keller Market neighborhood was transformed into a man-made hell of flying fists and bricks and bottles. Finally the darkness brought a temporary truce. Rumors spread wildly throughout the night that Negroes were going to burn down Keller School and that White Leaguers would put colored schools to the torch. Bands of bitter men—Negroes armed with pistols and knives and straight razors and White League squads ready to renew the work of restoration interrupted by the Federals in September— patrolled the streets until dawn. One White League unit, allegedly fired upon from a Negro church on the corner of First and Freret streets, riddled the building with bullets, but the only casualty was a Leaguer shot accidentally in the foot. Apart from that, the night passed without bloodshed.

On the following day the task of "purifying" the public schools went on. Taking a cue from their elders, the white children at Bayou Bridge School ejected their colored classmates.

The Central High School vigilantes returned to the Lower Girls' High School and removed six colored girls overlooked in the confusion of the day before. A mob of white men visited several grammar schools, forcing a number of Negro children out of the Fillmore and St. Philip street institutions. When their tour of duty took them to the Beauregard School, on the corner of St. Claude and Union, the white mob was persuaded to abandon its activities by a group of Negroes with drawn pistols. But none of these incidents sparked a renewal of the rioting.

Then the tumult died. The School Board prudently closed all public schools a week early for the Christmas holidays. With no mixed schools in session, the vigilantes called a halt to their endeavors, confident that the victory was theirs. They had forced Superintendent Charles W. Boothby to sign a statement condemning school mixing and they had read in the *Times* that Judge Henry C. Dibble now supported school segregation. They had even read in the *Republican*, official mouthpiece for the enemy, that "society would be more at peace . . . were race relations reconciled by separation." On December 19, the *Times* laid the desegregation experiment to rest, telling its readers, "There is no danger that mixed schools will be forced upon us here. That point is settled."

But the rejoicing proved premature, for the public schools were still desegregated when they resumed classes on January 11. Few colored children came back at first, but when no new white violence developed the others soon followed. Emboldened by their success at resisting white wrath, Negroes moved to mix the Boys' Central High School, the very storm center of the December disturbances. On February 18, 1875, a young Negro named Roxborough became the first member of his race ever to attend the school. Most of the white boys walked out, but the move failed to attract the public support given the December boycotts and Central High School remained mixed. Desegregation soon spread to the school's faculty with the appointment of a Paris-educated octaroon named Edmonds as instructor of mathematics. This latter development provoked a mass meeting in Lafayette

Square, instigated by the militantly racist *Bulletin*. Segregationist resolutions were passed, but nothing was done.

Public school desegregation dragged on for two more years, until Radical Reconstruction itself died in the spring of 1877. But it never regained its pre-riot momentum and each new move to mix white facilities stirred tensions and hatreds anew. In September, 1876, a longtime holdout fell when two colored girls were enrolled in the Paulding School. They were driven away by the white boys and when one returned on the following day, she was again repelled with stones and mudballs. The incident reached the newspapers and evidently became an overnight symbol for Negroes, for an army of colored children appeared at the school on the next day to demand admission. Most of the white pupils were promptly withdrawn. This incident, staged during the very twilight of Reconstruction, showed again that the Negroes had not lost their determination to desegregate nor the whites their will to resist.

Radical Reconstruction in New Orleans was laid to rest in April, 1877, when President Rutherford B. Hayes withdrew the federal troops from Louisiana and the Republican regime quietly dissolved itself. Negro dreams of a society without segregation were buried with the party that had given them political life ten years before. If the Democratic "redeemers" who came to power in 1877 disagreed among themselves on the proper place of the Negro in Louisiana life, they all believed that segregation must survive to maintain the sovereignty of the white race.

The political turnabout was the death warrant for New Orleans public school desegregation. The new conservative school board that took control in April deferred the execution until September, fearing that racial reassignments in the last month of the term would lead to unnecessary confusion. When the city schools reopened in the fall, thirty-seven schools were allocated to whites and twenty-two to Negroes. Despite a board directive to all personnel that no colored children would be allowed in the white schools, some three hundred of them were enrolled in forbidden facilities. School officials soon remedied the situation, however, and by the Christmas holidays of 1877 mixing was only a memory.

The prouder Negroes did not surrender without a struggle. When the board made known its intentions in June, a delegation of New Orleans Negroes led by the aged colored Creole patriarch Aristide Marie took their protest to Governor Francis T. Nicholls, who advised them that "the courts are open, and there lies your redress." A suit entered by Negro editor Paul Trevigne was dismissed in October because the childless plaintiff could prove no personal injury. Another action, brought by Negro Arnold Bartonneau after his two children had been barred from Fillmore School, dragged on into 1879, when United States Circuit Judge W. B. Woods ruled that school segregation was legal if both races were afforded equal facilities. With that the protests died.

After 1877, New Orleans Negroes again studied in separate schools, dined in separate restaurants, and imbibed in separate saloons. A few houses of prostitution in the squalid sin district along Dauphine and Burgundy streets continued to offer white and colored girls to a mixed clientele, but they had become rarities by 1880. White baseball teams played exhibitions against colored nines until the middle 1880's; colored jockeys rode against white riders until 1890; and white boxers met Negroes in the prize ring until 1892. Both races rode on the same street cars until a state law passed in 1902 put an end to the practice. By then the segregation of the races was virtually universal in city life.

The first crusade against the color line scored some unique victories before it ran its course. Racial equality in public places was written into the law of Louisiana. A few New Orleans Negroes ate in white restaurants, drank in white taverns, and sat in white theatre boxes. Some of their children went to school with white classmates. Yet the movement was a failure. Its accomplishments were token at best, and none of them long outlived the Republican regime that made them possible. Despite a decade under seige, segregation survived every Negro effort to kill it.

New Orleans Politics-The Greatest Free Show on Earth

Hermann B. Deutsch

There is no such thing as a valid condensation of two and a half centuries of history, especially when it is a history so complex, so varied, and so stressful that my scholarly colleague, Charles L. Dufour, pithily entitled his recently published chronicle of Louisiana Ten Flags in the Wind.

It is all very well for teachers of English composition and other authoritarians to point out that when setting down their report the Bible's chroniclers compressed into ten words the story of all creation, to wit:

"In the beginning God created the heaven and the earth."

But where would mankind be today without the rest of the Holy Scriptures, and even the Dead Sea Scrolls?

It is beyond denial, however, that there must be a golden mean somewhere between ten-word "condensations" and a ten-volume encyclopaedia in which any story can be told, if not in the fullest detail, at least without obvious errors of omission, commission and chronology. In this account of Louisiana's political beginnings I have sought to attain at least a gilded mean.

Until after it was purchased from the first Napoleon for approximately four cents an acre, Louisiana had no political history to speak of, save as a colonial pawn. LaSalle had claimed the entire watershed of the Mississippi, from its source to its mouth, for the Sun King, Louis XIV, who was a capable, even brilliant, administrator and no more dissolute than was the custom among monarchs and nobles in 1682. But he remained curiously blind to the potentials of the all but incalculable wealth LaSalle had placed at the disposal of the Crown, and did not trouble to authorize or finance a settlement of colonists from the motherland in what is today Louisiana.

Thomas Jefferson more than doubled the area of the United States by the purchase for which he will always be remembered. It included not only the western watershed of the Mississippi, but the Isle of Orleans as well. This gave Louisiana possession and control of both banks of the Mississippi River's mouth, which in itself was worth far more than the beaver pelts and buffalo hides which the Western watershed produced in lieu of the gold for which, like every other European monarch, Louis XV, great-grandson and successor of the Sun King, lusted.

In short, up to 1803 Louisiana was simply the shuttlecock of the European power-political badminton game and had no politics of its own as such. To be sure, there was the inevitable hostility which inspired all the Latins, French and Spanish alike, to unite against the Americans who came down the river on keelboats or rafts.

In time, five-year-old King Louis XV's psycho-somatic development reached a stage where girls became objects of consuming interest. The heir to the Sun King's throne was married at age 15 to the daughter of an exiled Polish king. By this legitimate spouse he begot no less than seven legitimate children, while concurrently launching a career of extra-curricular libertinism which eclipsed even the exploits of his great-grandsire. He left matters of state to his regent whenever possible.

That individual, Philip of Orleans, summoned to the empire's aid and his own, a remarkable Scotsman, John Law, whom the French populace ultimately dubbed Jean L'As, and who, according to historian-writer Charles L. Dufour "would build up Louisiana and bankrupt France." He was a half-and-half blend of promoter and mathematical genius.

Bienville was administrator of Law's Company of the West and in the name of that company he laid out a fortification some eighty miles above the great river's shifting mouths, naming it New Orleans. As a private enterprise, Louisiana threatened to become a sort of glorified penal colony until Law, despairing of turning France's deported smugglers, pimps, cut-purses, and trollops into solid agrarian citizens, imported shiploads of Nova Scotians from Canada and Germans from the Rhine Palatinate so that a core of decent, hard-working citizens was implanted in outlying settlements of today's "Greater New Orleans Area," where they still flourish after the passage of two and a half centuries.

The first major split which divided Louisianians along a quasi-political cleft followed the irascible revolt of Louis XV against established diplomatic patterns. After harvesting nothing but headaches instead of treasure from Louisiana, he made a gift of the whole ball of wax to his royal cousin, Charles III, King of Spain.

Before this dénouement to the great experiment, a final effort promised to provide a cure for the colony's ailment. No one then realized more acutely than Law that deported prostitutes and pickpockets were not the sort of helpmeets the stable colonists desired, and vice versa. No one at this late date can say with certainty who suggested the organization of *filles à la cassette.* The "hope chest girls" were the decent daughters of impecunious farm families in France. Each such girl who would agree to migrate to Louisiana under the aegis of the Ursulines, and there marry a Louisiana colonial approved by the *religieuses,* would receive from the Crown as dowry a chest of linens and other basic household necessities plus a small purse of gold. Until they were married, subsistence would be provided for them by the Ursulines at their new convent.

These were the future mothers of proud Creole families. Their descendants made common cause with Nova Scotian, German and Spanish elements against the Anglo-Saxons politically and socially. The cavalier fashion in which they were bandied about, almost like chattel slaves, by Louis XV's gift of Louisiana to Spain's Charles III in 1762 outraged them. But when "Bloody" Alejandro O'Reilly arrived with a major military force, New Orleans surrendered without firing a shot. Five rebellious ringleaders were executed.

Thus the first revolt of an American colony against the mother country in Europe preceded by some thirteen years the signing of a great Declaration of Independence, proclaimed in July of 1776. An event which would even more profoundly affect the politico-economic future of Louisiana occurred in the 1790's, when Étienne de Boré devised a practical process for granulating sugar. Slave holding sugar barons ultimately led the way to a conservatism that would manifest itself as late as the national election of 1964.

The Spanish occupation of "Luisiana" lasted only until 1803, by which time the French Revolution had unseated the Bourbons, and the authoritarian First Consul, Napoleon, who substituted golden bees for the stylized *fleur-de-lys* on the banners of the Republic, had come to power. He had Louisiana retroceded to his France, and twenty days after his title to the returned territory was validated, sold the entire tract to the young republic of the United States.

With that, the formation of what we now recognize as political parties was begun. Most of the growing "American" population in New Orleans was settled in the Second Municipality, upstream from the Vieux Carré; the French-Creole population of the supposedly walled and fortified city in the First Municipality; and the largely Spanish-Criollo population in the Third Municipality, downstream from the Old City.

Nationally, the country's population was divided into the opposing forces of Alexander Hamilton's conservatives, known as the Federalists, who favored government by a sort of ruling class operating through a strong central government, and Thomas Jefferson's followers who, under his masterful leadership, favored a broad base of local government with a central government empowered to exercise only those functions specifically granted to it by the Constitution.

In the beginnings of their fixed opposition to the Federalists, Jefferson's followers were known as Republicans, or Democratic Republicans. The party did not officially become the Democratic party until Jackson's successful campaign for the presidency, when all the various cliques which had joined forces under the leadership of John Quincy Adams and young Henry Clay headed what became known as the National Republican party until the 1830's when they were officially reorganized as the Whig party. This was in general terms the party of conservatism until it was split into a multitude of sects once more by the slavery v. abolition issue, and was succeeded by the Republican party of Lincoln.

New Orleans, and Louisiana in general, paid little attention to these labels. Locally politics was based on the rivalry between the so-called Creole groups of French and Spanish descent, and the "Americans" whose numbers began rapidly to swell after the purchase of Louisiana. In time, *L'Abeille* would editorialize more in sorrow than in anger that it was a distressing thing to note that "the pictures in our political gallery" show so many citizens supporting "the candidate of their ancestors' enemies." In general though, the issue that divided all the country in the first half of the nineteenth century was slavery, followed in turn by secession, and Abolitionist Reconstruction's fifteen defiled years of carpetbaggery.

In seeking to present a rational condensation of the political shifts and changes during the nineteenth and twentieth centuries, it is necessary to disregard such violently but briefly divisive factors as the Ku Klux Klan terror in 1923–24, or the occasionally very bitter flurries of anti-Catholic feeling between Protestant North Louisiana and the largely Roman Catholic southern half of the state which defeated Catholic Congressman Hale Boggs for the governorship once, and Catholic Mayor "Chep" Morrison of New Orleans for that same high office in three consecutive campaigns.

But slavery was no occasional issue. The feeling was that if slavery were abolished a feudally administered economy, based on the production of sugar and cotton, faced absolute ruin. The importance of this issue outweighed considerations based on the otherwise simple contention that states which freely entered into a federation with one another were just as free to withdraw from that union when a majority of their voters decided to do so.

The war did "ruin" Louisiana. A radical abolitionist wing of Republicans passed a reconstruction bill over President Johnson's veto. Texas and Louisiana were lumped into one military district commanded by General Phil Sheridan, who summarily ousted the Mayor and the entire City Council of New Orleans from office, replacing them with appointees of his own selection. When riots followed the announcement by a Sheridan-appointed governor that Louisiana had ratified the Fourteenth Amendment, a federally-commanded "Metropolitan Police Force" was created to supersede the municipal peace officers. Most of the Metropolitans were Negroes.

In 1875 a mass meeting of armed citizens fought a pitched battle involving heavy loss of life on both sides, routed the Metropolitans, seized the state capitol—the Mechanics' Institute building on Dryades street—and proclaimed themselves the de facto as well as the de jure government of Louisiana.

President Grant promptly dispatched General Emory to New Orleans with additional federal troops to restore the Carpetbag Governor, William Pitt Kellogg, to office. Three years later the story was different. Francis Tillou Nicholls was again elected governor by a coalition of Democrats and Moderate (as distinguished from Radical) Republicans, decisively defeating Stephen Packard, the Carpetbag candidate. But the Carpetbag returning board fraudulently certified Packard as the victor, so that for a time Louisiana had two governors, two state capitols in New Orleans, and two legislatures.

This took place in the presidential election year of 1876, while Ohio's Hayes and New York's Tilden campaigned against one another. Having two state administrations, Louisiana sent two sets of returns to the electoral college (as did also Florida and South Carolina). In each case one certified Tilden electors, the other Hayes. Confronted by a situation for which the Constitution made no provision, Congress appointed a special commission composed of five representatives, five senators and the five justices of the Supreme Court to determine which of the electors should be legitimatized.

It has never been incontrovertibly established that any sort of political *quid pro quo* was discussed, but the Commission did certify the coalition (that is to say Hayes) delegates from Louisiana. It was said at the time that Hayes, if elected, had agreed in advance to end the occupation of New Orleans by federal troops; but all that can now be set down with complete certainty is that within a month of his inauguration, the troops were at last ordered out on April 24, 1877.

As the soldiers embarked at the foot of Canal Street for Jackson Barracks, Carpetbag legislators began their exodus from the old St. Louis Hotel (on a site now occupied by the Royal Orleans Hotel), to which the Packard administration had transferred the capitol. Next day the Nicholls administration was formally installed and for the first time since 1862 Louisiana was again a free state in which what was at least nominally the Democratic party would dominate all state politics for the next 86 years.

Corruption in public office is an almost inevitable concomitant of one-sided political power. In the 1880's, a special catalyst of venality was the Louisiana Lottery. It had purchased from the "Carpetbag" legislature of 1868 a twenty-five-year franchise, the term of which was due to expire in 1893. And in the city the Ring, composed of city ward leaders, held sway. Finally in 1888 the feeling of outrage generated by the Lottery's all-out effort to perpetuate itself, caused even the Ring's incumbent Mayor Guillotte to join in the support of a reform slate headed by a former mayor, Joseph A. Shakespeare, which swept the field.

Thus the Lottery faced hostile Governor Nicholls and a hostile Mayor Shakespeare. Undismayed, its spokesmen dealt with a venal Legislature, purchasing the votes needed to renew the Lottery charter for an additional 25 years, beginning with the expiration of its original permit in 1893. Thereupon Governor

Nicholls vetoed it. But in the final analysis the Lottery could not manage to run even until its first and only charter expired. By congressional action the federal government closed not only the mails, but all interstate transportation to tickets, reports, and other lottery paraphernalia; and therewith the big gamble finally passed out of existence.

Reform Mayor Shakespeare was therefore confident he could coast to victory in the next New Orleans municipal election. The head of the city machine was Captain John Fitzpatrick. Under no illusion as to the portent of earlier reverses, he spearheaded the municipal campaign by becoming the mayoral candidate himself. Along with their candidate, the Reform organization leaders likewise assumed that victory would come to them by first intention.

This is an almost invariably fatal political conceit. Moreover, the Shakespeare-led reformers also overlooked the fact that the Republicans were split down the back like an old coat. The so-called "black-and-tan" Radical faction was so bitter against the Moderate wing headed by former Governor Henry Clay War-moth that they supported Fitzpatrick rather than aid in Shake-speare's re-election. The upshot of it all was that Fitzpatrick swept to victory along with almost his entire ticket.

Fitzpatrick, scrupulously honest in his personal affairs, was undeniably a capable executive. None the less, after the so-called "Boodle Council" scandal he was impeached by a committee of citizens, the charges being brought to trial before Judge Fred D. King of the Civil District Court, who found him "not guilty" on every count. This prompted the *Times-Democrat* to suggest editorially that a mass meeting be held in Lafayette Square publicly to burn the city charter, since "it was obviously not worth the paper it was written on."

John Newton Pharr, St. Mary Parish sugar planter, was the Republican candidate for governor in the 1896 election. He was credited with having received 90,138 votes, which came to 44 per cent of the ballots cast. Seriously alarmed by the possibility of a return to power for the party which had imposed "Carpetbag" government on Louisiana, the Democratic administration called the Constitutional Convention of 1898 into session and wrote into the organic law of the state the Grandfather Clause which withheld suffrage from everyone whose grandfather had not been a property owner.

In addition, an unwritten understanding made possible the "white primary." It was agreed that since political parties were private organizations which, like any other club, could accept or reject applicants for membership at pleasure, all hands would register as Democrats and would reject Negro applicants for membership. It was further agreed that future political differences would be settled not between two parties but between two factions of the same party, all voters pledging themselves to abide by the result of the Democratic primary. In this way, general elections at which Negroes, if registered, could vote, would be deprived of further significance. Thus the virtual extinction of the Republican party in Louisiana was the major political turning point of the so-called mauve decades. Fitzpatrick was succeeded by Walter C. Flower, whose administration saw the creation of three agencies which shaped the entire future of New Orleans, as well as the future of Louisiana. These were the Levee Board, the Dock Board (officially the "Board of Commissioners of the Port of New Orleans"), and the Sewerage and Water Board.

The history of the levee system runs from the days when each planter was responsible for dikes along the river at his plantation to 1928 when the prevention of such disasters as the overflows and crevasses of 1927 was at last recognized by the Reid-Jones flood control act as a federal responsibility. However it was not until the Constitution of 1898 was adopted that these various boards were validated in the state's organic charter. Similarly destined to influence the course of municipal politics for decades to come was an ordinance introduced by Alderman Sidney Story, which stands as perhaps the greatest piece of legalistic double talk ever inscribed in any code of laws in all history. It was an attempt to legitimatize prostitution by prohibiting it.

In the mid-nineteenth century, an effort to license bawdy houses in New Orleans was so unsuccessful that it was soon abandoned. But in the latter 1890's public sentiment crystallized against the uncontrolled and swiftly expanding areas given over to licentiousness. Alderman Story proposed the ordinance which was finally adopted in January, 1897, and which made it unlawful for any "woman notoriously abandoned to lewdness" to occupy any house outside of a district enclosed by Customhouse (now Iberville), Basin, St. Louis and N. Robertson streets ". . . provided that nothing herein shall be so construed as to authorize any lewd woman to occupy any house, room, or closet in any portion of the city."

Alderman Story was displeased to find himself the *parrain* of one of the country's most notorious red light districts which, after the enactment of his ordinance, became generally known as Storyville, and the name stuck until the First World War in 1917 abolished the "District" as being within five miles of a Naval station.

It was likewise during the Flower administration that a new charter for New Orleans was finally enacted by the Legislature which divided New Orleans into seventeen wards with one alderman to each.

Apparently feeling that his record of achievement would assure his reelection, Mayor Flower and his backers made no strenuous effort to organize an effective campaign. The Regulars on the other hand redoubled their efforts to gain control of the new aldermanic council and the mayoralty. Moreover, instead of choosing a ward leader as candidate for the top spot, they persuaded Paul Capdevielle, a gentleman of the old school, the scion of distinguished Creole ancestry, to make the race, and he won the election.

Capdevielle launched twenty uninterrupted years during which the Old Regular machine maintained its hold on the mayoralty of New Orleans. Generally speaking, this coincided with the era of personal bossdoms which sprang up in many of the nation's major cities: Tweed and Croker in New York, Ruef in San Francisco, Curley in Boston, Cox in Cincinnati, Thompson and Lundin in Chicago.

In New Orleans the man who became boss was Martin Behrman. Five times elected to the office of mayor, he was beyond dispute one of the most remarkable men ever to monopolize Louisiana's municipal spotlight.

He was born in New York on October 14, 1894 and was moved to New Orleans by his parents while still a baby. He had not grown out of infancy when his father died. His mother supported the family by operating a dry goods stall in the notions section of the French Market, but her death when he was twelve put an end to his formal schooling.

One kinsman living in Algiers, where he operated a retail grocery, took him in. Another, also a grocer, numbered among his sons one of Martin Behrman's cousins who became famous in World War II as General "Lightning Joe" Collins. Shortly after his marriage at twenty two, Behrman was made clerk in the assessor's office of his district at $150 a month, a substantial increase over his earnings as a grocery salesman, but a year later, when Joseph Shakespeare was elected, he was summarily dismissed to make room for a Reform appointee. In 1904, newly elected to the post of state auditor, he was selected to run for mayor as the Ring candidate and won handily.

His régime was enormously popular in his first term, but a different and more turbulent course marked the close of his second quadrennium. For one thing, the Regulars were split wide open over the governorship in 1912. Colonel Robert Ewing, publisher of the *Daily States* and a leader of the Tenth Ward, refused to endorse the candidacy of Congressman James B. Aswell, as approved by the majority of the Behrmanite caucus, and put forth one of the ward bosses, John T. Michel, as rival nominee. The Reform leaders, organized this time under the name of the Good Government League (and promptly nicknamed "The Goo-goos" by Machine stump speakers) persuaded Luther Hall, a North Louisiana jurist newly seated as a justice of the Supreme Court, to run for governor. With the Regular forces and their allies divided, and the "Goo-goo" contingent in city and country solidly united, Hall was nominated in the primary; and by this time Democratic nomination was tantamount to election.

His first legislative session brought about a major change in the city charter of New Orleans. Instead of a seventeen-man aldermanic city council whose members were each elected by the vote of his own ward only, a commission council of five members was set up, each elected by the vote of the city at large. In this way, the reform element hoped to break up the insular solidarity of the Ring, whose ward leaders would no longer be able to concentrate on a relatively small bailiwick's tight organization. The Regulars shrewdly chose a group of outstanding citizens for their council candidates; and their victory was overwhelming. It laid the groundwork of the Ring's disintegration as a monolithic political force.

Up to this point in the city's political evolution, the ward bosses had derived their powers directly from the people. They won—or lost—their positions of leadership at the polls in their respective districts. Once the election by wards was abolished, vacancies in the Old Regular caucus were filled through appointment by Martin Behrman.

He had the human failing of selecting those bosslets who were first of all loyal to himself. As the knights of his political round table became a palace guard their potential at the polling place began to wane, and in 1913 the first of a number of important defections deprived him of one of his best proconsuls. This was John Patrick Sullivan, a giant of a man physically, colonel of a Louisiana regiment in the Spanish-American war, a man of great personal popularity—and the son-in-law of Captain John Fitzpatrick, Behrman's political sponsor and mentor. For the moment, however, Behrman continued to ride the crest of popular support.

It was during his first term, in 1905, that the city's last bout of yellow fever was halted in its very inception. Martin Behrman had been elected to the mayoralty only a year before this spectacular achievement. In 1908 he and his ticket were returned to office without opposition, and again in 1916, after the Regulars had successfully backed Ruffin Pleasant's candidacy for governor in both the primary and in the ensuing general election, the only significant one held for local office in Louisiana up to that time after the Constitution of 1898 went into effect. John M. Parker, running for governor on the "Bull Moose" Progressive ticket against Democratic nominee Pleasant, was defeated, of course, but polled a total of 53,000 votes, a trifle more than 33 per cent of all ballots cast.

Later that year Parker ran for vice-president on the national Progressive ticket, though it had no candidate for president, and vigorously supported Democrat Woodrow Wilson for re-election. After the latter's victory, Parker officially cancelled his registration as a Progressive and re-registered as a Democrat. This was tantamount to a formal notice of his availability as a primary candidate for governor in the election to be held on January 20, 1920. The campaign began on July 4, 1919.

A Behrman emissary of the Old Regular City Ring went to Monroe, Louisiana, to tender its support to Colonel Frank P. Stubbs, recently returned from France where he had commanded the First Louisiana Infantry regiment. Next, a great mass meeting in New Orleans, with delegates from all parts of the state summoned John Parker to lead the anti-Ring crusade, as reform candidate. Among its leaders were John Sullivan, and such other former Ring allies as ex-governors Pleasant and Sanders.

Behrman pledged to Colonel Stubbs the 25,000 votes which he had once incautiously boasted he could swing to either side of a disputed issue on twenty-four hours' notice. He delivered them. The New Orleans tally stood 25,004 for Stubbs as against 20,603 for Parker. But the country parishes came through with a thumping 16,600 majority for Parker, so that he was nominated (equivalent to election) by 77,000 to 65,000. Incidentally, this was the last state election in Louisiana in which only men voted.

Among Parker's principal platform planks had been one es-

pousing virtual rebirth for the state university which was then
housed in a hodge-podge of ancient buildings, some of which
had been used by Union troops as cavalry stables during the
Civil War.

To finance this last without additional property taxation he
proposed the levy of a severance tax on every natural resource
"severed" from the seas and soil of Louisiana. The principal such
resource was petroleum, of course, but there were others: natural
gas, furs (Louisiana at that time produced more furs, principally
muskrat, than any other state in the Union and more than the
entire Dominion of Canada); shrimp, of which Louisiana produced half the annual take of the nation; salt, sulphur, gravel,
timber, and the like.

Some weeks before his inauguration, he laid this proposal
before representatives of the interests to be affected by it. He
conceded quite frankly that by bringing suit against the constitutionality of such a tax—the rate was to be two per cent—the levy
could be delayed for perhaps as much as two years. But he
offered this bargain: if the interests from whom this toll would
be collected did not seek to block its imposition by court action,
he in turn would pledge that the two per cent rate would not be
increased during his administration.

One of the attorneys for the Standard Oil Company asked:
"How can we be sure of that?" Governor-designate Parker passed
the documents across the conference table to him and said:
"You write the bill; if my legal advisers can't find any joker that
you might slip into it, it will pass exactly as you wrote it."

This was hailed as a great achievement by the public. But to
at least two of the professional politicians who had backed Parker's candidacy it was sheer anathema. One was a young man
from Winnfield, who had recently moved to Shreveport, name
of Huey Pierce Long; the other was the outgoing governor of
Louisiana, Ruffin G. Pleasant. These two were implacable foes.
At a Hot Wells meeting the previous July 4 where six candidates
had thrown their hats into the gubernatorial ring, Long had

referred to Pleasant as "the pliant tool of the Standard Oil trust" and to one of Pleasant's appointees as "the official bar-fly of Louisiana."

However, Pleasant had accurately gauged the political situation in 1919, had pledged his support to Parker and turned over to the Parker campaign forces the large patronage of the Dock Board and other state agencies. Still hostile to one another, Long and Pleasant had been as one in supporting Parker. The former hoped to get legislation enacted making common carriers of all oil and gas pipe lines. Pleasant hoped to force an increase in the severance tax and use this as a springboard toward election to the United States Senate. Both saw in the agreement with Standard Oil on the severance tax a severe political set-back.

The Legislature met and the Parker program went through without a hitch, even to the calling of a constitutional convention.

Women were eligible to vote in the election of convention delegates. The nineteenth amendment had been ratified in August by Tennessee, the 36th state to do so. Louisiana had rejected the amendment two months earlier.

By that time the anti-Berhman coalition of essentially incompatible New Orleans elements had finally settled on Andrew James McShane, hide merchant, as reform candidate for mayor. He had had some prior record as police commissioner, and as unsuccessful candidate for the Commission Council. Reared in an orphanage, he had married into a family long established as socially prominent; in short, his background was in itself calculated to assure political success.

No more eloquent tribute could be paid to the hold Martin Behrman had on the people of his city than the fact that with everything in his favor, McShane managed to defeat him by only some 1400 votes. The Ring landed only one place on the Commission Council in the election of Paul Maloney.

McShane took office as mayor in May of 1921, and within a matter of months the city hall was a shambles. He had boasted during his campaign that in building up his business he never borrowed a penny from a bank or any one else and seemed utterly bewildered by the discovery that New Orleans, at that time a city of almost half a million inhabitants, simply could not be administered on such a cash and carry basis. Within a year he was virtually nonenityized.

The Constitutional Convention of 1921 was followed by a special session of the Legislature to enact the statutes which would put the new provisions into effect. There had been a wild flurry in the convention over the severance tax. Ruffin Pleasant manœuvered into adoption a raise of this levy from two to three per cent, with the proviso that the added one per cent go to the treasury of the parish in which the tax was collected.

Regarding this as a betrayal of his pledge, Governor Parker called in those of his supporters who had let themselves be persuaded to assist enactment of this proposal. Very bluntly he informed them he would veto their measures in the Legislature if they made it impossible to keep his word not to raise the severance tax during his term as governor. The action was rescinded. In consequence, ex-Governor Pleasant refused to sign the new constitution.

The proposal to make pipe lines common carriers likewise fell by the wayside, whereupon the thin thread of Railroad (now Public Service) Commission Chairman Huey Long's patience snapped. During the ensuing special session he typed out, stencilled, mimeographed and laid upon the desk of every member of the House and Senate a statement declaring in effect that Louisiana's laws were now being written at 26 Broadway (the offices of the Standard Oil Company) and that Governor Parker was distributing state patronage at that corporation's direction.

Parker was not the sort of man to pass this off as mere political give-and-take. He filed charges of criminal libel against Long, who, in November, 1921, was found guilty and sentenced to pay a fine of one dollar and serve one hour of imprisonment. The judge—later Justice Harney Brunot of the Supreme Court—who handed down this verdict and pronounced the sentence, paid the dollar out of his own pocket, and directed that the jail term be served in his chambers.

New Orleans' next mayoral election was not held until 1925. City Commissioner Paul Maloney, one of the leaders representing an uptown ward, argued that he should be the Old Regular candidate since he had been the only Old Regular to survive the debacle of 1920. When he saw that he could not hope to win the endorsement over Behrman, he and the representatives of four other wards withdrew to form a separate group which chose Maloney as its candidate.

Thus the 1925 city campaign was really between two Old Regulars. However, a promoter of electric light companies, who had been denied a franchise by Maloney, backed McShane to run, in order to split off some of the Maloney vote, and in so doing, he defeated him. The Behrman-Maloney totals were so close that McShane's scant 4,487 votes were enough to deny either of them a clear majority. Ordinarily, this would have made a second primary mandatory. But one of the ward leaders who had supported Maloney abruptly returned to the Behrman fold in a second primary, and in view of this it would have been futile for Maloney to enter a run-off, so he withdrew and Behrman became the Democratic nominee. In May he began his fifth term as mayor of New Orleans while his followers, whose campaign rallying cry had been "Papa's coming home!", changed it to a jubilant "Papa's back!"

Within a year, suffering from chronic myocarditis, he took to his bed, and on January 13, 1926, he died. There was no Democratic primary to select his successor. The Old Regulars chose City Treasurer Arthur J. O'Keefe as their standard bearer, and no other candidate entered the lists.

Meanwhile a significant change had taken place in the gubernatorial situation. Henry Fuqua had been elected in 1924 with O. H. Simpson of New Orleans (who had been Senate clerk for the previous 20 years) as his lieutenant governor. Two others had entered the race: Hewitt Bounchaud, outgoing lieutenant governor, and Huey Long who announced his candidacy on

August 30, 1923, the day on which he attained the age of 30 years, prescribed in the state constitution as requisite minimum for eligibility to serve as governor.

Any tendency to take his candidacy lightly was erased when, in spite of foul weather that turned the country roads into quagmires on election day, Long came up with some 77,000 votes. This was only a little less than the tally he needed to make him one of the two finalists.

With a plurality of 9000 or so over Fuqua, Bouanchaud stubbornly entered a run-off, but the times were against him. This was the peak year of Klan and anti-Klan bitterness, and Hewitt Bouanchaud was a Catholic. The result was that except in South Louisiana, he was snowed under.

Henry Fuqua, a moderate who had pledged himself to have the Legislature enact statues forbidding both secrecy of membership and the wearing of masks in public except on such occasions as Mardi Gras, made good this promise early in his administration. But death struck him down abruptly in mid-term and Simpson succeeded to the governorship, making no secret of the fact that he proposed to run for election on his own account at the close of what had begun as the Fuqua term.

However, in 1928 when Huey Long once more ran for governor, John Sullivan, who had correctly gauged the portent of Long's phenomenal 77,000 votes in 1924, allied himself with the Kingfish-to-be, became his city campaign manager, and publicly played upon a cliché of the day by adopting as his slogan: "It *will* be Long now!" The Old Regulars selected Congressman Riley D. Wilson from North Louisiana as their candidate, Simpson had already nominated himself, and once again a three-cornered race for Baton Rouge seemed to center in New Orleans.

Long came romping to the finish line with an overwhelming plurality amassed in the rural districts. This was not enough to overcome the combined total of Simpson and Wilson ballots. Simpson immediately offered to support Long in the second primary, if one were held, in consideration of various deals, at least one of which was the support of Paul Maloney for Congress. In the face of the combined Long-Simpson vote, Riley Wilson's backers threw in the towel and did not demand a run-off.

Thus did the Kingfish enter upon his tyrannical seven-year dictatorship over Louisiana. He was preparing to run for the presidency of the United States against Roosevelt in 1936 when, on September 8, 1935, an assassin's bullet ended his reign and his life.

It has been truly said that the era of Huey Long was like a nettle rash, irritating and at times painful, but never tedious. Within a year he was impeached by the House of Representatives. Long had offended many legislators. He had boasted publicly to a New Orleans gathering that "I hold all 52 cards at Baton Rouge, and I shuffle and deal them as I please." He told a group of officials from West Feliciana parish about their member in the House of Representatives that: "I bought him like you'd buy a sack of potatoes to be delivered at your back door."

He proposed to levy a special processing tax against the Standard Oil Company in an era when at least 18,000 of Baton Rouge's then 25,000 inhabitants were directly supported by a breadwinner on the Standard's refinery payroll. Standard countered by detouring a shipment of machinery for a proposed eight million dollar Baton Rouge plant expansion from the docks at New Orleans to Bayonne, and threatened to withdraw from the state. All legislators who harbored resentment against the self-proclaimed Kingfish allied themselves with a move to impeach him.

However, the ouster was aborted by having one charge tried and dismissed, and voiding all the others with a round robin which fifteen Senators signed to the effect that because of a technicality, they would refuse to convict the Governor on any of the remaining charges, regardless of evidence. Since fifteen signers constituted two more than one third of the elected Senate membership of thirty-nine, and a two-thirds vote was required for conviction, the stymied anti-Long contingent adjourned the session and went home.

In an atmosphere of gathering storm, New Orleans approached the 1930 election for its city-parish officials. Both major candidates for Mayor were anti-Long: one was Francis Williams, who, with his brother Augustus, had been city manager for Long's first gubernatorial campaign in 1924, but had quarreled with him and was now among the bitterest of his enemies.

The other candidate was T. Semmes Walmsley, whose family was of the socially elect. Semmes' father, Sylvester P. Walmsley, had been Rex in 1890, and his brother-in-law, Leon Irwin, had been Rex in 1928. His brother Pierce was Captain of the Mystic Club. Semmes had captained the football team at Tulane University, the Louisiana equivalent of the Ivy League's Princeton; he had been commander of the Louisiana Department of the American Legion, had served as assistant attorney general in the probe of the Morehouse parish Klan murders . . . in short, his career and background were the very antithesis of what one would expect to find in a successful machine politician.

None the less, he won the 1930 mayoral election in a walk, receiving substantial though not overt help from the Long leaders and defeating Williams by a majority of some 10,000 votes. One of the major political achievements of his administration was the working out of a sort of guarded truce between the Old Regulars and Huey Long, who though elected to the United States Senate in September, 1930, while his gubernatorial term still had two years to run, did not actually go to Washington until February, 1932, after securing the election of his boyhood friend, Oscar K. Allen, to succeed him as governor.

His reason for remaining in Louisiana even after his election to the Senate was spelled out with no effort to disguise the facts. By that time he had broken with his lieutenant governor, a Jeanerette (South Louisiana) dentist, Paul Cyr. In mid-term, the Legislature had defeated Long's proposal for a great highway bond issue. It scraped through to the necessary two-thirds majority of the elected membership in the house, but in the senate two bitter-enders—William Boone who only the year before had been one of the Round Robin's fifteen signers, and John Caffery, a sugar planter—filibustered it to death.

In a sense, Long welcomed this defeat, announcing he would take the issue to the people by running for the United States Senate in September. But even after he won, he refused to give up his office as governor until it was certain Lieutenant Governor Cyr could no longer succeed him.

He sent his credentials to the Senate, but remained in Louisiana, with highway police guarding his office in the old capitol, and the mansion, against any intrusion by Dr. Cyr. The latter finally lost patience and took the oath of office as Governor before the clerk of court in Shreveport, went to Baton Rouge, set up executive offices in a hotel, and filed suit to have the "usurper" Long ousted from the governorship. Once again, as during the death throes of the carpetbag era, Louisiana had two governors.

When this bit of litigation finally got to the Supreme Court in 1932, that body decided that since Huey Long had never taken oath as a Senator, he had not "vacated" the governorship of Louisiana; but Dr. Cyr *had* taken the oath of office as Governor and had thereby vacated the post of Lieutenant-Governor, making himself ineligible to continue to exercise any of the functions of that office.

Within two days Huey and a jubilant retinue of partisans were en route to Washington. The Louisiana House of Representatives not only withdrew the impeachment charges technically still pending against Long, but passed his bond issue program.

The session was the first held in the new state capitol, built on what had previously been the Louisiana State University campus. The 31-story structure was erected at a cost of $5.5 million or thereabouts, and it must be conceded that it is doubtful whether it could now be duplicated for five times its 1932 cost.

At the same time Senator Long, resentful of the fact that the Tulane University Board of Administrators was almost unanimously anti-Long, paid LSU enough cash for two other buildings to launch a new medical school as competitor to the century-old one at Tulane.

The entente between Long and the Old Regulars in New Orleans could not endure. As the city election of January, 1934, approached, the rupture arose over the endorsement of District Attorney Eugene Stanley for re-election. The Old Regulars endorsed for re-election not merely the Mayor and the other incumbent members of the Commission Council, but the District Attorney as well. Long promptly put forth a ticket of his own, selecting a universally respected engineer, John Klorer, as candidate for Mayor along with council members of similar civic status. Francis Williams, corrosively bitter against his former ally, Long, entered the race for Mayor, along with a full slate of officials, who called themselves the Independent Regulars, and opposed both Walmsley and Klorer.

Walmsley held a commanding lead in the first primary, receiving 48,700 votes, to Klorer's 31,800 and Williams' 26,600. As one of the top two candidates, Klorer could have called for a second primary. But Long, always a realist, knew Williams would at once throw in his lot with Walmsley and therefore withdrew his candidate. But on the heels of this he launched a series of special legislative sessions without parallel in the history of republics. Via a long roster of so-called "dictatorship laws" he deprived all parishes and cities of local self-government and concentrated this in special hand-picked boards at Baton Rouge. With malicious humor, he labeled one of these his civil service board.

A final special session of the nominally Allen legislature was called for ultimate consolidation of Long's authoritarianism when on the second night of the five-day meeting, Long was shot, bringing to a close the fantastic era his inauguration had initiated.

A period of confusion followed. The anti-Long contingent selected for its gubernatorial candidate an inept campaigner, a pro-Roosevelt congressman from Alexandria, Cleveland Dear, whom Huey's heirs promptly dubbed the leader of the assassination ticket. After a wild overnight schism, in which the Reverend Gerald L. K. Smith tried to proclaim himself the new Kingfish, the Long heirs prevailed on Richard Leche to surrender the virtually life-time tenure of his place as judge on the Appeals Court bench and run for governor. On his ticket were also Oscar Allen to serve out the two years remaining of Huey Long's term as senator, Allen Ellender to run for the six-year term that would follow, and Earl Long as lieutenant governor. Russell Long, Huey's then seventeen-year-old son, made his debut in the political arena as one of the speakers touring the state on behalf of this ticket.

The election was almost unbelievably one-sided. The dispossessed country folk who had looked up to ol' Huey as their share-our-wealth Messiah, were opposed by a poor speaker who projected a diffident image at best. Hence, Richard Leche was elected by the largest majority ever accorded a governor up to that time.

He did a great deal to restore harmony to a state that had been strife-ravaged politically for eight years. He made his peace with the Roosevelt administration, restoring the flow of federal patronage to Louisiana. He immediately had his Legislature repeal the act that made all public school employees dependent on the whims of the state administration for appointment to and retention of their positions, and followed this with the enactment of a genuine teacher tenure law. Before the Legislature's 1936 session was half over, Mayor Walmsley resigned.

The New Orleans Democratic committee thereupon put forward only one candidate, Robert S. Maestri, wealthy real estate operator, and head of what was then known as the Conservation Commission, with full control over all natural resources, animate or inanimate. As the Democratic nominee with no opponent, he was not even under the necessity of being voted on at the general election of August 17. Hence Robert Maestri became mayor of New Orleans without a single vote having been cast for him.

Maestri made a remarkable record during his first term as

mayor. Within less than two years he put the bankrupt city of New Orleans on a cash basis. He was of a taciturn bent, and when he did say anything his speech was likely to be earthy as well as forthright, which shocked a good many persons. He would cruise about the city with an engineer friend each morning, noting every sidewalk that needed repair, every street that should be resurfaced, every city building that must have a coat of paint and the like. At the city hall he would repair to a desk in the large public reception parlor, never entering his private office during normal business hours. In this way he could say to some caller who was prolonging his visit unduly:

"Look, pal. I got all these people waiting to talk to me too, so tell me the rest of it some other time."

When the six years were up, the anti-machine contingent was hard put to it to find an opponent to pit against Maestri, but finally came up with an eloquent young attorney who, despite an energetic campaign, was swamped. The easy victory worked some sort of change in Maestri. He spent more and more time in his private office, inaccessible to the public. He concentrated less and less on touring the city to see conditions for himself; more and more in masterminding the political activities of the coalition of Long and Old Regular ward leaders which he headed. One reason for this was that the grip Huey's heirs had maintained on the state administration was broken in January, 1940.

It all began when James Monroe Smith, president of Louisiana State University, called on Governor Leche and said in what must still be regarded as one of the world's great masterpieces of understatement: "Governor, I'm afraid I've done something foolish." The something foolish to which he referred was the fact that with forged Louisiana State University bonds as security, and on the authorization of forged minutes of the University's Board of Supervisors (of which the governor was ex officio chairman), he had borrowed $200,000 from one bank in the University's name, $200,000 from another, and $100,000 from a third, and had lost all of it in the wheat market.

With his wife, daughter and son-in-law he left that night for parts unknown, registering enroute as "J. M. Southern," which would match the initials on his hand luggage . . . He was traced to Canada, arrested, and returned to Baton Rouge by the police to face some forty-six state and federal charges. A number of other officials were tried, found guilty and convicted, serving various sentences in state or federal correctional institutions. At the height of what was dubbed "The Scandals," Governor Leche resigned, with nearly a year of his term yet to run, and his lieutenant governor, Huey's younger brother Earl, stepped up to the governorship. But the effect of the Scandals was not to be gainsaid. True, in the first primary, Earl Long led his nearest competitor, Attorney Sam Houston Jones of Lake Charles, by the staggering plurality of some 73,000 votes. But a third candidate in the race, the same Senator James A. Noe who had served as acting governor for four months between the time of Oscar Allen's death and Judge Leche's inauguration, was third man, and joined forces with Sam Jones for the run-off election.

Jones was a persuasive campaigner, and had the good government contingent solidly behind him. Noe was still looked upon as a staunch disciple of Huey. The quid pro quo of his support for Jones in the run-off was a frankly admitted pact stipulating that state patronage would be split fifty-fifty between the Jones and Noe supporters. That deal foreseeably carried within itself the swiftly germinating seeds of its own destruction. Jones won. Those who had supported him from the first felt they were entitled to a majority of the plums. The Noe supporters insisted that since Jones could not have won without them, half was not enough and furthermore they were being short-changed by receiving far less than even half.

By contrast the serene stability of the city's fiscal situation made it easy for Maestri to defeat his two 1942 opponents. This was the first real year of American participation in the Second World War and politics of the seamy sort was subordinated to war-winning. Baton Rouge, for instance, was more concerned with the progress of the "cat crackers" turning out aviation gas in the world's largest high-octane refinery—the Esso plant just north of Baton Rouge—and in the Polymer Corporation plant and others turning out synthetic rubber by the carload.

This was borne out by the results of the state election of January, 1944. Earl Long chose to run for Lieutenant Governor on the ticket headed by Lewis Morgan of Covington. Sam Jones had personally selected an all-but-unknown hillbilly singer and band leader, a former school teacher who had been elected one of the city commissioners of Shreveport, the son of a Jackson Parish sharecropper, Jimmie (not James) H. Davis, as the candidate he and his reform faction would endorse.

Davis, campaigning with his hillbilly musicians and the theme-song "You are my Sunshine" whose authorship is credited to him, was high man in the first primary in January, but Earl Long was high man for Lieutenant Governor, and Joe Cawthorn, a North Louisiana state senator, was high man for Attorney General. According to the primary law as it then stood, in the event no run-off was required for Governor, the plurality leaders for all lesser state offices were declared party nominees. In Louisiana that was still tantamount to election.

Since Davis did not have a majority of the votes cast, he could be forced into a second primary if Lewis Morgan, with the second-high vote total, demanded it. Earl Long and Joe Cawthorn, realizing that they would automatically be elected if Morgan did not demand a run-off, asked him to withdraw. He flew into a fury and announced he would insist on a run-off. Thereupon the Louisiana voters elected the whole Davis ticket and likewise a Legislature of what were for the most part sincere public servants. They maintained intact the greatest single accomplishment of the Jones administration: redemption of the Port of New Orleans from its earlier sink of politicalization. One of the commissioners appointed under the Allen regime had been at the time of his appointment a handbook operator. Before every city and state election the payrolls had been fantastically padded.

Governor Jones had sponsored a constitutional amendment that took the Board permanently out of such political mismanagement. In essence it limited the governor to appointments made from a list to which the universities, the chamber of commerce, and other such civic organizations each contributed three names. The appointments were so staggered that no more than two or three ever fell to any one governor during the course of his four year term.

Victory in Europe and in Japan, and what has proved to be a very uneasy peace, came to the world at last, and with this came the realization that New Orleans Democrats were about to nominate—which is to say elect—a mayor. Primary day was set for January 22, 1946.

The reform element which automatically opposed the Maestri-Regular organization was searching high and low for a candidate who might unseat him. Meanwhile he spent much of his time closeted in his private office, wheeling and dealing with ward leaders and precinct captains, when the Reform caucus decided to support Joachim O. Fernandez against him.

Fernandez had been an Old Regular state senator in 1930, when he switched his allegiance from Walmsley and the City Hall to Huey Long and was rewarded with Huey's support for the congressional seat held by veteran James O'Connor. Huey Long was also running for the Senate at the time. In St. Bernard parish he and those on his ticket received 2700 votes or so; his opponent received 7. The astonishing figures added the words "a St. Bernard count" to Louisiana's colloquial speech. Fernandez stayed in Congress until 1940 when, on the crest of the Reform wave that enabled Sam Jones to defeat Earl Long, City Editor F. Edward Hebert of the *New Orleans States* defeated him and has retained the seat from the first Louisiana district ever since.

Ex-Congressman Fernandez was taken care of by federal patronage, first as a Navy lieutenant-commander in the intelligence section and later by a federal appointment as collector of internal revenue at New Orleans. He was still serving in this capacity when a Reform caucus incredibly tapped him as their candidate against Maestri for mayor in 1946.

Then, two days before the final filing date for primary candidates, Fernandez shocked all New Orleans out of its complacent preoccupation with such matters as preparation for the first post-war renewal of Carnival activity by announcing his withdrawal from the race! This would leave Mayor Maestri unopposed.

At this juncture, with less than 48 hours before the entry list for candidates would be closed, Colonel de Lesseps "Chep" Morrison, one of New Orleans' representatives in the State Legislature from the twelfth ward, returned from overseas. Like a number of other office holders he had been re-elected *in absentia* while on military service. Still wearing his uniform, Representative Morrison was rushed to the office of the Orleans Parish Democratic Committee and became a candidate for the Democratic nomination for mayor. He felt, as did most of his backers, that he was leading a forlorn hope. Maestri's machine was close-knit and well organized. Morrison actually had no organization in the strict sense of the word, and yet . . .

Captain "Mike" O'Leary, manager of the more-than-a-century-old St. Charles (now Sheraton Charles) Hotel, where Winfield Scott had run up appalling bar bills in his day, and a dethroned John L. Sullivan awoke to the realization, after his fight with Gentleman Jim Corbett that he could no longer "lick any _____ in the house," compressed what happened into the best post-election summary ever set to words when he said:

"The day after election, the two most surprised individuals in New Orleans were Maestri and Morrison!"

Small wonder! Morrison had taken not merely the lead, he—the last minute second choice of even his most ardent supporters—had scored a first primary majority, and there would be no run-off!

He was elected mayor of New Orleans four successive times. His most meaningful election was the second one, in January, 1950. Two years before, Earl Long, running against a miscellany of candidates as Jimmy Davis' term drew to a close, had swamped Sam Jones, not only in a first, but in a second primary as well.

Long's dossier of vengeful legislation had for its target the city of New Orleans. The Maestri defeat of 1946, swung the Old Regulars to Long in the second primary, after they had backed another candidate who ran last in the first round. (He actually ran third in the city of New Orleans). The city Machine's legislators agreed to vote for all of Long's anti-New Orleans spite bills provided Long would change the charter of New Orleans to establish a modified councilmanic form of government, so that only the mayor and one other councilman would be elected on a city-wide basis. Realizing they could no longer carry a city-wide vote they proposed to gerrymander the municipality into seven districts, each of which would elect only one councilman. They tailored the district boundaries so weirdly that Machine picked candidates would win in six, and with luck in all seven.

This would effectually nullify Morrison's political power, giving him nothing but the title of the mayoralty. To make certain that nothing went wrong, they incorporated into the new statute a clause by which the citizens of New Orleans were specifically barred from voting on the adoption or rejection of the change in their community's form of government.

Resentment over this dossier of anti-New Orleans statutes was so wide-spread and bitter that the elaborately planned gerrymander defeated itself. On election day only one of the Old Regular aldermanic candidates received enough votes to get into a second primary, in which he was later elected over his Morrison-sponsored opponent. Instead of insuring a 6 to 1 Old Regular majority they provided Morrison with a ready-made organization, the Crescent City Democratic Association, which became dominant for the next 16 years.

The lesson was not lost on Governor Long. He appointed a city charter commission to work out a new organic statute for New Orleans. The commission did so, leaving the quasi-aldermanic separation of legislative and executive functions in effect, but resetting the boundaries of the absurdly gerrymandered districts, reducing these to five in number and providing that the mayor and two councilmen-at-large be elected city-wide, the five remaining council members from their respective districts which now were approximately equal in population. Victor H. Schiro and Glen Clasen were the first councilmen-at-large to win the office which carried with it the duty of presiding over council meetings and serving as vice-mayor during the mayor's absence from the city.

That September Russell Long was victorious in his first bid for a full six-year term in the United States Senate. When John H. Overton had died in 1948, two years of his term remained. Russell Long, serving as administrative assistant to his newly inaugurated Uncle Earl, became a candidate in the September primary. Resentment was still strong in New Orleans over the city spite bills Earl had dragooned through the Legislature two months earlier. Although he had been high man in the New Orleans vote in January, New Orleans gave a 25,000 majority against Russell in September. Two years later the bitterness had subsided. Russell won the election for a full term handily; and by 1962 the city gave him a literally overwhelming majority.

In 1952, Mayor Morrison made what proved to be a costly political error. Instead of supporting Judge Robert Kennon, he brought out (or joined in supporting) his one-time partner, Congressman T. Hale Boggs, as Crescent City Democratic Association candidate for governor. Boggs did not place among the top two and so was eliminated in the first primary, which gave Judge Kennon the second-largest vote. In the run-off, Kennon was elected by a substantial majority.

His administration was remarkable in several respects. He had pledged that taxes would be reduced, and he repealed the two cent raise Long had added to the retail per-gallon tax on gasoline, and substantially increased personal state income tax exemptions. In place of the Jones civil service statute which Long had found it so easy to repeal, he accepted from Charles Dunbar, head of the Civil Service League, a draft statute which his floor leader, Senator (now federal judge) Robert Ainsworth, steered through to enactment by an overwhelming vote as a constitutional amendment. When ratified its repeal could never even be submitted to a popular vote without a two-thirds majority of the elected membership of each house of the State Legislature, and repeal itself would be subject to a vote of the people. He made the use of voting machines mandatory in every one of Louisiana's 2300 or so precincts, instead of merely in large communities whose citizens voted to adopt them.

Meanwhile, a city campaign once more reached its quadrennial climax in 1954, with Morrison running for a third term in a field of no less than nine candidates, only four of whom were to be taken seriously. Some of the nine cheerfully paid their qualification fees for the satisfaction of getting their names and pictures into the newspapers and a share of any multilateral TV programs on which candidates appeared.

The serious opponents to Morrison were Councilman Thomas M. Brahney, the only Old Regular to survive the backfiring gerrymander of 1948–50; Criminal Sheriff John Grosch who had left the Old Regulars to endorse Morrison four years earlier; and Francis Williams who had run for mayor in 1934 and for secretary of state in 1936.

Morrison had built up a truly remarkable record of constructive city improvements. Notably, he had sponsored a bond issue by which a relatively few over or under-passes eliminated a great many hazardous rail and vehicular grade crossings within the city limits. He had also projected the clearance of a central slum area, where a new city, state, and federal office building complex (all now complete), arose.

The record was impressive, and so was the political step Mayor Morrison sponsored in having the city charter amended to provide that no mayor of New Orleans could thenceforth be elected for more than two successive terms. Since this did not go into effect until 1954, it enabled him not merely to become a candidate for what was in actuality a third term, but to run again for a fourth term in 1958.

He reached the crest of his popularity in 1954 at the close of his second term, when he was swept back into office in the first primary.

But he ran for governor against Earl Long and three other candidates two years later and was one of those sharing what was tantamount to a rout when "Ole Earl" was returned to office by a clear majority of first primary ballots. No one has ever come up with a satisfactorily rational explanation of what brought about this astonishing reversal of Morrison's fortunes.

It was a strange race, with one member of Governor Kennon's official family already in the race when the governor put in another candidate, a virtual unknown. The Kennon nominee would have been different had Morrison not so needlessly increased the governor's unforgiving hostility by assuring his defeat.

However, Earl Long's growing unpopularity was climaxed when his wife, his nephew, his sister and other members of the family, took him by plane to Galveston and had him confined in a mental institution there.

He won a court release from this hospital, promising to submit to medical treatment on his return to Louisiana. But on arrival at Baton Rouge, he went directly to the state capitol. Before he could get out of his car there, he was examined in his automobile by Coroner Chester Williams, who pronounced him mentally incompetent and directed that he be confined in a nearby state mental hospital on the outskirts of Mandeville. With his attorney's aid he swiftly maneuvered his release by having the hospital superintendent dismissed and securing the appointment of a successor who promptly pronounced him mentally sound and released him.

He then strove by every conceivable stratagem to evade the constitutional prohibition which barred him from being reelected as his own immediate successor. One device he considered was to resign shortly before his term expired, letting his lieutenant governor, Lether E. Frazar, become governor for a month or so. Since he would thus not technically campaign for office as his own "immediate successor" he could be declared eligible to run.

But the joy ride was over. When he summoned the Legislature into extraordinary session to carry this or some similar plan into effect, one of his own floor leaders made a motion the moment the meeting began that the assembly adjourn *sine die,* and it did so without further ado.

However, convinced that even as candidate for the second place on the ticket he could not win, he stopped campaigning and was eliminated. Jimmie Davis was once more elected to the governorship, defeating Chep Morrison who had been high man in the first primary. Thereupon, Earl Long ran for Congress from the district his late brother George had long represented in Washington, and handily won the Democratic nomination, but died of a heart attack a few days later, before he could be "elected."

Chep Morrison, defeated in his second gubernatorial campaign in 1960, had already been re-elected Mayor in 1958 to serve a second term under the new charter provision barring more than two successive incumbencies. Since this would keep him from seeking re-election in 1962, a campaign was launched by his supporters to have this provision repealed, in spite of the fact that Morrison had vigorously campaigned originally for its adoption. The proposal was voted down.

By this time President Kennedy had been inaugurated and he offered Morrison an appointment as United States ambassador to the Organization of America States. He had to resign the mayoralty to accept it. This set off a wave of disaffection among a number of his CCDA ward leaders. Morrison went to Washington as OAS ambassador and acting Mayor Schiro became a candidate for mayor in the 1962 municipal primary. He was opposed by State Senator Adrian Duplantier whom Morrison backed unreservedly, in a public statement in which he announced he had cast an absentee ballot for the entire Duplantier ticket "from top to bottom."

Duplantier led in the first primary but Schiro, second high, received the united support of the two next highest candidates, and the result was a foregone conclusion.

The next state campaign's result was directly determined by the assassination of the President on November 22, 1963, just a fortnight prior to the Louisiana Democratic party primary for state and parochial offices. Of the eight or nine gubernatorial candidates who were at least nominally in the race, only four were regarded as actual aspirants for Democratic nomination to this post, nomination being for the last time, perhaps, tantamount to election. As a matter of fact it was no longer a foregone conclusion that Democratic nominees would automatically sweep the boards in a general election. Charlton Lyons, a wealthy Shreveport oilman, had been chosen by the Republicans as their standard bearer, and he was already at work with the help of an adequate and thoroughly organized staff, campaigning busily and effectively.

The four seekers after Democratic nomination were former New Orleans Mayor, and currently U.S. Ambassador to the Organization of American States, deLesseps Morrison, seeking the governorship in a third effort, having met with defeat in two previous tries; former Governor Robert F. Kennon; Congressman Gillis Long, actively supported by Huey's two sons, Russell B., who had succeeded to his late father's seat in the U.S. Senate, and Palmer R.; and Public Service Commissioner John McKeithen, who was supported politically by Earl Long's widow.

Every knowledgeable observer of the then current political scene in Louisiana, took it for granted that Morrison would be high man by a substantial plurality, still far short of an overall majority, in the first primary. Up to the 22nd day of November most of them were agreed that Kennon would lead the other two and in the run-off would win, since Morrison would have polled his full potential in the first primary. But in a matter of the few moments during which Kennedy lost his life in Dallas his image was transformed from that of a controversial figure who had barely squeaked through to victory over Richard M. Nixon in 1960 to that of a sort of haloed martyr, who had laid down his life for his people.

Judge Kennon had pitched his entire campaign on his implacable opposition to the newly sainted martyr, declaring openly that if the President were renominated by the Democrats—a virtual certainty—he, running for the Louisiana governorship as a Democrat, even when elected and thus *ipso facto* the head of Louisiana's Democratic party, would support Kennedy's Republican opponent, as he had supported Eisenhower in '52 and '56.

There was no time in which to eradicate public reaction to what was suddenly a heartless attitude, or to replace it with an updated platform. As a result, candidate Kennon ran fourth instead of second, and so was eliminated from the general election when the Democratic standard would be carried by McKeithen. The latter's principal appeal to the voters had been a non-factional "I want to he'p you. Won't you please he'p me to do so?"

As predicted, he defeated Morrison by a near-landslide, and was thus pitted against Charlton Lyons in the first meaningful Louisiana general election in nearly a century. The jubilant inference which GOP pundits drew from the fact that Lyons had actually received some 200,000 votes to the effect that Louisiana had "become a two party state again" was specious, to say the least. There had always been two parties in the state, even though both of them were labeled "factions within the Democratic party," however bitterly they might do battle against one another.

Various Supreme Court decisions which followed in due course on President Eisenhower's 1953 appointment of Earl Warren to be Chief Justice of the United States, had already reversed the separate-but-equal concept of keeping the public schools segregated wherever a majority of the local citizenry desired this. It had also decided that political parties were not the type of private organizations which had the right to pick and choose among applicants for membership, denying admission to those who otherwise met every expressed constitutional qualification for the suffrage.

Because of Louisiana's inherent politico-economic conservatism, and its long-standing racial prejudices, Republican registration swelled. So did that of the Democrats. Almost half the newly re-enfranchised Negro voters registered as Democrats. In the general election of 1964, two members of the 105-man state House of Representatives were Republicans, the first to be seated in that chamber since carpetbaggery was stamped out. However, no one can say with any approach to certainty what will be the effect on future elections of the so-called anti-liberal backlash engendered by resentment over the wave of lawless violence, Black Power demonstrations, protest sit-ins, love-ins and draft-card burnings that marked the middle 1960's.

However, it is reasonably safe to assume that any city which survived foreign wars and enemy occupation during history's bloodiest fratricidal strife, the community which learned at first hand what it means to lose a war, a people who succeeded in throwing off the dictatorship of the Carpetbaggers in the 1870's and the unparalleled autarchy of the Long regime in the 1940's can not indefinitely be deprived of its essential dignity or the enjoyment of its pursuit of happiness.

It would not come amiss to stress here the marginal note that this does not refer only to the city of New Orleans and the state of Louisiana, and is coupled with the earnest hope that the pendulum may not swing back too far in its retrograde arc.

Mardi Gras

Laurraine Goreau

In New Orleans, its business head askew atop its Creole spirit, fantasy is never very far away.

For New Orleans takes its pleasure seriously, and the pivot of its pleasure is Mardi Gras, a vast fantasia of magic and madness, rolled into mirth, bursting upon more than a million persons who are both cast and audience of the greatest free show on earth.

It is a standard New Orleans gambit that an upper-class family begins working on a daughter's becoming queen of a Carnival ball on the day of her birth.

A young man of seven currently is dedicated to two things: knights and his avowed future status as King of Carnival. He is already seriously preparing for his kingly responsibility by wearing his long underwear to Carnival parades even when it's too warm for it, "because kings do."

The boy's great-great-grandfather was one of the founders of Rex in 1872. His great-great-aunt was Rex's consort, Queen of Carnival; so was his great-aunt. His mother was maid to the Queen of Carnival and herself Queen of Oberon, among the oldest of society's *bals masqués*. At seven, he doesn't grasp all this, but he doesn't need facts; he senses the portents of the Cult of Carnival.

New Orleanians, sensitive to signs and symbols, know that Mardi Gras was fixed into the city's fabric from the first night that Pierre Le Moyne, Sieur d'Iberville, bent on perpetuating a colony for France, made camp on Louisiana soil some 30 nautical miles from the mouth of the Mississippi River.

It was Mardi Gras, March 3, 1699. D'Iberville named the site Pointe du Mardi Gras. The stream which emptied into the Mississippi at this point became known as Bayou du Mardi Gras.

There is no record of New Orleans's earliest Mardi Gras revelry, but Louis XIV is said to have issued a decree permitting Carnival frivolities in the colony without penalty of law. However, masking was not then linked exclusively with the Carnival season as it is today. It was a frequent fillip to the continual round of balls and *soirées* (less formal gatherings) with which the colonists danced through flood, famine, plague, fire, hurricane, rebellion, hordes of mad dogs, thugs who infested the streets, and a virtual roulette of possession between France and Spain with periods of no government at all, and the final shock of finding themselves "owned" by the Americans in 1803.

The pattern was set by the Marquis de Vaudreuil, who arrived in 1743 as governor of the province after the resignation of the city's founder, Jean Baptiste Le Moyne, Sieur de Bienville (Iberville's younger brother), who was finally overwhelmed by the magnitude of the colony's problems and the inadequacies of his facilities to cope with them.

Vaudreuil's lavish balls, state dinners served on gold plate, and extravagant pomp and ceremony quite captured the colonists. His Carnival entertainments were spectacular.

In his 10 years' stay, de Vaudreuil's grandeur of manner, his dashing style, his fostering of music and drama set the mode and manners for generations; just as his civil corruption and tolerance of vice confirmed the course on which the colony seemed bent, that of a "sin city of pleasure."

Fortunately for the future of Carnival it was rooted in the pre-Christian celebrations of the advent of Spring, rescued from their maelstrom of pagan debauchery, cleansed into Christian rite, and transmuted into the feast of the flesh before the fasting commenorating Christ's fast, the period of revelry which the volatile Latins of Italy, France and Spain required before the austerity of the forty days of Lent (excluding Sundays) preceding Easter. The Carnival season thus fell conveniently into the weather dictates of a New Orleans social life, with dancing before the hot summer set in—if "conveniently" may be applied to the rainiest, coldest, most capricious season of the year, when New Orleanians for over two centuries have prayed fervently for a "good day" for Mardi Gras and, latterly, for the broad stretch of Carnival parades.

Many of the first mentions of Mardi Gras maskers in New Orleans streets were ballgoers in fancy dress going to and from both public and private *bals masqués.*

The élite attended subscription balls whose invitation lists were rigidly select, even if a sum as high as $10 or as little as $3 were exacted for the privilege of attending, as was the custom.

Public "balls," minus formality, were held at least as frequently as the society balls, with admission usually free for the "ladies" (no Creole gentlewoman could have with propriety attended) and 50 cents to $1 for the men. Such balls were advertised so as to ape the select events of the upper strata.

From 1790 to 1812, a simple wooden structure, La Salle Condé, was the scene of most *haut monde* masquerade balls. Then the Condé lost favor to the new Theatre St. Philip, the first of a succession of theatres. New Orleans was growing vastly more prosperous as flatboats, keel boats, tugboats, steamboats came 'round the bend and deposited undreamed-of wealth along with a cargo of adventurers, gamblers, and roustabout desperadoes. This motley crew quickly filled the public dances at the Condé Street ballroom, which became as notorious a haunt as was La Salle de l'Harmonie on St. Peter Street. It advertised masked balls every Monday and Wednesday, $2 for men; women, free. In time the St. Philip Theatre too became outmoded and, renamed the Washington Ballroom, became an arena for scandal and frequent murders.

Much of the blame was laid to the masking. Masquerades had been under intermittent fire during the uneasy years of

Spanish rule, and a series of edicts for their control was issued, surreptitiously disobeyed, allowed to lapse, then when the situation grew sufficiently alarming, revived.

One such edict grew out of the increasing frequency with which colored men and women (chiefly, free men and women of mixed blood) were found to be slipping into the white public masquerade balls, and mingling with the white maskers on the streets. By law, such racial mixing was forbidden. The new Spanish countermeasure was a decree that "only Caucasians may masquerade." Later, masquerading was prohibited entirely, a prohibition which lasted through nearly the first two decades of the American régime.

But who was to tell a Creole not to masquerade? As soon tell him to stop his blood from flowing. The private society balls masked in secret, and were later given official exemption. The public balls would not be gainsaid either, and even intermittent penalties could not suppress New Orleans's favorite pastime. Besides, Carnival served a very substantial social function, as indicated in a letter of September 18, 1810, addressed to the mayor and City Council by "Lucinda Sparkle" (possibly a pseudonym), and published in *The Louisiana Gazette*. It petitioned that a suitably genteel, tree-shaded promenade be established to foster matrimony for "the best female society," who were losing out to the quadroons who promenaded the levee and ensnared the eligible gentlemen of the city.

"During the Carnival," wrote Lucinda, "when our young gentlemen from custom and the pleasures of dancing are frequently in company with our belles, feelings of the most pure and tender nature are often excited; but . . . time passes, the Carnival ends, and the period of female seclusion again returns, and there remains nothing to counteract the baneful vices complained of by your petitioner."

With a suitable public promenade and "every inducement" held out to young ladies for its use, Lucinda expressed hope that "the favorable and honorable impressions made during the Carnival might be renewed; new conquests might be made."

Since 1791, New Orleans had had America's first resident theatre company; later it was to have America's first opera house; its love for concerts had been long established. Of equal importance, its distinctive cuisine had evolved, born of an inspired palate.

All these came into play by the mid-1820's, as élite masquerade balls took on added dimension: Carnival tableau balls. Using the dual facilities now offered by the Théâtre d'Orléans and the adjoining Salle d'Orléans, these Carnival balls began with a theatrical presentation; then, by elevating the orchestra pit, the extended stage was used for dancing as well as the ballroom; the whole followed by a sumptuous supper.

The exclusive Carnival balls of today are not too removed from this pattern except for their restriction of general dancing, which would have frustrated earlier Creoles intolerably. However, watching dancing was second choice to dancing itself, even in the 1880's when the popular craze was for dance marathons, thus the current tradition has its roots in the old. The far more popular krewes of today with their masquerade extravaganzas hark back to the equally honorable tradition of the elaborate *bal masqué*, thus the twin streams of New Orleans's Mardi Gras celebrations flow side by side, but far more peacefully than in the old days.

So rowdy, so murderous were the public masquerade balls in the 1820's, so many were the outbreaks on the streets that in 1825 attempts were made to persuade the city aldermen to abolish all masquerades and masked balls.

That year the Duke of Saxe-Weimar Eisenach, governor of the Dutch West Indies, visited New Orleans. He was taken to two Mardi Gras balls, the first, a society subscription ball at the Théâtre d'Orléans, $2 for gentlemen, $1 for ladies. This ball, the duke discovered, couldn't compete with the second he attended that night, a masquerade ball at the St. Philip Theatre, by then solely a dance hall far down the social scale but the talk of points as distant as London, for this was now the site of the celebrated quadroon balls.

At the society ball, wrote the duke, "most of the gentlemen . . . hastened away to the quadroon ball." So many men left that many of the ladies "were obliged to form *bredouille* (tapestry).

Four years later, on Feb. 17, 1829, *The Louisiana Gazette* (the first English-language newspaper) reported "many occasions for disorder because of the disguises, but police were so active . . . there were no incidents of rioting." Under new stricture, all canes, swords, sticks or arms of any nature were deposited at the entrance, "and from the ball at the Opera to the lowest dive that formality was religiously observed."

Ultimately, it was a unique complaint which once more brought absolute prohibition: Many white women, masked, were attending the quadroon balls, held two or three times a week. "The most dissolute class," said Acting Mayor Culbertson to a City Council reluctant to act.

Not so, said *The Bee* editorially, after a visit to the Washington Ball Room. Many of the white women, it declared, were reputedly "usually considered respectable in their sphere of life."

Their motives were obscured more effectively than their faces were concealed, but Alderman Allard defended the right of married white women to be present if masked, "to surprise husbands *flagrante delictu*."

The debate raged a year. The public scandal grew. On Dec. 19, 1836, 24 days before the Carnival season opened on Twelfth Night, all masquerades and masked balls were prohibited under penalty of $500 fine.

Before another Carnival rolled 'round, the ordinance was repealed, on Oct. 25, 1837, and a resolution passed permitting masked balls in the Orleans Ball Room (Salle d'Orléans), Davis' Ball Room, the St. Philip Street Ball Room, and the Washington Ball Room. The first two were the locales of society balls; the latter two, of public balls. A license for each ball was $20, half to the city, half to the Catholic Association for Destitute Orphans. Masked balls admitting both white and colored women were to be fined $50 the first time, $100 thereafter, half to the informer, half to the city. No masked balls were to be held before Nov. 1 nor after May 1.

Masquerade balls contracted to the Carnival season, and so it has remained.

Proscription of masquerade balls *per se* has long fallen by the wayside. But even today, by state law, street masking is permitted only on Mardi Gras, and then masks must be removed at sundown. By tacit accord the law is not applied to the krewemen riding high on their glittering floats.

The earliest description of an organized street masking group on the New Orleans scene is of one in 1827, when a group of students back from Paris organized themselves to parade the streets in costume on Mardi Gras. Soon one observer noted that "parading about is getting to be as important as the ball."

Only the indomitable Creole zest for entertainment could have produced the first organized Mardi Gras parade in 1837, for it was a period of gloom and mounting financial disaster, climaxed three months later when all 14 banks folded, the second major crash in 17 years. Crop failures, yellow fever, cholera had struck as well. But the Creoles bounded back with that incurable *joie de vivre* and shrug-ability characteristic of New Orleans even today.

The French press took no notice of that 1837 parade. The new American paper, *The Picayune,* dismissed the costumes as "outlandish and grotesque," labelled the parade "noisy" (as if *that* were a Mardi Gras drawback), and frowned on the "riffraff" following in its wake.

The 1838 parade was bigger and better. Both the French and American press applauded and *La Créole* reported, "The whole town doubled up with laughter. . . . The beautiful and joyous cavalcade wound its way at full speed. . . . What noise! What hubbub! And what fun! . . . The masked ball brought the day to a fitting close."

"Many of them were dressed in female attire," reported the enthusiastic *Picayune*, "and acted the lady with no small degree of grace." So successfully, in fact, that rumors spread through the crowd that ladies were riding through the streets and distributing favors, a scandal to the wellborn. Actually, the gentlewomen viewed the proceedings discreetly, from balconies. The tossing of sweetmeats to them is the earliest of Carnival parade "throws."

The parade was timed to wind up at the Théâtre d'Orléans, where Auber's opera *Gustave III* or *Le Bal Masqué* was being performed, so that the parading masqueraders could rush on stage and join the cast in the finale, a grand march and gallopade, after which cast and audience joined in dancing. This was so successful that *Gustave* became a Carnival staple, with its climactic finale addition from the Mardi Gras parade.

Each year the street procession became more elaborate. In 1841, some 300 to 400 brilliantly costumed Bedouins, a group of leading citizens, staged an imposing parade with which other maskers fell in. They wound through the streets for three hours, romped on stage for the *Gustave* finale, then adjourned for a feast and private costume ball in the fashionable new City Exchange (later St. Louis Hotel). Another such ball was held at the American Hotel. The latter won patronage when the St. Charles Hotel, reeling under pressure from its guests for invitations to the now-famous balls, advised the sponsors that they would have to provide admission to hotel guests, or move the ball elsewhere. The élite elected to move rather than dilute their prestigious list, a practice clung to up to the present day despite pressure which would long ago have burst the bounds of less iron resolve in matters social.

The Bedouins were an increasingly prominent feature of Mardi Gras for some years. In 1852, their parade sparked a procession of thousands on foot, on horse, or on wheels.

These flashes of brilliance and fun, though, were overshadowed by the general rowdiness. An American visitor in 1835 wrote of Mardi Gras, "The authorities countenance it reluctantly. . . . It is a custom to which the old citizens were and their descendants are much attached, and it will be difficult to prevent its continuance."

The ensuing years did nothing to help matters, and Mardi Gras revelry drew further disfavor. Street masking waned, so that in 1850, the editor of *The Bee* told his readers that Mardi Gras was on its way out. "We are not sorry this miserable annual exhibition is rapidly becoming extinct. . . . It originated in a barbarous age, and is worthy of only such."

The New Orleans of the day was suffering its own barbarous age. The city was engulfed in the muddy, turbulent waters of virtual civil strife in the 1850's. Political corruption allowed bands of thugs to roam unchecked. Murder was commonplace; so was every other brand of violence.

Death by murder was as nothing to the yellow fever epidemic in 1853 which struck over 40,000 and turned the city into one vast stinking grave.

This pestilential hell did little to clear the political atmosphere in the ensuing years. The police were so demoralized that gangs took quarrels into their own hands.

Since the Americans were in control, the Creoles blamed them for the whole mess and had as little to do with them socially as possible.

In this atmosphere, Mardi Gras brought concerted outcry in both the American and the Creole press. Said the *Delta*: "Mardi Gras has become vulgar, tasteless, and spiritless." *L'Union*: "Each year Mardi Gras loses its gaiety." *The Bee*: "As for genuine Mardi Gras of former days . . . that has passed forever." *The Crescent*: "We hope we have seen the last of Mardi Gras."

Then came Comus riding into the night. Elegant, allegorical, tasteful, lively, dramatic. The secrecy with which the surprise had been kept, the surrounding degradation which it denied, made its achievement the more spectacular that Mardi Gras night, 1857. It was everything the press had mourned as lost.

It was also the first time the Americans had taken a dominant hand in Mardi Gras. For Carnival, a new world was aborning.

The project was that of six young men, all Anglo-Saxons originally from Mobile, who decided in late 1856 to organize a Mardi Gras parade such as Mobile's Cowbellion de Rakin held on New Year's Eve night. By Feb. 8, 1857, their ranks had grown to 83: Charles M. Churchill was elected parade captain; Joseph Ellison was made chairman for costumes, key to the whole enterprise; and a name was adopted: The Mistick Krewe of Comus, son of Bacchus and Circe, the god of revelry and mirth. The "Mistick" connoted both allegory and the secrecy which was a basic tenet for the group, and the pattern for all Carnival organizations to come. The spelling conveyed mock-antiquity.

The Krewe would present a parade, a tableau ball and a supper, borrowing the Cowbellion costumes.

The sun shone brightly on New Orleans that February 24, 1857, but there was little else for decent citizens to exult over. The *Daily Crescent* commented that "The street maskers were a God-forsaken and man-forsaken set." Most respectable citizens stayed indoors. The toughs, masked or otherwise, ruled the day. Instead of the customary flour, they threw lime and bricks. The newspapers implied that it wasn't safe to be on the streets. The upper classes waited for night, when they would costume and attend their *bals masqués*.

But there was something else to pique the curiosity of low and high alike. Rumor had spread that the Americans would have something new, something special, abroad that night. The Mistick men had woven a fine web. Expectant throngs waited for they knew not what.

Suddenly the fashionable uptown area of Julia and Magazine Streets was aflame with torches, their fumes and smoke an effective aura for the two elaborate floats which rolled forth, Comus on one, Satan high atop another, his Palace of Lucifer ablaze with gold and diamond brilliance. The floats were preceded and followed by every variety of devil, with a band setting a lively tempo. Negroes carrying flambeaux lighted the street for blocks. New Orleans had never seen its like, and never before had had a Carnival torchlight parade. Comus was an instant popular success.

Down Magazine they went, to Theatre Alley and through the stage doors of the Gaiety Theatre, which fronted on Gravier Street and was filled with their eager guests. The Krewe offered four lavish tableaux: "Tartarus," "The Expulsion," "Conference of Satan and Beelzebub" and "Pandemonium." Dancing followed on stage until midnight, then the masqueraders trooped to a banquet hall nearby where their accomplishments were toasted until daylight.

Next day the American press was lavish in its praise. The Creole press was another story. The *Daily Orleanian* described other balls in detail, but did not even admit the Comus ball had occurred, nor mention its parade. The *Daily Creole* held to its insistence that Carnival be abandoned at once, that it was in undesirable hands. The *Daily Delta,* deploring the day's rowdy, drunken, damaging display, said "matters were not mended by the Mistick Krewe of Comus, each man habited rather as a 'goblin damned' than a human being." Their "infernal tableaux" were labelled "more startling than pleasing." The *Bee* admitted the pageant had been brilliant, but lambasted its parading uptown rather than in the Vieux Carré. In the main, to the Creoles it seemed too much that the Americans, who had taken over so much else in the city, should capture Mardi Gras too.

Before Mardi Gras 1858, however, the proof of the pudding was in the eating: The Anglo-Saxons had invited applications for membership, and accepted a considerable infusion of Creole blood into their ranks. The Creole press was mollified, and thousands strove to wangle invitations to the ball. What Creole of New Orleans could resist a parade, a masquerade, dancing— and a secret?

Thus augmented, the electrified crowd learned on the night of February 16, 1858 that Comus in 1857 had merely been twirling his cape. Flaming torches lit 30 resplendent *tableaux roulants* bearing the Gods and Divinities of Olympus, paced smartly by marching bands.

Mardi Gras had had its face lifted. It was never to sag again. With Carnival revitalized, new *bals masqués* and entertainments dotted the calendar. Americans and Creoles joined common cause.

It took a war to make Mardi Gras stumble. There could be no float building in 1861, the first year of the War Between the States, but an unquenchable Comus and his Krewe brightened the public Mardi Gras with a street procession on foot, then entertained the élite with the now-traditional tableau ball. In the four gruelling, wretched years which followed, not phantom gods but hunger, disease, and federal troops stalked the streets.

In 1866 Reconstruction racked what was left of the city, but Comus rolled forth on his float, golden goblet in hand, loyal krewemen behind on foot, a symbol to a miserable city. Carnival was on the rise again, and Comus regularly set forth with determined merriment. Even the Carpetbagger régime ackowledged Comus's special status, for in 1870, when a police order was issued that each group of maskers must have at least one person unmasked, the Krewe of Comus was excepted.

In 1872, Comus left Olympus and indulged in defiant political satire. "The Missing Links to Darwin's Origin of the Species" mocked prominent carpetbaggers who infested the city. No repercussions are recorded. But in 1877, the floats of Momus, God of Laughter and Ridicule, splashed biting mockery across the Carpetbagger rule—from President Grant and his cabinet down to local scalawags—so tellingly that Governor Nicholls, contesting for the right to elected government, feared Washington would clamp down. Despite the wild cheering with which New Orleanians had greeted this personification of the feelings of most, the governor wired Washington that "the sentiment of the whole community is opposed to what occurred . . . the act of a few private individuals, unauthorized and unknown, and universally condemned and regretted."

Actually, Governor Nicholls was active in Carnival krewe circles and could surely have named names. His wire seems to have been sufficient balm, however, for no federal action was taken. In reprisal, however, the local Republican press printed those names of the Momus committee which it ferreted out. Among the Momus ringleaders named was Edward Douglas White, later Chief Justice of the United States. On sober reflection, the Carnival leaders' consensus was that politics and Mardi Gras should not mix, nor have they since, in any serious sense.

The 1872 parade was the first one wholly designed and constructed in New Orleans. Previously, parts of floats had been ordered from France, as were costumes and masks. Today, the same French firm supplies Comus the identical masks it first shipped in 1857, only the material has changed from waxed linen to plastic. France and Austria still supply Carnival with its crowns, scepters, diadems, ornate collars; Rex's giant animated figures come, in the main, from Germany, Italy, France, Spain, according to Blaine Kern, floatbuilder for Rex and largest parade producer in the city.

Comus made one last gallant bow toward the Lost Cause. In 1884, for the tableau ball at the French Opera House, the proscenium box on the right was occupied by Confederate President Jefferson Davis and General A. D. Hill and their daughters, Varina Davis and Nannie Hill; the daughters of General Robert E. Lee, Mildred and Mary Lee, and Julia Jackson, daughter of General Stonewall Jackson. Comus called out as his partner for the first quadrille, Mildred Lee, thereby winning her place in Carnival history as his first queen. The four other daughters of the Confederacy were called out by Comus's courtiers, becoming officially the first maids of honor. The precedent was established, and each year since, Comus has had a queen and court.

Twelfth Night Revelers gamboled onto the scene in 1870, firmly fixing the pendulum swing of New Orleans Carnival from January 6 through whatever date becomes Mardi Gras. Twelfth

Night signifies the visit of the Magi to the infant Jesus, with gifts and rejoicing. The Revelers were ambitious; that first year they paraded 18 floats. They meant to present Carnival's first queen then, too, at the ball which followed, but too many cooks spoiled the cake. Romping through their paces at this merriest of society balls (as it is today), the Revelers handed out slices from a giant Twelfth Night Cake to the young ladies in the French Opera House box seats. In one slice was a golden bean, which would make the finder their queen, but the Revelers grew so enthusiastic about tossing the cake that the bean was lost completely.

More decorum was decreed next year, and luck tapped Miss Emma Butler for the honor. Sheer chance ruled for some years after that. At least once, a young winner was so unprepared she was sent home to change her red dress for queenly white. Chance became mischance again in 1876, when the queen of 1872, Miss Ada Bringier, drew the bean again. Today, although the traditional motions are meticulously carried out, the Twelfth Night Revelers make their choice in advance from among the débutantes of the season and notify the girl's parents, who are sworn to secrecy. Sometimes they can keep the secret, as in 1964, when Courtney Manard was so surprised at finding the bean that she fainted. Even with this "sure" recipe, though, the cake ritual has occasionally crumbled, and the wrong girl been handed the golden bean. Such is Carnival that the Revelers cheerfully retrieve the bean and the ball proceeds without skipping a step.

After 1876, the Revelers contracted to simply staging a ball. Until well into the twentieth century, the parade field was carried in the main by the Big Four of Mardi Gras: Comus; Momus, who first rolled in 1872 on New Year's Eve, but because the ladies left the ball too early to attend to New Year's duties with their families shifted to the Thursday before Mardi Gras; Proteus, the Sea Deity who rose in 1882 out of the depths of the waiting lists for Comus and Momus membership with Comus's blessing; and Rex, King of Mardi Gras.

Rex was puffed into being entirely of the gossamer stuff

which clothes the Carnival, so light of spirit it cannot be submerged.

There was no one "king" of Carnival and none might ever have been agreed upon had not Russian playboy Alexis Romanoff Alexandrovitch, His Imperial Highness, Grand Duke Alexis, visited "incognito" in America early in 1872. Though traveling as "Lieutenant Romanoff" he was accompanied by three vessels of the Imperial Russian Navy. He followed actress Lydia Thompson to New Orleans, where she was to star in *The Burlesque of Bluebeard* at the Academy of Music.

Alexis was the most royal notable due since the visit in 1798 of three French princes (including the future King Louis Philippe). When it became evident that the Carpetbagger government wasn't going to organize suitable entertainment for him, the honor of Orleanians was at stake. It was near Mardi Gras, which meant, of course, a parade and a ball.

As had Comus on its birth, Rex went into action with remarkable rapidity. Prominent citizens formed the Rex organization. Young banker Lewis J. Salomon quickly raised the necessary $10,000, and was rewarded by becoming the first Rex. Donors became his dukes. A flood of audacious and imaginative proclamations was issued through the press, including one proclaiming Rex's rule for Mardi Gras, another proclaiming it a general holiday, another asking persons on the parade route to reinforce their balconies (still a wise precaution) and decorate with the royal colors, green for faith, gold for power and purple for justice. At the last minute the City Council had a reviewing stand erected, and Rex became official.

Vehicles were commandeered and hurriedly decorated. Rex borrowed tragedian Lawrence Barrett's Richard III costume, and the Varieties Theatre wardrobe provided the rest of the accoutrements for him and his dukes. On Mardi Gras, mounted on chargers, they led hundreds of maskers escorting the Boeuf Gras (the live, gaily decorated fat bull of French Carnival tradition), followed by decorated vehicles and a crowd of general maskers which swelled to some 5,000 by the time they greeted the Duke.

Someone, his name lost to posterity, had the inspired idea of putting band tempo to Miss Thompson's hit, "If Ever I Cease to Love," known to have captivated Alexis. Band after band played the frothy bit, and from that day it became Mardi Gras' official song, its words part of the fantasy: "If ever I cease to love . . . May sheepsheads grow on apple trees . . . May the moon be turn'd into green cheese . . . May oysters have legs and cows lay eggs, If ever I cease to Love." Ironically, the Duke did—cease— only to begin again. When Miss Thompson left, Alexis stayed to ogle Lotta Crabtree, appearing in *The Little Detective*.

Romantic New Orleans loved everything about Rex. The organization increased its membership from 40 to 100 and was chartered as the "School of Design," authorized to advance art; entertain, amuse and instruct the people; "and do other things which will redound to the good of society, the State and the Nation."

In its second year Rex opened its reception and ball to the general public, who turned up in everything from formal evening dress to makeshift costumes bedraggled from the day's wear. Seeking a queen, Rex (E. B. Wheelock) circled the hall twice before singling out a startled young onlooker in black dress and black bonnet, Mrs. Walker Fearn (nee Fanny Hewett). "It wasn't even my best dress!" she exclaimed later.

After the public experiment, Rex adopted the closed invitation list for his ball. It didn't hurt his popularity. He had given the public its biggest boon in popular history, an official holiday on Mardi Gras. The yeast was already in ferment; Rex provided the time and the space for it to expand.

The ball list grew. For tableau balls, besides Twelfth Night Revelers and their merry bakers, by the turn of the century there were Atlanteans, Oberon, Nereus, Olympians; then Athenians, Mystery, Osiris, Mystic (whose court gives matrons a second time around), Dorians, Achaeans. In 1926 society's offspring were restored to formal observance with the Children's Carnival Ball.

(As adult-court pages, many were already deeply involved and committed.) And Harlequins, which started with a high school age membership, raised its age limits so the original dancers could continue in the organization until *their* children, the Quins, could participate in the ball.

Formal tableau balls became an engrossing passion for tens of thousands among the general public. New krewes crisscrossed like paper serpentine, some to fix firmly onto the Carnival structure, many to flash only briefly; but for each which died, others were forming in the wings, money in their hands, dreams of one night's splendor in their heads. Women's krewes became popular. Mardi Gras clubs and peripheral parties showered like confetti into every nook and cranny of the complex city's existence; at every age, at every level.

A major impetus for the Carnival ball explosion was the opening of Municipal Auditorium in 1930. Rental fees were within reach of any major group, both concert hall and larger auditorium were available, and staging and seating facilities for balls were excellent. It became *the* place to give a ball.

Competition for dates became so fierce that the city and the krewe captains drew up formal rules, the foremost, that seniority prevailed in choice of dates. In 1951, when no balls were held because of the Korean War, most krewes paid full Auditorium rent to preserve seniority.

In 1946, when Carnival resumed after the World War II hiatus, 31 balls were staged at the Auditorium. In 1968, 61 were booked, most of them elaborate extravaganzas as distinct from the more sedate society balls. In a short Carnival such as 1967, the season stretched backward (the only direction it could expand) and 11 Carnival balls were given before Carnival officially opened. With Easter on a pendulum, the Carnival interval may be as few as 28 days, as many as 63.

With age, the makebelieve became a cult. Tradition became the bible, its commandments so cloaked as law that in 1956 the women's Krewe of Adonis sued to regain its "traditional" date at

Municipal Auditorium, assigned an older sister krewe, Iris, because of the compacted season. City officials were named with
Iris as co-defendants.

After four days' deliberation, Judge Viosca dismissed Adonis's
suit with, ". . . it is not the function of the courts to make rules
for the operation of Municipal Auditorium."

In one season, with krewe members as hosts who share the
full cost among themselves, well over 200,000 guests in formal
attire attended Carnival balls in Municipal Auditorium, each in
a fresh and lavish setting. More formal gowns are sold in New
Orleans than in any city in the U.S., including New York.

Ball invitations are avidly sought. Comus once advertised a
$2,000 reward for the return of two which had gone astray,
appalled at the prospect of having two uninvited persons among
its assemblage. The reward was never collected, but neither were
the invitations used.

Hundreds of lesser balls are staged in other halls throughout
the city.

When Hurricane Betsy and the ensuing flood devastated
much of New Orleans on Sept. 9, 1965, costumes, ball scenery
and floats were well in progress. But only one krewe (Anubis)
failed to come forth for Carnival in full splendor, even though
losses were not covered by insurance and for some it meant
starting over.

So epidemic had the Carnival fever become by 1950 that
Rex of 1931, Edward E. Soulé, in a speech to the Rex organization admonished, "You have all heard . . . that we are going
Carnival crazy in New Orleans and that we are all overdoing this
Carnival idea. With so many Carnival balls and so many day and
night parades of both men and women, it would seem no doubt
to many of you that we should perhaps call a halt and revise our
Carnival season. . . . I say to you, in all seriousness, that all the
well-meaning critics are wrong, absolutely, positively, and decidedly wrong. . . . Every good citizen, like yourselves, is entitled to
participate in the joys and pleasures and mysteries of a masked

ball or a Carnival parade. . . . The answer must be—'More organizations, if necessary.' "

Any other answer than Soulé's would have been shouted down by an indignant public with an insatiable appetite for more and more Carnival.

Street parades multiplied and grew more spectacular, some with giant figures and animation. If Druids fell by the wayside, larger and more glamorous Hermes and Babylon cavorted onto the scene. Neighborhood groups formed, then expanded and rolled downtown. New krewes mounted suburban processions; others rolled in new-born grandeur. Mid-City, Carrollton, Freret, Thoth, Helios, Jason, Okeanos, Pegasus, Zeus, Endymion, the list ebbs and flows with the years but the tide steadily swells. Venus (first women's krewe to mount floats) and Iris are among the hardiest women's krewes, on parade year after year in part by renting their floats from a larger krewe, which is permitted with the reservation that no float may be seen more than twice on Canal Street.

The working man by now had become a king; he could live all year on a day's reign. On the West Bank—that part of the city across the Mississippi River—Alla, Grela, Poseidon, Arabi, Choctaw, Cronus delight their "subjects." Thousands never cross the river to see Rex; they're having too good a time with their own.

Looped in and under and around the major framework, an intensely personal Mardi Gras is conducted by each born or bred Orleanian.

Some 10,000 of them gained a special way, a special status, and a new look for Mardi Gras through the rainy day inspiration in 1933 of a disgruntled masker, Chris R. Valley, aboard a truck which had been barred from the congestion of the main streets.

The "truck ride" for years had been a humble but happy way for masked Orleanians, mostly in their teens and 20s, to celebrate Mardi Gras. Sometimes clubs, sometimes pick-up groups (ads often appeared for so many places open on a truck with such-and-such costume), they would split the cost of a truck, hire a jazz combo, put food, soft drinks and beer aboard and roll, self-sufficient even unto a dance floor. They went where they could, when they could. They had a permit to be on the streets, but there were frequent wrangles with harried police trying to maintain parade routes and control the crowds which closed in immediately after.

Why be stepchildren? thought Valley. Why not organize into a krewe, with a parade permit to follow Rex?

Valley was a born organizer. He formed the Krewe of Orleanians under the aegis of the Elks, with whom he was active. Ground rules were well laid out before a public call went out in early January, 1935, inviting decorated trucks with at least 30 maskers aboard to register and draw for position. The newspapers gave enthusiastic support, especially *New Orleans States* columnist F. Edward Hebert, later Louisiana's senior Congressman, who wished Valley's "experiment" success.

That year the Chamber of Commerce had appealed for more general masking. The Young Men's Business Club had made this an official project. Depression-hit masses were concentrating on beans, not baubles. Watchers of the public weal were uneasy about the future of the total public involvement which had become New Orleans' Mardi Gras.

Public debate over whether 30 or 40 maskers formed the proper complement to qualify, prompted *The Times-Picayune* to editorialize, "The important thing is that the fraternal order is organizing, for the first time, one of the most interesting activities of our Mardi Gras, and thereby is giving notable encouragement to picturesque display."

On Mardi Gras 1935, 56 trucks rolled toward rendezvous, jazz blaring happily, and struck a sour note. They were scattered in almost 56 directions. Before the next year, though, Police Traffic Chief Tom Depaoli counseled the krewe. In 1936 they assembled at a den, as did their parade elders, instead of at a street intersection, and fell in smoothly behind the grandeur of Rex, to the delight of the crowds.

Valley had proved to skeptics that the krewe of "amateurs" could handle a Carnival parade, a complex undertaking. A twin device assured that it grow steadily more ambitious: prizes for the best floats, with enough categories to be stimulating; and lead-off positions in next year's parade for the winners.

From a modest start, the Krewe of Orleanians has become the most significant new feature on the face of Carnival. In 1967, 181 floats with some 9,000 maskers aboard of all ages (including babes in arms) rolled in the longest parade on earth. The trucks, now mostly long flatbeds normally carrying bales of cotton or newsprint or drums of oil, vanished under elaborate papier mâché settings (the stuff of the formal parades) or a variety of other ingenious disguises. Each was a theme in itself.

Directly behind those 181 floats, which followed Rex's "big time" 23, were 61 more truck floats of a newer group, the Krewe of Crescent City. And still the crowd would have welcomed more.

Packed densely into a relatively small stretch of Canal Street, the Civic Center area, Bourbon Street, Royal Street, St. Charles up to Lee Circle, and, in thinning ranks, the remainder of the parade route, on Mardi Gras 1967 were over one million people. Weaving through that mass in the happy 12-ring circus that is Mardi Gras were the marching clubs. Fanciful, audacious, cavorting with a delight which communicates, the marching clubs never march; to the merriest of jazz, they prance, dance, strut and sometimes stagger as the hours and the drinks begin to tell.

Oldest are the Jefferson City Buzzards ("21 beer stops on our route"), on the march since 1889 and not in the least exhausted. A new crowd favorite is the Half-Fast Walking Club organized in 1962 by clarinetist Pete Fountain.

Pete and most of his marchers are musicians foregoing impressive professional fees to dress up and play for free, for the crowd, for themselves. Phil Harris, Charles "Bud" Dant, Frankie Laine, Charlie Weaver, Eddie Miller have come across country in various years for the privilege.

Only the city which produced jazz could have evolved New

Orleans Mardi Gras of today. During Carnival, every musician able to crawl is busy, for pay or for fun. High school bands from throughout the city strike a jazz beat for the strutting Negro flambeaux carriers lighting night parades and for long-limbed twirlers flashing sticks in the sun. Jazz combos play for society Carnival clubs, the Bourbon Street Bounders, the Royal Street Rounders, the Friars; for the let-your-hair-down suppers which follow the formality of the balls; for the scores of parade-route parties and day-long festivities at every possible reception point in the city. Jazz is camped on the streets for spontaneous dancing; it's snaking through the crowds with the marchers; it's riding high on the floats. You are never out of earshot of jazz, the day of the Mighty Madness.

Mardi Gras, in turn, has provided that essential nourishment for musicians: inspiration, and jobs. It is no coincidence that the birthday of the New Orleans Jazz Club is, officially, Mardi Gras, the day of, and the source of, its inception in 1948. Armand Hug, one of New Orleans' finest traditional jazz pianists, dates his ambition to become a musician from the 1924 Mardi Gras when he stood spellbound, a boy of nine, drinking in the Dixieland of a saxaphone, bass and guitar trio playing at a parade viewing stand outside a clothing store. Later he was to play hundreds of Carnival "gigs," both public and private. Major bands get Carnival bookings as far as two years in advance; lesser groups get all the work they can handle before the season rolls around, and there's always a hole for an unknown to work into with every professional night spot in the city running full blast, every private group setting a Carnival fête, and every débutante party drawing on jazzmen.

Yet there was a period when the élite of New Orleans scorned this child of their city as debased, unfit for society; and they cast it out. But not at its birth. When ragtime, the earliest jazz, came bouncing out of the dance halls and bordellos of New Orleans before the turn of the century, it was hailed by the lighthearted krewemen of the era as "good time music," just right for Carnival.

During the next two decades, both white and Negro marching bands were parade fixtures. Others hired out to ride around in advertising wagons making a joyful pitch for some of the small commercial balls extant at the time, which sold tickets (a practice long since vanished). Names historic in jazz annals were often aboard: Tom Brown, who took Tom Brown's Band from Dixieland to Chicago in 1915, the first full jazz group to head north in a body; The Original Dixieland Jazz Band, which made the first jazz recording issued just one week after Mardi Gras, 1917; the New Orleans Rhythm Kings, another pioneer group which made history in recording.

The biggest jazz entrepreneur of all time, "Papa" Jack Laine, had as many as six white bands busy simultaneously during Carnival, dubbing them Reliance #1, #2, #3, etc. He marched with Reliance #1 with Rex for many years, such a crowd favorite that a "second line" of admirers followed along, dancing in the streets.

It was a warm union of talent and use until two factors brought on a chill which may have contributed to the trek north which began about this period: the Musician's Union organized the bands and priced them out of the krewes' budgets, and beyond the reach of most of the private parties.

It was just the ammunition needed for a growing faction within the old line krewes to scuttle jazz. With age had come increasing decorum among the Carnival hierarchy. They objected to jazz as illiterate; they wanted "better-class" music for their enterprise. Throughout the major parade krewes, there was a general dropout of jazz and in marched the high school and college bands ("football music," frowned a detractor). These they could get for nothing, for the prestige of the occasion.

Jazz, of course, survived and thrived among the popular celebrations in "combos" . . . but under censure.

It is an ironic footnote that in 1915, august Comus felt its popularity beginning to wane and moved to draw in some young blood. It gave a dance Mardi Gras night at the Pickwick Club (its affiliated organization) and invited a young Tulane University campus band to play, the popular "6-⅞ Band," which included young Edmond Souchon, later to become an obstetrician as well as musician; and law student E. Howard McCaleb, later Judge McCaleb. The infectious music began immediately after Comus's parade, and instead of going to their hosts' ball, the young elegants stayed to dance. Long after Rex had been received at midnight by Comus to signal the end of Mardi Gras, Comus's guests at the club danced on.

They danced to jazz, which was to change the course of music around the world, and win America acclaim for a truly original contribution to the arts.

In 1966, Rex made handsome amends. Leading the parade was an official bandwagon bearing a foot-stomping basic Dixieland group, the Crawford-Ferguson Night Owls. The Eureka Brass Band—whose impressive family tree is rooted in the very origins of jazz—marched on foot.

In 1967, Rex augmented its jazz arrangement with Sherwood Mangipane and a picked group aboard a second bandwagon—in all, 22 of the finest New Orleans jazz musicians in a city where new groups now emerge as fast as they can learn to blow, often to get their first major exposure in the parade not with, but right behind, Rex.

In 1968, still a third New Orleans group was booked to ride high, Sharkey Bonano and his band aboard "A Streetcar Named Desire."

Thus Carnival has again made room at the top for the city's natural-born son, recognizing that the spirits are fused, the heartbeat is mutual. The beat is up-tempo . . . up, up, up, up. . . .

What's the biggest impression you get, riding on a Rex float? a veteran of many parades was asked. "Noise," was the prompt reply. "It comes up like a solid wave; it never lets up. It's like you could touch it."

"Throw me something, Mistah!" is the clarion call of Carnival. Many uninitiates assume the act symbolizes the bestowing of largess on the peasants by royalty and nobles. Actually, it is a much more romantic spoof: In the earliest parades, young bloods tossed sweetmeats as marks of favor to ladies they were courting, or wished to.

Other "throws" were not so pleasant. Early chronicles speak of bands of masqueraders, en route to and from their balls, throwing flour at bystanders in a spirit of fun. Shortly appear references to flour being thrown by onlookers at masqueraders, and at each other. With organized, rolling parades, a bag of flour became standard equipment, being thrown up at balcony viewers and down onto the people below. When it rained, as it often does at Mardi Gras, the maskers had a bag of paste on their hands.

In subsequent years, street rowdies converted relatively innocent flour-throwing to sticks, bricks, stones, dust and even lime, which in 1860 revived demands from an indignant press that Mardi Gras be suppressed.

Perhaps the fact that in the hungry Civil War years flour at $23–$30 a barrel was too scarce to throw away, played a part in the vanishing of the disagreeable practice.

Beads and other baubles beloved of Carnival crowds were unknown until another of those small events occurred on which Mardi Gras is apt to pivot: In the rollicking 1871 Twelfth Night Revelers parade, among the float figures attending "Mother Goose's Tea Party" was a jolly Santa Claus. The imaginative masker playing Santa filled his bag with trinkets to toss to the crowd, and modern-day "throws" were born.

Today, virtually every float-rider plays Santa. A parade without a satisfying supply of throws to last the whole route is a failure at the end of the line.

The nineteenth century's light favors for lady-loves grew in later years to be items of some value, handed to each dance partner at the ball at the conclusion of each "call-out" dance—but vigilant parents have been known to step in when the token has stretched the bounds of decorum. A particularly romantic act is the tossing of a special gift from a float, such as the pearl necklace which Rex of 1903 (J. Thornwell Witherspoon) threw to the first Rex's wife, Mrs. Lewis J. Salomon, on the balcony of the Boston Club.

Among the millions upon millions of throws since, there's scarcely a penny's worth apiece except for the Mardi Gras phenomenon of the 1960s: The Great Doubloon Stampede. It has not only dethroned beads as the most prized catch of parades; it has affected the fabric of civic, social, business and even religious life, and created the most popular single hobby in history among Orleanians: doubloon collecting.

It started casually enough. Although Carnival traditions are its commandments, Rex is noted for adding fresh elements to the expanding Carnival. In 1960, the krewe ordered aluminum and gold-anodized aluminum medallions made to throw among its trinkets, engraved with the Rex image, the Rex motto, "Pro Bono Publico," and the parade theme, "The Wonderful World of Let's Pretend." Some genius (unnamed, since all members are anonymous except for Rex) dubbed them "doubloons." The discs weren't even dated.

On Mardi Gras, the crowd was galvanized by the glint of coins flashing through the air. If there had been a scramble for beads, there was ecstatic riot for doubloons. The craze was launched, fueled in part by the connotation of pirate treasure in a city where the memory of Lafitte, the pirate, is very much alive; spurted soon after by word from coin dealers that the then-worthless pseudo-coins would grow valuable with age.

By 1967, the 1960 undated plain aluminum Rex doubloon was listed at $15, according to coin dealer William Taylor. The gold-anodized one, $45–50. The 300 of the latter which 1960 Rex (Gerald Andrus) had dated and gave to friends to commemorate his reign, was quoted at $175. The 1960 silver doubloon struck for Rex's court was quoted at $1200–1500, when available. The 1961 aluminum, $10; gold-anodized, $25–30.

Big krewes, little krewes, showered their own issues. The Half-Fast Walking Club led a whole group of other clubs into the swift new current. King Zulu's doubloon was more coveted than his coconuts. The Krewe of Orleanians created the "Elkoin." Others called them medallions. A "Mardi Gras medal" appeared with the seal of the city, for groups unable to afford a personal coin issue. No matter what the technical name, to the public they were "doubloons" and avidly sought.

In 1965, Comus, Momus, and Proteus joined the more than 30 Carnival groups flinging "coins." Orders for the 1968 season more than doubled that number, with one firm, Blaine Kern Associates—one of four major doubloon makers in the city— minting more than a million.

Non-Carnival groups meanwhile awakened to the possibilities and many of them coined their own commemorative doubloons.

It doesn't take doubloons, however, to keep Carnival in evidence year-'round in New Orleans. A significant part of the population spends all or part of its working time entirely on Carnival's trappings: costume designers, seamstresses, headdress fabricators, beadwork experts, wig makers, float designers, scenic designers, artists, sign painters, hairdressers, souvenir makers, every phase of the building trades, caterers, dress shops, musicians, vendors, the hotel-motel industry, importers. . . . The complexity of Carnival today is bewildering, its scope astounding. Still entirely privately financed, essentially for the financers' own pleasure with the public as invited guests, Mardi Gras has become a multi-million-dollar business, one of America's great tourist attractions.

The one important and unique parade least concerned with the outside world but beloved by New Orleanians at large is the Zulu Social Aid and Pleasure Club's free-wheeling procession. A Negro parade, it was founded in 1909 as a burlesque of the bigshot white folks uptown, and with intermittent attacks of social consciousness, has retained the spirit of "There Never Was and There Never Will Be a King Like Me." That was the title of the skit in the musical comedy *Smarter Set* which inspired William Story, the first Zulu, and his cronies, and sent Story forth with lard can crown and a banana stalk for a scepter.

Today, Zulu's float is called the Royal Barge, since early in Zulu history he mocked Rex (who initially arrived the day before

Mardi Gras by royal yacht on the Mississippi, from a mythical land) by arriving from Africa on the New Basin Canal by skiff. As the parade grew more ambitious, the skiff became a Mississippi River barge. (The canal was filled in.)

Mardi Gras 1967, somewhat after the 8:30 a.m. starting target (nothing about Zulu is cut and certainly not dried), a beaming King Zulu (Milton Bienamee) arrived in high Afro-Orleanian style aboard the riverboat Mark Twain, surrounded by his "tribesmen" and equipped with 1500 coconuts carved with monkey faces or warrior heads or elaborately trimmed with sequins and beads. By long standing tradition, the coconuts were thrown to the crowd in burlesque of the other parades' trinkets.

Transferred to floats, tightly hemmed in by a delighted crowd of both Negroes and whites, the entourage rolled on a route announced beforehand but inclined to wander as the spirit (bottled) moved them, in true Zulu tradition. All barrooms along the way toast the Zulus, which in itself was enough reason to abandon following Rex, a practice of the 1930's. It was too dry downtown.

At the queen's reviewing stand at Gertrude Geddes Willis Funeral Home on Jackson Avenue, Zulu toasted his queen with champagne. Actually, she was on her own float that year, behind the king, but that didn't alter her toast.

The Witch Doctor, a key figure; the Big Shot From Africa; jungle cats; African warriors in grass skirts with spears at the ready; the jazz band following in rags and tatters; it was, said King Zulu with satisfaction, "a real African parade."

The NAACP had lost to the spirit of Mardi Gras. The two previous years, Zulu had abandoned its traditional roaming, whomping mock-African guise and, at behind-scenes NAACP urging, presented parades embodying the dignity of the race. All went smoothly, except it wasn't any fun, even for the first "reform" king, Milton Bienamee. Outraged, he battled for club control and by late 1966, he won. Mardi Gras, 1967, as zealously as any of his counterparts in uptown mansions, Bienamee led his people back to "the old-time traditions."

Several times those traditions have been shared by a visiting king, Louis "Satchmo" Armstrong.

The biggest celebrity stir since Grand Duke Alexis, however, occurred when Edward, Duke of Windsor, ex-King of England, and his Duchess arrived for Mardi Gras, 1950.

Two raging issues occupied the élite beforehand: Would the duke, royal prince, former king, bow to Rex, mock King of Carnival? The second concerned whether the queen's court would have to curtsy to the duchess. A solid contingent of conservative family representatives declared they would not; to them, she was still "that woman" who caused a king to lose his throne.

To the audible satisfaction of all, the duke bowed to Rex. No occasion arose to curtsy to the duchess.

The duchess had full approval from the most conservative socialite, however, when she curtsyed deeply to the Carnival monarch.

Subsequently, America's First Lady, Mrs. Harry Truman, and her daughter Margaret attended Carnival and failed to bow to Rex, launching a flurry of unfavorable comparison at having "stood there like sticks when real royalty did the right thing." Unfortunately, an insider confessed later, no one had thought to coach the White House ladies on Carnival protocol.

That protocol proved beyond the White House security forces in 1966, when Lynda Bird Johnson arrived for Mardi Gras. A Secret Service agent asked to screen the Comus invitation list, and the krewe captain responded courteously, "That won't be necessary; we've already screened you."

Carnival honors have become so vital that they are the *raison d'être* of the entire social season. One débutante bowed a year early because the Mithras throne, for which she was eligible, was already firmly committed for "her" year and the next. Another débutante at the last possible moment was announced for an early début at her father's persuasion, because he, in poor health, feared he might not survive to enjoy her Carnival honors.

When one father discovered that his débutante daughter had

not been invited to mount a single throne, despite his community prominence, he organized an entire new Carnival krewe so she might be queen. Furthermore, her court was composed entirely of débutantes of the season, the criteria for social standing of a ball.

Possibly apocryphal but credited in some circles is the account of the grandmother whose dearest wish was to see her granddaughter reign over the krewe with which the family had a long Carnival tradition. The girl was chosen queen, but the day before the ball, grandmother died suddenly. Horrified, the family took the only consistent action: They delayed announcement of the death and put the body in the attic. Daughter reigned at the ball, and the queen's supper at their home was a triumphant affair while grandmother lay, content they were sure, above. When word of this got about, a socially oriented New Orleanian gasped, then added, "What else could they do, with everything ready?"

Court deportment is deemed so cardinal that kings are coached and "queen's lessons" teach the technique of walking with a heavy mantle. The queen also learns how to carry a scepter ("it never falls below your waist; that's a sign of fallen royalty," explained one).

"Maid's lessons" include the technique of a good court curtsy, not easy, with a book on your head as you sink to the floor—and what to do with the bouquet.

No training at all is necessary for a special category of queen during Carnival, one which outnumbers all the formal queens of Carnival many times over. Long before the general public ascended to parade and tableau grandeur, teenage queens were reigning with teenage kings in the humblest New Orleans neighborhoods at the cherished "King's Cake Parties." Rooted in the same tradition as the elite Twelfth Night Revelers but reshaped to fit the players, these are weekly at-home dances which begin with Twelfth Night and last until Mardi Gras.

During this period, bakery ovens turn out tens of thousands of King's Cakes, an oval circlet of distinctive, almost breadlike, consistency decorated with the Carnival colors and containing a lucky bean. If the bean is found in her slice by a girl guest, she's next week's queen and gives the party. She chooses a king, who provides the cake. If the bean goes to a boy, he chooses a queen, who must then give the party, with the boy providing only the King's Cake. During the Depression era and the parallel languishing of traditional jazz in its birthplace, music was often simply by record. With the resurgence of homegrown talent and teen-age dance bands in particular, music is apt to be live. In either case, there's little or no ceremonial homage to the king and queen.

Among the older New Orleanians, King's Cake retains such favor that it's apt to show up in business offices, for coffee breaks, or for party buffet.

There has been but one major change in the growing tradition of Carnival. Today the parade floats are tractor drawn. Until 1950, mules in medieval white trappings were the usual power. But the once-large mule colony had dwindled by then until the only ones left were the city garbage mules. For some years, tired mules hauled garbage by day and glitter by night. Finally, that year, Comus, Rex, Momus, Proteus and Hermes, the five largest of ten parades, were pulled by tractors. Mules had had their day.

It's all a part of Carnival, and Carnival is many parts.

Carnival is a girl's clear voice piping, "Are you a boy or a girl?" . . . A plump, greyhaired woman on a balcony with arms outflung in ecstasy at first sound of the bands . . . Newfound friends singing "Alouette" in uncertain French, arms linked . . . A tot eying a bracelet her father caught for her, with "That's not a bracelet, daddy; that's a hole." . . . White-sheeted, dark-skinned flambeaux carriers strutting down Royal Street and scrambling for coins tossed by admirers, heedless of scattered drops of flaming oil . . . Girls teetering by on sailors' arms . . . Families mounted on ladders hauled onto sidewalks . . . Chic ballgoers, blowsy women . . . A business suit blossoming with strings of beads . . . A dignified matron on St. Charles Avenue throwing her ample skirts over her head at first sprinkle of rain, with a crisp, "My hat is brand new and my legs are 65 years old." . . . A police team hustling off a young tough who's trying to prove he is . . . An Esplanade hostess explaining to a non-coffee-drinking guest who refused her heady Café Brulôt, "But there's practically no coffee in it!" . . . Upthrust arms clutching the same beads, which burst in a bright spray . . . An Auditorium parking attendant surveying the jammed lot as more cars clamor for entrance and murmuring, "Washday and no soap." . . . Newcomb college students heading for parade trucks with "survival kits" packed by their food services director . . . A howling child in the Roosevelt Hotel lobby screaming, "I don't see no Mardi Graw-w-ws!" . . . A waiter, looking over Kolb's Restaurant balcony at marching girls, declaring, "I wouldn't let my daughter go skimpy like that." . . . Hot corn on the cob and hot dogs slathered with yellow mustard; becoming Creole hot dogs with substitution of Creole mustard . . . A Midwesterner clutching her eye with, "How'll it sound to Blue Cross that I'm a bead casualty?" . . . A police charge for "Barking at people" . . . Cars passing with dummy clown atop one car, papier mâché zebra atop another, nodding to each other as they pass by . . . Baroness Renée Klaudy Dewitz walking into her Old Europe patio and discovering a masker's stray skunk eating her dog's food . . . A quiet clot of boys and girls singing softly to themselves in Pirate's Alley, ignoring the parade beyond . . . A teenage pirate grinning happily to a Mickey Mouse, "I traveled twenty hours yesterday to get here from St. Louis, and I have to leave tonight, but boy, I wouldn't trade this day for a straight-A report card." . . . A dense mob around a wooden stand on Bourbon Street watching the female impersonators having their day in the open, preening in gorgeous costumes for showy trophies . . . A taxi driver explaining to a suspicious traveler that on parade nights and Mardi Gras, you can't get across Canal Street downtown . . . A grandmother doing the can-can with her granddaughter as a space opens up before City Hall . . . A tired father halting beside his complaining son with, "Boy, Our Lord walked from Jerusalem to Calvary with a cross on His back. He was barefoot and He walked on rocks. You got shoes on and you're walking on Burgundy Street. Come on." . . .

Mardi Gras is 30 men with eight trucks, two sweepers and two frontend loaders in the French Quarter and on Canal Street and a like staff on St. Charles from Louisiana to Lee Circle hauling away 172 tons of beer cans, newspapers, boxes, bits of costume and general débris as Ash Wednesday dawned in 1967. The same crews had already borne away 478 tons of débris from the week's festivities.

And Mardi Gras 1967 was three persons killed and hundreds treated at Charity Hospital for injuries sustained in violence or accident among a million celebrants.

Rex of 1967, banker Morgan L. Whitney, in his Rex proclamation commanded that "Melancholy be put to rout, and joy unconfined seize our subjects, young and old of all genders and degrees . . . that the spirit of make-believe descend upon the realm and banish from the land the dull and the humdrum and the commonplace of daily existence."

A man of modest means, a member of no Carnival club, was asked by a curious outsider what masking on Mardi Gras meant for him. "Is it worth all the trouble and expense to dress yourself up for one day?"

The Orleanian thought. "Well, I'll tell you," he said. "I guess it's one day you can be anybody you want, and you're just as good as the next guy. Nobody shoves you around. Everybody's happy. You're not worrying about the troubles that go with who you are; you're somebody else. All you got on your mind is having a good time. Let the world wait. It'll all be there tomorrow."

The Orleanian feels, with Emerson, that "He who laughs, lasts."

Index

LAKE PONTCHARTRAIN.

COPY AND TRANSLATION
From the Original Spanish Plan dated 1798.
SHOWING THE
CITY OF NEW ORLEANS,
ITS FORTIFICATIONS AND ENVIRONS.

1798

CYPRESS SWAMP

CYPRESS SWAMP

CYPRESS SWAMP

CYPRESS SWAMP

CYPRESS SWAMP

Fort ST. JOHN

Bayou Gentilly
Gentilly and Chef Menteur Road

Bayou Tchoupitoulas

Metairie Road

Concession to Antonio Rivaro, 28 Oct. 1708
Concession to Nicolas, alias Delon, Oct. 1708
Concession to Bapt. Portier, 28 Oct. 1708
Maturino Gerbon sold to Ant. Rivaro, June 1720, with consent of Governor Bienville, three arp.
Peter Dreux, alias Mr. Lepage, sold to Anton Rivaro, 4 Oct. 1720.
Concession of Ant. Rivaro, 5 Feb. 1721
Seventeen arpents front belonging to Mrs. Wwe. Lawrence.
Madame Juazante, absent heiress 2⅓ arp. front.

Lands of Stephan Roquigny, Esq., successive heir to John Girardy, declared proprietor of 14 arp. front by the government.

Concession of Stephen Langlois and Daniel Provanches, dated 20 October, 1720, and April 21st, 1721. Lands at present occupied by Mr. Louis Blanc.

Lands of John Bte Macarty

Boundary of John Bte Macarty

CYPRESS SWAMP

Canal

Carondelet

CYPRESS SWAMP

Boundary of the plantation of John Gravier

Lands of John Gravier, part of the plantation of the Jesuits, confiscated through his very christian Majesty, 13 arpents front on the Mississippi River

Land of Delor Sarpy and part of the former Jesuit plantation

CYPRESS SWAMP

CYPRESS SWAMP

Plantation of Peter from Lorenzo Sigur dication took place on this same plantation pents and high per this acr high per this plantation belong expressive, king are ing to the king on the Mississippi

Concession of Mr. de Morand dated 8 June, 1796

Concession of Mr. de Morand, dated 19 June, 1795

de Marigny Esq. bought it appears that the adju the late Mr. Dubreul, was sold for several pents and 12 toises from front for it says pents and 12 toises to it a king, without superficial or Front these 2 king, belong Signed CARLOS TRUDEAU

The Mill Royal Road

RIVER

MISSISSIPPI

WATER LINE IN 1875

WATER LINE IN 1875

WATER LINE IN 1875

PLAN
OF THE CITY OF
NEW ORLEANS
AND
THE ADJACENT PLANTATIONS,
Compiled in accordance with an Ordinance of
the Illustrious Ministry and Royal Charter,
24 December, 1798.

Signed: CARLOS TRUDEAU.

CYPRESS SWAMP.

Scale of Toesas.
0   100   200   300   400   500   600   700   800 toesas